QUESTIONS & ANSWERS
TO HELP YOU PASS THE REAL ESTATE
Exam

SEVENTH EDITION

John Reilly, Paige Bovee Vitousek,
Tim Meline, Consulting Editor

Dearborn™
Real Estate Education

This publication is designed to provide accurate and authoritative information in regard to the subject matter covered. It is sold with the understanding that the publisher is not engaged in rendering legal, accounting, or other professional service. If legal advice or other expert assistance is required, the services of a competent professional person should be sought.

President: Roy Lipner
Vice-President of Product Development and Publishing: Evan Butterfield
Associate Publisher: Louise Benzer
Development Editor: Caitlin Ostrow
Managing Editor, Production: Daniel Frey
Quality Assurance Editor/Typesetter: David Shaw
Creative Director: Lucy Jenkins

Published by Dearborn™ Real Estate Education,
a division of Dearborn Financial Publishing, Inc.®
30 South Wacker Drive
Chicago, IL 60606-7481
(312) 836-4400
http://www.dearbornRE.com

Printed in the United States of America.

06 07 10 9 8 7 6 5 4 3

CONTENTS

CHAPTER 18
Property Management, Lease Agreements, and Securities   267

APPENDIXES

INTRODUCTION

USE THIS BOOK TO PASS THE EXAM THE FIRST TIME

This book was designed specifically for the dedicated real estate student who wants to pass the licensing examination on the first try.

You can acquire all the necessary knowledge of basic real estate principles through the classroom, the textbook, and the guidance of a skillful teacher. Even so, you may be like many examinees who still lack the confidence that they can "ace" the exam on the first try. *Questions & Answers* is a book of tests similar to the licensing exams that can be used for practice, building confidence, discovering weak areas, learning how to avoid mechanical errors, and improving test-taking time.

This workbook is ideally used

■ as a supplement to the text in a basic real estate course;

■ by one who has completed the course, yet wants to review while waiting to take the state exam; or

■ by one not enrolled in any formal class but who needs to refresh those ideas and concepts.

Whatever the reason, *Questions & Answers* simulates the real examination and enables you to approach the exam with complete confidence in your ability to pass.

Not all states use the same examination. The Association of Real Estate License Law Officials (ARELLO) encourages all real estate regulatory agencies to require certified examinations to test the competency of the applicant. Certified test providers include Applied Measurement Professionals (AMP) located in Lenexa, Kansas; Experior Assessments LLC located in St. Paul, Minnesota; Promissor located in Bala Cynwyd, Pennsylvania; and Psychological Service Inc. (PSI) located in Glendale, California.

For the address, fax, and telephone numbers of every real estate regulatory agency, go to *www.arello.org* and click on Regulatory Agencies. For regulatory Web addresses go to *www.reea.org* and click on Resource Links/Regulatory Web Site Links. For your reference these Web sites are alphabetically listed.

Alabama
http://www.arec.state.al.us/

Alaska
http://www.dced.state.ak.us/occ/prec.htm

Arizona
http://www.re.state.az.us/

Arkansas
http://www.state.ar.us/arec/arecweb.html

California
http://www.dre.cahwnet.gov/

Colorado
http://www.dora.state.co.us/real-estate/

Connecticut
http://www.dcp.state.ct.us/licensing/realestate.htm

District of Columbia
http://www.dcra.org/main.shtm

Delaware
http://www.state.de.us/research/profreg/realcomm.htm#topofpage

Florida
http://www.state.fl.us/dbpr/re/index.shtml

Georgia
http://www.grec.state.ga.us/

Hawaii
http://www.hawaii.gov/hirec/

Idaho
http://www2.state.id.us/irec/

Illinois
http://www.obre.state.il.us/

Indiana
http://www.state.in.us/pla/bandc/estate/

Iowa
http://www.state.ia.us/government/com/prof/realesta/realesta.htm

Kansas
http://www.ink.org/public/krec/

Kentucky
http://www.krec.net/

Louisiana
http://www.lrec.state.la.us/

Maine
http://www.state.me.us/pfr/olr/

Maryland
http://www.dllr.state.md.us/license/real_est/reintro.html

Massachusetts
http://www.state.ma.us/reg/boards/re/default.htm

Michigan
http://www.Michigan.gov/realestatelicense

Minnesota
http://www.commerce.state.mn.us/mainre.htm

Mississippi
http://www.mrec.state.ms.us/default.asp

Missouri
http://www.ecodev.state.mo.us/pr/restate/

Montana
http://www.com.state.mt.us/License/POL/pol_boards/rre_board/board_page.htm

Nebraska
http://www.nol.org/home/NREC/

Nevada
http://www.state.nv.us/b&i/red/

New Hampshire
http://webster.state.nh.us/nhrec/

New Jersey
http://www.naic.org/nj/realcom.htm

New Mexico
http://www.state.nm.us/clients/nmrec/

New York
http://www.dos.state.ny.us/lcns/realest.html

North Carolina
http://www.ncrec.state.nc.us/

North Dakota
No Web page is available at present for the agency. However, there is an e-mail address: *pjergenson@state.nd.us*

Ohio
http://www.com.state.oh.us/ODOC/real/

Oklahoma
http://www.orec.state.ok.us

Oregon
http://bbs.chemek.cc.or.us/public/orea/orea.html

Pennsylvania
http://www.dos.state.pa.us/bpoa/recomm/mainpage.htm

Rhode Island
http://www.dbr.state.ri.us/

South Carolina
http://www.llr.state.sc.us/POL/RealEstateCommission/

South Dakota
http://www.state.sd.us/dcr/realestate/Real-hom.htm

Tennessee
http://www.state.tn.us/commerce/trec/index.htm

Texas
http://www.trec.state.tx.us/

Utah
http://www.commerce.utah.gov/dre

Vermont
http://www.vtprofessionals.org/real_estate/

Virginia
http://www.state.va.us/dpor/reb_main.htm

Washington State
http://www.dol.wa.gov/realestate/refront.htm

West Virginia
http://www.state.wv.us/wvrec

Wisconsin
*http://badger.state.wi.us/agencies/drl/Regulation/licensee_services/
real_estate/re1000.htm*

Wyoming
http://realestate.state.wy.us/

THE SUBJECT MATTER

This book consists of multiple-choice questions and answers divided into topics consistent with those subjects covered on most real estate licensing examinations. The main topics covered include Real Property and Laws Relating to Ownership; Valuation of Real Estate; Financing of Real Estate; Transfer of

Property Ownership; Real Estate Brokerage; and Mathematics. Each main topic has subchapters and a series of questions followed by explanatory answers. In addition, there are appendices that cover typical state-specific licensing laws, mathematics, review exams, and sample final exams for salespersons and brokers.

CRAM GUIDE

If you find yourself with this book in hand and relatively little time in which to prepare, or if you feel you are already prepared, we suggest you first take the review quizzes and practice final examinations in the back of the book. If you miss questions on a specific topic, concentrate your remaining study time on those particular areas of the book.

We have also included specific "quick review questions" or "cram questions" (designated by the shaded box over them) that convey the essential points from each chapter. Do these cram questions as a minimum. If you have the time later, go back and complete the remaining questions.

BROKER QUESTIONS

For a speedy broker review, certain broker-level questions are designated with a bull's-eye in the margin (◎). However, broker candidates should still answer all of the questions in this book and not simply those marked with a bull's-eye. Broker tests cover the same topics as those found on a salesperson's examination and include additional questions that deal with office organization, office management, and human resource development.

Let's go over some of these types of broker questions and answers.

■ If the expenses of an office, consisting of 24 full-time equivalent associates, are annually $480,000, what is the desk cost? The solution is determined by dividing the number of full-time associates (24) into the annual expenses of $480,000. The answer, then, is $20,000.

■ What amount is remaining after all commissions, sales, and referral fees are paid out? The answer is *company dollar*.

■ If a broker wanted to avoid the possible loss of personal assets from a lawsuit against the brokerage firm as well as double taxation, the *BEST* form of business structure would be a
A. Chapter S Corporation.
B. limited partnership.
C. sole proprietorship.
D. general partnership.

The answer is A. Chapter S Corporation.

■ The 100 percent commission arrangement is *MOST* advantageous to whom?

The answer is an agent whose productivity is relatively high.

■ Employment applications may ask for applicants'
A. age and race.
B. religion.
C. former places of employment.
D. spouse's employment.

The answer is C. former places of employment.

Also, broker candidates should pay special attention to Part D (Transfer of Property Ownership) and Part E (Real Estate Brokerage).

HOW TO USE THIS BOOK

There are two approaches that you can use for the most effective study and learning. It is really a matter of individual preference as to which approach is most effective for you.

One technique is like eating an elephant: take one bite at a time. Answer only five or six questions at a time and after each set of questions, look up the answers, then do another set, and so on. This method will build your confidence as you go along and give you immediate feedback. Sometimes, if you answer large numbers of questions at one time without looking up the answers until later, you can't remember why you made the answer choice you did.

The other technique is to answer the entire exam before looking at the answers, allowing one minute per question. Many people feel this not only builds reading speed but also allows them to compare the percentage correct with the test goal (70 percent to 75 percent) and dramatically increases their confidence in their testing skills.

Whichever method is used, we feel you should not circle your answers in the book, but rather, put them on a separate piece of paper so that when you want to restudy the material, you can't see the previous answers. Likewise, if you save this paper, you can compare the results the second time around.

When you have mastered all of the chapters and appendix material, go ahead and complete the practice final examinations. Reserve enough uninterrupted time to take the final and review exams under simulated testing conditions.

A STRATEGY FOR STUDYING

1. Organize your study time into two-hour to four-hour segments. Cover no more than four review chapters at a time. Lengthy cram sessions are less productive. The same advice holds true if you are studying over the Internet or from a CD.

2. Unfortunately, just reading the review material isn't going to prepare you for the test. To arrive at a thorough understanding of the material, it is wise to outline your study material and make up in your mind subject-related true/false questions.

3. Also, after reading, use the vocabulary words from each review chapter to make flash cards and then ask someone to quiz you. Or, use a tape recorder to record the vocabulary words and then listen to your voice reciting the definitions. Play these tapes in your car as you go to work or do errands.

4. In addition to using this book, if you are in a prelicensing class, form a study group with two or three others.

5. The testing providers weight Part E, Real Estate Brokerage, heavier than most of the other areas. Double your review time on Agency, Listings, Valuation of Real Estate, and Sales Contracts.

Simulation Test-Taking Tips

1. Find a quiet place (no phones or outside distractions) to take the tests in this book.

2. Never leave a question blank. Narrow your choices and make an educated guess.

3. Because you could outsmart yourself, don't look for trick questions. However, choosing the best answer may require you to watch out for those answers that are only partially correct.

4. If the question is read carefully, first impressions are generally correct. As a general rule, don't change an answer unless you discover later that it was misread or unless a future question "triggers" your memory.

5. After taking the tests in this book, check your results. Don't just evaluate those questions correctly answered, but review all of them. Understanding why an answer was correct and why the other choices were incorrect is the key to mastery.

By using this book in the preceding manner, you will acquire an instinct for the actual examination and gain confidence by knowing the answers to similar problems.

ACTUAL DAY OF TESTING TIPS

1. Test anxiety comes from worrying about passing the exam. It is important to realize that test anxiety is normal, so expect a few butterflies. If your testing site is near enough, consider driving there and back a week or so ahead of time to eliminate the apprehension associated with not knowing where you are going. While in the parking lot visualize yourself sitting down and taking

the exam and then walking back to your car. Let your mind visualize the experience so that when you return to take the real test your butterflies will be in formation.

2. Get a good night's rest instead of cramming the night before the test. Eat lightly both the night before and the morning of the exam.

3. Try not to pay any attention to the other candidates. Attitude is crucial. Have confidence in yourself and the fact that you are well prepared.

4. For most candidates, there is an ample amount of time to take the exam. Pacing, though, is important. The test questions are all weighed the same. A simple vocabulary question is scored the same as a long, difficult math problem; both are scored as one point. Therefore, if you don't know how to work a time-taking math problem, skip it and return to it after completing the rest of the test. Knowing that you are using your time wisely helps to reduce testing anxiety.

5. If you are nervous, the first several questions may appear more difficult than they actually are because your concentration is off. So, start with the first question you do know and then return to those that you skipped.

6. Watch out for the "none of the above" solution to a math problem. It is an excellent way to tell if someone really knows how to work a problem.

For example, what is the PI payment for a $145,000 loan, amortized over 30 years at 7 percent interest using a factor of $6.65?
A. $864.25
B. $974.25
C. $1,064.25
D. None of the above

The answer is $145 \times \$6.65 = \$964.25$

Looking at the plausible solutions, answer D is *by default* the correct answer. If you know that you've worked a problem correctly and the solution isn't there but none of the above is one of the possible answers, feel empowered to answer the question as none of the above.

7. Stopping halfway through a problem is a concern. Crucial to passing the exam is carefully reading each question and asking yourself what the question asks.

For example, if a person put 20 percent down on the purchase of a home and paid a one-point origination fee of $1,500, what was the price of the home?
A. $102,500
B. $150,000
C. $187,500
D. None of the above

Ask yourself, "what does the question ask me to solve?" Answer: the question wants me to compute the price of the home. Right, *not the loan amount*.

To solve the problem, though, you must compute the loan amount first, and this amount is used as a detractor in the answer key. By not being careful, you could stop halfway and assume that you have answered correctly because the answer calculated appears as one of the answers.

To solve the problem, the $1,500 must be divided by one percent ($1,500 divided by 1% = $150,000). Next, the $150,000 must be divided by 80 percent in order to answer the question, *what is the price of the home?* $150,000 divided by its percentage of the whole, 80 percent, equals $187,500. In order to make sure that the math problem was worked correctly, it is a always a good habit to work it backwards. $187,500 − 20% = $150,000 × 1% = $1,500.

8. Another math trick is to use the answer key and work each one of the stated answers backwards until discovering the correct answer. The process of elimination takes time, but if you understand that one of the answers has to be correct, it is a good trick to remember.

   A. $102,500 − 20% = $82,000 × 1% = $820   Wrong Answer
   B. $150,000 − 20% = $120,000 × 1% = $1,200   Wrong Answer
   C. $187,500 − 20% = 150,000 × 1% = $1,500   Right Answer
   D. None of the above

9. Watch for superfluous facts that are not needed to answer the question and be prepared to make a value judgment on those questions that ask for the BEST ANSWER.

10. Because questions are industry-related, you have to really know your real estate vocabulary. The day before the test, spend at least two hours reviewing the vocabulary from each chapter.

11. On a final note, beware of test questions that give you two right answers. Be sure to read every answer for the BEST response, not necessarily a right answer. For example, if a question asks you to compute for a homeowner's monthly tax but you select the solution that correctly describes the annual tax, you'll be wrong because it asked for monthly, NOT annually. Another example might ask, if a broker discharged a salesperson, the real estate license should be (A) returned to the real estate commission or (B) returned to the real estate commission by the broker. Solution (B) is the BEST response even though solution (A) is also correct.

ACKNOWLEDGMENTS

The authors express their gratitude to all those who contributed to the development of this edition of *Questions & Answers*.

In particular, we wish to thank the following people:

- **John Anjos**, Anjos Realty Institute, Acushnet, Massachusetts

- **Gerald Cortesi**, Harper College, Palatine, Illinois

- **Dr. Lawrence Hasbrouck**, Real Estate Training Institute, Biloxi, Mississippi

- **Barbara G. Samet**, DREI, Pocono Real Estate Academy, East Stroudsburg, Pennsylvania

- **Robert Troyer**, Troyer School of Real Estate, Huntington, Indiana

- **Randall S. van Reken**, Southern Nevada School of Real Estate, Las Vegas, Nevada

John Reilly, DREI, is a member of the New York, California, Hawaii, and Federal bars, and is a licensed real estate broker in Hawaii and California. He has been an adjunct professor of real estate law and an instructor for both salesperson and broker classes. He is author of the leading text on agency, *Agency Relationships in Real Estate*, 2nd Edition, and *The Language of Real Estate*, 5th Edition, and coauthor of *Agency Relationships in California Real Estate*, 2nd Edition (with Martha R. Williams), and *Texas Real Estate Agency*, 3rd Edition (with Donna K. Peeples and Minor Peeples III). John is a founder of the Internet Crusade, an electronic publishing and training organization dedicated to helping people make sense of the Internet: *http://InternetCrusade.com*.

Paige Bovee Vitousek, DREI, is an author, lecturer, and instructor in the field of real estate principles and practices, and has been president/owner for more than 25 years of Hawaii's largest real estate school. She is an active real estate broker and a Graduate, REALTORS® Institute. She is the first educator in Hawaii to receive the prestigious Distinguished Real Estate Instructor (DREI) award from the Real Estate Educators Association. She has also authored *Principles and Practices of Hawaiian Real Estate*, a textbook geared to practice in her home state.

ABOUT THE CONSULTING EDITOR

Tim Meline, GRI, DREI, is the Director of Sales Training for Iowa Realty and Director of Iowa Real Estate School. He has been a licensed real estate trainer and instructor since 1978. In 2002 he assisted in the creation of *Iowa Real Estate Basics* and *Iowa Real Estate Exam Prep*, also published by Dearborn™ Real Estate Education. In 2003 he was consulting editor on the 5th Edition of *Guide to Passing the PSI Real Estate Exam*. He has served as President of the Des Moines Area Association of REALTORS® and has chaired three Habitat for Humanity builds. He was recognized by his board as REALTOR® of the Year in 2000 and in 2004 was awarded Humanitarian of the Year.

A

Real Property and Laws Relating to Ownership

This part contains questions on the topics of

■ the legal concepts of real property;

■ ways title to property may be held;

■ methods to legally describe property;

■ the role of encumbrances, easements, and restrictions on property ownership;

■ the government's rights and restrictive powers; and

■ aspects of condominium and cooperative ownership.

Expect about 20 percent of the national portion of the examination to contain questions on the topics covered in Part A.

Forms of Ownership

The question of title arises when the listing broker reviews the seller's ownership and determines who legally must sign the listing contract. It arises again when the buyer is asked to declare the method of taking title from the seller's deed because the method of taking title to real property has serious tax and legal consequences.

Questions in this chapter will test your comprehension of the following topics:

■ Differences between the various ways to hold title to real property (e.g., tenancy in common, joint tenancy, tenancy by the entirety, tenancy in severalty)

■ Other forms of ownership: corporate, time-share, limited partnership

■ Ways in which a tenancy can be terminated

■ Who should advise the buyer on how to hold title

KEY WORDS

Co-ownership: Co-owners having an undivided interest and equal rights of possession. Forms of ownership are tenancy in common, joint tenancy, and tenancy by the entirety. Once made, a tenancy can later be changed if certain legal formalities are met.

Corporation: A separate, legal entity created and regulated by state law that has perpetual existence and the right to sell shares of ownership to the public. One corporation disadvantage is double taxation of income. It is important to obtain a corporate resolution showing proper authority to bind the corporation. The limited liability company (LLC) is becoming a more popular form of real property ownership because of the single tax feature and limited liability.

Joint tenancy: Two or more natural persons with the right of survivorship. They can sell, encumber, or lease but cannot leave by will—a sale by one tenant will convert the joint tenancy into a tenancy in common. Upon death of a joint tenant, the interest vests in the surviving tenants, without probate. It requires the four unities of *Time, Title, Interest, and Possession.* A corporation cannot be a joint tenant because it has perpetual existence.

Partition: The dividing of common interests in real property owned jointly by two or more persons.

Partnerships: An association of two or more persons who carry on a business and share in profits and loss. In a general partnership, each partner is liable for all the firm's debts. Real estate may be taken in the name of the individual partners or the partnership. Death of a partner usually dissolves the partnership. In a limited partnership, the limited partners are not liable for the firm's debts—however, the management and operation of the business is under the exclusive control of the general partners. Partnership files but does not pay income tax—each partner pays his or her own tax.

Sole ownership: When one person owns property, it is known as *tenancy in severalty*—it could be either a legal person, such as a corporation or association, or a human being.

Survivorship: The right of survivorship is that special feature of a joint tenancy whereby all title, right, and interest of a decedent joint tenant in certain property passes to the surviving joint tenants by operation of law, free from claims of heirs and creditors of the decedent.

Tenancy by entirety: Similar to a joint tenancy with right of survivorship, but tenants must be husband and wife. In essence, the marriage owns the property—thus one spouse cannot sell or partition the property, nor can a creditor of one spouse force a sale. Upon divorce, the parties become tenants in common.

Tenancy in common: Two or more persons without the right of survivorship. Each has an undivided interest in the whole property; it does not have to be equal shares. Any cotenant can sell without the other cotenant's consent. They can leave by will—subject to probate; it does not pass to surviving cotenants. No one cotenant can claim possession of any specific physical portion of the property.

The "Methods of Ownership" chart in Figure 1.1 summarizes the differences in tenancy types that you studied in your prelicense course.

FIGURE 1.1
Methods of Ownership

	Tenancy in Severalty	Tenancy in Common	Joint Tenancy	Tenancy by Entireties
DEFINITION	Property held by one person, severed from all others.	Property held by two or more persons with no right of survivorship.	Property held by two or more individuals (not corporation), with right of survivorship.	Property held by husband and wife with right of survivorship.
CREATION	Any transfer to one person.	By express act; also by failure to express the tenancy.	Express intention plus four unities of time, title, interest, and possession (with statutory exception).	Express intention, only husband and wife in most states. Divorce automatically results in tenancy in common.
POSSESSION	Total.	Equal right of possession.	Equal right of possession.	Equal right of possession.
TITLE	One title in one person.	Each co-owner has a separate legal title to his or her undivided interest; will be equal interests unless expressly made unequal.	One title to the whole property because each tenant is theoretically deemed owner of whole; must be equal undivided interests.	One title in the marital unit.
CONVEYANCE	No restrictions (check release of marital rights if any).	Each co-owner's interest may be conveyed separately by its owner; purchaser becomes tenant in common.	Conveyance of one co-owner's interest breaks his or her tenancy; purchaser becomes tenant in common.	Cannot convey without consent of spouse.
EFFECT OF DEATH	Entire property subject to probate and included in gross estate for federal and state death taxes.	Decedent's fractional interest subject to probate and included in gross estate for federal and state death taxes. The property passes by will to devisees or heirs, who take as tenants in common. No survivorship rights.	No probate and cannot be disposed of by will; property automatically belongs to surviving cotenants (last one holds in severalty). Entire property included in decedent's gross estate for federal estate tax purposes, minus % attributable to survivor's contributions, i.e., the net value.	Right of survivorship, so no probate. Same death taxes as joint tenancy.
CREDITOR'S RIGHTS	Subject to creditor claims.	Co-owner's fractional interest may be sold to satisfy his or her creditor. Buyer becomes tenant in common.	Joint tenant's interest also subject to execution sale; joint tenancy is broken and purchaser becomes tenant in common. Creditor gets nothing if debtor tenant dies before sale.	Only a creditor of both spouses can execute on property.
PRESUMED BY LAW	None.	Favored in doubtful cases; presumed to be equal interests.	Not favored, so must be expressly stated.	Must be expressly stated.

QUESTIONS

1. Only a husband and wife may hold title to real property as
   A. joint tenants.
   B. tenants by the entirety.
   C. tenants in common.
   D. tenants by the severalty.

2. One of the advantages of a joint tenancy is that it
   A. cannot be terminated without the consent of each tenant.
   B. can be held in different fractional shares.
   C. avoids the delays and expenses of probate.
   D. can exist only between husband and wife.

3. Which of the following events creates a tenancy in common?
   A. Transfer of one joint tenant's interest to a third party
   B. Death of one of two joint tenants
   C. Transfer of one joint tenant's interest to the other joint tenant
   D. Death of one of four joint tenants

4. A tenant in common may transfer his or her interest under which of the following circumstances?
   A. Only with the permission and approval of the other tenants in common
   B. At any time, without permission or approval, even under protest
   C. Only at the expiration of the lease
   D. Only for a valuable consideration

5. A woman and her brother hold property in joint tenancy. What results if the woman deeds her part to herself and her husband?
   A. The deed to the husband is invalid.
   B. The joint tenancy is severed.
   C. All three now hold title in joint tenancy.
   D. The joint tenancy remains the same.

6. A property is purchased by a brother and sister with equal shares. This could be a
   A. tenancy by the entirety.
   B. joint tenancy.
   C. tenancy in community.
   D. tenancy in severalty.

7. Two sisters, Florence and Mary, inherit real property from their mother with no stipulation except that one-third is to go to Florence and two-thirds to Mary. Which of the following is *TRUE?*
   A. Florence and Mary are joint tenants of the property.
   B. Mary may not mortgage her interest in the property without Florence's consent.
   C. Upon Florence's death, her part of the property reverts to Mary.
   D. Upon Mary's death, her share passes to her heirs or devisees.

8. If title to a farm is held in tenancy by the entirety, which of the following is *TRUE?*
   A. A specifically enforceable contract to sell the farm must be signed by husband and wife.
   B. A creditor of one spouse can assert a valid lien on the farm.
   C. Either husband or wife may partition the property.
   D. The shares may be unequal.

9. When purchasing real estate, the form or method of ownership (severalty, tenants in common, joint tenants) would BEST be determined by a
   A. broker.
   B. buyer and attorney.
   C. seller and CPA.
   D. salesperson.

10. Tom and Sam take title to a farm as joint tenants. Assuming Sam dies, which of the following is *TRUE?*
    A. Tom holds title with Sam's heirs.
    B. Tom holds title to the whole farm subject to the marital interest of Sam's surviving wife.
    C. The farm may be sold to satisfy Sam's creditors.
    D. Tom is the sole owner of the property.

11. In a joint tenancy among five people, all of the following are true *EXCEPT*
    A. shares must be equal.
    B. any party may convey his or her share without consent of the others.
    C. any of the five parties may will away his or her share.
    D. one of the owners may sell to another person, who now owns a one-fifth tenancy in common.

12. A joint tenancy may accomplish all of the following *EXCEPT*
    A. sell the interest.
    B. give away the interest.
    C. encumber the interest.
    D. devise the interest.

13. Tenancy in common is a form of
    A. survivorship.
    B. ownership.
    C. probate.
    D. partition.

14. An action brought by a co-owner of property to compel the severance of respective interests is an action for
    A. foreclosure.
    B. quiet title.
    C. forfeiture.
    D. partition.

15. A tenancy in common must have the unity of
    A. time.
    B. title.
    C. interest.
    D. possession.

16. When someone owns property to the exclusion of all other persons, this person is said to hold the property in
    A. personalty.
    B. common.
    C. severalty.
    D. secret.

17. In the case of three tenants in common owning a property, which of the following is *TRUE?*
    A. A tenant's estate ends upon his or her death.
    B. There is just one title to the property representing the undivided interests of all cotenants.
    C. Each tenant has a separate and distinct interest.
    D. The last surviving tenant would hold title in severalty.

18. A tenant in common can do which of the following?
    A. Encumber the whole property
    B. Convey any part of the property so as to bind the interest of another tenant in common
    C. Sell the entire property
    D. Own two-thirds of the property

19. ◎ A husband and wife contact a broker about selling their home. The wife has a number of outstanding debts. Which is *TRUE* of this property, which is held as tenancy by the entirety?
    A. The listing broker should get both husband and wife to sign the listing.
    B. The wife's creditors have a right to take one half of the property in settlement of the debts.
    C. The property should not be sold until the debts have been paid.
    D. The debts of both spouses are of no importance to the broker listing the property.

20. Which of the following statements applies equally to two joint tenants and to tenants by the entirety?
    A. There can be no right to file a partition suit.
    B. The last living tenant becomes sole owner.
    C. A deed signed by one party will convey a fractional interest.
    D. A deed will not convey any interest unless signed by both spouses.

21. Where two cousins hold title to property, one having a one-third interest and the other having a two-thirds interest, title is held in
    A. joint tenancy.
    B. tenancy by the entirety.
    C. tenancy in common.
    D. tenancy in severalty.

22. Abe conveys property to Ben and Carlie, who are unrelated and not joint tenants. When Ben dies, what most likely happens to ownership of the property?
    A. Carlie is the sole owner.
    B. Ben's share goes to his heirs.
    C. Property reverts back to Abe.
    D. Ben's share escheats to the state.

23. All of the following tenancies would permit partition if the husband and wife cannot agree on the sale of the property *EXCEPT*
    A. joint tenancy.
    B. tenancy by the entirety.
    C. tenancy in common.
    D. tenancy in partnership.

24. ◎ Which is *TRUE* regarding the liability of a limited partner?
    A. Liability is to the extent of his or her investment.
    B. Liability is without limits.
    C. Liability is limited to short-term debts of the partnership.
    D. Personal liability is limited to a stated percentage of partnership debts.

25. Bob and Carlos have a concurrent unequal interest in the same property. Regarding this type of ownership interest, which *BEST* describes Bob and Carlos's title?
    A. Bob and Carlos both hold title as joint tenants.
    B. Bob and Carlos both hold title as tenants in common.
    C. Bob and Carlos would be classified as tenants by the entirety.
    D. Bob and Carlos would be classified as tenants for years.

26. The four unities of title, time, interest, and possession normally are found in which of the following?
    A. Tenancy in common
    B. Partnership
    C. Mortgage or trust deed
    D. Joint tenancy

27. A corporation and an individual cannot hold title to real property as joint tenants because
    A. it is in violation of the Securities Act.
    B. a corporation has perpetual existence.
    C. it is difficult to list all stockholders in the deed.
    D. a corporation cannot convey title to real property.

28. Alex, Brad, and Curt own property as joint tenants. Curt dies, then Brad sells his interest in the property to Dan. The property is now owned by
    A. Alex, Dan, and Curt's widow and Earl (his sole heir) as joint tenants.
    B. Alex and Dan as joint tenants.
    C. Alex and Dan as tenants in common, each with one-half interest.
    D. Alex, Dan, and Brad's wife.

29. The *BEST* term that describes a group of investors who pool their financial resources to acquire real property is
    A. rental pool.
    B. syndication.
    C. consolidation.
    D. limited liability company.

30. ◎ Which is usually *TRUE* under commonly accepted principles of tenancy law?
    A. Unless otherwise specified, a conveyance of property to a man and woman is automatically construed as a "tenancy by the entirety."
    B. Tenancy by the entirety is characterized by a right of survivorship, which may be severed only by divorce or by joint conveyance of the husband and wife.
    C. A joint tenancy may be created by operation of law rather than by intent of the parties.
    D. Tenants by the entirety may will away their separate halves of the property.

31. Cindy, Barb, and Sue are tenants in common. If Barb dies
    A. Cindy's share in the property is unaffected.
    B. Barb's interest goes to Cindy.
    C. Barb's interest goes to Cindy and Sue.
    D. Barb's interest automatically goes to her surviving spouse.

32. The right of survivorship is a feature of which of the following types of tenancy?
    A. Joint tenancy
    B. Tenancy in common
    C. Tenancy in severalty
    D. Tenancy for years

33. One of the distinguishing characteristics of joint tenancy is that
    A. tenants possess separate estates.
    B. tenants may possess unequal interests in a single estate.
    C. interests of a deceased tenant pass to the remaining tenants.
    D. interests of a deceased tenant pass to heirs rather than to the other tenants.

34. Which of the following methods of ownership could result in double income taxation?
    A. Joint tenancy
    B. S Corporation
    C. Corporation
    D. Partnership

35. A joint tenant in real property who wishes to dispose of the interest
    A. may not file for partition.
    B. has no recourse except to sell the interest to other joint tenants.
    C. may convey to a nontenant who becomes a tenant in common.
    D. has no recourse except to buy out the other joint tenants.

36. When owners of a tenancy by the entirety are divorced, they
    A. become tenants in common.
    B. become tenants at sufferance.
    C. remain tenants by entireties.
    D. automatically become joint tenants with right of survivorship.

37. ◎ All of the following are in harmony with joint tenancy ownership *EXCEPT*
    A. probate.
    B. survivorship.
    C. undivided interest.
    D. equal shares.

38. A buyer is thinking of purchasing an interest in a resort condominium that would guarantee possession of a specific two-bedroom unit for March of every year. Which of the following forms of ownership might a broker recommend?
    A. Time-sharing
    B. Corporate
    C. Cooperative
    D. Syndication

39. If two friends were partners in a business and invested in a parcel of real estate as tenants in common, which of the following would be *TRUE* about the investment?
    A. They would have equal interests.
    B. They would have unity of time.
    C. They would have to sell at the same time.
    D. They both would have equal rights of possession.

40. Which of the following *BEST* describes a tenancy in severalty?
    A. Property held by several people with right of survivorship
    B. Property held by a corporation and a partnership together
    C. Property held by several people whose interest passes to their respective heirs
    D. Property held by one person, whose ownership rights are severed from all others

41. A broker helped buyers prepare an offer to purchase a three-bedroom home. The buyers asked the broker whether they should hold title as joint tenants. The broker should advise them to
    A. take title as tenants by the entirety.
    B. consult a title company.
    C. take title as tenants in common.
    D. consult an attorney.

42. In a will, a father left a farm to a daughter and a brother—the daughter to take a three-quarters interest and the brother a one-quarter interest. The father stated that there would be "a right of survivorship between them." How will they hold title?
    A. As joint tenants
    B. As tenants in common
    C. As tenants by the entirety
    D. As tenants in severalty

43. A testator prepared a will leaving his farm to his wife and daughter, the wife to have a two-thirds interest and the daughter a one-third. Title would be held as
    A. tenants by the entirety.
    B. joint tenants.
    C. tenants in severalty.
    D. tenants in common.

44. A mother and son could hold property in which manner?
    A. Tenants by the entirety
    B. Community property
    C. Joint tenants
    D. Tenancy in severalty

45. Carl and Samuel own a farm as joint tenants. Which of the following statements is *TRUE?*
    A. Samuel's wife has a dower interest in the property.
    B. Carl can transfer his interest in the property by will.
    C. Upon Samuel's death his interest will pass to his widow.
    D. Carl can sell his half interest in the farm without Samuel's consent.

46. Your client plans to get divorced shortly before closing on a property she and her boyfriend just purchased and asks you about how to hold title to the property. You should suggest she
    A. get divorced first.
    B. conceal the pending divorce.
    C. consult an attorney.
    D. choose joint tenancy.

47. ◎ When a person who owns real estate in severalty dies testate, the property
    A. goes entirely to the surviving joint tenant.
    B. is probated and distributed according to the will.
    C. is solely vested in the remaining tenant in common.
    D. reverts to the county by escheat.

48. ◎ Assume a real estate broker incorporates her real estate firm. Which is *TRUE?*
    A. The firm is a separate legal entity, distinct from the broker.
    B. The broker is liable for the debts of the corporation.
    C. The broker can advertise solely in her individual name.
    D. The shareholders must have real estate licenses.

49. In what way is tenancy by the entirety different from joint tenancy for a husband and wife?
    A. The right of survivorship exists.
    B. There is equal undivided interest.
    C. Creditors of both can claim the property.
    D. One spouse can sell only with the other's consent.

50. ◎ In the sale of real property owned by a limited partnership, who must sign the sales contract or deed for it to be valid?
   A. Each limited partner
   B. Any limited partner
   C. Each general partner
   D. Any general partner

51. ◎ In some states a husband has a 50 percent interest in property acquired by his wife during marriage. This is known as
   A. dower.
   B. curtesy.
   C. community property.
   D. tenancy by the entirety.

ANSWERS

1. **B.** The *marital unit* (husband and wife) actually owns the property. Husband and wife could also hold title as (A), (C), or (D) in severalty, if each holds different property separately. Tenancy by the entirety exists in a minority of states.

2. **C.** There is no interest left in the deceased joint tenant's estate. Because it passes to the surviving tenant, there is nothing to probate. A joint tenancy can be severed by transfer of one tenant's interest. Shares must be equal, and anyone but a corporation can be a joint tenant. Consent from all is needed to sell the property, not an interest.

3. **A.** The third party would be a tenant in common with the remaining joint tenants. The original tenancy would be severed. In (D) the three remaining owners still would be joint tenants with one another.

4. **B.** To avoid this result, some cotenants enter into a right of first refusal agreement, whereby any sale must be first offered to the other cotenants. Choice (D) is wrong because there could be a gift of a tenancy in common interest as well as a sale.

5. **B.** The joint tenancy is severed on the transfer, with the brother owning one-half undivided interest and the husband and wife owning the other half, which could be held as tenancy by the entirety, joint tenancy, or tenancy in common. They are tenants in common as to their respective half interests.

6. **B.** Only husband and wife can be tenants by the entirety. It could also be a tenancy in common, but this is not one of the choices.

7. **D.** There is no right of survivorship with tenancy in common. In a joint tenancy, the shares must be equal. Just as tenants in common can transfer their interest, they can also mortgage it, although most lenders do not prefer to hold a tenancy-in-common type of security.

8. **A.** If only one spouse had signed such a contract, the buyer could not obtain specific performance against the nonsigning spouse. The creditor must be a creditor of the marital unit, which explains why lenders often insist on both spouses signing loan agreements or mortgages.

9. **B.** Such a determination involves the practice of law, especially because there are important estate tax ramifications. A broker should be able to describe the differences among the various types of tenancies; however, the broker should not make a recommendation or the ultimate decision.

10. **D.** Joint tenants hold the property free from claims of dower or curtesy of spouses, free from claims of creditors or heirs of a deceased joint tenant, and free from the laws of descent.

11. **C.** A will is ineffective to transfer a joint tenant's interest because the interest ceases at death of the joint tenant and passes to the surviving joint tenants. Shares must be equal, and any person may convey his or her share without the consent of the others. If one of the owners sells his or her ownership, the joint tenancy is broken, with regard to this conveyance, so the new owner holds a one-fifth interest as a tenant in common with the remaining four owners, who remain joint

tenants. For example, if Number one conveyed a one-fifth share to a sixth person, then Numbers Two, Three, Four, and Five would be joint tenants with each other, with a total of four-fifths undivided interest, while Number Six would be a tenant in common with a one-fifth undivided interest.

12. **D.** There is no property left to transfer by will (devise) because the remaining joint tenant(s) has survived to the decedent's interest.

13. **B.** Tenancy in common is a popular form of *ownership*. It is joint tenancy that deals with survivorship.

14. **D.** If the cotenants cannot reach an agreement on splitting the property, then any one tenant can petition the court to partition the property. They can try to physically divide the property (partition in kind) or else sell it and split the net proceeds. Most courts first attempt a partition in kind, but this is sometimes impossible—for example, in the case of a studio condominium property.

15. **D.** Although a joint tenancy traditionally requires all of these four unities, each tenant in common has only an undivided interest to possess the whole. Thus, in a tenancy in common involving two people, each person owns a 50 percent interest in 100 percent of the property.

16. **C.** This person's ownership is severed from that of anyone else. *Personalty* (A) is another word for personal property.

17. **C.** Each cotenant has an undivided interest in the entire property. There is no right to possess any specific portion of the property. Thus, one tenant cannot stake a claim to the portion he or she uses. (A), (B), and (D) refer to joint tenancy.

18. **D.** Choices (A), (B), and (C) require the consent of all cotenants.

19. **A.** Many courts still would enforce a listing against the sole signing spouse (meaning the one signing could be liable for a commission), but it is best to get both to sign. Both spouses must owe the creditor for the possibility of executing against the home to exist. (There may be a different result if they are joint tenants.)

20. **B.** (A) and (D) are true in a tenancy by the entirety. (D) is false as it relates to joint tenancy. (C) is true as it relates to a joint tenancy. (A) is false because in most areas joint tenants can partition.

21. **C.** The key to this question is the unequal shares.

22. **B.** Bob and Carlie are tenants in common. The interest of the deceased tenant in common passes to his or her heirs.

23. **B.** The marital unit owns the property in tenancy by the entirety, so one spouse cannot seek partition.

24. **A.** A general partner usually is liable for all the debts of the partnership. A limited partner loses limited liability if he or she participates in the management of the partnership.

25. **B.** The unequal interests indicate there is a tenancy in common. Joint tenancy and tenancy by the entirety require equal interests.

26. **D.** Many state statutes have relaxed the traditional rules of these four unities and thus allow one person to transfer title to himself or herself and another as joint tenants or to use a nominee.

27. **B.** Because corporations have perpetual existence unless dissolved, the corporation always would be the surviving joint tenant.

28. **C.** Alex and Dan are not joint tenants because they have separate titles created at different times. Alex and Brad were fifty-fifty joint tenants after Curt's death, and then Dan bought Brad's interest; this severed the joint tenancy.

29. **B.** The word *syndication* refers to a group of people united for the purpose of making and operating an investment. It may take the form of a limited partnership or a general partnership. A *rental pool* (A) refers to an arrangement whereby participating owners of rental apartments agree to make their apartments available for rental and share in the profits and losses according to an agreed-upon formula. A *limited liability company* is often a professional business form of organization.

30. **B.** In most states, a tenancy involving survivorship must be created by clear and definite words. Otherwise, it will be construed as a tenancy in common. In a few states, however, the mere conveyance to husband and wife automatically creates a tenancy by the entirety.

31. **A.** Barb's interest goes to her heirs.

32. **A.** Tenant-in-common interests pass to the heirs or beneficiaries of the will rather than to the surviving tenant in common.

33. **C.** This is the right of survivorship.

34. **C.** A corporation is subject to tax on its profits, and the stockholders will be taxed again on any dividends distributed to them. On partnerships and S Corporations, income and expenses are passed through to the owners, so taxes are paid only once.

35. **C.** Joint tenancies may be severed by transfer of one's interest in the property. In some cases, the parties agree to give their cotenants a right of first refusal.

36. **A.** Because the marital unit is ended, the tenancy by entirety also ends. Often there is a property settlement agreement that resolves who gets the property, or the owners may elect to form a joint tenancy or a tenancy in common. Otherwise, by operation of law, property is held in tenancy in common.

37. **A.** An attractive feature of joint tenancy ownership is that it avoids the delay and expense of probate. Contrary to popular belief, however, it does not avoid the payment of death taxes by the estate of the deceased joint tenant.

38. **A.** Time-sharing is a recent development in communal living. Different people purchase the right to use a piece of real property (typically a condominium unit) for a set period each year for a definite or indefinite period of years. The different owners could be tenants in common (called *time-interval ownership*), members of a special club, or lessees under a vacation lease plan.

39. **D.** Tenants in common can have different interests and need not acquire the property at the same time or from the same deed. The only unity required is that of possession—an undivided interest to possess the entire parcel.

40. **D.** Tenancy in severalty is ownership of property severed from anyone else's ownership. Choice (B) describes a tenancy in common. (Corporations can't hold title as joint tenants.)

41. **D.** Brokers should not determine the best tenancy for those with whom they deal. Because of the important tax and estate implications of such a selection, an attorney should be consulted. Title companies insure good title; they don't advise how to select the method of holding title.

42. **B.** *A* may have wanted to create a joint tenancy, but joint tenants must have equal shares. The law favors tenancy in common, so the courts in this case will keep the shares at three-quarters and one-quarter but eliminate the right of survivorship.

43. **D.** Devisees under a will frequently obtain title to the deceased's real property as tenants in common. Because the interests are unequal, they cannot be joint tenants. Only husband and wife can be tenants by the entirety.

44. **C.** Choices (A) and (B) are forms of ownership requiring the parties to be husband and wife.

45. **D.** Dower does not apply to joint-tenancy property. There is no property left in the estate to pass by will because the remaining joint tenants survive to the interest of the deceased joint tenant.

46. **C.** The client can be best served by having an experienced real estate attorney discuss the best type of tenancy based on the pending divorce.

47. **B.** A tenant in severalty is the sole owner of the property; if he or she dies leaving a will (testate), the property passes according to the terms of the probated will.

48. **A.** The corporation is a separate legal entity under state law; thus, the broker is not responsible for its debts. Under (D), only the principal broker needs a broker license.

49. **D.** One joint tenant spouse can sever the joint tenancy, whereas only the marital unit can sell tenancy by entirety property.

50. **C.** The contract or deed must be signed by each general partner unless the partnership agreement designates a specific partner. Limited partners need not sign either, as they have no participation in management and are treated as investors only.

51. **C.** States such as California and Washington are community property states. If property was acquired prior to marriage, it remains separate property.

2

Interests in Real Property

Although houses in a neighborhood might look the same, each property is unique. The real estate agent needs to understand what bundle of rights attaches to each property and a title report provides helpful information and insight on those rights.

Property describes the rights or interests a person has in the thing owned, commonly called the "bundle of rights," which includes the right to possess, to use, to encumber, to transfer, and to exclude. Property is either personal or real. It is important to distinguish between real and personal property because the law treats them differently for purposes of transferring ownership, taxes, probate, and enforcement of liens.

The interest one acquires in real property is called an *estate,* reflecting one's "status" of ownership. It describes the degree, nature, quantity, and extent of a person's interest in property. There are "freehold" and "leasehold" estates.

Questions in this chapter will test your comprehension of the following topics:

■ Estates and interests in real property such as fee simple and life estates

■ The difference between fixtures and personal property

■ The effect of riparian and littoral rights on ownership

■ The creation of interests in real property under a last will and testament

K E Y   W O R D S

Bundle of rights: An ownership concept describing all those legal rights that attach to the ownership of real property, including the right to sell, lease, encumber, use, enjoy, exclude, will, etc.

Fee simple: The largest estate one can possess in real property. A fee simple estate is the least limited interest and the most complete and absolute ownership in land: it is of indefinite duration, freely transferable, and inheritable.

Fixture: An article that was once personal property but has been so affixed to the real estate that it has become real property (e.g., stoves, bookcases, plumbing). If determined to be a fixture, then the article passes with the property even though it is not mentioned in the deed.

Intestate: To die without a valid will.

Less-than-freehold estate: An estate held by one who rents or leases property. This classification includes an estate for years, a periodic tenancy, an estate at will, and an estate at sufferance.

Life estate: Any estate in real or personal property that is limited in duration to the life of its owner or the life of some other designated person.

Probate: The formal judicial proceeding to prove or confirm the validity of a will. The will is presented to the probate court, and creditors and interested parties are notified to present their claims or to show cause why the provisions of the will should not be enforced by the court.

Property: The rights or interests a person has in the thing owned; not, in the technical sense, the thing itself. These rights include the right to possess, to use, to encumber, to transfer, and to exclude, commonly called the *bundle of rights.*

Real property: All land and appurtenances to land, including buildings, structures, fixtures, fences, and improvements erected upon or affixed to the same, excluding, however, growing crops.

Riparian: Those rights and obligations that are incidental to ownership of land adjacent to or abutting on watercourses such as streams and lakes.

MISTAKEN IDENTITY

The following words are often confused with one another. Note the difference in meaning of these mistaken identity words and phrases.

Remainder/Reversion: At the termination of a life estate, the property may revert back to the grantor (reversion) or transfer away from the grantor when a third party remainderman is designated.

Executor/Testator: A *testator* writes a will, whereas an *executor* (also called a *personal representative*) executes or carries out the terms of the will after the testator dies.

Devise/Demise: A *devise* is a transfer of real property by will; a *demise* is a transfer by lease of the (demised) premises.

Testate/Intestate: To die with a will is to die *testate;* to die without one is to die *intestate* (in which case the state writes the will).

QUESTIONS

1. When a deed does *NOT* specify the estate being conveyed, it is presumed to transfer a(n)
   - A. defeasible fee.
   - B. fee simple absolute.
   - C. estate for years.
   - D. life estate.

2. One is seized of property when he or she
   - A. is the lawful owner.
   - B. is a trespasser.
   - C. is in possession of property under a lease.
   - D. has fulfilled the required period for adverse possession.

3. ◎ If Alycia deeds property to Bernice and her heirs, with the stipulation that if Bernice leaves no heirs the property will then go to Cynthia, then Cynthia now holds which type of estate?
   - A. Contingent life estate
   - B. Contingent reversion fee
   - C. Contingent remainder fee
   - D. Reversionary interest

4. In a deed that states "to Arlo for his life," the grantor has what type of interest?
   - A. Life estate
   - B. Remainder
   - C. Reversion
   - D. Right of reentry

5. A life estate may be granted
   - A. only when it is for the duration of the grantee's life.
   - B. for the duration of the life of someone other than the grantee.
   - C. for a definite term.
   - D. only to a grantee over the age of majority.

6. A freehold could be any of the following *EXCEPT* a(n)
   - A. life estate.
   - B. fee simple estate.
   - C. estate for years.
   - D. defeasible fee estate.

7. Fee simple is all of the following *EXCEPT*
   - A. an estate of inheritance.
   - B. a freehold estate.
   - C. a less-than-freehold estate.
   - D. indefinite as to its duration.

8. A hospital receives a gift of real property from an elderly couple who reserve to themselves a life estate. The hospital is which of the following?
   - A. Grantor
   - B. Remainderman
   - C. Reversionary party
   - D. Donor

9. An owner of a life estate can do all of the following *EXCEPT*
   - A. sell.
   - B. mortgage.
   - C. devise.
   - D. lease.

10. A widow who is willed the use of the family home for the rest of her natural life, with provision that title shall pass to the children upon her death, holds a(n)
    - A. fee simple estate.
    - B. leasehold.
    - C. easement.
    - D. life estate.

11. ◎ Which of the following is *CORRECT* regarding a life estate?
    - A. It must be measured by the life of one person only.
    - B. Because it is based on life, it may not be encumbered by the holder.
    - C. It may be created by will or deed.
    - D. It requires that the holder make principal payments on any encumbrances.

12. The degree, quantity, or nature of a person's interest in real property is known as his or her
    - A. estate.
    - B. dower.
    - C. curtesy.
    - D. possession.

13. The return of land to the grantor or grantor's heirs when the grant is over is *BEST* described as
    A. remainder.
    B. reversion.
    C. kickback.
    D. surrender.

14. An estate in land vested in a grantee "until he or she marries" is properly classifiable as
    A. an estate in equity.
    B. a defeasible fee.
    C. less than a freehold estate.
    D. a life estate.

15. An example of a less-than-freehold estate is a(n)
    A. life estate.
    B. leasehold estate.
    C. estate on condition subsequent.
    D. mortgaged estate.

16. With respect to real property, the term *estate* is *BEST* described as
    A. all property left by the deceased.
    B. a bequest of a specific property in a will.
    C. fee simple ownership of property.
    D. the nature and degree of an interest in real property.

17. Which of the following provides the greatest assurance that you are getting fee simple ownership?
    A. The owner will give a general warranty deed.
    B. The owner can furnish title insurance.
    C. The deed contains the covenant of seisin.
    D. The habendum clause states that a fee estate is what is being conveyed.

18. The interest in real property with the *LEAST* bundle of rights is
    A. tenancy at will.
    B. fee simple absolute.
    C. fee simple subject to condition subsequent.
    D. tenancy at sufferance.

19. All of the following are characteristics of a fee simple estate *EXCEPT*
    A. freely transferable.
    B. freely inheritable.
    C. definite duration.
    D. unlimited duration.

20. An estate for life that a husband takes at the death of his wife in one-third of the real property of which she was seized at the time of her death is called
    A. fee simple estate.
    B. dower.
    C. curtesy.
    D. estate in remainder.

21. If Heloise possessed a fee simple estate, she could do any of the following to the property *EXCEPT*
    A. sell it.
    B. subdivide it.
    C. use it contrary to zoning regulations.
    D. will it.

22. An estate for years in real estate can also be called a
    A. leasehold.
    B. fee simple conditional.
    C. fee.
    D. joint tenancy.

23. Of the following, the largest estate or ownership in real property is a(n)
    A. estate at sufferance.
    B. estate at will.
    C. life estate.
    D. fee simple estate.

24. ◎ The holder of which of the following would be a "nonfreeholder"?
    A. Life estate
    B. Defeasible fee
    C. Unrecorded vendor's deed
    D. Estate for years

25. The grantor of a life estate can do all of the following *EXCEPT*
    A. grant title using an assumed name.
    B. receive title upon the death of the life tenant.
    C. take back fee title at any time.
    D. create a life estate for the life of more than one person.

26. A licensee is concerned about a construction project going on next to a property she is selling. Where would she be *BEST* advised to go to clarify any question about an encroachment?
    A. City attorney
    B. Planning department
    C. Licensed surveyor
    D. Tax office records

27. With what type of estate is the phrase "of indefinite duration" *MOST* usually associated?
    A. Estate of inheritance
    B. Tenancy at sufferance
    C. Leasehold estate
    D. Estate for years

28. An example of personal property is
    A. household furnishings.
    B. wall-to-wall carpeting.
    C. built-in dishwasher.
    D. garbage disposal.

29. Which of the following is typically personal property?
    A. Gas and mineral rights
    B. Water rights
    C. A beneficiary's rights under a real property trust
    D. Trees on a farm

30. Which of the following *BEST* defines real property?
    A. Land and the air above it
    B. Land and the area below and above the surface to infinity and all the improvements thereon
    C. The land, buildings thereon, and anything permanently affixed to the land and/or buildings
    D. Land and the mineral rights in the land

31. Generally, things or objects of a temporary or easily movable nature are
    A. realty.
    B. devices.
    C. personalty.
    D. appurtenances.

32. Assume the contract for the sale of real property includes the sale of certain removable items, such as paintings and furniture. Upon delivery of the deed, the seller should also deliver a(n)
    A. bill of sale.
    B. estoppel certificate.
    C. chattel mortgage.
    D. satisfaction piece.

33. Each of the following is an appurtenance *EXCEPT* a(n)
    A. barn.
    B. orchard.
    C. fence.
    D. trade fixture.

34. The *MOST* important factor in determining whether something is a fixture is
    A. the method of its attachment.
    B. its size.
    C. its weight.
    D. the intention of the party who attached it.

35. All of the following are required for a valid bill of sale *EXCEPT*
    A. signature of the seller.
    B. description of the items.
    C. date of transaction.
    D. name of buyer.

36. Which of the following *BEST* describes personal property?
    A. Chattel
    B. Appurtenance
    C. Fixture
    D. Improvement

37. ◎ "Littoral" property is located on
    A. a hillside.
    B. the seashore.
    C. the boundary line.
    D. a stream.

38. In real estate, the term *improvements* most
    nearly means
    A. fences, wells, drains, and roadways.
    B. additions to the original structure.
    C. everything artificial or constructed except
       the land.
    D. upgrades to the interior.

39. The rights of ownership, including the right to
    use, possess, enjoy, and dispose of a thing in
    any legal way so as to exclude everyone else
    without rights from interfering, are called
    A. corporeal ownership.
    B. incorporeal ownership.
    C. bundle of rights.
    D. survivorship.

40. An appropriation of land for some public use
    made by the owner and accepted for such use
    by or on behalf of the public, such as streets
    in a platted subdivision, is called
    A. an easement.
    B. dedication.
    C. a public grant.
    D. condemnation.

41. An owner of real property is in doubt whether
    riparian rights are included. This can *BEST* be
    determined by reviewing the
    A. water department records of the county
       recorder.
    B. title policy.
    C. grant deed.
    D. appropriate state law.

42. ◎ The boundary of a property is changed by
    A. accretion.
    B. avulsion.
    C. encroachments.
    D. construction of a fence.

43. A riparian owner is one who owns land
    bounding on
    A. municipal property.
    B. a waterway.
    C. a national forest.
    D. unsurveyed public lands.

44. In a physical sense, real estate may be said to
    include everything *EXCEPT*
    A. the surface of the earth.
    B. the air above the surface.
    C. personal property.
    D. the subsurface.

45. Riparian rights are those rights possessed by
    A. an owner living in a townhouse subdivi-
       sion.
    B. an owner living on a waterway.
    C. an owner entitled to ripened fruit from
       crops.
    D. owners of land granting easements for
       city water pipes.

46. The removal of land when a stream suddenly
    changes its channel is
    A. adverse possession.
    B. breach.
    C. avulsion.
    D. accretion.

47. ◎ A landowner who sells a one-acre farm
    must
    A. specifically reserve the mineral rights
       therein, or they will automatically pass
       to the buyer.
    B. specifically describe the air rights in the
       deed for the buyer to gain title thereto.
    C. sign a quitclaim deed to release air
       rights.
    D. release any riparian rights.

48. ◎ A father deeds a life estate in the farm to
    his son. The son sells this interest to a friend.
    What happens to the farm when the friend
    dies?
    A. It goes back to the son.
    B. It goes to the father.
    C. It goes to the friend's heirs.
    D. It goes to the state.

49. The loss of one's real estate by the gradual wearing away of soil through the operation of natural causes is
    A. erosion.
    B. escheat.
    C. curtilage.
    D. obsolescence.

50. An important characteristic of land is that it may be modified or improved. Such improvements tend to increase the value of real estate. All of the following are improvements *EXCEPT*
    A. a new access road.
    B. utilities.
    C. a new house.
    D. planted crops.

51. All of the following types of property are normally real property *EXCEPT*
    A. water rights.
    B. appurtenances.
    C. air space rights.
    D. furniture.

52. Riparian rights are *BEST* described as those rights
    A. specifically granted for a specified source of water.
    B. found in the records of the county recorder's office.
    C. an owner has from a natural watercourse abutting or crossing the land.
    D. obtained by the purchase of fixtures.

53. An example of a right, privilege, or improvement that belongs to and passes with a property is described as a(n)
    A. emblement.
    B. appurtenance.
    C. restriction.
    D. encroachment.

54. The word *fee* used in connection with real property means
    A. the money charged by a broker for services rendered.
    B. an estate of inheritance.
    C. the charge made for searching title.
    D. leased land.

55. The rights to the space above the ground within vertical planes are *BEST* described as
    A. air rights.
    B. the bundle of rights.
    C. solar rights.
    D. riparian rights.

56. Crops that grow on land and require annual planting and cultivation are called
    A. emblements.
    B. fructus naturales.
    C. real property.
    D. fixtures.

57. All rights in the land that happen to pass with the conveyance of the land are *BEST* described as
    A. reversion interests.
    B. warranties.
    C. tenements.
    D. reservation interests.

58. Items that are affixed as appurtenances to land are usually real property. All of the following are real property *EXCEPT*
    A. growing trees.
    B. trade fixtures.
    C. buried water tanks.
    D. buildings.

59. A man dies testate, leaving a wife and minor son. He leaves all of his property to his son. His wife claims her elective share under the Uniform Probate Code. His property will be distributed as follows:
    A. All to the wife
    B. All to the son
    C. Part to the wife and part to the son
    D. None to the wife

60. A man who makes a will is called a(n)
    A. testator.
    B. executor.
    C. testatrix.
    D. administrator.

61. A woman who acquires real property under the terms of a will is known as a(n)
    A. personal representative.
    B. executrix.
    C. devisee.
    D. testatrix.

62. A devisee receives
    A. real property by will.
    B. personal property under a bill of sale.
    C. property by escheat.
    D. property through foreclosure.

63. The word intestate *MOST* nearly means to die
    A. leaving a will.
    B. without leaving a will.
    C. without leaving an heir.
    D. leaving property to the state.

64. Real property conveyed by a codicil to a will is conveyed by
    A. demise.
    B. devise.
    C. decree.
    D. degree.

65. *Probate* means an action to
    A. cure a defect by a quitclaim deed.
    B. prove title by adverse possession.
    C. process a will to establish its validity.
    D. process a partition of property.

66. A devise is a
    A. gift of real estate.
    B. trust in perpetuity.
    C. real estate gift by last testament.
    D. plan or scheme of development.

67. The property of a person who dies intestate passes by
    A. succession.
    B. accretion.
    C. acquisition.
    D. prescription.

68. When a person dies intestate and no heirs can be found for intestate succession, the real property will revert to the government through a process known as
    A. reconveyance.
    B. reversion.
    C. escheat.
    D. succession.

69. When a person dies testate, the real property
    A. escheats and is sold at an auction by the state.
    B. goes to the next of kin.
    C. passes to the devisee.
    D. goes to the administrator.

70. Personal property bestowed in a will would be all of the following *EXCEPT* a
    A. codicil.
    B. gift.
    C. bequest.
    D. legacy.

71. Title to an owner's real estate can be transferred at the death of the owner by which of the following?
    A. Warranty deed
    B. Special warranty deed
    C. Trustee's deed
    D. Last will and testament

72. The word *escheat* refers to the
    A. feudal custom of the king's seizure of land.
    B. right of the government to take private property for a public purpose upon payment.
    C. acquisition of title by adverse possession.
    D. right of the government to acquire title where the owner dies without a will and without heirs.

73. In probating an estate, which of the following is the last to receive payment, if any?
    A. Holder of the second mortgage
    B. Creditors
    C. Heirs
    D. The government for taxes

74. Which of the following words is *NOT* associated with the others in the group?
    A. Testator
    B. Devise
    C. Intestate
    D. Will

75. What document is prepared to evidence that personal property is pledged to secure a loan?
    A. Bill of sale
    B. Chattel mortgage
    C. Bargain and sale deed
    D. Partial release

76. All of the following instruments transfer an interest in real property *EXCEPT* a(n)
    A. option.
    B. lease.
    C. bill of sale.
    D. agreement of sale.

77. ◎ A man executed a will. After his death, the probate court declared the will invalid because it did not meet the state law requirements. Which of the following will receive title to the man's real estate?
    A. The devisees named in the will.
    B. Those entitled under the state laws of intestate succession.
    C. The property escheats to the state.
    D. The previous owners of the property.

78. Who usually selects the executor of an estate?
    A. Probate court
    B. Administrator
    C. Testator
    D. Heirs

79. If a property owner dies without a will, his or her real property will go to which of the following?
    A. The government by escheat
    B. The heirs by descent
    C. Whoever was living on the property at the time
    D. The original grantor

80. Under which of the following conditions would a property owner have riparian rights?
    A. When minerals are discovered under the land
    B. When the land is contiguous to a stream
    C. When the property is in a geothermal area
    D. When the property borders on the ocean

81. When a person dies testate, his or her real property will
    A. escheat to the government.
    B. pass to the next of kin.
    C. descend to the survivors.
    D. pass to the devisees.

82. ◎ Which of the following statements is *FALSE* about a party wall built on the property line between two lots?
    A. Each owner is responsible for one-half of the maintenance fees.
    B. Each owner owns the half of the wall on his or her side and has an easement on the other half.
    C. Only one owner is responsible for the maintenance on the wall.
    D. Neither owner may destroy the wall without the other's permission.

83. ◎ The main purpose of the Uniform Commercial Code is which of the following?
    A. To prevent fraud in the proof of fictitious oral sales contracts
    B. To regulate personal property items pledged in a sale contract
    C. To make real property transactions more uniform
    D. To regulate commercial leasing

ANSWERS

1. **B.** While a defeasible fee (one subject to a condition) and a life estate can be transferred by deed, they must be clearly specified. An estate for years is transferred (demised) by lease. A fee simple absolute is one that is not qualified (or conditional).

2. **A.** Seisin (sometimes spelled "seizin") was the ancient equivalent of ownership; it required some possession coupled with a freehold interest. Seisin had to be delivered to the new owner ("livery of seisin").

3. **C.** A reversionary interest under choice (D) is when the property will return to the grantor or the grantor's heirs. Here the property will "remain" away from the grantor and Cynthia will be the fee owner, provided that (contingent upon) Bernice dies leaving no heirs. Remainders are either vested (owned now) or contingent.

4. **C.** When Arlo dies, his life estate ends, and the property will revert back to the grantor. Rights of reentry are found in leases and also in a fee simple subject to a condition subsequent in which the condition is broken or violated.

5. **B.** The measuring life for a life estate can be that of someone other than the grantee—Abe to Ben for the life of Carl. Thus, upon Carl's death the property will revert back to Abe. If Ben predeceases Carl, Ben's heirs will have an interest in the property until Carl dies. This is called an *estate pur autre vie.*

6. **C.** An estate for years is a leasehold. Next to the fee simple absolute and the defeasible fee, the life estate is the most common freehold estate today. While it is not an estate of inheritance, it is an estate for an indefinite, or unpredictable, duration.

7. **C.** One of the key features of a fee simple is that the property can continue in the same family line through inheritance. The two most popular forms of freehold estates are fee simple (including absolute and conditional fees) and life estates.

8. **B.** After the death of both spouses, the life estate will end and ownership will *remain* away from the grantor's estate. The hospital's remainder interest then will ripen into a fee simple absolute estate. Here is another way to remember what a remainder estate is—it is the estate that remains after the existing life estate terminates.

9. **C.** A devise is a transfer by will (do not confuse with demise, which is a transfer by lease), but there is no estate left for heirs after the owner of the life estate (life tenant) dies. Because the buyer, lender, and lessee take their interest with knowledge, subject to the life estate, their interests cease when the life estate ceases. Lenders rarely lend on a life estate; if they do, they may require a term life insurance policy or an agreement with the remainderman as further security. Incidentally, any buyer of a life estate would then own a "life estate pur autre vie."

10. **D.** During her life she has ownership of a life estate. Her children have a remainder interest. Despite having ownership rights in the property, the widow can't commit "waste," such as tearing the structure down or converting it into a triplex rental.

11. **C.** Life estates are frequently created by will—the husband leaves the home to his wife for life and then to their children. There could be several "life tenants, or the survivor of them." The owner of the fee (grantor of life estate) is responsible for any mortgage principal payments, but the life tenant is responsible for carrying charges, such as interest, taxes, and maintenance.

12. **A.** This is the classic definition of *estate* (Latin for "status"). It ranges from absolute ownership to mere possession.

13. **B.** A *reversion* occurs when the land returns to the grantor or heirs of the grantor. A *remainder* occurs when the land remains away from the grantor or heirs.

14. **B.** This is a freehold estate in fee simple, which can be terminated upon the happening of an event such as marriage. It is also called a *determinable fee* or *qualified fee.*

15. **B.** Leaseholds are less than freehold based on ancient feudal classifications in which only "freemen" had protection of the courts and the serfs had no interest in land, although they had possession under leases.

16. **D.** (A) and (B) could include personal property, and (C) is just one example of an estate.

17. **B.** Under (A) and (B) you would have a claim for money damages if it turned out the grantor did not have the title as promised. There is more assurance of recovering money from the title company than from a grantor. For example, perhaps some defect in the title, owing to some off-record risk (such as forgery in the chain of title), prevents clear ownership of title. Title insurance companies only insure the title subject to stated exceptions; they cannot correct the actual defects that may be found in the title. Also under (C), a deed could be used to transfer a life estate, which is not fee simple ownership.

18. **D.** This involves a tenant who stays in possession after lease termination without the consent of the lessor. A trespasser might try to claim title by way of adverse possession—the tenant cannot because his or her claim is not hostile.

19. **C.** It is indefinite in time; unless conveyed to another, it will come to an end only in the event the owner dies without having left heirs or a valid will (in which case escheat occurs).

20. **C.** Dower is the wife's interest upon the husband's death. The technical rules of dower and curtesy vary greatly from state to state. Many states, usually community property states, have abolished these ancient marital estates and replaced them with the "spouse's right of election"—the right to receive a certain percentage of the deceased spouse's estate.

21. **C.** All but (C) are within the "bundle of rights." Heloise has a fee simple estate. She may not violate the governmental limitation.

22. **A.** It is a leasehold interest for a definite period of time, whether it is one year, ten years, or even ten days.

23. **D.** The largest bundle of rights attaches to a fee simple estate.

24. **D.** An estate for years is the only "less-than-freehold" estate listed here. An unrecorded vendor's (seller) deed would transfer a freehold estate, provided the grantor owned one and there was valid delivery (recording is advised but not required).

25. **C.** Grantors *should* grant title using the same name in which they acquired title. If they don't, this may cause title search problems. However, all that is required for a valid transfer is delivery, and that involves the *intention* of the grantor to relinquish all control to the grantee. Under choice (B) the grantor can structure the transfer so he or she keeps a reversionary interest. A life estate can be for the life of more than one person.

26. **C.** While public records may contain maps of the proper boundaries, these records do not usually reveal any encroachments, such as a fence two feet over a line. The licensee should retain a surveyor to verify the boundaries and reveal any encroachments.

27. **A.** An example is the freehold estate called a *fee simple.*

28. **A.** (B), (C), and (D) are generally treated as being fixtures (chattels real), and thus title passes with the land on its sale. Unless the contract of sale provides otherwise, the seller can remove personal property prior to closing.

29. **C.** The beneficiary does not own the real property, only an interest in the trust. All contracts involving the sale or transfer of property should be executed by the trustee, not the beneficiary only.

30. **B.** Real property includes rights in the land, air rights, subsurface rights, and improvements.

31. **C.** (A), (B), and (D) involve real property. *Personalty* is another word for chattel or personal property.

32. **A.** A bill of sale is especially useful to investors for purposes of allocating values to personal property that can depreciate at faster rates than real property for income tax purposes.

33. **D.** A trade fixture such as a merchant's display case does not become a part of the landlord's property during the term of the lease. Trade fixtures are removable by the tenant.

34. **D.** While (A), (B), and (C) are factors, most courts emphasize the intention test, particularly as noted in the listing and sales contracts.

35. **C.** While the date is frequently given, it is not as essential as the other items. Nevertheless, anyone preparing a bill of sale should insert a date.

36. **A.** Chattel is derived from the word *cattle,* one of early man's most prized possessions. A synonym is personalty.

37. **B.** Littoral property borders on the ocean or sea. Riparian property is located on a watercourse or over an underground nonnavigable stream.

38. **C.** The definitions of (A), (B), and (D) are not quite as broad as (C); thus, (C) is more comprehensive.

39. **C.** Real property is a collection of all one's rights in a certain parcel.

40. **B.** A dedication is, in effect, a grant *to* the public, which may be either a fee simple or an easement. Condemnation is the government's taking private property for a public use with just compensation.

41. **D.** Riparian rights are those rights an owner has to the adjoining nonnavigable water, such as rights to swim, boat, or irrigate. These rights are created by operation of state law. If in doubt, an owner should check with a local real estate attorney.

42. **A.** Accretion is the gradual addition of soil (alluvion) to the shoreline (littoral accretion) or to the land bordering a stream (riparian accretion), which then becomes the property of the shoreline owner or the streamside owner. Avulsion is the tearing away of land caused by a sudden natural occurrence, but the original property line stays intact.

43. **B.** A littoral owner has land that bounds on the ocean. If the land borders on a navigable waterway, then there are no riparian rights because the government would have control over this property.

44. **C.** This is the vertical concept of ownership, which includes subsurface and air rights, as opposed to horizontal ownership such as is found in condominiums.

45. **B.** Such riparian owner would be the beneficiary of any increased land due to accretion and could take some of the water for personal use.

46. **C.** The key word here is "suddenly"; no change in ownership results.

47. **A.** Mineral rights and air rights are typically part of the real estate being sold and, unless reserved to the grantor, will automatically pass to the grantee. However, some states, and sometimes a previous grantor, already may have reserved the mineral rights before the owner obtains title. Therefore, it is important to check state law and the status of the owner's title before taking title.

48. **C.** Note that the question asks what happens when the friend dies, not the son. The life estate is valid until the son dies; thus, it passes to the friend's heirs upon the friend's death. It is an estate for the life of another (an estate *pur autre vie*).

49. **A.** Erosion will result in a loss of one's property. *Curtilage* describes the enclosed space of ground and buildings immediately surrounding a dwellinghouse, such as a courtyard or fenced-in area.

50. **D.** Improvements refer to human-made constructed additions or developments, such as roads, buildings, or fences, which are usually part of the real estate. Planted crops are usually personal property, technically known as *fructus industriales.*

51. **D.** Furniture is personalty unless it is a built-in fixture.

52. **C.** These riparian rights arise by operation of law, and attach to property bordering on a nonnavigable stream.

53. **B.** Appurtenances are rights in land that pass to the new owner. Emblements are annual crops produced by cultivation and are treated as personal property.

54. **B.** Fee refers to a fee simple, which is a freehold estate of inheritance. The broker typically earns a "commission."

55. **A.** The air rights are just one of many of the bundle of rights that go with ownership. Many highrise office buildings and condominiums are built after the developer purchases the air rights. Solar rights involve easements to give access to light and air.

56. **A.** Note that trees and shrubs *not* requiring annual cultivation would be real property, called *fructus naturales.*

57. **C.** *Tenement* is a broad term covering rights to buildings, fences, easements, and rents. Reversion interests return to the grantor in the future and reservation interests remain with the grantor. Warranties may be expressed in the deed.

58. **B.** Trade fixtures such as display cabinets, storage systems, or barber chairs can be removed by the tenant upon expiration of the lease. They are considered personal property. Growing trees are classified as *fructus naturales.*

59. **C.** In those states that have adopted the Uniform Probate Code, she would be entitled to one-third absolute interest in all his property (i.e., she could elect to renounce the will).

60. **A.** A testatrix is a female. Executors (those named in a will) and administrators (those named by the court) handle the settlement of the deceased's estate—a more popular name today is "personal representative."

61. **C.** Real property conveyed by will is called a *devise,* and the recipient is called a *devisee.*

62. **A.** A bequest is a gift of personal property. (A legacy is a gift of money to a legatee.)

63. **B.** In the case of intestacy, the state will, in effect, write a will under its laws of intestate succession (or laws of descent).

64. **B.** A codicil is an addition to a will that must be executed with the same formality as the original will. A demise is a transfer of a real property interest by lease.

65. **C.** When a testator dies, it is necessary to prove the validity of the will and give notice to any creditors that they may file claims. This is all part of the process of transferring title out of the name of the deceased owner.

66. **C.** The devisee must wait for the probate process to settle the decedent's estate and pay the just debts before the devisee will obtain marketable title.

67. **A.** Each state has its own rules as to who will succeed to the intestate person's property. In effect, the state writes the will.

68. **C.** Most state laws allow a long period between death and title passing to the government so that next of kin have sufficient time to file claims.

69. **C.** Testate means to die with a valid will in which real property is passed by way of a devise.

70. **A.** A codicil is an addition to a will and could transfer real property as well as personal property. Bequest is the transfer of personal property, and a legacy is money.

71. **D.** A will differs from a transfer by deed in that a provision in a will is effective only after death and probate. A deed is effective on delivery during the grantor's lifetime. A will can be rewritten any time prior to the death of the testator.

72. **D.** Escheat also applies to abandonment of real property. Choice (B) refers to eminent domain.

73. **C.** Secured creditors, the government, and unsecured creditors all receive payment before the heirs. Sometimes a devisee finds out that the real property he or she was to receive had to be sold to pay all of the debts of the deceased.

74. **C.** Intestate means there is no will, while the rest involve a will prepared by a testator. A devise is real property passing by will.

75. **B.** In those states that have adopted the Uniform Commercial Code, the chattel mortgage is called a *security agreement;* it is the financing statement that is recorded.

76. **C.** A bill of sale is used to transfer title to *personal property* and is sometimes used in real estate transactions, so the seller will warrant that there are no unpaid liens on the title. (A), (B), and (D) all transfer an equitable interest in real property.

77. **B.** In the event of the death of a person who did not leave a valid will, state law will specify which relatives are entitled to succeed to the real and personal property. This is sometimes referred to as the *state laws of intestate succession* or *laws of descent.*

78. **C.** The deceased person usually designates the executor in the will. If one was not designated or the one designated does not qualify, then the probate court will appoint an administrator. In some states, the executor and administrator are referred to as *personal representatives.*

79. **B.** Each state has its own set of rules (of descent) for the method by which property will pass on intestacy. Escheat occurs only if there are no surviving relatives as well as no will.

80. **B.** Riparian rights belong to owners whose land borders a watercourse. They are rights to acquire title to accreted land and rights to boating, swimming, and so forth.

81. **D.** When a person dies testate, the real property will be devised to those people named in the will. If the person dies intestate, then state law determines to whom the property will descend.

82. **C.** Party walls are more frequently used in large city tenements. They involve reciprocal easements of support.

83. **B.** Where personal property is used as security in a land sales contract, the creditor-seller should, under the UCC, perfect the lien by filing a financing statement that describes the particular personal property.

3

Condominiums and Cooperatives

Condominium is a legal concept that describes an ownership system consisting of individual co-owners residing in multiunit structures who have joint ownership in common areas known as common elements. Each unit has an individual deed, is separately assessed for property taxes, can be individually mortgaged, and is eligible for title insurance as a separate piece of property. Condominium owners have the same legal rights of ownership as any other property owners. They have the exclusive use of their interior airspace and can use their units as collateral to obtain financing and homeowners insurance. They can file for homestead and take income tax deductions for mortgage interest and property tax payments. Also, resulting from the Taxpayers Relief Act of 1997, co-owners benefit, up to the legal limits, for any appreciation in value.

Outside of the individual's ownership is property owned in common by the association of co-owners. This interest is in respect to the common areas and facilities that are part of the entire building and land. From among the co-owners, an elected board of directors perform the governing functions, including the legal right to assess for operational costs, maintenance, insurance, and property taxes.

For consistency, state legislatures have drafted condominium laws, legally referring to them as horizontal property regime acts. These statutes outline the structure for creating, establishing, and sustaining condominium ownership. They are essential for developers of condominium projects and serve as a legal blueprint when submitting the *declaration of condominium* for approval. The rules governing the use of the common elements are found in the bylaws and enforced by the association of co-owners. The co-owners own a percentage of interest in the common elements, and often their percentage of ownership mirrors their voting rights too.

Conversion is the required legal process to convert an apartment building or rental housing into condominium ownership.

Cooperatives are residential multiunit buildings whose title is generally held by a corporation, owned and operated for the benefit of the owner-tenants. These persons are the shareholders of the corporation and sign a proprietary (privately owned and managed) lease. Because stock is personal property, the tenant-owners don't legally own real estate as do their condominium owner counterparts. The operation and management are determined by the corporation's bylaws. The corporation is responsible for operational and maintenance costs on the common property as well as individual apartments. Budgeted items are assessed monthly to the shareholders like the common area assessment in a condominium association. Unlike a condominium association that has lien authority against individual owners, the remaining tenants in a cooperative must carry the full burden of delinquent and defaulted assessments. Cooperative owner-tenants enjoy some tax benefits, such as deductible loan interest and property tax contributions.

Only general questions on the condominium and cooperative forms of ownership will appear on the national portion of the exam while specific state laws may appear in the state portion of the test.

Questions in this chapter test your comprehension of the following topics:

■ The difference between owning a condominium and a cooperative

■ Documents involved with condominiums, including bylaws, declaration, and master deed

■ Condominium conversions

K E Y   W O R D S

Air space: Ownership area within a condominium unit that goes from wall to wall and floor to ceiling.

Amenities: Those areas located outside one's owned property that enhance its value. In condominium projects, amenities can include golf courses, clubhouses, swimming pools, tennis courts, gardens, and proximity to shopping, schools, and public transportation. In contrast, features are always located within a property.

Apartment: An architectural term used to describe a residential condominium unit.

Articles of incorporation: Those documents required by state law to establish nonprofit corporations. These documents name the condominium association and identify its purpose and powers.

Assessment: This is a monetary obligation imposed by associations against unit owners for operational costs and common area maintenance (CAM). If the monthly association dues or special assessments are unpaid, the association has the legal authority to place a lien and foreclose on any assessed unit. In addition, a delinquent owner's voting rights may be suspended.

Association: A nonprofit corporation legally created to manage a condominium development sometimes called the homeowner's association. The co-owners' board of directors is responsible for its governance.

Boards of directors: They are defined in the bylaws as elected individuals who oversee the association's business. The bylaws often determine the board's size, term of office, removal, compensation, and authorized actions that can be taken without a meeting.

Bylaws: Recorded documents that name and state the location of the association and define used vocabulary words. They establish the organizational right to conduct association meetings and create the association's board of directors and officers and define their duties. They create the association's assessment authority and indemnification responsibilities and establish amendment authority.

Common area maintenance (CAM): The co-owner's proportionate share of the association's utility bills, insurance premiums, property taxes, general maintenance, repairs, and replacement costs.

Covenants, conditions, and restrictions (CC&Rs): The operational procedures used to describe the rights and prohibitions of co-owners. The CC&Rs begin with definitions and then describe the rights co-owners have in the common areas and illustrate their membership and voting rights. They describe too how the covenant for assessment actually works. Other topics include a description of the association's insurance coverage and their right to levy an assessment for the insurance; easement and encroachment situations; parking rights; party walls; architectural controls; signage; use restrictions; and general provisions. For example, some of the rules deal with outdoor grill usage, exterior decorating, holiday decorating, planting, garbage container placement, payment of association dues, garage usage, garage sales, parking, satellite dish placement, pets, flags and flag poles, signage, structural changes, leasing, snow removal, violation notices, and even mailbox placement.

Common elements: Mutually owned and commonly used property rather than individually owned property in a condominium development. These areas may include the external structure of the unit owner's building and association-owned buildings, such as clubhouses, interior hallways, lobbies and elevators, exterior courtyards, and association-owned streets.

Condominium ownership: Condominium is a legal concept created by state laws that subdivides airspace over a parcel of land and establishes co-ownership in community property. It is an estate in real property consisting of an individual interest in an apartment or commercial unit and an undivided common interest in the common areas such as the land, parking areas, elevators, stairways, and the like. Simply stated, a condominium apartment is an owned dwelling with a common wall and/or ceilings and floors with co-owner neighbors.

Condominium apartment building: This architecturally describes a building that is mutually owned by the co-owners in an association.

Cooperative ownership: Cooperative ownership of an apartment unit means that the apartment owner has purchased shares in a corporation that holds title to the entire apartment building.

Conversion: The legal process required to convert an apartment building or rental housing into condominium ownership.

Density: The number of people who live in close proximity to each other. Lower density relates to fewer owners, less noise, and often more enjoyment of recreational amenities.

Features: Those things found within one's property. In condominium apartments and townhouses they include its square footage and number of bedrooms and bathrooms and garages. They also include walk-in closets, storage areas, wall coverings, floor coverings, cabinets, and basements. In contrast, amenities are those things outside the property that enhance a property's value.

Fee simple title: A legal phrase that describes the ownership rights co-owners have in their units. However, by agreement, some of these rights may be abridged. The co-owners can either hold title to the common areas or the homeowner's association can hold title.

Interior surfaces: The ownership interest inside a condominium apartment unit. If included in the condominium unit's legal definition, these surfaces need to be insured. Interior surfaces include kitchen cabinets, countertops, wall coverings, floor coverings, interior doors, light fixtures, and window treatments.

Limited or restricted common areas: Areas limited in use to individual unit owners or possibly a block of unit owners within the condominium development. These are areas not found within the defined boundaries of a unit or lot but are designed for their exclusive use. Examples could be exclusive easement rights to decks, patios, and storage areas. Here the association controls the use of them while the unit owner enjoys the privacy provided by their limited use. Laundry facilities located on certain floors of a development could be limited for the use of those co-owners living on that floor.

Party wall: A dividing wall or fence that separates co-owners. The CC&Rs describe the responsibility for maintenance, impose restrictions on alterations and replacement, and establish maintenance access rights.

Percentage of interest: The percentage share of common area owned by the individual co-owners.

Proprietary lease: A written lease in a cooperative apartment building between the owner-corporation and the tenant-stockholder, in which the tenant is given the right to occupy a particular unit.

MISTAKEN IDENTITY

The following words are often confused with one another. Note the difference in meaning of these mistaken identity words and phrases.

Proprietary lease/Condominium apartment deed: The seller conveys a cooperative apartment by way of a *proprietary lease* and a condominium apartment by way of a condominium *apartment deed.*

Common interest/Common element: Each condominium apartment is assigned a percentage of undivided common *interest* in the project's common *elements* described in the declaration (e.g., elevators, roofs, land, and foundations).

QUESTIONS

1. The purchaser of any of the following units could have a fee simple interest *EXCEPT* for the purchase of a
   A. condominium.
   B. cooperative.
   C. town house.
   D. time-share.

2. Under the condominium law, all of the following are true about apartments *EXCEPT*
   A. individual apartments may be mortgaged.
   B. title insurance may be issued on individual apartments.
   C. taxes are assessed on individual apartments.
   D. rents are paid on the common elements.

3. Common elements in a residential condominium usually include all of the following *EXCEPT*
   A. girders and stairways.
   B. parking stalls assigned to particular apartments.
   C. elevators.
   D. roofs.

4. Able purchased a two-bedroom condominium. Able now holds a
   A. freehold interest in the unit.
   B. proprietary lease.
   C. reversionary interest.
   D. leasehold estate.

5. ◎ All of the following are accurate concerning properties registered under the condominium law *EXCEPT* each apartment
   A. has its own deed.
   B. may be conveyed or encumbered as if it were separate and distinct from all other apartments.
   C. is assessed its own maintenance fee.
   D. has its own proprietary lease.

6. A condominium apartment owner can avoid payment of the apportioned share of common expenses by
   A. not using certain common elements.
   B. abandoning his or her apartment.
   C. leasing his or her apartment.
   D. no means, because payment is always required.

7. The owners of an apartment in a condominium can do all of the following *EXCEPT*
   A. convey a freehold title to a grantee.
   B. hypothecate the apartment as security for a mortgage.
   C. lease their unit.
   D. partition the common elements.

8. ◎ Which of the following statements is *TRUE* about apartment ownership?
   A. In a condominium, each owner is responsible for his or her own mortgage payments as well as those of the other owners.
   B. In a cooperative association, if one or more members fail to pay their share of the mortgage, the other owners must make payments for the defaulting members or risk foreclosure on the entire property.
   C. In a condominium, each unit owner is a voting member of the association of owners.
   D. In a cooperative association, taxes are collected twice a year.

9. All owners of condominium units have all of the following *EXCEPT* their own
   A. real estate tax bills on their units.
   B. deeds to their units.
   C. maintenance dues on their units.
   D. deeds to the common elements.

10. The swimming pool in a condominium project is usually a common
    A. interest.
    B. element.
    C. profit.
    D. tenancy.

11. A condominium project restricts the type of window air-conditioning units that can be installed. In what document would this restriction *MOST* likely be found?
    A. Bylaws
    B. Master Deed
    C. Apartment Deed
    D. Articles of Incorporation

12. All of the following condominium fees are most likely to be paid by a condominium owner *EXCEPT*
    A. recreation fees.
    B. maintenance fees.
    C. stock-transfer fees.
    D. hazard insurance.

13. All of the following are true concerning apartment ownership *EXCEPT*
    A. ownership in a cooperative usually requires purchase of shares of stock in the cooperative corporation or association.
    B. individual apartments in a condominium are conveyed and are financed as if they were single-family dwellings on separate pieces of land.
    C. cooperative owners usually can sell their units only with prior board-of-directors approval.
    D. cooperative owners receive a deed.

14. Which of the following is *TRUE* concerning the difference between owning a condominium and owning a cooperative?
    A. A buyer can be deeded fee simple title to a condominium unit.
    B. The owner of a cooperative apartment unit owns an undivided tenancy in common interest in his or her unit.
    C. Only the condominium owner is entitled to exclusive possession.
    D. Only the cooperative owner is entitled to property tax deductions.

15. ◎ Which of the following is *TRUE* about condominium ownership?
    A. The definition of common elements includes any basements, gardens, lodging for janitors, recreational facilities, and interiors of apartments.
    B. The Declaration of Horizontal Property Regime, also called the *Condominium Declaration,* need not include a description of the limited common elements because property is restricted to use by a certain limited group.
    C. It applies only to residential buildings.
    D. Owners have the same tax benefits as do owners of single-family homes.

16. Which of the following is *TRUE* concerning condominium ownership?
    A. If the bylaws require the board of directors to secure property insurance, the insurance premiums shall be common expenses to be apportioned among the owners according to their percentage of common interest.
    B. If a mortgagee forecloses on Anne's apartment and Betty purchases the apartment at the foreclosure sale, Betty is liable for all the unpaid common expenses that existed prior to the sale.
    C. The board of directors of the association consists of community leaders who have no ownership interest.
    D. No unit can be sold without the prior approval of all owners.

17. An individual owner in a condominium can normally do which of the following?
    A. File a suit for partition of the common elements
    B. Be exempt from paying part of the common expenses by waiving or abandoning the use or enjoyment of the common elements
    C. Sell the limited common elements separate from the apartment
    D. Cast a vote at association meetings

18. The bylaws governing a property that is subject to the condominium law generally would include all of the following *EXCEPT*
    A. provisions for election of a board of directors of the association of apartment owners.
    B. the method by which each apartment owner's share of the common expenses will be collected.
    C. provisions for conducting association meetings.
    D. the percentage of common interest for each apartment.

19. If the board of directors of a condominium project obtains insurance coverage
    A. the premiums are common expenses.
    B. individual apartment owners cannot insure their own apartment contents.
    C. the premiums are refundable.
    D. the insurance covers theft losses in individual units.

20. An owner or lessee may submit his or her property to the Horizontal Property Act, and it will become a condominium by terms of the act when
    A. the certificate of completion is issued by the appropriate county official.
    B. all the units have been sold.
    C. the final report is issued.
    D. the declaration is recorded.

21. Which of the following terms *BEST* describes a modern form of real property ownership that involves the guaranteed right of occupancy and use of a specific property for a specific portion of each year for either a fixed number of years or forever?
    A. Time-sharing
    B. Recreation lease
    C. Periodic tenancy
    D. Life estate

22. ◎ Which of the following is *TRUE* concerning condominium conversion?
    A. An owner might favorably consider converting an apartment building to a condominium in an area with strict rent controls.
    B. Condominium conversions receive universal support from city managers and governments.
    C. Condominium conversions are illegal and fraudulent.
    D. Tenants have no right to buy their converted units.

23. All *EXCEPT* which of the following practices are generally true in a conversion of an apartment building to a condominium?
    A. The existing tenants on month-to-month leases are given longer than 30-day notices to relocate.
    B. The existing tenants are given the first right to purchase their units.
    C. Renovations are made to individual apartments.
    D. The tenants can extend their leases for five years.

24. What can the taxing agency do when a condominium apartment owner defaults on paying his or her real property tax?
    A. Seek to foreclose against the apartment owner
    B. Seek to recover from the condominium association
    C. Put locks on the front door
    D. Collect from the lender

25. A woman owns Apartment 22 in the Blueridge condominium development. What part of the condominium does she own?
    A. The entire floor, walls, and ceiling of the unit
    B. An equal share of each unit in the Blueridge
    C. The air space within Apartment 22
    D. The parking stall and swimming pool

26. ◎ Which of the following statements comparing condominium ownership with cooperative ownership is *TRUE?*
    A. The financing arrangements in a cooperative situation make it a more attractive purchase than a condominium.
    B. Cooperative associations generally exercise much more rigid control regarding the qualifications of new buyers and tenants of buyers than do condominium associations.
    C. Cooperative ownership is less expensive.
    D. Cooperative ownership offers greater tax benefits.

27. Traditionally, one of the principal advantages of a condominium over a cooperative has been
    A. lower maintenance.
    B. greater security.
    C. better location.
    D. easier financing.

28. All of the following documents are used in the typical condominium project *EXCEPT*
    A. association bylaws.
    B. a master deed.
    C. a proprietary lease.
    D. a declaration.

29. In a residential condominium project, which of the following events requires an amendment to the condominium declaration?
    A. Purchase and installation of a new air-conditioning unit
    B. Negotiation of a new property management agreement
    C. Relocation of the boundaries of several units
    D. Renegotiation of the building's master insurance policy

30. Which of the following is *TRUE* regarding ownership of a cooperative apartment unit?
    A. Each unit is taxed separately.
    B. Each unit can receive title insurance for its fee simple interest.
    C. Each unit is owner-occupied.
    D. Each unit is conveyed by a proprietary lease.

31. In recent times, the time-share condominium has become a very important influence in marketing real estate in resort areas. It has generally caused a reduction in the
    A. cost of ownership.
    B. number of occupants.
    C. real property taxes.
    D. maintenance fees.

ANSWERS

1. **B.** A co-op purchaser would obtain a proprietary lease plus stock in the corporation or association that owns the entire building. The condo purchaser could own a fee interest in the air space, even if the land on which the condo was constructed was a long-term leasehold estate.

2. **D.** Because individual apartments (fee ownership) are considered as "homes in the sky," an owner has most of the same bundle of rights that exist for a single-family home. The purchaser can obtain separate financing, and a title company will insure his or her interest. Owners pay a pro rata share of, not rent on, common expenses.

3. **B.** Common elements consist of those areas used in common by all owners and include elevators, lobbies, recreation areas, and laundry rooms. Areas assigned for the exclusive use of individual owners are called *limited common elements* (such as storage closets and reserved parking stalls). Different rules that relate to maintenance responsibility and permission to make additions or alterations apply to limited common elements.

4. **A.** Note that this freehold interest is a recent creation of state condominium legislation. Choice (B) involves a cooperative apartment in which there can be no separate fee ownership.

5. **D.** Condominium apartments have separate and distinct ownership qualities. Each is subject to the liens and encumbrances of its individual owner.

6. **D.** If owners were allowed to reduce their monthly maintenance expenses (association dues) by electing not to use the swimming pool, for example, there would be much chaos in managing the condominium. Likewise, until title to the abandoned apartment is transferred, the owner is still liable for common expenses.

7. **D.** The owners can convey, mortgage, lease, and encumber, just as if they owned a single-family home. However, they generally cannot partition the common elements.

8. **B.** In a condominium, the owners are not responsible for the mortgage payments of other owners. But in a cooperative, because there is usually one blanket mortgage, all owners must make up the defaults of other unit owners to avoid foreclosure of the one mortgage. Of course, they would place a lien on the defaulting owner's interest to the extent of their cash advances. If ten people own one unit, they are not all voting members; usually it is one member per unit.

9. **D.** Taxes and special assessments are levied against each individual apartment and not on the building as a whole. Title to common elements is held in common.

10. **B.** Under (A) the common interest is the percentage of ownership in the common elements. Each owner is responsible for a share of maintaining the common elements such as the swimming pool. A common profit would be profit from some venture, such as coin-operated vending machines, that generates money for the association. This profit then would be shared among owners according to their common interest.

11. **A.** The bylaws contain the major operating rules for the condominium. Minor restrictions are found in the house rules. The master deed establishes the condo project as a legal form of ownership; the apartment deed conveys title to the unit; and the articles of incorporation set up the condominium association as a legal entity.

12. **C.** Stock-transfer fees are paid in connection with the transfer of a cooperative apartment.

13. **D.** In addition to stock purchase, the cooperative purchaser becomes a lessee under a proprietary lease to the specific apartment unit, not a grantee under a deed.

14. **A.** The cooperative owner does have an undivided interest in the common areas, although it stems from the individually held stock and lease ownership and not from any deed, as in a condominium.

15. **D.** Common elements do not include apartment interiors. The limited common elements must be specifically described in the declaration and it must be noted to which units they are appurtenant. Condominiums may include commercial or industrial land uses.

16. **A.** Apartment owners should still obtain insurance for damages within their respective units. The unpaid expenses are generally made part of the association's overall common expenses and apportioned among all owners, including the purchaser at the foreclosure sale.

17. **D.** The common elements are not usually the subject of an action for partition. Payment of expenses for common elements is not based on how much they are used by each owner.

18. **D.** The board is a powerful voice in managing the operations of the condominium project. The owner's proportionate responsibility for the common expenses is usually fixed according to his or her percentage of common interest. The board, however, generally determines the most efficient method to collect and disburse these funds.

19. **A.** Failure of the board to obtain such coverage could be a basis for liability for negligence. Each person should obtain individual coverage for apartment contents.

20. **D.** The declaration is the critical document in creating the condominium. To sell the condominium, many other steps must be taken to acquire the necessary government approval.

21. **A.** Many time-sharing projects are structured as vacation leases, club memberships, or time-interval ownership. For example, each unit may have several tenant-in-common owners who have agreed on the time when each is entitled to occupancy during the year.

22. **A.** If an owner were subject to rent controls that prohibited or made it difficult to raise rents to achieve the return desired, the owner probably would want to convert. City managers and governments are considering laws to limit conversion because it removes rentals from the market and increases the housing shortage for people not financially secure enough to buy.

23. **D.** Most states require a minimum of 90 days' notice and generally require that the developer give tenants the first right to purchase their units. There is a growing trend toward governmental regulation in the area of condominium conversion owing to the housing problems created by frequent relocation of tenants and the reduction in the number of available rental units. Long lease extensions are not granted.

24. **A.** Most state laws require that state real property taxes be assessed against individual units and not against the property as a whole. Thus, the association is not liable.

25. **C.** Condominium ownership is ownership of air space in a horizontal plane. The floors, walls, and ceilings are typically common elements.

26. **B.** Until recently, individual financing for cooperative units was impossible because no lender could be subject to the blanket mortgage on the building. The 1980s gave rise to a trend in state laws toward easing this financing restraint. While some condominium associations require prior approval of buyers and tenants, this practice is much more prevalent in cooperative associations.

27. **D.** Until recently, buyers of cooperative units were unable to obtain individual financing because there already was a blanket mortgage on the cooperative. Some states are legislating to remove this financing obstacle.

28. **C.** The proprietary lease along with a stock or trust certificate is typically used in a cooperative housing project.

29. **C.** While the board of directors is empowered to handle operational decisions, as in (A), (B), and (D), any major changes in the established boundaries usually require unanimous owner approval (along with all mortgagees' consent as well).

30. **D.** The basic cooperative concept is that the corporation (or trust) owns the building and the cooperative unit owner owns a proprietary lease to the unit. The fee simple interest is in the corporation and taxes are assessed against the property as a whole, with each unit owner being assessed by the corporation for his or her respective share. Some cooperatives require owner occupancy.

31. **A.** Because the total cost of the unit is divided up among the many time-share owners, a person can acquire an interest in a unit at a relatively low cost. The trade-off is that use is limited to a certain period.

Encumbrances: Easements, Restrictions, and Liens

There are two general classifications of encumbrances: (1) those that affect the *title,* such as judgments, mechanics' liens, tax liens, and mortgages, to secure a debt or obligation and (2) those that affect the *physical condition* of the property, such as restrictions, easements, and encroachments. Note that all liens are encumbrances but that not all encumbrances are liens.

Easements are the most common type of encumbrance affecting the physical condition or use of property—a right to use the land of another for a specific purpose. The two classes of easements are *easements appurtenant* and *easements in gross.*

- Easements appurtenant are said to "run with the land," meaning they are automatically transferred to a buyer even though this is not stated in the deed. There are two tracts of land: one receives the benefit of the easement (dominant estate), the other the burden (servient estate).

- Easements are best created by express grant in a deed of easement, but they can be created also by implied grant or reservation, prescription, condemnation, necessity, or dedication.

- Easements are permanent and irrevocable, whereas a license is a personal, revocable, and nonassignable permission to use the land of another. What may look like legal access to a property may turn out to be a mere license, revocable at the will of the neighbor—check for recorded easement rights of access.

- Other types of nonmonetary encumbrances are private restrictions (sometimes found in CC&Rs, that is, covenants, conditions, and restrictions, a recorded document that runs with the land and binds future owners), encroachments, lateral support, and party walls. Public restrictions affecting the use of real property are zoning, building codes, and variances.

- If a zoning ordinance and a deed restriction are in conflict, the more strict often controls.

■ Private restrictions can be found in restrictive covenants in a deed, a mortgage, or CC&Rs. Such restrictions can be terminated, but only if all affected parties sign a quitclaim deed.

The questions in this chapter test your comprehension of the following topics:

■ Various types of easements, including easements appurtenant, in gross, and prescriptive

■ The creation and termination of easements

■ Easements and license distinguished

■ Restrictive covenants in deeds and leases

■ Encumbrances affecting the title to real property (tax and mortgage liens)

KEY   WORDS

Covenants and conditions: Covenants are promises contained in contracts, the breach of which would entitle a person to damages. Conditions, on the other hand, are contingencies, qualifications, or occurrences on which an estate or property right would be gained or lost.

Declaration of restrictions: A statement of all the covenants, conditions, and restrictions (CC&Rs) that affect a parcel of land.

Easement: A property interest that one person has in land owned by another that entitles the holder of the interest to limited use or enjoyment of the other's land.

Easement in gross: The limited right of one person to use another's land (servient estate), which right is not created for the benefit of any land owned by the owner of the easement; that is, there is no dominant estate, as the easement attaches personally to the owner, not to the land.

Encroachment: An unauthorized invasion or intrusion of a fixture or other real property wholly or partly on another's property, thus reducing the size and value of the invaded property.

Encumbrance: Any claim, lien, charge, or liability attached to and binding on real property that may lessen the value of the property but will not necessarily prevent transfer of title.

Party wall: A wall that is located on or at a boundary line between two adjoining parcels and is used or is intended to be used by the owners of both properties in the construction or maintenance of improvements on their respective lots.

Prescription: The acquiring of a right in property, usually in the form of an intangible property right, such as an easement or right-of-way, by means of adverse use of property that is continuous and uninterrupted for the prescriptive period.

Restrictions: Limitations on the use of property. Private restrictions are created by means of restrictive covenants written into real property instruments such as deeds and leases.

Restrictive covenant: A private agreement, usually contained in a deed, that restricts the use and occupancy of real property.

Running with the land: Rights or covenants that bind or benefit successive owners of a property, such as restrictive building covenants in a recorded deed that would affect all future owners of the property, are said to *run with the land.*

MISTAKEN IDENTITY

The following words are often confused with one another. Note the difference in meaning of these mistaken identity words and phrases.

Lienor/Lienee: The creditor (*lienor*) has a lien on the property of the debtor (*lienee*) to satisfy a claim or debt.

Encroachment/Encumbrance: An *encroachment* is an unauthorized intrusion of one property onto another property; it is an *encumbrance* on both properties until court action or agreement resolves the issue.

Easement appurtenant/Easement in gross: An *easement appurtenant* benefits and runs with the land, whereas an *easement in gross* does not benefit any land. It is personal to the owner (e.g., utility company); there is no dominant estate (see below).

Dominant estate/Servient estate: The *dominant estate* is the property benefited by the easement; the *servient estate* is the property burdened or subject to the easement.

Easement/License: An *easement* is a permanent right in property, whereas a *license,* which is not an interest in real property, is a temporary right to use that may be revoked at any time.

QUESTIONS

1. Which of the following statements about deed restrictions is *FALSE?*
   A. They are frequently encountered in residential subdivisions.
   B. They are called *restrictive covenants.*
   C. They terminate on the death of the grantor.
   D. Once established, they run with the land and are limitations on the use of future grantees.

2. An easement appurtenant
   A. is the usual type of easement granted to utility companies to permit them to run electric lines across the property.
   B. runs with the land.
   C. has only a dominant estate.
   D. benefits the servient estate.

3. Restrictions in a deed that benefit only the grantor
   A. cannot be removed by the grantor.
   B. must be more lenient than current zoning laws.
   C. may be removed by the grantor's issuing a quitclaim deed.
   D. may be changed by a subsequent grantee.

4. An easement created by adverse use is said to have been created by
   A. express grant.
   B. reservation.
   C. implication of law.
   D. prescription.

5. Restrictive covenants in a deed
   A. must be consistent and not at variance with the zoning.
   B. cannot be more strict than the current zoning use.
   C. are the same as conditions in a deed.
   D. are an encumbrance on the property.

6. All the following events will terminate an easement *EXCEPT*
   A. when dominant and servient tenements merge.
   B. when the particular purpose for which the easement was created ceases.
   C. absence or nonuse of the easement for several years.
   D. when the dominant tenement sells the property to a new owner.

7. ◎ When an easement appurtenant exists between two parcels of land that are separately owned, the
   A. dominant tenement has use of this easement only for ingress and egress.
   B. servient tenement must have created the easement in writing.
   C. dominant tenement is benefited by the easement.
   D. servient tenement may revoke the use of easement by giving proper notice.

8. Which of the following creates deed restrictions?
   A. Local building inspector
   B. Authorized authorities
   C. Planning commission
   D. Grantor

9. All of the following restrictions are government restrictions *EXCEPT*
   A. police power.
   B. covenant.
   C. escheat.
   D. eminent domain.

10. A restriction is considered to be which one of the following?
    A. Lien
    B. Color of title
    C. Encumbrance
    D. Abstract

11. To the holder of the dominant tenement, an easement is a(n)
    A. encumbrance.
    B. appurtenance.
    C. restriction.
    D. encroachment.

12. A deed subject to a restrictive covenant involves which one of the following?
    A. Zoning restriction
    B. Encumbrance
    C. Life estate
    D. Defective title

13. The right of a water company to lay and maintain water mains along the rear of a lot is called a(n)
    A. appurtenance.
    B. riparian right.
    C. easement in gross.
    D. right of encroachment.

14. ◎ Which of the following statements is *TRUE?*
    A. The owner of the servient tenement generally has rights to subsurface profits.
    B. The owner of the dominant tenement has the right to drill an oil well on the servient property.
    C. The servient estate benefits from an easement.
    D. The servient estate can terminate an easement by abandonment.

15. A recorded easement may be removed from the records by
    A. recording a quitclaim deed signed by the owner of the easement (the dominant tenement).
    B. instituting a lis pendens action.
    C. filing a marginal release.
    D. giving a three-day notice followed by an Unlawful Detainer Action.

16. ◎ Which of the following statements is *TRUE?*
    A. When an easement has been created, it remains in effect even after the dominant and servient properties are merged into one.
    B. The mere nonuse of an easement right is sufficient evidence to prove abandonment.
    C. An easement is created for the benefit of the servient tenement.
    D. Easements are encumbrances affecting the physical use of land.

17. A property owner, by use of a deed restriction, may do all of the following *EXCEPT*
    A. prohibit a use of property that would be allowed under existing zoning laws.
    B. limit the size and shape of the buildings.
    C. change the zoning of the property.
    D. limit the placement of a dwelling on a lot.

18. A party wall would be found
    A. along a property line.
    B. between the dining and living rooms.
    C. facing the direction from which bad weather usually comes.
    D. between the upper and lower stories of a structure.

19. An easement would *MOST* likely be involved with which of the following?
    A. Right-of-way
    B. Subordination
    C. Defeasance
    D. Estoppel

20. When one has permission to use land but has no other rights, one has a
    A. tenancy in common.
    B. leasehold estate.
    C. tenancy at sufferance.
    D. license.

21. An easement is most commonly terminated by
    A. abandonment.
    B. quitclaim deed.
    C. the owner of the servient tenement.
    D. operation of law.

22. ◎ The most practical method of imposing restrictions on all lots in a large new subdivision is by
    A. publishing the restrictions in a newspaper of general circulation.
    B. including the restrictions as covenants in all deeds.
    C. recording the restrictions, prior to any sales, in the manner provided by law.
    D. posting the restrictions on the property.

23. Which of the following deed restrictions is valid?
    A. Limitations are placed on materials used or the type of architecture.
    B. The property cannot be sold to persons of a certain race.
    C. Property must not be used for religious purposes.
    D. The restriction must always be the same as the existing zoning.

24. If, after a buyer purchases a property, she has a survey made and finds that her neighbor, through error, has recently built an ornamental fence two feet over her land, this would be a basic example of
    A. a party wall.
    B. an encroachment.
    C. an appurtenance.
    D. adverse possession.

25. ◎ A person owning beachfront property sells the two lots between his lot and the public road. This person would be best advised to reserve from the transfer which type of right-of-way?
    A. Easement in gross
    B. Easement of necessity
    C. Easement appurtenant
    D. License

26. In what type of easement is there a dominant estate and a servient estate?
    A. Easement in gross
    B. Easement appurtenant
    C. Easement for profit
    D. Easement by license

27. The right to enter upon the property of another and to fish in the pond on the property is called a(n)
    A. trespass.
    B. license.
    C. riparian right.
    D. encroachment.

28. All of the following create an easement EXCEPT a(n)
    A. express grant.
    B. prescription.
    C. assignment.
    D. implied grant.

29. Which of the following statements is TRUE about restrictive covenants found in deeds?
    A. They are encumbrances.
    B. They automatically expire upon violation.
    C. If the restriction violates another law, the entire deed is void.
    D. They must be the same as local zoning laws.

30. A landowner wants to give her neighbor the right to cross over her property, but the landowner does not wish to make this a permanent, irrevocable right. The broker should advise the owner to consider granting what type of right?
    A. Easement in gross
    B. Right-of-way
    C. License
    D. Easement appurtenant

31. Encumbrances that are considered liens on real estate can be created by
    A. special assessments and improvement taxes.
    B. covenants that restrict the use of the property.
    C. easements.
    D. personal restrictions.

32. All of the following statements regarding restrictive covenants on real property are true EXCEPT that they
    A. run with the land.
    B. are enforceable in court unless contrary to public policy.
    C. are limited to a specific time period.
    D. may be removed from the record without legal action.

33. Of the following liens, which normally takes priority over all other liens?
    A. Judgment lien
    B. Mortgage lien
    C. Mechanic's lien
    D. Real property tax lien

34. The priority of a mechanic's lien depends on the date
    A. of recordation.
    B. of the contract.
    C. of completion.
    D. on which work commenced.

35. ◎ A materialman's lien is superior to which of the following?
    A. A first mortgage recorded prior to the time of the visible commencement of work
    B. A lien for delinquent real property taxes
    C. Mechanic's lien for broker's commission
    D. Previously recorded judgment liens

36. The lender wants to ensure the first priority of its lien. The lender should make sure of which of the following?
    A. All other liens are removed from title or subordinated from the property being used as collateral.
    B. The borrower has an unconditional fee simple estate with no liens.
    C. The borrower's father has cosigned the note.
    D. The loan is insured.

37. In order to become effective, which of the following must be recorded?
    A. Quitclaim deed
    B. Warranty deed
    C. Mechanic's lien
    D. Easement

38. All of these professionals may file a mechanic's lien after completing work and not being paid *EXCEPT* a(n)
    A. carpenter.
    B. real estate broker.
    C. electrician.
    D. engineer.

39. All of the following are both encumbrances and liens *EXCEPT* a
    A. mortgage.
    B. judgment.
    C. restriction.
    D. tax.

40. Encumbrances that are also liens on real estate can be created by
    A. federal income taxes.
    B. a subdivision declaration of restrictions.
    C. zoning regulations.
    D. building permit requirements.

41. A recorded notice of a current lawsuit involving title to real property is termed a(n)
    A. lis pendens.
    B. writ of execution.
    C. attachment.
    D. order to show cause.

42. ◎ In distinguishing between an attachment lien and a judgment lien
    A. an attachment is made after judgment.
    B. an attachment lien applies to all property of the debtor.
    C. a judgment lien is a general lien.
    D. a judgment lien can be obtained prior to a court decision.

43. The discharge of certain property from the lien of a judgment, mortgage, or claim is a
    A. release of lien.
    B. lien binder.
    C. lien statement.
    D. tax.

44. ◎ An easement by necessity is *MOST* appropriate in which one of the following situations?
    A. Landlocked parcel
    B. Profit a prendre
    C. Party wall
    D. Encroachment

45. A chattel mortgage is a lien on
    A. real property.
    B. personal property.
    C. encumbrances.
    D. land.

46. A court-issued order to sell property to satisfy a judgment is known as a(n)
    A. easement.
    B. encumbrance.
    C. attachment.
    D. writ of execution.

47. Which of the following statements is *TRUE?*
    A. All liens are encumbrances.
    B. All encumbrances are liens.
    C. Specific liens affect all property of the debtor located in the state.
    D. Judgments are specific liens.

48. A legal right of a creditor to have a debt or charge satisfied from the personal property of the debtor is a(n)
    A. mortgage.
    B. lien.
    C. right-of-way.
    D. escheat.

49. Which of the following encumbrances constitutes a lien on real property?
    A. Easement
    B. Encroachment
    C. Restriction
    D. Mortgage

50. Usually a mechanic's lien is removed from public record by
    A. court order.
    B. payment in full.
    C. recording a release.
    D. satisfaction of the judgment.

51. ◎ A mechanic's lien filed for record today for work commenced two weeks ago usually has priority over all *EXCEPT* which one of the following?
    A. A mortgage filed five days ago
    B. A second mortgage recorded three days ago
    C. An unrecorded mortgage that was given a month ago
    D. A three-week-old judgment lien

52. ◎ Which of the following liens will have top priority in the event of foreclosure on the subject property?
    A. State income tax lien recorded first
    B. Federal estate tax lien recorded second
    C. Mechanic's lien for work commenced before any other lien was recorded
    D. Real property tax lien recorded last

53. Which of the following is *TRUE* regarding an encumbrance on real property?
    A. An encumbrance effectively prevents the passing of title from grantor to grantee.
    B. An encumbrance may indicate a lien.
    C. Encumbrances are liens that restrict use of the property.
    D. Encumbrances are restrictions that transfer title to property.

54. A laborer on a parcel of real property can do which of the following if she or he is not paid for their work?
    A. Post a bond
    B. File a lien
    C. Start foreclosure proceedings
    D. Remove his improvements

ANSWERS

1. **C.** Restrictive covenants run with the land. They are not terminated by death but may expire at the end of a stated time or upon release by all benefiting owners.

2. **B.** One of the features of an easement appurtenant is that it runs with the land. Also, it is granted in writing. It has both a dominant and a servient estate. Choice (A) refers to an easement in gross that doesn't benefit any adjacent parcel of real estate.

3. **C.** For example, assume a grantor who owned Lot 1 reserved an easement to benefit neighboring Lot 2. At any time, easement interest in Lot 1 could be released by way of a quitclaim deed. While a more lenient deed restriction may limit a building to three stories, it will not have priority over a zoning law that permits only two stories, for example.

4. **D.** Prescriptive easements usually require open, notorious, and hostile use for the same statutory period as adverse possession.

5. **D.** Restrictive covenants and zoning regulations are often at variance with each other; the one that is more strict or severe will control the use of the affected property, except in certain situations where a deed restriction is against public policy or in violation of law.

6. **D.** Regarding choice (A), if the owner of Lot 1 buys Lot 2, any easements over Lot 2 that benefit Lot 1 will cease because an easement is an interest in *another's* land. An easement to cross the pasture to fish in the lake will cease when the lake is filled in and converted to a shopping center. Regarding choice (D), easements are considered rights of way that "run with the land."

7. **C.** The dominant tenement is the benefiting property that is served by the other. Easements appurtenant are generally irrevocable, and the stated purpose may be for more than ingress and egress.

8. **D.** (A), (B), and (C) involve public restrictions, such as zoning and building code regulations.

9. **B.** Covenants (promises) involve private restrictions. Police power is the general governmental power to pass rules to protect the health, welfare, and safety of the community—for example, zoning, licensing laws, and building codes.

10. **C.** A lien is a charge against a property for a debt, whereas an encumbrance is anything that limits the value or use of the property. All liens are encumbrances, but not all encumbrances are liens.

11. **B.** To the servient tenement, the easement is an encumbrance. To the dominant tenement, it is something that attaches to the land and benefits it.

12. **B.** Restrictive covenants are private restrictions found in deeds and leases that encumber the property.

13. **C.** Easements in gross are rights in the land of another person that benefit someone else (legal or natural), but there is no dominant estate as with an easement appurtenant. Appurtenances are property rights that attach to and benefit a parcel of land; riparian rights are water rights.

14. **A.** The owner of the servient tenement owns the land and has the entire bundle of rights except the easement created for the benefit of the dominant tenement. This easement is limited to the purpose for which it was created (i.e., if it is a right-of-way, then there is no right to drill).

15. **A.** A quitclaim deed is effective to release the easement interest of the grantor. Lis pendens gives notice of a pending lawsuit; it is not an actual lawsuit. Marginal releases involve the satisfaction of mortgages.

16. **D.** On merger, there is no longer any land of *another,* an essential element of an easement. To terminate an easement by nonuse, there must be clear acts of abandonment, such as building a cement wall across the former easement right-of-way.

17. **C.** Whichever is the more strict—a restriction or a zoning regulation—will control the use of the property. A popular restriction is to limit the height of buildings and sometimes even the minimum cost or size of the structures.

18. **A.** A party wall is a shared wall between two adjoining buildings. Each party owns one-half of the wall and has an easement of support in the other half. Party wall agreements should be in writing because they involve an interest in real property, according to the statute of frauds.

19. **A.** A right-of-way is a right to cross over someone's property, usually to gain ingress and egress to a neighboring property. *Subordination, defeasance,* and *estoppel* are terms used in financing.

20. **D.** Such permission is revocable, unlike an easement. For example, the right to enter a movie theater is a revocable license. In addition to a use right, a lessee may have the right to make improvements.

21. **B.** An easement can be terminated by abandonment or operation of law (merger), but it is normally terminated by the owner of the dominant tenement quitclaiming his or her interest in the servient tenement.

22. **C.** Because a declaration of restrictions (*CC&Rs,* or *covenants, conditions, and restrictions,* as they are sometimes called) can be quite lengthy, it is easier to record one set in the public record office and then, by incorporation by reference, make each deed subject to that prior recorded declaration of restrictions.

23. **A.** Racial and religious restrictions are barred under federal and most state antidiscrimination laws.

24. **B.** The buyer could bring a lawsuit to seek removal of the fence. Failure to do so for a long enough time might result in the neighbor's obtaining title to the disputed land by adverse possession. This would be an encumbrance on the buyer's land, not an appurtenance. A party wall is located on or adjacent to the property line, is usually created by agreement, and is for the support of each party's structure.

25. **C.** To maintain access to the road, the owner should clearly reserve in the deed an easement appurtenant that will benefit the beachfront lot and "run with the land" to bind successive owners of the two lots permanently. Under choice (A), an easement in gross would personally benefit the beachfront owner but may not be transferable to future grantees. This could reduce the marketability of the beachfront lot.

26. **B.** In most situations of easements appurtenant, the two properties involved are adjacent or contiguous. With an easement in gross, there is no dominant estate.

27. **B.** A license is a right or privilege to use another's property. Unlike an easement, it is revocable. A riparian right is the right of the owner of land bordering on nonnavigable water to the use of the water.

28. **C.** Grants are used to create rights, while assignments are used to transfer rights.

29. **A.** Because restrictions control the use of property, it is important that a potential buyer (or the buyer's broker) ascertain the extent of these encumbrances on the free use of the property *before* the buyer commits himself or herself to buy.

30. **C.** A license is a mere right or privilege to use another's property. This right can be revoked at any time. An easement appurtenant is irrevocable; an easement in gross often is irrevocable; and a right-of-way is a specific type of easement (it may be appurtenant or in gross).

31. **A.** Not all encumbrances are liens, although all liens are encumbrances. Liens are specific charges on real property for payment of a debt. They include mortgages, tax liens, or mechanics' liens. Restrictions are merely encumbrances.

32. **C.** Restrictive covenants found in deeds may have a specific time limit, but this is not a requirement. One method of removal is a quitclaim deed from all the beneficiaries of the restriction.

33. **D.** Real property tax liens have priority even over prior recorded special and general liens. Do not confuse them with income tax liens or estate tax liens, whose priority is set by the date of recordation.

34. **D.** The lien, once recorded, usually relates back to the date of visible commencement of work. Thus, buyers of property that shows evidence of recent construction should either obtain waivers from laborers or rely on an extended title insurance policy.

35. **C.** A mechanic's lien attaches from date of *commencement* of work, not from date of *completion*. Real property tax liens have priority; other liens usually have priority based on date of recordation. Brokers cannot file mechanics' liens.

36. **A.** Prior liens should be removed or placed junior through subordination. The lender usually would not want to lend on a *conditional* fee simple estate without further assurances against loss.

37. **C.** Most state statutes require public notice of mechanics' liens. An unrecorded deed is effective between the grantor and grantee. Judgments have legal effect on entry, but they do not become liens until recordation.

38. **B.** Most states do not treat a broker as a laborer, mechanic, or materialman, because he or she seldom does anything to enhance the property's value. The broker's legal remedy is to file a lawsuit if attempts to negotiate a settlement are futile.

39. **B.** A restriction is not a charge on property for the payment of a debt; it is a physical encumbrance.

40. **A.** Failure to pay federal income taxes can result in liens being placed on the property. Restrictive covenants and governmental restrictions are popular physical encumbrances on land but are not liens.

41. **A.** The lis pendens is the notice of suit, whereas an attachment is the actual seizure of specific property by a court pending the outcome of the lawsuit. The writ of execution is an order for the sale of property to satisfy the judgment.

42. **C.** Judgment liens usually apply against all the property of the judgment debtor.

43. **A.** Most releases are recorded.

44. **A.** Where a common grantor sells several parcels but fails to specify an access route to one of the parcels, courts often imply an easement across one parcel so the other parcel is not landlocked. This is also called an *easement by implied grant*. A *profit a prendre* refers to a right to take part of the land such as timber, coal, or produce.

45. **B.** The chattel mortgage has been replaced in some states by the security agreement and financing statement under the Uniform Commercial Code.

46. **D.** If a judgment is not paid or satisfied, the creditor can ask the court to execute on the property of the defendant.

47. **A.** Judgments (D) are general liens. Easements (B) are encumbrances but are not liens.

48. **B.** Judgment liens could be satisfied from proceeds of sale of debtors' personal property.

49. **D.** Choices (A), (B), and (C) are encumbrances but are not liens.

50. **C.** To clear the records, it is necessary to record a release.

51. **D.** The mechanic's lien relates back to the visible commencement of work.

52. **D.** Priority typically depends on date of recordation except in cases of governmental (state and county) real property tax liens and special assessments. The correct order of priority is (D), (C), (A), (B) because mechanics' liens relate to the date when work started.

53. **B.** Many grantees agree to accept title subject to certain disclosed encumbrances. All liens (mortgages, judgments, or taxes) are encumbrances, but not all encumbrances (easements, restrictions, or encroachments) are liens.

54. **B.** The laborer's most immediate remedy is to follow appropriate state law procedures for filing a mechanic's lien. If the mechanic obtains a judgment and the owner still refuses to pay the debt, then the property can be sold at a foreclosure sale with the mechanic getting enough of the proceeds to pay the debt and the owner getting the balance. Choice (D) is an example of self-help and would be a trespass.

Governmental Limitations: Zoning and Eminent Domain

Even a landowner with a fee simple absolute title may find that the use of the real property is often subject to governmental restrictions. Under the constitutional right of eminent domain, the government can take property for public use or public benefit if it pays just compensation.

Under the police power, the government can pass reasonable rules such as zoning and building codes to protect the health, welfare, and safety of society. In addition to these public restrictions, the property also may be subject to private deed restrictions. If there is a conflict between the public restrictions and the private restrictions, whichever is more restrictive normally applies.

The questions in this chapter test your comprehension of the following topics:

■ The difference between a variance and a nonconforming use

■ Eminent domain and condemnation

■ Zoning ordinances, building codes, and police power

KEY WORDS

Building permit: A written permission granted by a governmental building department and required prior to beginning the construction of a new building or other improvement (including fences, fence walls, retaining walls, and swimming pools).

Condemnation: Either a judicial or administrative proceeding to exercise the power of eminent domain (i.e., the power of the government to take private property for public use).

Eminent domain: The right of government, both state and federal, to take private property for a necessary public use, with just compensation paid to the owner.

Nonconforming use: A permitted use that was lawfully established and maintained but that no longer conforms to the current use regulations because of a change in the zoning.

Police power: The constitutional authority and inherent power of a state to adopt and enforce laws and regulations to promote and support the public health, safety, morals, and general welfare.

Zoning: The regulation of structures and uses of property within designated districts or zones. Zoning regulates and affects such things as use of the land, types of structure permitted, building heights, setbacks, and density (the ratio of land area to improvement area).

MISTAKEN IDENTITY

The following words are often confused with one another. Note the difference in meaning of these mistaken identity words and phrases.

Variance/Nonconforming use: A *variance* is an exception to the existing zoning, whereas a *nonconforming use* (also called a *grandfather clause*) arises when there is a change to the zoning but an existing one is still permitted to continue.

Police power/Eminent domain: When property is taken under *eminent domain,* there must be payment of just compensation; a taking under the *police power* (such as zoning) does not require compensation.

QUESTIONS

1. A landowner is advised by the government that a public utilities company plans to cross his property with a power line. If the landowner refuses, the utilities company can seek to acquire this right through the use of
   A. police action.
   B. eminent domain.
   C. accretion.
   D. partition action.

2. Which of the following is a variance?
   A. A large, new supermarket located in an area zoned for small retail shops
   B. An old grocery store located in an area recently rezoned residential
   C. Several choices of similar homes at the same price
   D. A restriction in a deed that differs from the zoning

3. All of the following are examples of public restrictions *EXCEPT*
   A. police power.
   B. encroachment.
   C. eminent domain.
   D. taxation.

4. ◎ When property represents a nonconforming use with regard to current zoning regulations, all of the following are true *EXCEPT*
   A. the use is legal and permissible as long as the building exists with no major structural changes.
   B. if the building is destroyed, no new structure may be erected on the land that is not in conformity with existing zoning.
   C. the use may continue even though it is in conflict with zoning.
   D. the use must stop.

5. The right of the government to place reasonable restrictions on the use of privately held land is known as
   A. restrictive covenant.
   B. police power.
   C. subordination.
   D. eminent domain.

6. If an area is rezoned industrial and a commercial establishment is given permission to continue its operation in that area, this is an example of which of the following?
   A. Variance
   B. Nonconforming use
   C. Variable zoning
   D. Restrictive zoning

7. Building codes have the ability to do all of the following *EXCEPT*
   A. influence architectural style of buildings.
   B. establish acceptable material and construction standards for buildings.
   C. regulate safety of buildings in certain areas.
   D. require that an attorney review each transaction.

8. ◎ When the owner of property suffers financial loss from the exercise of police power, such as through the application of zoning laws
   A. the owner must be justly compensated for the loss.
   B. there is a condemnation proceeding.
   C. the owners will never be allowed to continue their use under the former zoning.
   D. the owner can appeal to the zoning commission.

9. All of the following are used in municipal planning *EXCEPT*
   A. building codes.
   B. housing codes.
   C. subdivision regulations.
   D. subdivision covenants.

10. All of the following are limitations or regulations of property exercised by government *EXCEPT*
    A. police power.
    B. taxation.
    C. subordination.
    D. escheat.

11. An owner wants to extend the side of her house beyond the setback boundary. Which must she obtain?
    A. Variance
    B. Nonconforming use
    C. Subordination agreement
    D. Reservation

12. A government agency may acquire a certain property for public use by utilizing
    A. an attachment.
    B. the right of eminent domain.
    C. a suit to quiet title.
    D. a claim of adverse possession.

13. Eminent domain *MOST* nearly means
    A. sale to a public corporation.
    B. private use with consideration.
    C. public use without compensation.
    D. public use with compensation.

14. What is the greatest power the government has to affect the value of real property?
    A. FHA minimum housing standards
    B. Ad valorem taxes
    C. Zoning
    D. Declassification

15. ◎ A grandfather clause in a zoning ordinance may permit an owner to
    A. remodel the exterior of a building that is a nonconforming use.
    B. enlarge a building that is a nonconforming use.
    C. collect damages from the government.
    D. sue for specific performance.

16. Zoning ordinances control the use of privately owned land by establishing land-use districts. All of the following are usual zoning districts *EXCEPT*
    A. residential.
    B. commercial.
    C. rental.
    D. industrial.

17. Regulations established by local governments setting forth the construction requirements of structures are *BEST* described by which term?
    A. Conveyance
    B. Devise
    C. Common law
    D. Building code

18. Eminent domain, taxation, police power, and escheat are
    A. restrictions on the ownership of any property.
    B. benefits belonging to the owner of real property.
    C. private restrictions on personal property.
    D. factors that affect only owners of land abutting government-owned property.

19. Zoning is done by authority of
    A. the mayor.
    B. the law of eminent domain.
    C. police power.
    D. petition.

20. A landowner builds a small factory in the city. After the factory is built, the city adopts a zoning ordinance in which the area in question is designated a residential area. Which of the following statements about the owner's alternatives is *TRUE?*
    A. He must move his plant to a portion of the city zoned for industrial purposes.
    B. He may continue to operate as a nonconforming use.
    C. He should abandon the plant and sue the city for damages.
    D. He is entitled to a variance.

21. The provisions of county building codes are designed to establish minimum
    A. sideline and setback lines for buildings.
    B. construction standards for buildings within the county.
    C. standards for flood control.
    D. licensing requirements for contractors.

22. When a zoning regulation permits a specific use of a property but a private restriction contained in the deed limits that use of the property, the one that would prevail is the
    A. deed restriction.
    B. zoning law.
    C. master plan.
    D. building restriction.

23. Which of the following is the *BEST* description of the purpose of a building permit?
    A. Municipal control of the volume of building
    B. Evidence of compliance with municipal regulations
    C. Regulation of area and bulk of buildings
    D. Evidence that construction fees have been paid

24. There are several ways in which land use is regulated or controlled. All of the following are means *EXCEPT*
    A. resolutions passed by local REALTORS® boards.
    B. zoning ordinances.
    C. public ownership.
    D. restrictions contained in sellers' deeds.

25. Zoning ordinances usually cover such matters as
    A. base lines.
    B. setback lines.
    C. deed restrictions.
    D. prescription.

26. Government restrictions on land include all of the following *EXCEPT*
    A. title settlement.
    B. taxation.
    C. eminent domain.
    D. zoning.

27. The difference between police power and eminent domain can *BEST* be determined by whether
    A. the action was by sovereign power or by statute.
    B. any compensation was paid to the owner.
    C. the owner's use was affected.
    D. the improvements are to be destroyed.

28. The right of eminent domain refers to
    A. the right of every American citizen to own property.
    B. an organization's right to condemn property pending an improvement that is for the good of the community.
    C. an institution's or individual's acquiring land by grant from the government.
    D. the government's right to acquire or authorize others to acquire title to property for public use.

29. ◎ All of the following are true about the power of eminent domain *EXCEPT* that it
    A. may be exercised by a district school board seeking to obtain property for a public school.
    B. requires that just compensation be paid to the landowner when exercised.
    C. may be used when a city wants to take an owner's yard to widen the highway.
    D. may be used if a neighbor needs more access.

30. ◎ Compensation often follows a court action relating to which of the following?
    A. Trustee's sale
    B. Police power
    C. Condemnation
    D. Quiet title

31. The taking of private property for public use without compensation is authorized under the principle of
    A. escheat.
    B. police power.
    C. eminent domain.
    D. zoning.

32. ◎ An action brought by a landowner against the government in which the landowner claims money damages because her property value has been lessened due to government action is *BEST* called
    A. subrogation.
    B. attachment.
    C. inverse condemnation.
    D. lis pendens.

33. One owner wishes to develop a beauty shop on his property in an area zoned for single-family residences. What type of legal process should be requested?
    A. Nonconforming use
    B. Downzoning
    C. Building permit
    D. Variance

34. As defined in local zoning ordinances, the distance between lot lines and improvements is known as
    A. frontage.
    B. setback.
    C. buffer zone.
    D. depth.

35. All of the following are effective tools for the municipal planner *EXCEPT*
    A. subdivision regulations.
    B. building codes.
    C. subdivision covenants.
    D. zoning ordinances.

36. A zoning ordinance could validly affect all of the following *EXCEPT*
    A. height of a building.
    B. proportion of building area to land area.
    C. the use of a building.
    D. the amount of rent charged tenants.

37. ◎ A floodplain control regulation is an example of which type of governmental power?
    A. Eminent domain
    B. Police power
    C. Subdivision
    D. Attachment

ANSWERS

1. **B.** The powers of eminent domain to take private property (including an air space easement) with just compensation for a public purpose often extend to quasi-public agencies such as public utilities.

2. **A.** Choice (B) is a nonconforming use.

3. **B.** Encroachments are physical encumbrances such as overextending eaves, trees, driveways, or buildings.

4. **D.** As long as the nonconforming structure remains unchanged, the use is "grandfathered." However, the property will have to conform eventually to the new zoning.

5. **B.** The police power is given to the government by the constitution and enables the government to pass rules and regulations to protect the health, safety, and welfare of the community. Restrictive covenants are private restrictions found in deeds or recorded declarations.

6. **B.** A nonconforming (grandfathered) use is the continuation of a use that was permissible prior to the recent zoning change. A variance would be the introduction of a new use that varies from the current zoning.

7. **D.** Building codes directly regulate building materials and indirectly influence some architectural styles, especially in historic and preservation districts. There is no requirement for attorney review.

8. **D.** When property is taken by condemnation under eminent domain, just compensation is awarded, but generally not when property is regulated under police power, such as with a downzoning (e.g., from commercial to residential). Appeals are permitted within stated deadlines.

9. **D.** Subdivision covenants are private, not public, restrictions.

10. **C.** A fourth limitation by the government would be eminent domain.

11. **A.** One usually has to prove some hardship to justify a variance from the setback rule. A variance is an exception to a zoning regulation.

12. **B.** The government must pay "just compensation" to the condemnee for the taking. It pays less for acquiring an easement than for the fee simple title. If the government abandons the easement, clear title reverts to the condemnee.

13. **D.** Answer (C) is a taking by police power. An example of (C) would be the destructive taking of a building to protect some other buildings from a spreading fire.

14. **C.** A government decision to downzone a business district to residential could seriously affect property values.

15. **A.** The owner of a nonconforming use is "grandfathered" under the old law and generally can do cosmetic remodeling but can't make major structural changes.

16. **C.** Rental units are permitted in certain residential and commercial categories.

17. **D.** Building codes often are combined with plumbing and electrical codes.

18. **A.** In practice, escheat would have the least frequent impact on real estate ownership.

19. **C.** Police power is a constitutional power given to the government to pass rules and regulations to protect the health, welfare, and safety of the community.

20. **B.** Because the owner's use was permitted under the prior zoning, it will be allowed to continue.

21. **B.** Sideline and setback lines typically are established by zoning regulations.

22. **A.** Whichever rule is more strict—a government regulation or a private restriction—will control.

23. **B.** Building permits not only indicate compliance with building code requirements but also check conformity with the zoning regulations.

24. **A.** REALTORS® are active in monitoring local land uses but do not make actual regulations.

25. **B.** Base lines (A) are used in government survey descriptions. Choice (D) involves easements.

26. **A.** Title settlement refers to the closing of a real estate transaction.

27. **B.** If the value of property is lessened by government regulation under the police power as opposed to a taking under eminent domain, no just compensation is paid.

28. **D.** The government or a quasi-government agency (like a school district) can acquire property for public use upon paying just compensation, which is often determined in a condemnation proceeding with the government bringing suit against the condemnee.

29. **D.** A school board would be a quasi-government body authorized to exercise eminent domain powers. A private neighbor would not qualify (needs to be for a public purpose).

30. **C.** Condemnation is the legal proceeding brought under the constitutional right of eminent domain when the government and the landowner cannot agree on an appropriate amount of just compensation.

31. **B.** In emergency cases, such as a spreading fire, the government under the police power could destroy a person's property and not be liable for any compensation. Zoning (D) is the regulation, not the taking, of private property.

32. **C.** Inverse condemnation is, in effect, an action by the landowner demanding that the government complete a taking of the property and pay just compensation (e.g., if the state is constructing a highway and excavates part of the adjacent landowners' property).

33. **D.** A variance is a request for a change to the existing zoning, usually based on some hardship. Downzoning is an action by the local government to change the zoning to a lower classification, such as from commercial to residential. A nonconforming use is a use that is allowed to continue after the area has been rezoned; eventually, the use will have to conform to the new zoning.

34. **B.** Setback and sideline (or sideyard) requirements are helpful in keeping some open area around contiguous properties.

35. **C.** Subdivision covenants are private-use restrictions found in deeds and thus not directly available for public planning purposes.

36. **D.** Zoning ordinances frequently control building size, height, and density.

37. **B.** Under the police power, the government can pass regulations to protect the health, welfare, and safety of the general public, such as rules regarding types of structures in areas that are accessible to floods and requirements for special flood insurance before lenders can loan on property located in flood-prone regions.

Land Description

The three primary methods of describing real estate are as follows:

1. Government survey system
2. Metes and bounds
3. Subdivision lot and block number, also known as a recorded plat

In the salesperson examination, there may be a few questions involving legal descriptions. The problems may involve the metes-and-bounds description system, the subdivision lot and block number, or the government survey system. Brokers can expect to be tested on all three systems.

KEY WORDS

Check: Tracts of land repetitively located every 24 miles from a principal meridian and 24 miles from a defined base line. Guide meridians and correction lines define their boundaries, and they are 24 miles square consisting of 16 townships.

Correction lines: Standard parallel lines used to correct for the curvature of the earth and are repetitively located every 24 miles from a base line.

Government survey: A system of land description in which large blocks of land are divided into tracts bounded by imaginary lines conforming to the true meridian.

Guide meridians: Meridian lines used to compensate for heading North or South on a circular globe. They are repetitively located every 24 miles from a principal meridian.

Metes and bounds: A common method of land description that identifies a property by specifying the shape and boundary dimensions of the parcel, using terminal points and compass directions.

Ranges: A measurement, used in the government survey system, consisting of repeated strips of land six miles wide that run parallel from a principal meridian.

Section: An area one mile square that contains 640 acres.

Tiers: A measurement, used in the government survey system, consisting of repeated rows of land six miles wide that run parallel from a base line.

Township: An area used in the government survey system that measures six miles square. It is bordered by range line and tier lines.

GOVERNMENT SURVEY SYSTEM

A method of land description used in most states west of the Ohio and Mississippi rivers as well as in Florida is the government or rectangular survey system. It is based on a system of lines of longitude and latitude forming a checkerboard pattern of this portion of the United States. The north-south lines are called *principal* (or *prime*) *meridians* (of which there are 36 in the United States), and the east-west lines are called *parallel* or *base lines*. The largest squares in the government survey system are 24 miles in each direction, resulting in a unit of land approximately 24 miles square, called *checks*. (See Figure 6.1.)

To the east and west of each principal meridian are strips of land six miles wide that run in a north-south direction parallel to the meridian. These north-south strips (columns) are called *ranges* and are identified by consecutive numbers, beginning at the meridian and proceeding east or west from the principal meridian. To the north and south of each base line are also strips of land six miles wide that run in an east-west direction parallel to each base line. These are identified by consecutive numbers, beginning at the base line and proceeding north or south from the base line. These east-west strips (rows) are called *tiers*. To keep ranges and tiers straight, you might try to remember the word "CARRAT": *C*olumns *A*re *R*anges; *R*ows *A*re *T*iers.

FIGURE 6.1
Government Survey
System: Ranges and
Tiers

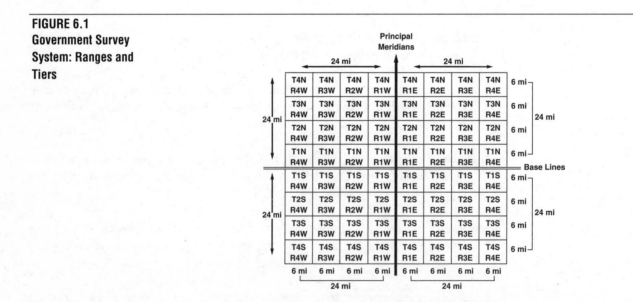

FIGURE 6.2
Government Survey
System: Township

6	5	4	3	2	1
7	8	9	10	11	12
18	17	16	15	14	13
19	20	21	22	23	24
30	29	28	27	26	25
31	32	33	34	35	36

Ranges and tiers form squares six miles by six miles called *townships*. Each six-mile-by-six-mile township is further broken down into squares of one square mile (640 acres) each, called *sections,* thus making 36 sections per township. Each section in a township is identified numerically, starting in the upper right corner and running from right to left for six sections, then dropping down to the next row and running left to right for six sections, etc., until each of the 36 sections is numbered. (See Figure 6.2.)

To further divide this 640-acre section into smaller areas, it is broken down into ½ sections (320 acres each), ¼ sections (160 acres each), etc. (See Figure 6.3.)

When locating or identifying parcels from rectangular descriptions, one reads backward from the general part of the description to the specific part at the beginning; more specifically, from the meridian, range, and township to the section or part of a section. Thus, a tract of land in the Southwest one-quarter of the Southeast one-quarter, Section 8, Township 3 South, Range 3 West of the 9th principal meridian (ordinarily abbreviated as SW 1/4, SE 1/4, S8, T3S, R3W 9th P.M.), would be identified by reading from right to left: first identifying the 9th P.M., then Range 3 West, then Township 3 South, then Section 8, then the Southeast 1/4 of Section 8, then the Southwest 1/4 of that quarter-section. (See Figure 6.4.)

FIGURE 6.3
Government Survey
System: Section

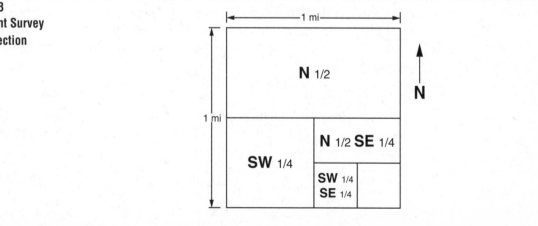

FIGURE 6.4
Government Survey System: Parcel Identification

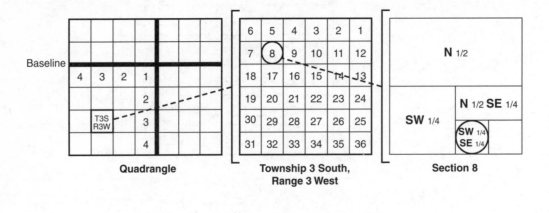

METES AND BOUNDS
================

Metes are measures of length, and *bounds* are boundaries. The purpose of these measurements is to allow a surveyor to walk the boundaries. Metes and bounds are commonly used in the legal descriptions found in deeds and are useful when it is necessary to describe tracts of land with irregular boundaries. Sometimes natural or artificial objects called *monuments* are used to locate the corners of a metes-and-bounds description and if a discrepancy occurs these objects will take precedence over the linear measurements. Old descriptions of this type used trees, stones, creeks, and other objects as markers, which often have since disappeared, moved, or otherwise been altered, thus making descriptions indefinite. Sometimes reference is made to "bench marks"; these are monuments used to establish elevation.

Permanent reference markers (PRM) are used to locate and subsequently originate metes-and-bounds descriptions. The actual description starts at a designated point called the *point of beginning* (POB) and then proceeds around the boundaries with reference to linear measurements, directions, and courses, ending at the POB. All directions are expressed in terms of angles from 0 through 360 degrees. A complete circle is divided into 360 degrees (360°); each degree is further broken down into 60 minutes (60'); and each minute is divided into 60 seconds (60"). This is extra credit material but a metes-and-bounds description can be by the *azimuth system* or the *bearing system.*

Azimuth System

In most metes-and-bounds descriptions, azimuths are measured clockwise from true north. An azimuth of 135 degrees, 45 minutes, would be written 135°45'. (See Figure 6.5.)

FIGURE 6.5
Metes and Bounds:
Azimuth System

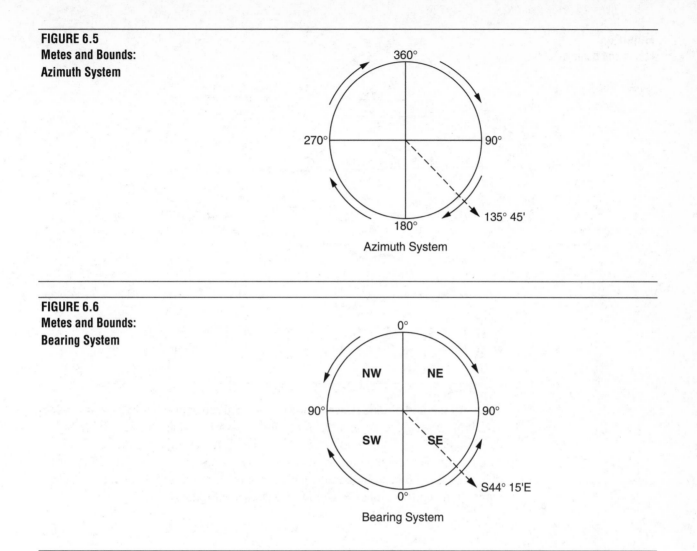

Azimuth System

FIGURE 6.6
Metes and Bounds:
Bearing System

Bearing System

Bearing System

In the bearing system, the complete circle is divided into four quadrants. The quadrants then are identified as northeast (NE), southeast (SE), southwest (SW), and northwest (NW). Each contains 90 degrees, measured from the north-south line (0°) toward the east or west. Using the bearing system, the azimuth shown in Figure 6.5 would read S44°15'E. (See Figure 6.6.)

Thus, Bearing S44°15'E is equal to Azimuth 135°45'.

An example of a metes-and-bounds description of the tract of land in Figure 6.7 might be as follows:

> A tract of land in Black Dog, Iowa, is described as follows: Beginning at the intersection of the east side of Mutt Road and the south side of Boxer Street; thence east along the south side of Boxer Street for 150 feet; thence south 45° east for 205 feet, more or less, to the north edge of Black Dog Gulch; then southwesterly along the north edge of said Gulch to the intersection with the east side of Mutt Road; then northerly 250 feet along the east side of Mutt Road to the point of beginning.

FIGURE 6.7
Metes and Bounds

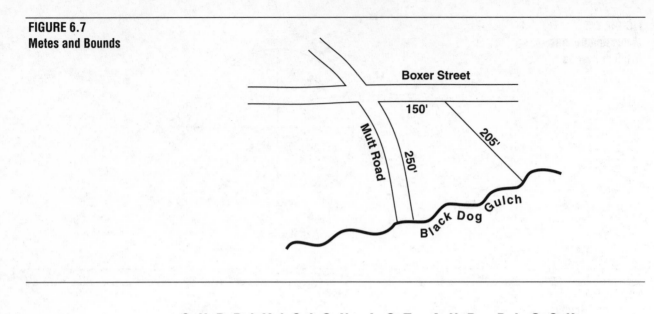

SUBDIVISION LOT AND BLOCK NUMBERS (PLAT AND PARCEL SYSTEM)

The third method of land description is by lot and block number in a recorded sub-division. A recorded plat book is a public record of maps of subdivided land, divided into blocks, lots, and parcels. After being recorded, these new additions or subdivision plats become the legal description. In describing a lot from a recorded plat, the lot and block number, the name or number of the subdivision plat, and the name of the county and state would be used. (See Figure 6.8.)

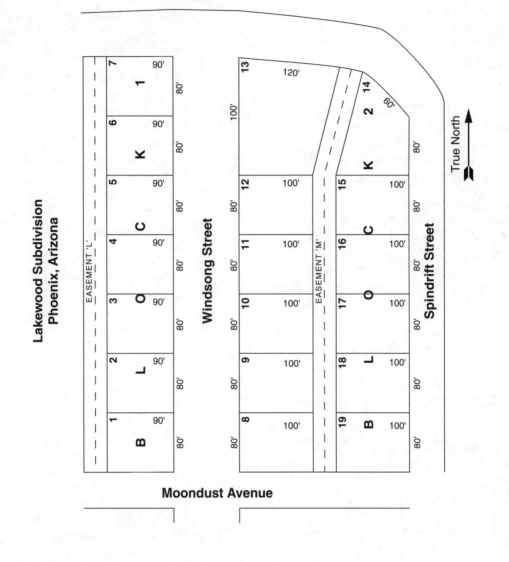

FIGURE 6.8
Lot and Block System

QUESTIONS

Government Survey System

1. The north-south lines that are 24 miles apart are called
   A. base lines.
   B. guide meridians.
   C. columns.
   D. ranges.

2. A range is numbered to the
   A. east or west of a principal meridian.
   B. north or south of a base line.
   C. north or south of a principal meridian.
   D. east or north of a base line.

3. A township contains
   A. 6 sections.
   B. 16 sections.
   C. 24 sections.
   D. 36 sections.

4. A tier is numbered to the
   A. east or west of a principal meridian.
   B. north or south of a base line.
   C. east or west of a base line.
   D. north or south of a principal meridian.

5. The NW 1/4 of the NE 1/4 of the SW 1/4 of Section 8 contains how many acres?
   A. 10
   B. 20
   C. 30
   D. 40

6. The horizontal distance between two township boundaries is
   A. 6 miles.
   B. 18 miles.
   C. 23 miles.
   D. 24 miles.

7. Which of the following contains the smallest parcel of land?
   A. 640 acres
   B. 9 square miles
   C. ½ of a township
   D. 36 square miles

8. Which of the following contains the largest parcel of land?
   A. 2 miles square
   B. 2 sections
   C. 10 percent of a township
   D. 130 acres

9. Section 11 in a township is
   A. north of Section 14 and south of Section 2.
   B. north of Section 17 and south of Section 5.
   C. north of Section 19 and south of Section 17.
   D. north of Section 22 and south of Section 10.

10. Section 2 in a township is directly south of what Section of the township directly to its north?
    A. 2
    B. 5
    C. 32
    D. 35

11. Each side of a square acre contains approximately
    A. 208 feet.
    B. 215 feet.
    C. 230 feet.
    D. 320 feet.

12. How many acres are in the N 1/2 of the SE 1/4 of the SE 1/4 of a section of land?
    A. 8
    B. 20
    C. 32
    D. 64

13. How many townships are there in a piece of land 24 miles square?
    A. 8
    B. 16
    C. 24
    D. 32

14. The NE 1/4 of the SW 1/4 of Section 8 contains
   A. 40 acres.
   B. 80 acres.
   C. 120 acres.
   D. 160 acres.

15. In any individual township, which of the following sections would be contiguous to Section 30?
   A. 19, 29, and 31
   B. 29 only
   C. 19, 20, 21, 31, and 32
   D. 19, 29, and 33

16. What is the shortest distance between the closest borders of Section 2 and Section 35 of the same township?
   A. 2 miles
   B. 4 miles
   C. 6 miles
   D. 12 miles

17. Which of the following is larger than a standard section?
   A. 16 parcels, 40 acres each
   B. 5,000 feet by 6,000 feet
   C. 1/36 of a township
   D. 5,280 feet by 5,280 feet

18. A section of land sold for $1 million. What was the price per acre?
   A. $22.95
   B. $15,625
   C. $22,960
   D. $1,562.50

19. How many square feet are there in the S 1/2 SW 1/4 SW 1/4 NE 1/4?
   A. 217,800
   B. 435,600
   C. 24,111
   D. 108,900

Metes and Bounds

1. The main purpose of a metes-and-bounds description is to
   A. allow a surveyor to walk the boundaries.
   B. assist the assessor in determining land value.
   C. help an owner determine a fence line.
   D. eliminate the rectangular survey system.

2. Which of the following is *MOST* nearly due south?
   A. S 89° 30'E
   B. S 0° 45'E
   C. S 0° 30'W
   D. S 1° 15'W

3. In a metes-and-bounds legal description, *bounds* refers to which of the following?
   A. Measures
   B. Distances
   C. Monuments
   D. Compass direction

4. In connection with metes-and-bounds descriptions, official markers on the property used to determine elevations are called
   A. metes.
   B. monuments.
   C. bench marks.
   D. encroachments.

5. Persons *MOST* apt to use a monument in their profession would be
   A. lawyers.
   B. carpenters.
   C. general contractors.
   D. surveyors.

Subdivision Lot and Block Numbers

To answer the questions below, refer to Figure 6.8 on page 65.

1. If all houses in Block 1 faced toward Windsong Street, which way would they face?
   A. East
   B. South
   C. North
   D. West

2. Which statement is *TRUE* about Lot 1 in Block 1, compared with Lot 18 in Block 2?
   A. Lot 18 has more front footage than Lot 1.
   B. Lot 1 has less access than Lot 18.
   C. Lot 18 is deeper than Lot 1.
   D. Lot 1 has homes on either side of it.

3. Lot 8 in Block 2 is how many square feet larger than Lot 6 in Block 1?
   A. 1,000
   B. 600
   C. 800
   D. 1,200

4. Which lot has the greatest front footage on Windsong Street?
   A. Lot 13, Block 2
   B. Lot 1, Block 1
   C. Lot 14, Block 2
   D. Lot 8, Block 2

ANSWERS

Government Survey System

1. **B.** Guide meridians are the lines 24 miles apart running in a north-south direction that form the east-west sides of a check (because range lines are 6 miles apart, every fourth range line forms the side of a check).

2. **A.** Ranges are the land strips running in a north-south direction that lie to the east or west of the meridian. They are thus numbered starting at the meridian, with the numbers getting larger as they move to the east or west of that meridian.

3. **D.** There are 16 townships in a check, and 36 sections in a township.

4. **B.** Tiers are the strips of land running in an east-west direction that lie to the north or south of a base line. They are thus numbered starting at the base line, with the numbers getting larger as they move to the north or south.

5. **A.** Multiply the denominators and divide the results into 640 acres. Thus, $4 \times 4 \times 4 = 64$; 640 acres $\div 64 = 10$ acres.

6. **A.** Each township is 6 horizontal miles across or 24 miles across a quadrangle.

7. **A.** 640 acres = 1 square mile (1 section) and ½ of a township = 18 square miles.

8. **A.** 2 miles square is equal to 4 square miles. Do not confuse the expression "miles square," which means shape, with "square miles," which means area or content. For example, a township is a 6-mile square (a square 6 miles on each side), containing 36 square miles.

9. **A.** See Figure 6.2.

10. **D.** See Figure 6.4.

11. **A.** $208 \times 208 = 43,264$. An acre equals 43,560 square feet.

12. **B.** Multiply the denominators and divide the results into 640 acres. Thus, $2 \times 4 \times 4 = 32$; 640 acres $\div 32 = 20$ acres.

13. **B.** See Figure 6.1.

14. **A.** Multiply the denominators and divide the results into 640 acres. Thus, $4 \times 4 = 16$; 640 acres $\div 16 = 40$ acres.

15. **A.** See Figure 6.2.

16. **B.** See Figure 6.2.

17. **B.** All of the other three choices equal one section.

18. **D.** 640 acres in a section ($\$1,000,000 \div 640 = \$1,562.50$ price per acre).

19. **A.** Multiply the denominators and divide the results into 640 acres. Thus, $2 \times 4 \times 4 \times 4 = 128$; 640 acres $\div 128 = 5$ acres.

Metes and Bounds

1. **A.** The purpose of a metes-and-bounds legal description is to allow a surveyor to walk the boundaries.

2. **C.** Choice (C) is only one-half degree to the west of due south.

3. **C.** A metes-and-bounds description starts at a well-marked POB and follows the boundaries of the land by courses and metes (measures, distances, and compass direction) and bounds (landmarks, monuments) and returns to the true POB.

4. **C.** Benchmarks are used in the metes-and-bounds method to describe elevation.

5. **D.** Monuments (as used by surveyors) are objects such as rocks, trees, rivers, etc.

Subdivision Lot and Block Numbers

1. **B.** The top of most maps is *north*.

2. **C.** Lot 18, Block 2 is 100 feet deep while Lot 1, Block 1 is only 90 feet.

3. **C.** Lot 8 is 8,000 square feet. Lot 6 is 7,200 square feet.

4. **A.** Lot 13, Block 2 has 100 feet.

Valuation of Real Estate

This part contains questions on the topics of

- the principles of value;

- commonly accepted approaches to value;

- the effect of depreciation on value;

- assessment of real property for tax purposes; and

- basic principles of federal income taxation of real property.

Expect about 15 percent of the national portion of the examination to contain questions on the topics covered in Part B.

7

Appraisal

Appraisal is the process of creating an opinion (estimate) about a property's value. An appraisal usually is required when a property is sold, financed, condemned, taxed, insured, or partitioned. An appraisal may be in the form of a lengthy written report, a completed form, a simple letter, or even an oral report.

The three approaches used to estimate the market value of a property are the (1) direct sales comparison approach, (2) the cost approach, and (3) the income approach. A shorthand income approach sometimes used is the gross income multiplier (GIM) or gross rent multiplier (GRM). The GIM uses annual income while the GRM uses monthly income to determine value.

Questions in this chapter will test your comprehension of the following topics:

- Use and reconciliation of the three methods of appraisal

- The different types of depreciation, including functional and external obsolescence

- The four elements of value

- The different types of value

- The capitalization of income to arrive at value

- Replacement cost and reproduction cost

- The gross rent multiplier technique

With the requirement that only licensed or certified appraisers can be used to appraise collateral for certain federally related loans, real estate licensees need to be careful not to present their opinions of value as appraisals. Brokers are still able to recommend listing and sales prices, but brokers are prohibited from charging a separate fee for such recommendations.

You can expect that some of the appraisal questions will involve math calculations as well.

KEY WORDS

Amenities: Neighboring facilities and services located outside of one's property that always enhance its value. Examples include proximity to parks and public transportation.

Appraisal: The process of estimating, fixing, or setting the market value of real property. An appraisal may take the form of a lengthy report, a completed form, a simple letter, or even an oral report.

Appreciation: An increase in the worth or value of property due to economic or related causes, which may prove to be either temporary or permanent.

Arm's length: Transactions for which a reasonable length of time has been allowed for market exposure and in which the buyer and seller are unrelated; well-informed about the property's value; acting without any undue pressure; and its financing isn't affected by any unusual financing. Another name for arm's length is market value. Those sales that are not arm's length would be considered less than arm's length.

Assessed valuation: The value of real property as established by the state government for purposes of computing real property taxes.

Building residual technique: A method of determining the value of an improvement, normally used in appraising income property.

Capitalization: A mathematical process for converting net income into an indication of value, commonly used in the income approach to appraisal.

Cap rate (capitalization rate): The percentage selected for use in the income approach to valuation of improved property. The cap rate is designed to reflect the recapture of the original investment over the economic life of the improvement, to give the investor an acceptable rate of return (yield) on the original investment, and to provide for the return on borrowed capital.

Comparables ("comps"): Recently sold properties that are similar to a particular property being evaluated and that are used to indicate a reasonable fair market value for the subject property.

Depreciation: As related to appraisal, loss in value due to any cause; any condition that adversely affects the value of an improvement.

Fair market value: The highest monetary price that a property would bring, if offered for sale for a reasonable period of time in a competitive market, to a seller, willing but not compelled to sell, from a buyer, willing but not compelled to buy, both parties being fully informed of all the purposes to which the property is best adapted and for which it is capable of being used. Also known as "arm's length."

Functional obsolescence: A loss in value of an improvement due to functional inadequacies, often caused by age or poor design.

Gross rent multiplier (GRM) and gross income multiplier (GIM): A formula used to estimate the market value of an income-producing residential property. To create the multiplier an appraiser must have recent sales and rental income data. A multiplier is derived by dividing the selling price of an income-producing property by its estimated monthly rents. After several properties have been identified, a statistical mean is used to average the gross rent multiplier (GRM). Once established, the appraiser multiplies a property's gross monthly rent by the multiplier in order to arrive at an estimate of value. For example, if a duplex had gross monthly rents of $1,600 and sold for $150,000, then the GRM would be computed by dividing $150,000 by $1,600 to arrive at 94 (93.75). Once the multiplier (94) is established, then a neighboring income property would be multiplied by 94 to compute a value of $188,000. Gross rents ($2,000) × Multiplier (94) = $188,000.

For the broker's examination, it is necessary to know how to compute the Gross Income Multiplier (GIM). Because commercial real estate generates more income besides rent, this multiplier uses the gross *annual* income of a property. To compute the GIM the appraiser divides the annual gross income into the selling price.

Income multipliers work because rents and value seem to travel in the same direction.

Highest and best use: That use which, at the time of appraising the property, is most likely to produce the greatest net return to the land and/or the building over a given period of time.

Income approach: An approach to the valuation or appraisal of real property as determined by the amount of net income the property will produce over its remaining economic life.

Obsolescence: A type of depreciation of property.

Plottage: The increased value and improved usability that results from the merging or consolidating of adjacent lots into one larger lot.

Reconciliation: The process of applying all three appraisal approaches (market, cost, income) on the same property to estimate its value. It is not a statistical mean, but rather, as determined by the appraiser, a weighted average of each approach.

Reproduction cost: The cost, on the basis of current prices, of reproducing an exact replica of property with the same material as that used in the original.

Useful life: That period of time over which an asset such as a building is expected to remain economically feasible to the owner.

Value: The power of a good or service to command other goods in exchange for the present worth of future rights to income or amenities; the present worth to typical users and investors of future benefits arising out of ownership of a property.

MISTAKEN IDENTITY

The following words are often confused with one another. Note the difference in meaning of these mistaken identity words and phrases.

Functional obsolescence/External obsolescence: A loss in value resulting from some internal (i.e., *functional*) factor (e.g., poor design, outdated equipment) as opposed to an *external* factor (e.g., neighborhood change, highway relocation).

Reproduction cost/Replacement cost: The cost to construct an exact replica (*reproduction cost*) as opposed to the cost to construct a building with similar material and use (*replacement cost*).

Assemblage/Plottage: *Assemblage* is the process of joining several parcels to form a larger parcel; the resulting increase in value is called *plottage*.

Capitalization rate/Recapture rate: The *capitalization (cap) rate* is the rate of return the investor wants on a property; it consists of the return *on* the investment plus the *recapture* (through depreciation) *of* the investment.

QUESTIONS

1. Of the three methods of appraising properties, the replacement cost approach is particularly appropriate and would give the *MOST* accurate value in the appraisal of a(n)
   - A. new home.
   - B. multiple dwelling.
   - C. old home.
   - D. medium-age home.

2. An appraiser measuring the area of a house would use the
   - A. net rentable area.
   - B. exterior dimensions.
   - C. room sizes.
   - D. interior dimensions, excluding partitions.

3. The capitalization rate for improvements is the
   - A. recapture rate only.
   - B. interest rate only.
   - C. overall rate.
   - D. interest rate plus recapture rate.

4. ◎ The economic life of a building has come to an end when the
   - A. building ceases to represent the highest and best use of the land.
   - B. value of the land and the building equals the value of the land only.
   - C. rent produced is valued at less than a similar amount of money invested elsewhere could produce.
   - D. reserve for depreciation equals the cost to replace the building.

5. The sales comparison approach to value is an indication of the
   - A. lowest value.
   - B. highest value.
   - C. future value.
   - D. range of probable value.

6. What type of reduction in value is present when a hydrogen gas storage tank is located next to a property?
   - A. Physical deterioration
   - B. External obsolescence
   - C. Functional obsolescence
   - D. Negligible obsolescence

7. All of the following are characteristic of value *EXCEPT*
   - A. utility.
   - B. scarcity.
   - C. transferability.
   - D. cost.

8. Physical deterioration *MOST* closely means
   - A. obsolescence.
   - B. wear and tear.
   - C. reversion.
   - D. recapture.

9. The sales comparison appraisal approach would be *BEST* used for
   - A. estimating the price for new homes in a new subdivision.
   - B. valuing vacant land.
   - C. establishing a price on a nonprofit hospital.
   - D. determining the best price for a small private school.

10. When capitalization is sought, a person is particularly interested in
    - A. potential future value.
    - B. cost value.
    - C. total capital invested.
    - D. evaluating income.

11. A capitalization rate incorporates
    - A. return on land and building and recapture of building.
    - B. return on land and building and recapture of land.
    - C. return on land and recapture of land and building.
    - D. return on building and recapture of land and building.

12. The purchase and putting together of several pieces of land is *BEST* called
    A. annexation.
    B. appreciation.
    C. assemblage.
    D. integration.

13. ◎ Concerning the valuation of residential property, which of the following is *TRUE?*
    A. The value of the ordinary single-family residential property should be based on the income it is capable of producing if rented.
    B. In valuing a residence, functional accessories such as built-in teak cabinets are seldom taken into consideration.
    C. An older home in a neighborhood of newer homes will retain its value and not be affected by the value of the other homes.
    D. Recently sold homes in a neighborhood give a fair indication of the value of similar homes.

14. When a landlord makes improvements to property, the investment should be recovered over a set period of time. The landlord should use a(n)
    A. amortization rate.
    B. discount rate.
    C. recapture rate.
    D. reformation rate.

15. If the replacement cost shows a higher value than the appraised value, which of the following has *MOST* probably occurred?
    A. Accrued depreciation
    B. Excessive appraisal value
    C. External obsolescence
    D. Inappropriate capitalization rate

16. In making an appraisal, the before-and-after method is used *MOST* often with
    A. condemnation.
    B. exchange.
    C. cost of reproduction.
    D. option.

17. ◎ An appraiser often makes a distinction between the physical life and the economic life of an improvement. Regarding these two ways to measure "life," which is generally *TRUE?*
    A. Economic life lasts longer.
    B. Economic life and physical age are usually parallel.
    C. Physical life is shorter.
    D. Economic life ceases first.

18. Which of the following facts might be classified as functional obsolescence?
    A. The exterior needs painting.
    B. The property fronts on a busy expressway.
    C. The property has a single-car garage.
    D. The neighborhood is 50 years old.

19. Assume that the trend in architectural design is toward more contemporary-styled homes. Because of this trend, a conservatively designed home will tend to
    A. decrease in value more rapidly.
    B. decrease in value less rapidly.
    C. stay the same.
    D. stay the same and then appreciate.

20. The useful life of a building, or period of time after which the income provided by it is *NOT* sufficient to warrant its maintenance, is called
    A. recapture limit.
    B. economic life.
    C. reversion limit.
    D. investment duration.

21. All of the following statements are true *EXCEPT*
    A. functional obsolescence is the result of factors within the property.
    B. external obsolescence is caused by factors outside the property.
    C. external obsolescence is the result of one's personal financial condition.
    D. deterioration is wear and tear.

22. The *MOST* widely used approach in the estimate of value of residential real property is the
    A. income approach.
    B. direct sales comparison approach.
    C. cost approach.
    D. gross income multiplier.

23. A broker usually appraises to determine
    A. assessed value.
    B. book value.
    C. market value.
    D. insurance value.

24. Market value could be determined *BEST* by considering which of the following?
    A. Acquisition cost, market data, replacement
    B. Comparison, income, replacement
    C. Purchase price, summation cost
    D. Income stream, acquisition cost

25. The value of a leased fee property is equal to
    A. rent to the landlord.
    B. rent plus leasehold interest.
    C. rent plus reversionary right.
    D. commission to broker.

26. The period of time through which a property gives benefits to its owner is *BEST* described as
    A. investment duration.
    B. physical life.
    C. value duration.
    D. economic life.

27. Real estate values are *MOST* affected by
    A. location.
    B. availability of money.
    C. appraisal.
    D. national trends.

28. A house with four bedrooms and one bath is an example of
    A. external obsolescence.
    B. functional obsolescence.
    C. overbuilt obsolescence.
    D. residual physical depreciation.

29. Which of the following is *TRUE* of real estate appraisers of property secured by federally related loans?
    A. They need a master's degree.
    B. They usually base their fees on a percentage of the appraised value.
    C. They must hold a state appraiser's license or certification.
    D. They usually do not inspect the property.

30. An official valuation of property for ad valorem tax purposes is *BEST* described as
    A. a capitalization.
    B. an assessment appraisal.
    C. tax depreciation.
    D. tax equalization.

31. ◎ Using the income approach to valuation, all of the following are proper deductions from effective gross income to determine net income *EXCEPT*
    A. reserve for replacement.
    B. interest payments on loans.
    C. maintenance expenses.
    D. management costs.

32. Capitalization is a process used to
    A. determine the value of most residential property.
    B. convert income into value.
    C. determine the total remaining capital.
    D. save money on an investment.

33. The difference between the cost of replacement and current valuation of a single-family residence is equal to
    A. accrued depreciation.
    B. assessed valuation.
    C. investment limitation.
    D. economic replacement.

34. In estimating the value lost by a structure due to physical deterioration, the appraiser places greatest emphasis on the
    A. age of the building.
    B. condition of the surrounding buildings.
    C. observed condition of the subject building.
    D. zoning of the neighborhood.

35. A residence located in an area where there are factories and plants, and where there is much smoke and dust, is suffering from
    A. physical depreciation.
    B. external obsolescence.
    C. residential regression.
    D. accrued depreciation.

36. A post office of unique design and construction is *BEST* appraised by which of the following approaches?
    A. Income
    B. Market comparison
    C. Land residual
    D. Cost

37. ◎ All of the following statements are true about loss in value due to obsolescence *EXCEPT*
    A. extra-large load-bearing columns in a 30-year-old commercial building represent incurable functional obsolescence.
    B. an unattractive storefront window represents curable functional obsolescence.
    C. a chemical plant located across the street from a private residence represents external obsolescence.
    D. a larger property next door sold for 20 percent below the listed price.

38. All of the following are examples of external obsolescence *EXCEPT*
    A. population density.
    B. direct effect of the elements.
    C. zoning.
    D. nearby highway realignment.

39. In using the direct sales comparison approach to value, the appraiser considers the
    A. sales price of comparable properties.
    B. acquisition cost to the present owner.
    C. income stream.
    D. vacancy and bad debt factor.

40. Of the following, which type of value equals the actual market value?
    A. Assessed value
    B. Insurance value
    C. Book value
    D. Comparable value

41. Market value is most closely related to
    A. comparable price.
    B. replacement price.
    C. income analysis.
    D. reproduction price.

42. ◎ In regard to the capitalization rate, the value of property
    A. increases as the rate increases.
    B. decreases as the rate decreases.
    C. decreases as the rate increases.
    D. neither increases nor decreases.

43. The capitalization rate of a property is the ratio between the
    A. equity of the owner and the selling price.
    B. net income and the market value.
    C. sales price and the mortgaged value.
    D. recapture rate and the land residual.

44. The gross rent multiplier (GRM) is calculated by dividing the sales price by the
    A. monthly net income.
    B. monthly gross income.
    C. annual net income.
    D. annual gross income.

45. All of the following are used to estimate value *EXCEPT*
    A. improvements.
    B. deterioration.
    C. owner's livelihood.
    D. economic life.

46. A factor by which the appraiser multiplies the total rental income from a property as an estimate of its value is the
    A. gross income multiplier.
    B. land residual process.
    C. building residual process.
    D. capitalization rate.

47. The cost of constructing a new building that has utility equivalent to the property under appraisal but is built with modern materials according to current standards, design, and layout is an appropriate definition of
    A. reproduction cost.
    B. replacement cost.
    C. residual technique.
    D. economic replacement.

48. A homogeneous community typically has what effect on real estate values?
    A. Stabilizes them
    B. Causes the values to increase
    C. Causes the values to decrease
    D. Does not have any effect on the values

49. When an appraiser adjusts the estimate of a home's value because of a poor floor plan, the adjustment is made because of
    A. physical depreciation.
    B. functional obsolescence.
    C. cost-adjustment ratio.
    D. structural depreciation.

50. Highest and best use is concerned with all of the following *EXCEPT*
    A. net yield to owner.
    B. utility of surrounding area.
    C. relationship to regional development.
    D. interest rate on investment loans.

51. If a building has an estimated remaining economic life of 50 years, the appropriate recapture rate will *MOST* likely be
    A. 2 percent.
    B. 3 percent.
    C. 6 percent.
    D. 18 percent.

52. An appraiser's fee is typically based on which of the following?
    A. Value of property
    B. Time and expense
    C. Percentage of value plus a flat fee
    D. State regulated fees

53. An appraisal of real estate does which of the following?
    A. Determines value
    B. Estimates value
    C. Guarantees value
    D. Ensures value

54. Which one of the following *BEST* describes the concept of highest and best use?
    A. Gross return
    B. Natural and legal use
    C. Greatest net return over a given period
    D. Homogeneous use

55. The collection of data and the analysis of different approaches to value is known as
    A. depreciation.
    B. amortization.
    C. reconciliation.
    D. accrual.

56. The formula used in direct capitalization of income property valuation is
    A. value equals cap rate divided by income.
    B. value equals income divided by cap rate.
    C. value equals income multiplied by cap rate.
    D. value equals income divided by net assets.

57. Replacement cost is *BEST* described as the
    A. original cost adjusted for inflation.
    B. cost of building a property of equivalent utility with modern materials.
    C. cost of purchasing an equally desirable property.
    D. cost of building an exact replica of the subject.

58. An appraisal is needed to judge all of the following *EXCEPT*
    A. market value.
    B. replacement value.
    C. loan value.
    D. book value.

59. ◎ In appraising investment property what does the owner deduct to arrive at the net effective income?
    A. Federal income taxes
    B. Capital improvements
    C. Vacancy and bad debt losses
    D. All ordinary expenses to the property

60. A man recently appraised a three-bedroom ranch home in a poor neighborhood. He found another comparable in a better neighborhood that sold for $80,000. The comparable also had a fireplace, which the subject property did not. He assigned the following adjustments: $2,000 for the fireplace and $5,000 for the neighborhood. The adjusted sales price for this comparable would now be
    A. $73,000.
    B. $83,000.
    C. $87,000.
    D. $92,000.

61. Lots are valued at $30,000. Reproduction cost of the dwelling is $170,000. If properties are now selling for $140,000, the accrued depreciation is
    A. $30,000.
    B. $50,000.
    C. $60,000.
    D. $80,000.

62. ◎ An appraiser used the three approaches to value for determining the value of a duplex. If the appraiser used 60 percent of the market approach, 25 percent of the cost approach, and 15 percent of the income approach, what process was the appraiser using to determine market value?
    A. Capitalization
    B. Reconciliation
    C. Recapture
    D. Replacement

63. The actual selling price of a piece of real property is *BEST* described as the
    A. book value.
    B. replacement value.
    C. selling price.
    D. market value.

64. An appraiser preparing a market analysis of a parcel of real property would be *MOST* sensitive to the recent market tendencies of
    A. buyers.
    B. lenders.
    C. brokers.
    D. appraisers.

65. Which of the following tends to lower a property's value?
    A. Neighborhood conformity
    B. Excessive demand
    C. Transferability
    D. Deferred maintenance

66. When a property has suffered a reduction in value due to dry rot and termite damage, appraisers refer to such reduction as
    A. functional obsolescence.
    B. external obsolescence.
    C. physical deterioration.
    D. residual loss.

67. The period of time necessary to recover an investment in a commercial building is *BEST* described as
    A. residual.
    B. reversion.
    C. recapture.
    D. recovery.

68. Which of the following conditions is an indication of functional obsolescence?
    A. Cracked foundation
    B. Neighborhood airport expanded to land jumbo jets
    C. Ceiling lower than customary
    D. Increase in special assessments

69. ◎ A buyer purchased a commercial warehouse for $750,000. Fixed expenses are $15,000 per year and operating expenses are $49,000 per year. If the buyer wants a 9 percent return, how much gross rental income does he need each month?
    A. $6,750
    B. $10,958
    C. $9,708
    D. $5,625

70. All of the following would be considered functional obsolescence in evaluating a commercial building *EXCEPT*
    A. architectural design.
    B. volume or capacity in relation to site.
    C. parking plan.
    D. supply and demand.

71. An appraiser who is evaluating an urban commercial warehouse would look for all of the following factors *EXCEPT*
    A. potential income from the property.
    B. the replacement cost and accrued depreciation.
    C. economic life of building.
    D. original cost of the building.

72. Which is the *MOST* appropriate appraisal method to use in evaluating a property for fire insurance purposes?
    A. Sales data
    B. Capitalization
    C. Replacement cost
    D. Comparison

73. All of these facts are important for an appraiser of a commercial shopping center to discover *EXCEPT*
    A. the person(s) entitled to possession and ownership.
    B. the rents and operating expenses.
    C. all existing encumbrances.
    D. the current rate for commercial loans.

74. Which of the following *BEST* describes the highest and best use for a particular property?
    A. The use that the owner wants
    B. Whatever is the present use
    C. The use that produces the greatest net return
    D. Whatever use produces the highest density zoning

75. A woman inherited a residence from her father. The property's value at the date of his death five years ago was $117,000. An appraiser hired to recommend a listing price would be primarily concerned with which of the following?
    A. The $117,000 figure and the average rate of appreciation of residences in the past five years
    B. The value of similar residences recently sold in the community
    C. The book value of the dwelling
    D. The equity at the time of the father's death

76. All of the following would be considered in the cost approach appraisal method *EXCEPT*
    A. operating expenses.
    B. depreciation.
    C. land value.
    D. replacement cost.

77. If a neighborhood greenbelt enhances the value of a new housing development, an appraiser considers it a(n)
    A. amenity.
    B. feature.
    C. benefit.
    D. attachment.

78. In making an informal appraisal for listing purposes, a broker finds comparable residences that recently sold for $92,000, $82,000, and $102,000. The broker should advise the seller that the residence should be listed at which amount?
    A. Highest
    B. Lowest
    C. Average of the three
    D. Price of the most similar property

79. Which of the following is the appropriate method of selecting a capitalization rate for an income-producing property?
    A. Gross income divided by value
    B. Net income divided by value
    C. Value divided by net income
    D. Gross expenses divided by net income

80. Assume that three rental buildings had sales prices and rents as follows: $107,250 and $16,500; $105,625 and $16,250; $112,125 and $17,250. What value would most likely be indicated on a similar building if rents were $16,750?
    A. $107,250
    B. $108,300
    C. $108,875
    D. $112,125

81. ◎ A buyer is looking for an apartment building with a 10 percent return. If an available building produces $78,000 in gross income with expenses at 60 percent of income, how much should the buyer offer for the building?
    A. $312,000
    B. $558,000
    C. $780,000
    D. $912,000

82. When evaluating an income property, an appraiser must take into consideration all of the following *EXCEPT* the
    A. correct capitalization rate.
    B. cost of the building next door.
    C. net operating income of the property.
    D. vacancy and bad debt rates.

83. In using the gross rent multiplier, Comparable A has a value of $88,000 with monthly net income of $880; Comparable B is $90,000 with $900; Comparable C is $95,000 with $950. If you receive $930 a month net income, what is your comparable value?
    A. $91,500
    B. $93,000
    C. $94,000
    D. $97,500

84. Which of the following is *FALSE* about the direct sales comparison approach?
    A. Offers to buy are helpful to set the lower limits.
    B. The type of financing for comparable sales is relevant.
    C. Asking prices of comparable homes are significantly relevant.
    D. Net operating income figures are not relevant.

85. The capitalization approach to valuation does *NOT* consider
    A. real property tax.
    B. vacancy rate.
    C. lot size.
    D. insurance costs.

86. The value of the land plus the reproduction cost less depreciation is the formula for which appraisal approach?
    A. Direct sales comparison
    B. Cost
    C. Income
    D. Gross rent multiplier

87. ◎ When properties of dissimilar value are placed together, the value of the more expensive property will be affected adversely. This principle of change is called
    A. regression.
    B. progression.
    C. substitution.
    D. decreasing return.

88. A new office building constructed in an old neighborhood is for sale. What is the *BEST* method of appraisal to use?
    A. Direct sales comparison
    B. New construction cost
    C. Income
    D. RCN minus depreciation plus land

89. What factors determine the capitalization rate for a building?
    A. Rent
    B. Expenses
    C. Interest and recapture of investment
    D. Mortgage

90. ◎ A commercial warehouse is located on a half-acre of land valued at $20 a square foot. The six-year-old building had an economic life of 50 years when it was built and measures 92 feet by 135 feet. Current replacement cost is estimated at $45 per square foot. Using the cost approach, what is the property's value?
    A. $994,500
    B. $491,832
    C. $558,900
    D. $927,432

91. In appraising income-producing property, the remaining useful life of a building is considered to be the time remaining
    A. in which the owner retains occupancy.
    B. that the property can be profitably used.
    C. for tax depreciation purposes.
    D. during which the property will be physically sound.

92. During a period of declining values and tight money, real estate is considered to be a
    A. source of tax shelter.
    B. nonliquid investment.
    C. high-yield investment.
    D. hedge against inflation.

93. Which of the following principles of value is involved with the economic principle of change?
    A. Conformity
    B. Contribution
    C. Progression
    D. Substitution

94. A purchaser is considering buying several single-family residential homes and renting them out. If a gross rent multiplier of 10 is used, what effect will a 5 percent increase in insurance and property taxes have on value?
    A. 5 percent decrease
    B. 10 percent increase
    C. No increase or decrease
    D. 5 percent increase

95. In appraising a single-family home, the appraiser makes adjustments to the sales price of three comparable properties. The estimate of value would *MOST* likely be the
    A. highest sales price of the three properties.
    B. median sales price.
    C. adjusted value of the comparable property that is most similar to the subject property.
    D. average of the adjusted value of the three properties.

ANSWERS

1. **A.** The older a building becomes, the more difficult it becomes to accurately adjust for depreciation. The approach is based on the principle of substitution—a buyer will not pay more for a structure than it would cost to duplicate it.

2. **B.** The appraiser is concerned with exterior dimensions.

3. **D.** In vacant land, the capitalization rate is the interest rate alone; however, because a building is a wasting asset, the investor must also "recapture" (or get a return of) the cost of the building.

4. **B.** Economic life is the period over which a building can be profitably utilized; it is often shorter than the physical life of the building.

5. **D.** The direct sales comparison approach, also called the *market comparison approach,* indicates probable range due to the principle of substitution; a property's value tends to be set by the cost of obtaining an equally desirable substitute property.

6. **B.** External obsolescence is loss in value due to external causes outside the property itself, such as a change in zoning.

7. **D.** The elements of value are utility, scarcity, transferability, and demand.

8. **B.** Loss in value due to wear and tear, such as damage from the elements (storms or snow), is physical deterioration.

9. **B.** Sales comparison is used most effectively in the appraisal of properties that are frequently sold in the marketplace. Choices (A), (C), and (D) would be the cost approach.

10. **D.** Capitalization is sought when one wants to determine the present value of a projected income stream; in other words, what a person would pay for the right to receive certain monies over a given period.

11. **A.** An investor would get a return *on* the investment in the land and building (similar to receiving interest) and a return *of* the investment in the building through recapture (similar to depreciation rate).

12. **C.** Assemblage is the formation of a parcel from two or more lots, to be distinguished from plottage, which is the end result.

13. **D.** In comparing properties, appropriate consideration is given to different amenities, and monetary adjustments are made for each feature. The income approach is not appropriate for residential properties.

14. **C.** Through depreciation, the landlord will recapture the investment in the building and improvements before the building reaches the end of its productive life.

15. **A.** If it would cost $100,000 to reproduce a five-year-old building valued at $92,000, an adjustment has been made for $8,000 of depreciation over the five years.

16. **A.** When there is a condemnation or partial taking of a property, it necessitates determining the value before and after the condemnation. For example, if a ten-acre parcel is worth $1,000 per acre before an eight-acre section is condemned and the remaining two acres are worth only $500 each after the condemnation, then the condemnee will receive $8,000 for the eight acres plus $1,000 for the loss in value to the two remaining acres.

17. **D.** The value of the building typically ceases before it becomes structurally useless.

18. **C.** Lack of desirability in terms of design or layout compared with the desirability of a new property serving the same function is functional obsolescence. Usually double garages are functionally more acceptable.

19. **A.** This is an example of loss in value due to functional obsolescence.

20. **B.** Economic life is the period over which a building may be profitably utilized.

21. **C.** Choices (A) and (B) are correct definitions of obsolescence; together with physical deterioration they result in depreciation or loss in value.

22. **B.** The market comparison approach (using comparables) is the approach most commonly used by real estate brokers and salespeople in their everyday estimation of market values.

23. **C.** A real estate broker is most concerned with knowing market value to assist a customer in buying, selling, or determining loan value. Assessed value is used for tax purposes and book value for accounting purposes.

24. **B.** All three are appraisal approaches to value. Under choices (A), (C), and (D), acquisition cost generally is not relevant to present value.

25. **C.** The purchasers of the fee will pay a price that relates to the receipt of rental income over the term of the lease, as well as the right to receive the property at the termination of the lease (the reversion).

26. **D.** Economic life is the period over which a building is profitably utilized.

27. **A.** A shack on Waikiki Beach would be far more valuable than a mansion in the middle of the Mojave Desert. The three most important factors affecting value are location, location, and location.

28. **B.** Lack of desirability due to function, layout, or design is an indication of functional obsolescence. One bathroom with four bedrooms is a poor design by modern standards.

29. **C.** Many states have passed laws requiring that appraisers be licensed or certified, with certification being the higher requirement. It would be unethical to have a contingent appraisal fee.

30. **B.** To tax property, the taxing body must first evaluate (appraise) the property. It then will be assessed at a certain percentage of its market value. For example, if the assessed rate is 60 percent and the fair market value is $100,000, the assessed value is $60,000.

31. **B.** Concerning income-producing property, neither principal nor interest payments on existing mortgages are deductible as operating expenses, nor is building depreciation.

32. **B.** Capitalization determines the present worth of future benefits. In other words, it is the evaluation of a projected income stream.

33. **A.** The value of a property under the cost approach is the cost to replace less the accrued depreciation. For this reason, the replacement cost approach is best suited to new properties because they have not accrued any depreciation.

34. **C.** Effective age, not actual age, is sought in a determination of depreciation through physical deterioration.

35. **B.** External obsolescence is loss in value due to conditions of the surrounding neighborhood. The question does not present any facts indicating this house suffered physical damage caused by the dust and smoke.

36. **D.** The cost approach (also called *summation approach*) is the best way to appraise a property where there is no rental income and no comparables recently bought or sold.

37. **D.** Replacing the wide columns would be economically unfeasible. A storefront window most likely could be made attractive at little cost to the owner.

38. **B.** Population changes, changes in zoning, or highway realignment might cause external obsolescence of the property. Direct effect of the elements (such as wind or snow) could result in physical deterioration.

39. **A.** Because the sales comparison approach uses prices of recently sold comparables, the acquisition cost of the property is irrelevant.

40. **D.** Assessed value usually is based on a percentage of market value. Insurance value is based on replacement cost less accrued depreciation, and it would not consider values of comparable properties.

41. **A.** Market value is the most probable price a ready, willing, and able buyer, not forced to buy, will pay to a ready, willing, and able seller, not forced to sell, allowing a reasonable time for exposure in the open market.

42. **C.** For example: $5,000 capitalized at 5 percent is $100,000 ($5,000 divided by 0.05 = $100,000); $5,000 at 6 percent is $83,333; at 4 percent it is $125,000.

43. **B.** This is usually expressed as a percentage. Capitalization rate is also the rate of yield that the investor expects on the investment.

44. **B.** The gross rent multiplier is used to determine value by multiplying a property's gross income by the multiplier. It is computed by dividing a property's sale price by the gross monthly rents. The gross income multiplier operates in the same way except it uses gross annual rents instead of gross monthly rents.

45. **C.** The livelihood of an owner (how one earns one's living) has little to do with property value, except as it relates to the homogeneity of a neighborhood.

46. **A.** A gross income multiplier is obtained by dividing the sales price by the annual gross income of comparable properties recently sold. Choice (B) is used in the income approach when the value of the building and net operating income (NOI) are known. Choice (C) is used when the value of the land and the NOI are known.

47. **B.** Reproduction cost is the present cost of reproducing the improvement with an exact replica, not one with just similar utility, as in the more frequently used replacement cost.

48. **A.** Similarity of homes, social patterns, and livelihoods in an area tends to stabilize values.

49. **B.** Functional obsolescence is a loss in value due to a decrease in the home's desirability because of poor design, layout, or style.

50. **D.** Highest and best use is that use, at the time of the appraisal, most likely to produce the greatest net return over a given period of time.

51. **A.** Using straight-line depreciation, a factor of 2 percent per year would result in a return of 100 percent of the investment over this building's 50-year useful life.

52. **B.** Appraiser's fees are never based on a percentage of value because one might then conclude that an appraiser would arrive at a higher value to obtain a higher fee. By charging according to time, expenses, and reputation, the appraiser ensures the integrity of his or her efforts toward a correct evaluation.

53. **B.** An appraisal neither ensures nor guarantees value, and the actual sale of the subject property is the best determination of value. Therefore, an appraisal is always considered to be only an estimate of value.

54. **C.** Highest and best use is one of the economic principles of value. Today's highest and best use for a property may be a parking lot, whereas next year it could be a shopping center.

55. **C.** Reconciliation (also called *correlation*) is more than just averaging the three approaches to value; it weighs many factors.

56. **B.** Conversely, if the rate is unknown, it may be determined by dividing income by value; if income is unknown, it is determined by multiplying value times rate. If in doubt on a question like this, make up a practical example to see what amount is divided by what.

57. **B.** *Replacement* cost is the cost of an item of similar utility, whereas *reproduction* cost is the cost of an exact replica.

58. **D.** The book value of a property can be determined by an accountant sitting in an office and computing the cost of the property plus improvements less depreciation. The other types of value require an inspection and appraisal of the property.

59. **D.** Expenses are deducted to arrive at net effective income. Vacancy and bad debt losses reflect the gross effective income.

60. **A.** $73,000. Adjustments are made to the comparable property, not to the subject property.

The subject property lacks the fireplace ($2,000) and the neighborhood ($5,000).

61. **C.** $140,000 – $30,000 = $110,000; $170,000 – $110,000 = $60,000.

62. **B.** Reconciliation is a process in which an appraiser, after using all three approaches on a single property, uses a weighted average to determine a single value.

63. **D.** Market value is the price paid by a willing buyer to a willing seller. The selling price paid to a seller under financial stress may not reflect the actual worth.

64. **A.** Buyers' desires as to types of construction, location, amenities, and so on will have a direct bearing on a property's evaluation.

65. **D.** Deferred maintenance could indicate possible physical deterioration.

66. **C.** Physical deterioration refers to loss in value due to wear and tear, direct effects of the elements, or other physical damage.

67. **C.** Because the recapture rate is based on the theory that the building will be worthless at the end of its economic life, a factor must be made to recover this "loss" beforehand.

68. **C.** Lower-than-usual ceilings illustrate conditions within the property itself that will cause a reduction in value. Choices (B) and (D) indicate external obsolescence, and (A) is physical deterioration.

69. **B.** A 9 percent return on a $750,000 investment is $67,500. Add the expenses ($67,500 + $15,000 + $49,000) and then divide by 12 months.

70. **D.** Supply and demand is an element of value. A poor parking plan could reduce the value of an otherwise excellent building.

71. **D.** In addition to income and replacement cost (less accrued depreciation), an appraiser might also look for comparable sales of similar warehouses.

72. **C.** The fire insurer is interested in the cost of replacing one structure with another structure of similar materials.

73. **D.** Title information is needed to identify properly the property and interest being appraised, especially in situations involving transfers of sandwich leases where several people have interests. It is also necessary to know the type of ownership (deed, lease, land contract) and existing encumbrances and restrictions on use. Choice (B) information is needed for the capitalization or income approach to value. Current loan rates are irrelevant to the value of this property.

74. **C.** The highest and best use for a parcel could be a parking lot today but an office building three years from now. It depends on the greatest net return, not necessarily the maximum number of units that can be built in a given space.

75. **B.** The appraiser would be most concerned with market comparison information. In appraising the residence, neither original cost nor valuation for death tax purposes would have much relevance to the question of what a ready, willing, and able buyer would pay *today* for the residence.

76. **A.** Operating expenses are more relevant to the income approach to valuation. The cost approach looks more toward what it would cost for a substitute property.

77. **A.** Amenities are those neighboring facilities and services that enhance a property's value, such as a swimming pool and tennis court located in a condominium association. Amenities are always located outside of one's property. Swimming pools and tennis courts located on one's property are called features.

78. **D.** The important aspect of the market comparison approach is making the necessary adjustments in the differences among the comparable properties so as to arrive at the most similar property. More is involved than just averaging sales prices.

79. **B.** The income approach utilizes *net* income and capitalization rate to arrive at value. Value times the capitalization rate equals net income (e.g., $100,000 ÷ 10 percent =

$10,000; so $10,000 ÷ $100,000 would equal a capitalization rate of 10 percent).

80. **C.** Based on the three properties, the gross rent multiplier is 6.5; in other words, the sales prices were 6.5 times the annual rent.

81. **A.** $78,000 less $46,800 (60% × $78,000) is $31,200 net income divided by a 10 percent return equals $312,000.

82. **B.** If the cap rate is off by just ½ percent, the difference in valuation can be drastic. One percentage point difference in the cap rate can make a 12½ percent difference in the value estimate. There are two methods to select the appropriate cap rate: (1) by evaluating net income figures and sales prices of comparable properties and (2) by analyzing the two component parts of the cap rate, that is, the return *on* the investment (interest) and the return *of* the investment (recapture). The cap rate is applied to the net operating income after deducting for bad debt and vacancy.

83. **B.** A = 88,000 ÷ 880 = 100; B = 90,000 ÷ 900 = 100; C = 95,000 ÷ 950 = 100. Therefore, the average gross rent multiplier is 100 + 100 + 100 = 300 ÷ 3 (statistical mean) = GRM of 100. Gross rents are $930 (GR) × the multiplier (M) of 100 = $930 × 100 = $93,000.

84. **C.** Listing or asking prices reflect what the seller wants, not what the market is willing to pay.

85. **C.** The net operating income after deducting expenses is important, regardless of the size of the lot.

86. **B.** The cost approach adds up the separate parts to obtain the whole.

87. **A.** Progression is the opposite.

88. **D.** The cost approach using the replacement method is most accurate, because there is as yet little depreciation.

89. **C.** Capitalization involves the return *on* and the return *of* the investment money.

90. **D.** 43,560 ÷ 2 = 21,780 × $20 = $435,600 (land value). 92 × 135 = 12,420 × $45 = $558,900 less depreciation of 6 ÷ 50 (12 percent) or $67,068, equals an improvement value of $491,832, plus the land value of $435,600 equals $927,432.

91. **B.** Also called *economic life,* useful life is the remaining time use of the property that will be economically feasible. It is important for purposes of choosing the appropriate capitalization rate, which includes the recapture of the original investment over the economic life of the building. The economic life is typically less than the physical life of the building.

92. **B.** Liquidity is the ability of an asset such as publicly traded stock to be converted to cash in a short time. Real estate is a longer-term investment, difficult to turn into cash when the economy is in a recession.

93. **C.** The principle of change holds that economic and social forces are constantly at work to affect real property values (i.e., the law of cause and effect). Progression states that the worth of a lesser property is increased by being located among better properties; it is the opposite of regression. Contribution states that the value of a part of a property depends on how much it contributes to the overall property value. Substitution states that a buyer will pay no more than the cost of acquiring a desirable substitute. Conformity holds that the maximum value is realized when a property is in harmony with surrounding properties.

94. **C.** The gross rent multiplier (GRM) does not take into account the effect of differences in the property's expenses. The GRM is a rough rule of thumb used to estimate the value of rental residential property. It is used to estimate value as a multiple of monthly gross rents.

95. **C.** The appraiser does not average the three adjusted values. Rather, the appraiser considers all three properties and makes a personal judgment as to which property best compares with the subject property. The adjusted value of that property most likely represents the market value of the subject property. The *median* sales price is the sales price in the middle of the total number of prices. For example, if three properties are valued at $109,000, $112,000, and $107,000, respectively, $109,000 would be the median value.

Taxes and Assessments

The federal government grants certain income tax advantages to individuals through real estate investment and ownership. One of the advantages is the depreciation allowance, which is a permissible deduction from income for the investor. Land is not depreciable, nor is a principal residence.

The Section 1031 Tax-Deferred Exchange involves the exchange of "like-kind properties" that are held for productive use in a trade or business or investment. It does not apply to the exchange of personal residences or properties located outside the country. The most common type of exchanges involve two parties in a "delayed exchange" in which the replacement property needs to be identified and closed within a specified period of time. To the extent one property is valued higher than the other (called *boot*), the difference is taxable income.

A homeowner can deduct real property taxes and interest on the mortgage but cannot claim depreciation or deduct for repairs. As a result of the Taxpayer Relief Act of 1997, a homeowner who lives in the home two of the last five years is entitled to specified dollar amount exclusion on the gain in the sale. Up to $250,000 of gain ($500,000 for married filing jointly) realized on the sale of a principal residence on or after May 7, 1997, is not taxable (not just deferred) if certain prerequisites are met.

Questions in this chapter test your comprehension of the following topics:

■ Section 1031 Tax-Deferred Exchanges

■ Levying special assessments

■ Tax deductions allowed on real property

■ Tax aspects of home ownership

Because the tax laws change so frequently, exam questions on taxes tend to be general. In practice, however, it is essential to keep up to date with the latest changes and to refer clients to competent tax advisers to meet their specific requirements.

K E Y   W O R D S

Ad valorem: Latin for "according to valuation," usually referring to a type of tax or assessment.

Assessed valuation: The value of real property as established by, usually, the county or township government for purposes of computing real property taxes.

Basis: The financial interest that the IRS attributes to the owner of an asset for purposes of determining annual depreciation and gain or loss on sale of the asset.

Boot: Money or other property given to make up any difference in value or equity between two exchanged properties.

Capital gain: The taxable profit derived from the sale of a capital asset.

Depreciation: For tax purposes, depreciation is an expense deduction taken for an investment in depreciable property.

Imputed interest: Interest implied by the federal tax law.

Tax lien: A general statutory lien imposed against real property for failure to pay taxes. There are federal tax liens and state tax liens.

Tax shelter: A phrase often used to describe some of the tax advantages of real estate investment, such as deductions for depreciation, interest, and taxes, that may offset the investor's other ordinary income to reduce the investor's overall tax payment.

QUESTIONS

1. ◎ What accounting concept is the primary source of real estate tax shelter investment?
   A. Recapture
   B. NOI
   C. Boot
   D. Depreciation

2. The term *boot* probably would be considered in connection with
   A. exchange.
   B. legal description.
   C. depreciation.
   D. leasehold title.

3. No depreciation for tax purposes is allowed for
   A. improvements over 30 years of age.
   B. land.
   C. buildings.
   D. leaseholds.

4. Unpaid real property taxes are usually considered to be
   A. promissory notes.
   B. restrictions.
   C. solvent credits.
   D. liens.

5. Laura is preparing her federal income tax return. She can claim depreciation on all of the following *EXCEPT*
   A. a vacant duplex.
   B. a home rented to a friend.
   C. vacant land held for investment.
   D. a rented single-family dwelling.

6. The compulsory charge the government imposes against property owners benefited by street improvements, sewer line installation, or road repairs is called a
   A. general tax.
   B. special excise tax.
   C. property use tax.
   D. special assessment.

7. An investor made an initial investment of $450,000 and subsequently made $200,000 worth of improvements. After subtracting depreciation from the initial cost and adding the cost of improvements, the resulting number is known as what?
   A. Salvage value
   B. Capital gain
   C. Basis
   D. Adjusted basis

8. To defer payment of a portion of federal income tax on realized gain, principal payments received in the year of the sale on an installment sale must remain under what percent of the total price?
   A. 29
   B. 30
   C. 35
   D. No limit

9. The federal income tax allows investors to gradually write off their original investment. Which of the following methods is used?
   A. Exchanges
   B. Installment
   C. Depreciation
   D. Acceleration

10. ◎ An investor who is retired would be interested in
    A. adjusted gross income.
    B. gross income.
    C. rental income.
    D. net spendable income.

11. Which of the following is used as a basis for real property tax assessment?
    A. Land only
    B. Building only
    C. Both land and building
    D. Neither land nor building

12. A taxpayer is allowed to deduct repairs made to which one of the following?
    A. Property held for investment
    B. Appliances in the home
    C. Personal residence
    D. Church property

13. Real property taxes are determined by which of the following ways?
    A. On an ad valorem basis
    B. According to the number of occupants
    C. Loan-to-value ratio
    D. Duration of ownership

14. A seller sold her rental property and reinvested the sales proceeds in a more expensive rental property the same day. At the end of the year when she pays income taxes, what will be the minimum she will have to pay on the profits?
    A. Capital gains tax
    B. Ordinary income tax
    C. No tax
    D. Gross excise tax

15. A person owns an apartment hotel on three acres of land. For tax purposes, which of the following can be depreciated?
    A. The land
    B. The improvements
    C. Rental income
    D. Net operating expenses

16. ◎ Examples of deductible expenses on an owner's tax return for a vacation home are all of the following EXCEPT
    A. mortgage interest.
    B. property taxes.
    C. mortgage principal.
    D. casualty losses.

17. Three individuals for investment purposes form a business alliance. If all three have equal managerial responsibilities and share equally in the profits and losses, they have formed a
    A. Real Estate Investment Trust (REIT).
    B. limited partnership.
    C. general partnership.
    D. Real Estate Mortgage Investment Conduit (REMIC).

18. Before calculating the gain on the sale of your home, you can do all of the following to offset the gain EXCEPT
    A. add closing costs from your original purchase.
    B. add capital improvements.
    C. deduct brokerage fees upon resale.
    D. deduct depreciation.

19. An individual owns a condominium apartment unit used as a rental apartment that was bought four years ago for $140,000. The land was then valued at $30,000. Using 27.5 years for straight-line depreciation, what is the adjusted basis of the property today?
    A. $128,000
    B. $110,000
    C. $88,000
    D. $98,000

20. Which of the following is BEST for the taxpayer?
    A. A deduction for $10,000
    B. A deferral of $10,000 gain
    C. A credit for $10,000
    D. An exemption for $10,000

21. A landlord owner can deduct against rental income all of the following EXCEPT
    A. loan interest.
    B. accelerated depreciation.
    C. repairs.
    D. condominium maintenance fees.

22. ◎ Who of the following are subject to withholding tax on the sale of real property they own?
    A. Students
    B. Military enlisted persons
    C. Foreign investors
    D. U.S. homeowners

23. For tax purposes, a taxpayer can depreciate which of the following?
    A. Land
    B. Personal residence
    C. Investment building
    D. Mortgage interest

24. Tax deductions on a personal residence include all of the following EXCEPT
    A. loan points paid by purchaser.
    B. prepayment penalties.
    C. real property taxes.
    D. depreciation.

25. In qualifying for the "like-kind replacement rule" in which the taxpayer seeks tax deferral, the replacement property may be
    A. vacant land where he or she lives in a tent.
    B. a mobile home or a houseboat.
    C. rental property.
    D. stock in a commercial property.

26. Boot is a factor to be taken into consideration in a
    A. purchase of FHA-insured property.
    B. transfer by conditional sales contract.
    C. tax-deferred exchange.
    D. commercial lease.

27. For tax assessment purposes, which piece of information is the *LEAST* important?
    A. Zoning
    B. Location
    C. Length of lease
    D. Physical condition

28. ◎ After the Taxpayer's Relief Act of 1997, to qualify for a tax deferral on capital gain, a homeowner must reinvest how much of the proceeds from the sale of his residence into the replacement residence?
    A. 30 percent
    B. 50 percent
    C. 75 percent
    D. None of the above

29. Items for which special assessments may be levied include all of the following *EXCEPT*
    A. sidewalks.
    B. curbs.
    C. street paving.
    D. front yard beautification.

30. Which is *CORRECT* about a tax credit?
    A. It applies against tax deductions.
    B. It offsets gross taxable income.
    C. It is a dollar-for-dollar reduction in taxes owed.
    D. It increases the tax exclusion.

31. ◎ If a broker exchanges a property listed by a cobroker with a property she has listed, under the usual cooperating situation the broker
    A. receives two sales commissions.
    B. receives the sales commission only on the property she listed.
    C. forfeits her commission.
    D. is paid a flat fee.

32. ◎ An investor bought a ten-year-old office building. The allowed method of depreciation with no recapture of depreciation would *MOST* likely be
    A. 100 percent.
    B. straight-line.
    C. 150 percent.
    D. 175 percent.

33. Straight-line depreciation provides for which of the following?
    A. The same rate each year
    B. The fastest amount of allowable depreciation in the first year
    C. An adjustable rate
    D. A steadily increasing rate

34. Tax-deferred exchange treatment is given on
    A. like property exchanged for like property.
    B. a personal residence exchanged for a commercial property.
    C. personal property traded for real property.
    D. short-term leases.

35. Under which circumstance can one take depreciation on a single-family dwelling for federal tax purposes?
    A. When one lives in it
    B. When one sells it
    C. When one exchanges it
    D. When one rents it

36. ◎ A seller sold his three-year-old rental vacation home for a $30,000 gain. He immediately reinvested all the proceeds in a more expensive house in which to live. For income tax purposes he will
    A. have the gain deferred.
    B. pay capital gains tax.
    C. pay ordinary income tax.
    D. pay no tax.

37. ◎ A buyer purchased an investment condominium apartment three years ago and paid
$82 per month as her pro rata share of real
property taxes. In paying her federal income
taxes for last year, she is able to deduct all
those taxes paid from her taxable income.
Assuming she was in a 28 percent tax bracket,
how much less does she pay in taxes because
of this real property tax deduction?
A. $246
B. $276
C. $669
D. $945

38. If a person purchases an apartment building as
an investment and then sells it after nine
months, profit on the sale is taxed as
A. long-term capital gain.
B. ordinary income.
C. short-term capital gain.
D. tax-deferred income.

39. A broker is advising an investor about invest-
ing in real estate or in stocks. One big differ-
ence found in real estate is
A. capital gain.
B. depreciation.
C. risk.
D. investment return.

40. The principal advantage of exchanging real
estate as opposed to selling is
A. depreciation.
B. less commission.
C. deferring tax.
D. higher appraisal

41. A man sells the residence for $115,000 that he
bought two years ago for $78,000. He added a
bathroom for $2,500 and a basketball court
for $6,000. He buys another house ten months
later for $125,000. The realized gain on the
sale is
A. $28,500.
B. $34,500.
C. $38,500.
D. $41,000.

42. ◎ Which of the following is *TRUE* regarding a
property having depreciation deductions that
exceed the amount of income from the property?
A. The property will devaluate more rapidly.
B. It is never advantageous to show a loss on
income property.
C. The loss must always be used to offset
other income.
D. Within legal limits, it can be deducted and
any excess depreciation may be applied
for future years.

43. ◎ A couple buys a residence for $80,000.
During the first year, they have expenses of
$4,100 in mortgage interest, $1,500 in real
property taxes, depreciation of $3,300, and a
fire insurance premium of $520. They also
added a guest room for $6,400. Deductions on
their tax return for the year will be
A. $1,500.
B. $5,600.
C. $6,120.
D. $12,520.

44. Which of the following expenses is deductible
by the homeowner during the current tax
year?
A. Painting
B. Family room addition
C. Property insurance
D. Mortgage interest

45. An investor receives 5 percent interest on a
real estate loan. The IRS can claim a higher
interest rate, which is called
A. implied interest.
B. imputed interest.
C. escalated interest.
D. inferred interest.

46. A woman sells her investment condo for
$150,000. She bought it for $100,000 and
owned it for ten years. She took $15,000 of
the allowable depreciation deduction of
$27,500. She will pay tax on which of the fol-
lowing?
A. $77,500
B. $65,000
C. $72,500
D. $27,500

ANSWERS

1. **B.** Any recognized gain is taxed at ordinary income tax rates, rather than the previously allowed lower capital gain tax rates. Improvements and major repairs are added to basis; any depreciation taken reduces basis. Only minor repairs on investment property are deductible.

2. **A.** Boot (anything received in an exchange, such as extra cash to equalize the values of two properties) may be the only immediately taxable portion of a tax-deferred exchange.

3. **D.** In real estate investments, depreciation is, for tax purposes, an expense deduction taken over the period of ownership.

4. **D.** Unpaid taxes on real property become a lien and could cause the involuntary sale of the property to pay the tax.

5. **C.** Land does not qualify for depreciation, but improvements on investment property do.

6. **D.** When specific properties are benefited by public improvements, the charge levied to pay for such an improvement is called an *assessment,* a *special assessment,* or a *betterment* (unlike a general tax).

7. **D.** The answer is adjusted basis. When a property is purchased the owner's basis is the cost of the property. The investor then adds to the property's value with capital improvements and takes as a tax deduction allowable depreciation. The result is the property's adjusted basis. When the property is sold, the amount by which the sales price exceeds the adjusted basis is called capital gain.

8. **D.** Installment sale treatment is automatic, unless the taxpayer elects *not* to use it. As principal payments are received, only a portion is taxed as gain. The IRS has eliminated the 30 percent maximum down payment rule.

9. **C.** Depreciation is a permissible deduction that allows taxpayers to deduct periodically a portion of their investment from annual income before tax calculation. Thus, each dollar deducted from income is a dollar not taxed.

10. **D.** A retired person generally is looking for net spendable income cash flow rather than other types that may offer tax shelter advantages to salaried persons or other persons with taxable incomes.

11. **C.** Real property taxes are assessed according to improvement and land values and called "ad valorem" meaning "according to value."

12. **A.** Repairs are deductible for only rental property. Major improvements to a personal residence will be added to the basis of the home on sale, thus reducing the amount of taxable gain.

13. **A.** An ad valorem tax is one that is levied in accordance with the value of the property.

14. **C.** She would qualify for a tax deferral on the profit made from the exchange of her property. If she had purchased a less expensive rental property, a portion of her profit would be taxable that year.

15. **B.** Depreciation on land is not allowed; one can therefore depreciate only the improvements.

16. **C.** Mortgage principal on an owner's vacation home, a principal residence, or any other investment is not a deductible item. However, the other choices are deductible for the residence as well as for the vacation home.

17. **C.** The answer is general partnership. Under a limited partnership, one party acts as a general partner while the other members are merely investors with little voice in operations and are therefore called limited partners. A REIT is a real estate investment trust where investors purchase certificates in the trust and the trust invests in real estate or mortgages.

18. **D.** Depreciation does not apply to one's personal residence. (A), (B), and (C) are used to adjust the "basis" of the property.

19. **A.** The improvements are subject to straight-line depreciation based on $1 \div 27.5$ per year. $\$110,000 \times (1 \div 27.5) = \$4,000$ or $110,000 \div 27.5 = \$4,000 \times 3$ years $= \$12,000$. $\$110,000 - \$12,000 = \$98,000 + \$30,000 = \$128,000$.

20. **C.** Because it applies against the amount of tax owed, a credit is more beneficial than a deduction or exclusion, which lessens the amount of income subject to taxation.

21. **B.** The landlord can deduct straight-line depreciation, not accelerated depreciation.

22. **C.** Under FIRPTA, the Federal Foreign Investment in Real Property Tax Act, the buyer must withhold 10 percent of the gross amount realized by the seller (i.e., the purchase price) and pay that amount to the U.S. Treasury within 20 days of closing.

23. **C.** An investor-owned building is a wasting asset that the owner is permitted to depreciate over its useful life. Neither land nor personal residences are depreciable assets for tax purposes.

24. **D.** Loan points and prepayment penalties are fully tax deductible as interest in the year paid if the security for the loan is the borrower's personal residence. If the security is investment property, these charges are deductible over the term of the loan and not in the year paid.

25. **C.** The Section 1031 tax-exchange rule applies to like-kind investment property. Stock would not be like-kind. Personal residences do not qualify.

26. **C.** Boot is the difference in equity between two properties exchanged. Boot is recognized as taxable income.

27. **C.** Taxes are based on the fee simple interest. There is not one tax for a leased fee and another tax for a leasehold estate.

28. **D.** The law does not require any reinvestment of the sale proceeds into the replacement. Thus, a seller could get 100 percent financing on the replacement residence and pocket the tax-free cash from the sale of the previous principal residence. To qualify for the exclusion, the taxpayer must have occupied the residence for two of the past five years. The exemption is $250,000 for a single person and $500,000 for a married couple filing a joint return.

29. **D.** Items such as sewers, curbs, street paving, and sidewalks are all included in special assessments. Owners' front yards are their own responsibility and do not fall into an assessment category by the taxing body.

30. **C.** A tax credit is a direct offset against taxes owed. Tax deductions are applied against gross income to arrive at taxes owed. For example, a developer might be afforded a tax credit as an incentive to develop low-cost housing for the elderly.

31. **A.** The broker will receive a sales commission on each of the properties because she has, in effect, sold two properties. The broker also will receive the listing commission on the property listed for sale. The broker should disclose to both parties this dual commission situation.

32. **B.** Straight line is the only allowable method of depreciation. The accelerated depreciation rules were abolished by the 1986 Tax Reform Act. Now, all property must be depreciated on a straight-line basis over a specified number of years.

33. **A.** Straight-line depreciation is the only type of depreciation that provides the same amount each year.

34. **A.** To qualify for a tax-deferred exchange, there must be like properties that are held for productive use in business or for investment. Personal residences do not qualify, nor do leaseholds under 30 years.

35. **D.** Depreciation is allowed on property held in a trade or business but is not allowed on a personal residence.

36. **C.** There is no deferral of gain because the property is not the principal residence of the taxpayer.

37. **B.** Solution: $82 × 12 = $984. If taxed at a 28 percent bracket, $984 would require approximately $276 in taxes that would have been due if she didn't have this tax write-off.

38. **B.** Long-term capital gain benefits were abolished under the 1986 Tax Reform Act. All gain is now treated as ordinary income.

39. **B.** While investment real estate normally can be depreciated to the tax advantage of the owner, this is not true of stock.

40. **C.** A properly structured IRS Section 1031 exchange will result in a deferral of capital gain tax on the sale.

41. **A.** Realized gain is computed by subtracting original cost (plus improvements) from sale price. Whether the gain is recognized now or deferred until a later date is not material to this question. $115,000 – $86,500 = $28,500.

42. **D.** The extra deduction may help shelter other income from taxes, hence the term *tax shelter*. Current tax limits offsets against other income (passive loss rules). Excess depreciation can be applied against that property's income in future years.

43. **B.** On a residence (as opposed to an investment property) the deductible items are mortgage interest and real property taxes.

44. **D.** (A) and (C) are not deductible, and (B) is added to the *basis* to lessen the gain upon resale.

45. **B.** Unless the minimum rate (set by federal law) is charged, the imputed interest rule allows the IRS to assert that the mandated interest rate was actually earned.

46. **A.** She owes tax on her gain, which is determined by deducting the *allowable* straight-line depreciation from the original basis. Thus, she is penalized for taking *less* depreciation than she is allowed.

Financing of Real Estate

This part contains questions on the topics of

- institutional sources of financing;

- government loan programs;

- seller carryback financing;

- functions of the secondary mortgage market;

- features of the mortgage document; and

- foreclosure upon default of the mortgage.

Expect 10 percent to 15 percent of the national portion of the examination to contain questions on the topics covered in Part C.

C H A P T E R

Sources of Financing: Conventional, Governmental, and the Secondary Mortgage Market

The primary money market is the source of funds available directly to borrowers. Some of the major sources of real estate mortgage financing in the primary mortgage market are mortgage bankers, commercial banks, savings associations, life insurance companies, and credit unions. Other sources of mortgage financing are seller-financed purchase-money mortgages, contracts for deed, and sale-leaseback arrangements.

The secondary mortgage market is the marketplace for the purchase and sale of existing mortgages. After a mortgage is originated and sold, the originating lender can either collect the payments from the borrower and receive a fee for servicing the loan or they can sell directly to an intermediary investor. These intermediaries then can both keep and service them or sell them to another investor. The three most known investors of home mortgage money are sources that don't lend directly to the public, but rather (as noted) buy mortgages originated by local lenders and acquired and packaged into larger bundles by intermediaries. These entities are known as Fannie Mae (FNMA), Freddie Mac (FHLMC), and Ginnie Mae (GNMA).

The two principal types of nonconventional mortgage financing are the Federal Housing Administration (FHA) insured loans and the Department of Veterans Affairs (VA) guaranteed loans. The FHA, which operates under the Department of Housing and Urban Development (HUD), neither builds homes nor lends money itself. Instead the loan is made by an approved lender to a qualified borrower, and repayment is merely insured by the FHA. VA loans are also made by the lender to eligible veterans, and at the same time the VA guarantees the lender that in the event the borrower defaults, the VA will repay the lender up to a certain amount. See Figure 9.1 on page 104 for a comparison of FHA and VA loan payments.

The questions in this chapter will test your comprehension of the following topics:

■ The operations of the secondary mortgage market

FIGURE 9.1
Comparison of FHA and
VA Loan Programs

Comparison of FHA and VA Loan Programs

Federal Housing Administration

1. Financing is available to veterans and nonveterans.

2. Financing programs for owner-occupied (1-family to 4-family) residential dwellings.

3. Requires a larger down payment than VA.

4. Different evaluation methods; like VA, there are prescribed valuation procedures for the approved appraisers to follow.

5. FHA valuation sets the maximum loan FHA will insure but does not limit the sales price.

6. No prepayment penalty.

7. On default foreclosure and claim, the FHA lender usually gets U.S. debentures.

8. Insures the loan by way of mutual mortgage insurance; premiums paid by buyer or seller. If by buyer, may be paid in cash or added to note.

9. No secondary financing is permitted until after closing.

10. Buyer pays a 1 percent loan origination fee.

11. Loans made prior to 12/1/86 are fully assumable; seller remains liable until the loan is paid off. Loans made between 12/1/86 and 12/15/89 are fully assumable after 12 months on owner-occupied loans; seller remains liable for 5 years. Loans made since 12/15/89 require prior approval of assumptor; seller is released from liability.

Department of Veterans Affairs

1. Financing available only to veterans and certain unremarried widows and widowers.

2. Financing is limited to owner-occupied residential (1-family to 4-family) dwellings; must sign occupancy certificate on two separate occasions.

3. Normally does not require down payment.

4. Methods of valuation differ. VA issues a certificate of reasonable value (CRV).

5. With regard to home loans, the law requires that the VA loan not exceed the appraised value of the home.

6. No prepayment penalty.

7. Following default, foreclosure and claim, the lender usually receives cash (if VA elects to take the house).

8. Guarantees loans according to a sliding scale.

9. Secondary financing is permitted in exceptional cases.

10. Borrower may pay discount points but cannot finance them in the loan; he or she can pay a 1 percent loan origination fee.

11. A funding fee from 1.25 to 3.00 percent must be paid to VA in addition to other fees. It may be paid by the seller or buyer. If paid by the buyer, it may be paid in cash or added to the note.

12. VA loan can be assumed by nonveteran without VA approval for loans made prior to 3/1/88; otherwise, approval is required.

13. For loans originated after 3/1/88, release of liability is automatic if VA approves the assumption.

■ The procedures for obtaining loans guaranteed by the Department of Veterans Affairs (VA)

■ The procedures for obtaining loans insured by the Federal Housing Administration (FHA)

■ Installment land contracts from the seller

■ Use of the sale and leaseback

■ Conventional financing

KEY WORDS

Arbitrage: The profitable difference between borrowing money at one rate and loaning it out at a higher rate.

Auction: Real property sold by obtaining bids. There are two types of auctions, absolute and reserve. Absolute means that whatever is bid, the property is absolutely going to sell. Reserve means that a certain threshold has to be bid or the auctioned parcel isn't going to be sold.

Balloon payment: The final payment of a loan that is larger than the previous payments because it pays off the remaining debt in full.

Certificate of reasonable value (CRV): A certificate issued by the Department of Veterans Affairs sets forth a property's current market value estimate, based on a VA-approved appraisal.

CLUE: The Comprehensive Loss Underwriting Exchange is used by insurance companies to assess the risk of both the property and the prospective policyholder. Homeowner's insurance must be applied for early in the buying process.

Conditional loan commitment: A commitment by a lender to loan a certain dollar amount (for an agreed period of time) to a borrower subject to an appraisal. Once the property appraises, qualified buyers receive a loan commitment.

Conforming mortgages: Loans that conform to standards established by the secondary mortgage market including ceilings on lending amounts; forms used such as the Uniform Residential Appraisal Report (URAR), the Uniform Residential Loan Application (URLA); mortgage insurance requirements; credit scoring; and qualification ratios.

Credit scoring: A three-digit score that assesses a borrower's credit risk and the probability of default based on past pay performances, outstanding credit card balances, installment and revolving charges, time on file, and number of recent search inquiries.

CRV: The Community Reinvestment Act of 1977 encourages banks to help meet the credit needs of their community's low-income and moderate-income citizens. Annually they report how their efforts are meeting those needs.

Discount points: Money expressed in the form of a percentage. One point equals 1 percent of the loan. Therefore, two points would equal 2 percent of the loan. Either the buyer or seller could pay the points. Sometimes discount points are used to buy down the interest rate to increase the buyer's borrowing power. For example, if a borrower qualified for a $150,000 loan at 6 percent for 30 years, using a rate of $6 per thousand, their PI payment would be 150 × 6 = $900. However, if a seller would pay enough discount points to buy the interest rate down to 5.5 percent then the borrower's amortization rate would drop to $5.68 per thousand. By dividing the qualified PI payment of $900 by 5.68 the increased borrowing power would be $158,450. The discount points required to permanently buy down the interest rate would be determined by the loan originator.

Equity: The difference between the market value and debt against a property.

Federal Housing Administration (FHA): The FHA was set up in 1934 under the National Housing Act to encourage improvement in housing standards and conditions, to provide an adequate home financing system by insurance of housing mortgages and credit, and to exert a stabilizing influence on the mortgage market.

Institutional lender: Financial institutions such as banks, insurance companies, savings associations, or any lending institution whose loans are regulated by law.

Mortgage banker: A corporation or firm that normally provides its own funds for mortgage financing.

Mortgage broker: A person or firm that acts as an intermediary between borrower and lender; one who, for compensation or gain, negotiates, sells, or arranges loans and sometimes continues to service the loans.

Novation: Replacing one party in an existing contract with a new player and releasing the first party of all liability. Closely related to novation is an assumption. The difference between the two is that with an assumption someone could assume another's loan without the lender releasing the responsibility for future payments on the original borrower. In most cases, though, lenders require buyers to be qualified before assuming anyone else's debt. Then the lender releases the original borrower from any future responsibility, and, in essence, a true novation takes place.

Preapproval letter: When a borrower gives to a loan originator (in advance) confidential financial information in order to obtain a letter that shows the lender's financial commitment. With preapproval, the borrower's agent can negotiate with more confidence. Normally the borrower's credit score is obtained, and alternate documentation is obtained to validate employment, income, and down payment.

Sale-leaseback: A transaction in which, typically, an owner sells his improved property and as part of the same transaction signs a long-term lease and remains in possession.

Secondary mortgage market: A market for the purchase and sale of existing mortgages, designed to provide greater liquidity for mortgages; also called *secondary money market.*

Straight note: A promissory note evidencing a loan in which "interest only" payments are made periodically during the term of the note, with the principal payment due in one lump sum on maturity.

Vendee: In a contract for deed transaction, the contract purchaser.

Vendor: In a contract for deed transaction, the contract holder.

Warehousing: A term used in financing to describe the process that loan correspondents employ of assembling into one package a number of mortgage loans that the correspondent has originated and selling them in the secondary mortgage market.

MISTAKEN IDENTITY

The following words are often confused with one another. Note the difference in meaning of these mistaken identity words and phrases.

Debenture/Mortgage: Unlike a mortgage, a *debenture* involves a note without any collateral to secure it.

Installment land contract/Purchase-money mortgage: Both involve seller carryback financing; the difference is that legal title remains with the seller in an *installment land contract.*

Second mortgage/Secondary mortgage market: A *second mortgage* is a junior mortgage, whereas the *secondary mortgage market* refers to the selling of existing mortgages to investors like FNMA, GNMA, and FHLMC.

QUESTIONS

1. A mortgage banker generally can do all of the following *EXCEPT*
   A. service loans for its clients.
   B. use its own money to make loans.
   C. list for sale property financed by one of its clients.
   D. quote terms and conditions of loans to prospective borrowers.

2. All the following agencies are primary sources of money for the secondary mortgage market *EXCEPT*
   A. Fannie Mae (Federal National Mortgage Association).
   B. the Department of Veterans Affairs (VA).
   C. Ginnie Mae (Government National Mortgage Association).
   D. Freddie Mac (Federal Home Loan Mortgage Corporation).

3. Under a VA loan, a veteran can do which of the following?
   A. Transfer the original VA loan to another home
   B. Sell the home and allow a nonveteran buyer to assume the loan with VA approval
   C. Use the VA loan to acquire a commercial building
   D. Use one loan to purchase two separate properties

4. Which of the following practices is prohibited under FHA regulations?
   A. Lender requires title insurance.
   B. Lender charges a prepayment penalty.
   C. Seller and buyer split the points.
   D. Buyer obtains a second mortgage.

5. A case in which the seller wanted to be relieved of all obligations under the VA mortgage that another veteran buyer would assume and substitute eligibility would be *BEST* described as
   A. subordination.
   B. novation.
   C. acceleration.
   D. subrogation.

6. The VA is authorized to
   A. make direct loans to veterans.
   B. regulate lending institutions that make VA loans.
   C. charge prepayment penalties.
   D. guarantee repayment of loans up to a specified amount.

7. Which of the following statements regarding federally insured or guaranteed loans is *TRUE?*
   A. An FHA loan may be granted to a qualified buyer who indicates intent to rent the entire property for which the loan is obtained.
   B. A VA loan may be granted to an eligible veteran who indicates intent to rent the entire property.
   C. FHA loans are freely assumable.
   D. FHA loans insure the lender up to 100 percent of any loss suffered.

8. All of the following are transactions involving a collateralized debt *EXCEPT* a
   A. chattel mortgage.
   B. debenture.
   C. mortgage.
   D. deed of trust.

9. The VA is authorized to make direct loans
   A. when the veteran agrees not to occupy the property.
   B. in a rural area where the veteran cannot find a lender to lend at rates of interest competitive with those in other areas.
   C. to anyone who can financially qualify.
   D. provided there is no secondary financing on the dwelling.

10. A requirement of a borrower under an FHA-insured loan is that he or she
    A. have cash for a down payment and part of closing costs.
    B. have the spouse sign as coborrower.
    C. certify that he or she will rent the premises.
    D. have a minimum annual income of $25,000.

11. The FHA serves to do all of the following *EXCEPT*
    A. help stabilize the mortgage market.
    B. improve housing standards.
    C. make direct loans in the primary mortgage market.
    D. stimulate housing activity.

12. The money used for FHA loans is supplied by which one of the following?
    A. Qualified lending institutions
    B. Fannie Mae
    C. The Federal Housing Administration
    D. The Federal Home Loan Bank

13. To qualify for a VA loan on a dwelling, all of the following requirements are true *EXCEPT*
    A. the applicant must sign a declaration that he or she intends to occupy the dwelling.
    B. there must be an appraisal from an appraiser approved by the VA.
    C. the applicant must have a certificate of eligibility.
    D. the borrower must pay the discount points at closing.

14. When a loan is approved by FHA
    A. the appraised value must not be less than the sale price.
    B. the government guarantees the value of the property.
    C. it must be for investment property only.
    D. there will be some required down payment.

15. The FHA will insure
    A. first mortgages.
    B. second mortgages.
    C. wraparound mortgages.
    D. junior mortgages.

16. ◎ A veteran who sells her or his house and permits the buyer to assume her or his VA loan has
    A. no further liability if she or he obtains a release from the buyer.
    B. no further liability.
    C. a primary liability until the loan is paid in full.
    D. no further liability if she or he obtains a release from the lender and the VA.

17. CLUE is an acronym used to describe an underwriting procedure for what industry?
    A. Appraising
    B. Title insurance
    C. Homeowner's insurance
    D. Banking

18. An installment contract for the sale of real estate gives the buyer all of the following *EXCEPT*
    A. the right to live on the property.
    B. the right to lease the property.
    C. the right of possession.
    D. legal title to the property.

19. ◎ A qualified borrower for an FHA 203(b) loan must do which one of the following?
    A. Be an owner-occupant
    B. Obtain a conventional appraisal
    C. Obtain a second mortgage for all down payment expenses
    D. Produce a certificate of eligibility

20. When the amortized payment of a mortgage remains constant over the period of the loan but leaves an outstanding balance to be paid at the end, this payment is called a(n)
    A. escalation payment.
    B. balloon payment.
    C. satisfaction payment.
    D. acceleration payment.

21. The amount a lender will loan is generally based on the
    A. listed price.
    B. appraised value for loan purposes.
    C. appraised value for loan purposes or the sale price, whichever is lower.
    D. final sales price.

22. A borrower bought a $200,000 home with no down payment and paid a funding fee. The loan was a
    A. conventional insured loan.
    B. VA loan.
    C. FHA loan.
    D. conventional loan.

23. If title to real property remains in the seller's name after it has been sold on a monthly payment plan, the buyer has purchased it under
    A. FHA financing.
    B. a guaranteed loan.
    C. a land contract.
    D. an option.

24. A promissory note providing for interest only to be paid during its term is *BEST* described as a(n)
    A. installment note.
    B. straight note.
    C. amortized note.
    D. non-interest-bearing note.

25. To compute the dollar value of a loan discount, each point is equal to 1 percent of the
    A. loan amount.
    B. down payment.
    C. appraised value.
    D. sales price.

26. A mortgage that covers more than one parcel of land is called a(n)
    A. junior mortgage.
    B. blanket mortgage.
    C. open-end mortgage.
    D. package mortgage.

27. Usury *MOST* nearly means
    A. making loans without benefit of cosigners.
    B. lending money at fluctuating interest rates.
    C. being capable of multiple usage.
    D. illegal interest.

28. ◎ If the seller agrees to provide financing on a nonrecourse basis, which of the following is *TRUE* after the buyer defaults?
    A. The buyer is personally liable for the full amount of the note.
    B. The seller can recover a deficiency judgment against the buyer.
    C. The seller is limited to what the property brings at foreclosure.
    D. The seller can recover punitive damages against the buyer.

29. When a seller takes back a purchase-money second mortgage from the buyer, the seller is responsible for preparing and executing which of the following?
    A. Deed
    B. Second mortgage
    C. Acknowledgment on the mortgage
    D. Continuation of title

30. All of the following are important to a loan company considering a loan application *EXCEPT*
    A. length of employment.
    B. irregular overtime pay.
    C. other indebtedness.
    D. base salary.

31. Which of the following is an agency of the Department of Housing and Urban Development?
    A. Federal Deposit Insurance Corporation
    B. Ginnie Mae
    C. Department of Veterans Affairs
    D. Mutual Mortgage Insurance Corporation

32. ◎ A prospective home purchaser can do which of the following?
    A. Pay more than the certificate of reasonable value (CRV) but not more than the FHA appraisal
    B. Not pay more than the CRV but pay more than an FHA appraisal
    C. Pay more than the FHA appraisal, provided there is a second mortgage
    D. Pay more than the appraisal, provided payment is in cash

33. A person would consider a purchase-money mortgage under which of these circumstances?
    A. When the buyer has only a small amount of cash for the purchase
    B. When the owner wants to obtain a second mortgage to pay for home improvements
    C. When an owner needs extra cash to add a new bedroom wing
    D. When the buyer will not take title until after paying all that is owed

34. The liquidation of a debt by periodic install-ment is *BEST* described as
    A. amortization.
    B. an annuity.
    C. acceleration.
    D. assemblage.

35. Both VA and FHA loans can be made by all of the following *EXCEPT*
    A. savings associations.
    B. commercial banks.
    C. mortgage companies.
    D. credit unions.

36. If a buyer can afford a $1,200 PI payment, amortized over 30 years at 5.5 percent, using the factor of $5.68 per thousand, what is the buyer's borrowing potential?
    A. $201,268
    B. $211,268
    C. $221,268
    D. $231,268

37. A savings association would be likely to make all of the following types of loans *EXCEPT*
    A. VA.
    B. conventional.
    C. FHA.
    D. Fannie Mae.

38. A borrower wishes to locate first-mortgage financing that will not charge a penalty if it is paid off before maturity. In most states, all of the following loan types generally will meet this need *EXCEPT*
    A. FHA.
    B. conventional.
    C. nonconventional.
    D. VA.

39. The term *refinancing* refers to
    A. obtaining a second mortgage on a prop-erty that already has a first mortgage.
    B. the repayment of an existing mortgage loan from the proceeds of a new one.
    C. changing one or more of the terms of an existing mortgage loan.
    D. a secondary mortgage market transaction.

40. The upper limit on the amount of a VA loan is
    A. the listed price.
    B. the amount of the CRV.
    C. nothing; there is no limit.
    D. an amount three times the VA entitlement.

41. Interest calculated on the total sum of unpaid principal and the simple interest accrued thereon is called
    A. simple interest.
    B. compound interest.
    C. penalty interest.
    D. interest rate.

42. ◎ Of the following types of financing, which pairing is synonymous?
    A. Take-out loan—Secondary financing
    B. Construction loan—Take-out loan
    C. Interim loan—Construction loan
    D. Obligatory advances—Installment loan

43. Which of the following is a source of primary mortgage funds for real estate developers?
    A. Federal Deposit Insurance Corporation
    B. Fannie Mae
    C. Federal Home Loan Bank
    D. Federal Savings and Loan

44. A debenture is a(n)
    A. mortgage.
    B. collateralized note.
    C. trust deed.
    D. unsecured note.

45. A seller sold her residence and took back a purchase-money first mortgage that she decided to sell. To do this, she would have to find a buyer in the
    A. primary mortgage market.
    B. real property securities business with a permit.
    C. secondary mortgage market.
    D. business of arranging primary financing only.

46. A vendee is one who
    A. sells or offers to sell.
    B. buys or offers to buy.
    C. loans money.
    D. borrows money.

47. All of the following elements are typical of junior financing *EXCEPT*
    A. a balloon payment.
    B. a short term.
    C. private lenders.
    D. full amortization.

48. An impound or reserve account *MOST* benefits the
    A. borrower.
    B. lender.
    C. trustee.
    D. trustor.

49. The lender is not insured or guaranteed against a loss by reason of the borrower's default in repayment under which type of loan?
    A. FHA loan
    B. Conventional loan
    C. VA loan
    D. GI loan

50. The lender under a conventional loan normally compensates for the additional risks brought on by lack of government insurance or guarantee by doing all of the following *EXCEPT*
    A. requiring higher down payments.
    B. charging higher interest rates.
    C. requiring private mortgage insurance.
    D. requiring the purchase of title insurance.

51. ◎ A VA loan may be granted for the purchase of a one-family to four-family dwelling if the
    A. veteran certifies the rent collected will equal the mortgage payments.
    B. loan will be amortized for not more than 20 years.
    C. down payment will be at least 10 percent.
    D. veteran agrees to live there.

52. When a borrower defaults on an FHA-insured loan, any losses sustained by foreclosure are made up through
    A. the Federal Treasury.
    B. the Mutual Mortgage Insurance Plan.
    C. an attachment lien against the borrower.
    D. an assessment against the lending institution.

53. A land contract (or contract for deed) and a seller-carryback purchase-money mortgage are similar in that
    A. the seller assumes no financial risk.
    B. the title is conveyed immediately to the buyer.
    C. the seller is the lender.
    D. a mortgage is required.

54. Fannie Mae performs which of the following functions?
    A. Regulates commercial banks
    B. Makes VA and FHA loans
    C. Loans conventional mortgage funds
    D. Operates in the secondary mortgage market

55. What element is peculiar to the sale-lease-back transaction?
    A. The seller gets a return on the purchase in the form of rental.
    B. The property is sold on condition that the new owner lease it back to the seller at the time title passes.
    C. The buyer keeps capital in inventories, rather than in realty.
    D. The rental that the seller pays is not income-tax deductible.

56. The seller under a land contract is called the
    A. grantor
    B. grantee.
    C. vendor.
    D. vendee.

57. Under a VA loan, which of the following is *TRUE?*
    A. All closing costs must be paid in cash by the seller.
    B. World War II veterans are not eligible.
    C. The buyer pays the discount points.
    D. The loans do not contain prepayment penalties.

58. The FHA does all of the following *EXCEPT*
    A. insure loans to qualified buyers.
    B. protect lenders in case of default.
    C. require a down payment.
    D. loan its own funds.

59. The payment of an old loan with a new loan is termed *refinancing*. All of the following are most likely a purpose for "refinancing" loans *EXCEPT* to
    A. acquire the property.
    B. pay for rehabilitation or modernization.
    C. get a more advantageous loan than was on the property.
    D. raise money for purposes of satisfying a balloon payment.

60. One function of Fannie Mae is selling seasoned mortgages and trust deeds to individual investors and financial institutions. A *seasoned mortgage* is a mortgage that
    A. is in existence for some time that has a good record of repayment by the mortgagor.
    B. has a long record of assignments.
    C. contains a subordination clause.
    D. contains a novation.

61. Which of the following statements is *TRUE* concerning the FHA?
    A. It insures up to 80 percent of the loan amount.
    B. It is a part of the Department of Housing and Urban Development (HUD).
    C. It insures 60 percent or $46,000, whichever is less.
    D. It makes loans only to veterans.

62. For which type of loan must the applicant be an owner-occupant?
    A. VA loan
    B. Straight loan
    C. Conventional loan
    D. Amortized loan

63. ◎ The VA can give direct loans
    A. when the borrower/veteran agrees to rent the property.
    B. when the property is located in an area where conventional loans are not easily available.
    C. if the borrower puts up additional down payment.
    D. if the veteran agrees not to pay more than the CRV.

64. ◎ An FHA lender will allow all of the following *EXCEPT* the
    A. seller is willing to pay all closing costs for the buyer.
    B. buyer is to give the seller a second mortgage as part of the purchase price in which the total borrowed will exceed the maximum FHA loan.
    C. buyer is to prepay the loan without prepayment penalty.
    D. buyer is to refinance the loan when 80 percent of the loan can be paid off in 30 years.

65. Discount charges charged on a loan result in
    A. higher yield to the lender.
    B. longer time period of loan repayment.
    C. lower overall cost to borrower.
    D. higher purchase price in the secondary mortgage market.

66. Which of the following is considered a conventional loan?
    A. FHA-insured
    B. VA-guaranteed
    C. Commercial bank loan
    D. Fannie Mae mortgages

67. A veteran of the Vietnam War applies for a VA loan. Which of the following statements about VA financing is *CORRECT?*
    A. The veteran is prohibited from using a second mortgage.
    B. The veteran can use the loan to purchase an investment summer vacation rental property.
    C. The VA will guarantee the lender against loss up to certain amounts.
    D. The VA will loan the money directly to the veteran.

68. When an applicant applies for VA financing,
    A. the VA uses approved appraisers.
    B. the VA must accept the appraisal of an MAI.
    C. an appraisal is not required.
    D. an appraisal is required only if the applicant is applying for 100 percent financing.

69. Under an FHA graduated payment mortgage, which of the following fluctuates over the term of the loan?
    A. Interest rate
    B. Monthly payments
    C. Finance charge
    D. Annual rate

70. A seller has owned a property for one year. The buyer is paying all cash. The seller is *MOST* likely to pay a prepayment penalty with which type of loan?
    A. VA
    B. FHA
    C. Debenture
    D. Conventional

71. How many digits are there in a credit score?
    A. One
    B. Two
    C. Three
    D. Four

72. All but which of the following are *TRUE* of conventional loans?
    A. They are made to the buyer without governmental insurance or guarantee.
    B. The policy requirements of their lenders are not uniform.
    C. The requirements to qualify are uniformly fixed by state law.
    D. They require a higher down payment than nonconventional loans.

73. All of the following transfers can result in the lender's exercising its rights under the due-on-sale clause, based on the rules of Freddie Mac, *EXCEPT* a(n)
    A. recorded land contract.
    B. lease with option to purchase.
    C. unrecorded land contract.
    D. second mortgage.

74. A buyer wants to take out an FHA loan. The broker should refer the buyer directly to
    A. any approved lending institution such as a bank or savings and loan.
    B. an FHA appraiser in the area.
    C. the Federal Housing Administration Office.
    D. Fannie Mae.

75. The penalty for complete prepayment of an FHA-insured loan during the first ten years is
    A. 2 percent of the face value of the note at time of payment.
    B. 90 days interest on the remaining balance.
    C. 1 percent of the original amount of the loan.
    D. nothing.

76. Who would *MOST* probably pay the initial 1 percent origination fee allowed by VA on guaranteed loans?
    A. Seller
    B. Lending institution
    C. Buyer
    D. Escrow

77. The maximum amount that may be loaned to a qualified veteran on a VA-guaranteed loan is limited to
    A. the assessed value of the property.
    B. 60 percent of the appraisal.
    C. $60,000.
    D. the amount shown on the Certificate of Reasonable Value (CRV).

78. ◎ Which is *TRUE* regarding the secondary mortgage market?
    A. Ginnie Mae underwrites loan pools consisting of FHA and VA loans.
    B. The secondary mortgage market refers to lending institutions that loan money to homeowners, who then use their equity in the home as security in the form of a second mortgage.
    C. The entire market is headed by a federal commissioner.
    D. Loans are deemed securities and are regulated by the Securities and Exchange Commission.

79. The federal agency of HUD that buys and sells mortgages for subsidized low-income properties is known as
    A. Fannie Mae.
    B. Ginnie Mae.
    C. Freddie Mac.
    D. Farmer Mac.

80. When you purchase property under an installment contract of sale (agreement of sale), you have all of the following *EXCEPT*
    A. an insurable interest.
    B. an equitable interest.
    C. legal title.
    D. a transfer of possession.

81. As used in real estate financing, the term *impounds MOST* nearly means
    A. moratorium.
    B. reserves.
    C. attachments.
    D. penalties.

82. A federal savings association must belong to which of the following?
    A. Savings Association Insurance Fund
    B. Federal Land Bank
    C. Federal Reserve Board
    D. Federal Depository Board

83. ◎ Which of the following *BEST* describes the principal advantage of a sale-leaseback from the commercial buyer's point of view?
    A. Capital is not tied up.
    B. Rental payments are tax deductible.
    C. Capital gain benefits result.
    D. Allowable depreciation (cost recovery) can be claimed.

84. ◎ Which statement *MOST* accurately describes mortgage companies that act as mortgage loan correspondents?
    A. They prefer negotiating loans that can be sold on the secondary market.
    B. They are organized under federal laws and are subject to vigorous supervision.
    C. They do not service the loans they originate.
    D. They are not active in the field of government-insured loans.

85. Which of the following bank practices is prohibited by federal law?
    A. Charging an interest rate in excess of limits imposed by usury laws
    B. Charging points to increase the lender's yield
    C. Collecting three months' interest and taxes in advance
    D. Lending in certain ghetto areas of the inner city

86. All of the following practices in a real estate transaction involving a federally related mortgage loan under the Real Estate Settlement Procedures Act (RESPA) are prohibited *EXCEPT* that
    A. the lender requires a specific title insurer.
    B. the buyer pays referral fee to attorney.
    C. the broker requests kickback.
    D. escrow requires fee for services.

87. When a property is sold under an agreement of sale (land contract)
    A. legal title passes to the buyer.
    B. the buyer receives a deed at the close of initial escrow.
    C. the vendor retains possession.
    D. the buyer has equitable title until satisfaction.

88. The definition of an institutional lender includes all of the following *EXCEPT*
    A. state-chartered banks.
    B. pension funds.
    C. savings and loans.
    D. commercial banks.

89. The secondary mortgage market is *MOST* affected by the policies of
    A. Fannie Mae.
    B. unintentional investors.
    C. government-owned agencies.
    D. insurance companies.

90. A mortgage broker
    A. arranges loans between borrowers and lenders.
    B. is a lender.
    C. buys mortgages in the secondary mortgage market.
    D. buys mortgages and resells them at a profit.

91. A federal savings and loan institution must insure its deposits for up to
    A. $20,000.
    B. $40,000.
    C. $50,000.
    D. $100,000.

92. A financing arrangement under which the buyer does *NOT* become the legal owner of record is a
    A. trust deed.
    B. land contract.
    C. purchase-money mortgage.
    D. quitclaim deed.

93. Which of the following is a source of primary mortgage funds?
    A. Federal Deposit Insurance Corporation
    B. Fannie Mae
    C. Federal Home Loan Bank
    D. Federal Savings and Loan Association

94. The lender that specializes in real estate home loans, allows a high loan-to-value ratio, deals in nongovernment loans, services its own loans, and makes many medium-term to long-term loans is a(n)
    A. savings association.
    B. pension plan.
    C. insurance company.
    D. credit union.

95. A source of capital for real estate loans might come from all of the following *EXCEPT*
    A. life insurance companies.
    B. credit unions.
    C. savings association.
    D. mortgage brokers.

96. ◎ An individual wants to sell his industrial warehouse by way of a sale-leaseback. All of the following would be relevant factors for the buyer in such a transaction *EXCEPT*
    A. amount of lease payments.
    B. income tax deductions.
    C. book value of the warehouse.
    D. replacement cost.

97. Fannie Mae can do all of the following *EXCEPT*
    A. purchase certain conventional loans.
    B. sell mortgages to institutions.
    C. buy FHA-VA loans.
    D. originate federal loans.

98. When discount points are charged on FHA loans
    A. the purchaser must pay the discount points.
    B. the buyer or seller may pay them.
    C. only the buyer may pay the charge.
    D. the seller must pay all points.

99. Which of the following *BEST* describes the fee charged to make a loan?
    A. Reversion fee
    B. Origination fee
    C. Discount fee
    D. Transfer fee

100. An investor wants to buy five unoccupied rental units. He could obtain all the following loans *EXCEPT* a
    A. VA loan.
    B. bank loan.
    C. conventional loan.
    D. credit union loan.

101. How long does an FHA conditional loan commitment remain in effect?
    A. One month
    B. Three months
    C. Six months
    D. Twelve months

102. ◎ A buyer is purchasing a home by way of a VA loan. The closing statement reveals a payment of $1,200 in discount points. How would this payment appear on the closing statement?
    A. Reduction in the proceeds due seller
    B. Addition to the principal due from buyer
    C. Reduction in the buyer's down payment
    D. Addition to the proceeds due seller

103. The seller has an existing first mortgage. To limit exposure to further liability on the mortgage note, the seller should find a buyer ready to
    A. take title subject to the mortgage.
    B. subordinate his or her position to the mortgage.
    C. assume the mortgage and note.
    D. obtain his or her own financing.

104. When the lender under a deed of trust requires title insurance, who would be the *MOST* likely person to pay for it?
    A. Mortgagee
    B. Trustee
    C. Trustor
    D. Beneficiary

105. ◎ A buyer purchases a fee simple property for $70,000 by way of assuming a first mortgage of $50,000, paying $10,000 in cash and having the seller take back a purchase-money second mortgage for the balance. There is an existing $5,000 second mortgage on the property to be paid off. At settlement (close of escrow), what is the correct order in which to record documents?
    A. Assumption mortgage, deed, purchase-money second mortgage
    B. Deed, release of existing second mortgage, assumption agreement, purchase-money second mortgage
    C. Purchase-money second mortgage, deed
    D. Release of second mortgage, deed, purchase-money second mortgage

106. A couple is purchasing a home for $78,000 and the lender is giving a 90 percent loan at 10 percent interest, plus a 2 percent loan origination fee. How much is the loan origination fee?
    A. $1,404
    B. $1,560
    C. $1,650
    D. $7,020

107. When is legal title transferred to a vendee under an installment land contract (agreement of sale)?
    A. On payment of the conveyance tax
    B. On satisfaction of the purchase price
    C. At the initial closing
    D. When the vendee can guarantee payment to the seller

108. What is the primary purpose of an FHA conditional loan commitment?
    A. To insure a lender against default
    B. To guarantee against a borrower's default
    C. To qualify a buyer for an FHA loan
    D. To establish the market value of a property

109. Which of the following statements about conventional mortgages is *TRUE?*
    A. They are insured by the federal government.
    B. They may be neither prepaid nor assumed.
    C. The buyer must be an owner/occupant.
    D. They require a higher down payment than FHA or VA.

110. Which statement is *TRUE* regarding FHA loans?
    A. The FHA will insure first and second mortgages.
    B. To be insured, the loan must involve an FHA-approved mortgagee.
    C. There is a small prepayment penalty.
    D. They are funded by the federal government.

111. An owner is selling her house in a flood-prone area. Adequate flood insurance would be required in which case?
    A. Sale by way of FHA-insured loan or conventional financing
    B. Sale by way of purchase-money mortgage to seller
    C. Sale by agreement of sale (installment land contract)
    D. Sale by all cash

112. A certificate of eligibility is a prerequisite for which type of loan?
    A. Conventional
    B. FHA
    C. VA
    D. Fannie Mae

113. A borrower obtains a government-insured loan that allows paying a lesser amount each month during a fixed period of time and a greater amount each month during the next period of time. Which type of loan is this?
    A. Conventional rate loan
    B. VA direct loan
    C. FHA graduated payment loan
    D. Fannie Mae convertible loan

114. In which one of the following ways do mortgage brokers differ from mortgage bankers?
    A. Brokers service the loans they arrange.
    B. Brokers arrange junior financing.
    C. Brokers do not provide their own funds to originate loans.
    D. Brokers operate in the primary mortgage market.

115. Assume that a buyer is making fully amortized payments of $600 per month on a purchase-money mortgage. Which of the following is *TRUE?*
    A. The amount applied to principal decreases each month.
    B. The interest payment stays the same.
    C. Interest and principal payments are constant.
    D. The amount applied to interest decreases each month.

116. The borrower under a fixed-rate Section 203(b) FHA loan is notified that the total monthly PITI payment will increase $15 per month. What is the *MOST* likely cause of such an increase?
    A. Inflation
    B. Interest rate escalation
    C. Prepayment
    D. Tax increase

117. Where would a private investor go to insure a conventional loan?
    A. Federal Housing Administration
    B. Federal Home Loan Bank
    C. Fannie Mae
    D. Private mortgage insurer

118. A veteran sells his property to another veteran, who assumes the loan. Which of the following statements is *TRUE?*
    A. The seller is automatically released from liability upon the assumption.
    B. The seller is immediately eligible for a maximum new VA loan upon the assumption.
    C. There is a prepayment penalty.
    D. It may be assumed with VA approval.

119. The ceiling on the amount of interest that can be charged by the seller in a real estate loan is most directly regulated by
    A. Fannie Mae.
    B. Federal Home Loan Bank.
    C. Department of Veterans Affairs.
    D. state law.

120. All of the following statements are true about Freddie Mac *EXCEPT* it
    A. is a federal agency formerly called the Federal Home Loan Mortgage Corporation.
    B. buys and sells mortgages in the secondary mortgage market from savings associations.
    C. requires the use of standard loan documents.
    D. has a direct loan program up to $35,000.

121. A buyer signs a five-year interest-only installment land contract to purchase a farm for $100,000 with a $5,000 down payment. After diligently meeting her monthly payment obligations for three years, the buyer loses her job and defaults. A court would likely permit all of the following remedies *EXCEPT*
    A. foreclosure and sale.
    B. forfeiture of all payments.
    C. a suit to hold the buyer to the contract.
    D. a suit for repossession and balance due under contract.

122. Which one of the following is a source for investor loans?
    A. FHA-insured loans
    B. VA-guaranteed loans
    C. Ginnie Mae loans
    D. Conventional loans

123. Assume a couple is without enough combined income to qualify under acceptable "income-to-purchase price" ratios but whose prospects for rapid salary increases are great. For which type of financing program would it be *MOST* appropriate to apply?
    A. FHA 203(b)
    B. VA loan
    C. Fannie Mae loan
    D. FHA 245

124. ◎ A buyer is purchasing a house under an installment contract called a *contract for deed.* At the initial closing, the seller signed the deed and placed it with an escrow agent, who will hold it until the full amount is paid. Which of the following statements is *TRUE?*
    A. On default of the buyer, the seller can automatically get the property back, plus sue for the balance due.
    B. On the seller's death, escrow should surrender the deed to the probate court.
    C. If the seller dies during the contract period, the buyer will lose the house.
    D. The death of the seller should have no effect on the buyer's interest.

125. If buyers want to pay more than the FHA loan amount, what can they do?
    A. Increase the mutual mortgage insurance
    B. Increase the down payment
    C. Increase the points
    D. FHA rules prohibit paying more than the loan amount.

ANSWERS

1. **C.** Mortgage bankers often originate loans using their own money, then package them (warehousing) to larger investors, and continue to regularly service these loans.

2. **B.** The VA guarantees loans. Fannie Mae is now a private corporation that purchases VA, FHA, and conventional loans in the secondary mortgage market with money raised by selling debentures backed by the U.S. government.

3. **B.** VA loans are assumable with prior approval of the VA based on VA assumption guidelines. The VA loans are not transferable, and the veteran would need to have eligibility restored prior to getting a loan on another home. If the assuming buyer is also a veteran, the seller should see about getting the buyer to substitute his or her VA eligibility. Otherwise, the seller couldn't get his or her own eligibility fully restored until the buyer paid off the loan.

4. **B.** Under both FHA and VA loans, the lender may not charge a prepayment penalty. FHA permits second loans to cover a portion of the down payment, with restrictions on certain requirements such as length of loan and payment terms. The payment of points is negotiable between buyer and seller. RESPA prohibits lenders from requiring that borrowers obtain title insurance from a particular company as a condition of the loan.

5. **B.** Novation is the substitution of one obliged party for another. Note that the assuming buyer would have to substitute his or her own VA eligibility.

6. **D.** VA makes direct loans in rare cases, as in rural areas, where loans aren't readily available. While the VA does have certain lending standards, it does not regulate lending institutions, as do the Federal Reserve Board (banks) and the Federal Home Loan Bank Board (savings associations).

7. **D.** FHA once had investor programs, but it now requires the borrower to occupy the property. VA limits its loans to veterans who will occupy a single-family residence or at least one unit in a property not to exceed four units. FHA and VA loans now have certain restrictions and standards regulating loan assumption.

8. **B.** A debenture is an unsecured obligation. The FHA will sometimes offer to pay debentures to lenders who suffer a loss. A chattel mortgage uses personal property as the security.

9. **B.** The direct loan program is related to lack of comparable loans in certain areas, not to occupancy.

10. **A.** The borrower is prohibited from obtaining secondary financing to pay for the down payment and closing costs.

11. **C.** FHA sets standards for the loans. It also sets minimum property requirements (MPRs) for the secured properties.

12. **A.** The private lender makes the loan, which is then insured by FHA.

13. **D.** VA uses its approved appraisers and will lend only to owner-occupant veterans.

14. **D.** If the appraised value is less than the sale price, the purchaser must pay the difference in cash, not with a second loan. The government *insures* the lender against loss due to the borrower's default.

15. **A.** The FHA prohibits junior financing on properties it insures. After closing, the mortgagor can obtain further financing.

16. **D.** To get such a novation, the veteran could sell to a qualified buyer.

17. **C.** The Comprehensive Loss Underwriting Exchange (CLUE) is used in the homeowner's insurance industry.

18. **D.** The seller (vendor) retains legal title as security for payment of the balance due; the buyer (vendee) receives equitable title and possession.

19. **A.** The popular FHA 203(b) program now requires that the applicant be an owner-occupant. The loan is based on the FHA appraised value (not a conventional appraisal, although VA appraisals also are recognized). Secondary financing plus the first mortgage cannot exceed the maximum FHA limits on loan-to-value ratios (if so, a portion of the down payment must be paid in cash). VA loans use a certificate of eligibility.

20. **B.** For example, a five-year loan could be amortized on a ten-year basis with a balloon payment due at the end of the fifth year.

21. **C.** Typically the appraised value is lower in a sellers' market, because buyers are willing to pay higher prices to get the property.

22. **B.** There are no down payment requirements under the VA if the buyer and the property meet VA requirements. Thus, 100 percent loans are possible.

23. **C.** A land contract is also referred to as an *agreement of sale,* an *installment contract,* or a *contract for deed.*

24. **B.** A straight note is interest only. An amortized note would include interest and principal payments.

25. **A.** The percentage is based on the amount loaned. The amount loaned would be based on the lesser amount of either sales price or appraised value.

26. **B.** A blanket mortgage covers more than one parcel of land. Accompanying a blanket mortgage is a partial release clause allowing the developer to sell portions of real estate out from under the blanket.

27. **D.** Usury is a rate of interest that exceeds the legal maximum set by state law. Some courts will penalize the lender of a usurious loan by allowing recovery of principal only, and no interest at all. Federal rules control over state law.

28. **C.** In nonrecourse financing, the seller's sole recourse upon default is to look to the property. The buyer is not personally liable if the foreclosure sale fails to bring enough money to pay the amounts due.

29. **A.** Because the buyer benefits from having a mortgage loan to purchase the property, the buyer would pay for the cost of preparing the mortgage. Also, the seller does not sign the mortgage. The seller is obligated by contract to convey title to the buyer, so the seller pays for the cost of the deed.

30. **B.** The lender is primarily concerned with steady income, not irregular overtime, which may fluctuate greatly.

31. **B.** Ginnie Mae functions in the secondary mortgage market, especially in government-assisted projects.

32. **D.** The certificate of reasonable value (CRV) is used in VA loans. In either a VA loan or an FHA loan, the buyer can pay more than the appraisal.

33. **A.** Purchase-money financing often helps bridge the gap between the sales price and the amount of cash the buyer can produce through savings and other loans. While one could have a junior purchase-money mortgage, choice (B) describes a mortgage loan not given as part of the acquisition of the property.

34. **A.** A fully amortized debt is one in which there are equal periodic payments of principal and interest, resulting in a zero balance at the end of the stated period. While the amount is constant, the part of each payment applied to interest and that applied to principal varies, with the interest portion gradually decreasing and the principal portion gradually increasing. An annuity is the periodic payment of money for the duration of a person's life or other designated period of time.

35. **D.** Choices (A), (B), and (C) can make both conventional and nonconventional (VA and FHA) loans.

36. **B.** $1,200 ÷ 5.68 = 211.27 × 1,000 = $211,267.61. Rounded to $211,268.

37. **D.** All these loans named in (A), (B), and (C) are popular with savings associations. Fannie Mae does not originate loans.

38. **B.** Many conventional loans restrict prepayment and/or have a substantial prepayment penalty. Certain nonconventional loans by law contain no prepayment penalties.

39. **B.** An owner may pay off his or her five-year 10 percent loan with the proceeds of a recently negotiated 25-year, 9 percent loan (a primary market loan transaction). Naturally, the first lender would record a release of mortgage to clear the records of that encumbrance.

40. **B.** The CRV sets the upper limit of a VA loan.

41. **B.** Many states prohibit the charging of interest on the interest of a loan.

42. **C.** The construction loan is generally short-term during the interim of completing the building, and this loan is paid off or taken out by the final permanent take-out loan.

43. **D.** (A), (B), and (C) would not lend money directly to a borrower.

44. **D.** A debenture is an unsecured note. Fannie Mae raises money by selling debentures.

45. **C.** The selling of existing, primary loans involves the secondary mortgage market.

46. **B.** The buyer under an agreement of sale (land contract) from a vendor is called a *vendee,* who has acquired equitable title in the property.

47. **D.** Most junior loans are short-term, interest-only, or partially amortized with a balloon payment.

48. **B.** An impound or reserve account is to hold monies in reserve to pay for future charges on the property such as taxes or insurance, thus assuring the lender that the security will not be exposed to liens for delinquent payments.

49. **B.** Some lenders may, however, require some private mortgage insurance to protect against borrower's default.

50. **B.** Both government and conventional loan interest rates float with the open market. Lenders often require extra compensation or demand the purchase of private mortgage insurance and title insurance.

51. **D.** The only requirement is that the veteran certify that he or she will occupy one of the units.

52. **B.** The borrower formerly paid for the insurance on a monthly basis at the annual rate of ½ of 1 percent of the average annual loan balance. This fee is now paid at the start of the loan, or it may be financed.

53. **C.** Under a land contract, the seller retains legal title as security, whereas under the purchase-money mortgage, the seller retains no title interest in the property, only the lien interest of a mortgagee.

54. **D.** Fannie Mae buys and sells first mortgages in the secondary mortgage market. The Federal Reserve Board regulates commercial banks.

55. **B.** The buyer is relatively confident the seller will be a triple-A tenant. Rent is tax deductible as a business expense.

56. **C.** The vendor will become the grantor in the deed when the land contract is satisfied.

57. **D.** VA loans do not contain prepayment penalties. The veteran buyer can pay certain closing costs and discount points. VA loans are available to veterans of World War II and afterward.

58. **D.** Through a mutual mortgage insurance plan paid for by the borrower, the FHA will give lenders financial protection in foreclosure situations.

59. **A.** When acquiring a property, new buyers frequently obtain loans to pay sellers the purchase price, the proceeds of which the sellers use to satisfy their own mortgages.

60. **A.** Note that Fannie Mae also buys new mortgages from certain lenders that have a good track record in originating successful loans.

61. **B.** FHA, a federal agency of HUD, insures up to 100 percent of the loan amount.

62. **A.** A veteran can obtain a loan on a one-family to four-family dwelling, but the veteran must occupy one of the dwellings. FHA loans are available to both owner-occupants and nonoccupants, although the latter sometimes have to make a greater down payment (their loan-to-value ratio is lower).

63. **B.** VA does have a limited direct loan program, typically restricted to rural areas where financing is difficult to obtain.

64. **B.** Secondary financing is prohibited under FHA regulations if it makes the total borrowed exceed the FHA amount for the property.

65. **A.** Each point is computed as a percent. One point is 1 percent and two points equal 2 percent. The discount points increase the lender's yield. Borrowers today use points to buy down the interest rate. By artificially lowering the interest rate by paying discount points, the buyer's borrowing power increases. Either the buyer or seller can pay up to six discount points without having a negative influence on the appraisal.

66. **C.** In the event of default, conventional lenders look only to the borrower and the property to recover losses. FHA and VA loans are considered nonconventional loans because the federal government is called on to recover loan losses.

67. **C.** The VA will guarantee the lender up to $83,425. The veteran must sign an owner-occupant affidavit. Secondary loans are permitted with certain restrictions (buyer or seller have to pay closing costs in cash). The VA has a limited direct loan program in certain rural areas where conventional financing is not readily available.

68. **A.** VA does not have to accept the appraisal of anyone except its own approved appraisers.

69. **B.** Graduated payment mortgages appeal to younger people who expect their income to gradually increase so they will be able to handle higher payments in later years. Under an adjustable-rate mortgage, the interest would fluctuate.

70. **D.** Debentures are unsecured notes. FHA and VA prohibit prepayment penalties. Private lenders often include prepayment penalties in their mortgages.

71. **C.** The credit score is a three-digit number. The three-digit score assesses credit risk and the possibility of default against past paying experience. Factors weighed to

determine a credit score include past paying performance; outstanding debt including the actual number of open accounts; credit mix of retail, finance company accounts, installment loans, revolving charge accounts, and mortgage loans; time on file; and number of search inquires for new credit. The normal range is between 600 and 700. Above 700 is considered very good credit. To adjust for the risk, those borrowers with scores falling below 600 could be required to pay a higher (subprime) interest rate.

72. **C.** Each lender maintains its own unique practices and policies about originating conventional loans.

73. **D.** As a result of the federal Garn-St. Germain law, federal lending institutions are permitted to call in or accelerate their loans in the event the borrower transfers title to the real property securing the loan. Any transfer of legal or equitable title (including options or long-term leases) will trigger the due-on-sale clause, with a few exceptions such as transfer between husband and wife. This law does not apply to junior mortgaging, because no transfer of legal or equitable title is involved.

74. **A.** The FHA does not make the loan; the lending institution does.

75. **D.** No prepayment penalty is allowed on either VA or FHA loans.

76. **C.** Most likely the buyer would pay the origination fee. Either the buyer or seller could pay discount points to buy down the interest rate.

77. **D.** The CRV sets the ceiling on the loan. Assessed value refers to taxable value. Depending on the loan amount, VA will guarantee a loan up to a maximum of $83,425.

78. **A.** The secondary mortgage market refers to the marketplace for buying and selling loans that originated in the primary market. Such a program results in an increase in the flow of money available for further origination of loans. Ginnie Mae is a government agency that is active in the secondary mortgage market of VA and FHA loans.

79. **B.** Ginnie Mae, formerly the Government National Mortgage Association (GNMA), is in charge of the special assistance aspects of federally assisted housing programs. Ginnie Mae issues guaranty certificates backed by a pool of mortgage loans in its portfolio. The guaranty certificates provide for a periodic pass-through of principal and interest payments generated by the pool of loans. Freddie Mac was the Federal Home Loan Mortgage Corporation (FHLMC); Fannie Mae was the Federal National Mortgage Association (FNMA); and Farmer Mac was the former Federal Agricultural Mortgage Corporation.

80. **C.** Because of the vendee's equitable title, insurance on the property can and should be obtained.

81. **B.** An impound account is frequently required by mortgagees. The mortgagor advances monies for future payments of certain carrying charges, such as taxes and insurance. This protects the lender against problems that could arise if the buyer were to default on those charges.

82. **A.** Such membership is not required of state-chartered savings associations, although many voluntarily carry deposit insurance with the fund.

83. **D.** The buyer gets the tax advantages of ownership, plus the benefits of any later appreciation in value of the property.

84. **A.** They favor loans made with the standardized Fannie Mae and Freddie Mac application and document forms. Typically organized under state law, they often continue to service the loans they originate, which frequently are FHA and VA loans.

85. **C.** Under the Real Estate Settlement Procedures Act (RESPA), the lender can collect in advance in an escrow impound account no more than two months' advance payments. Federally related loans are not subject to state usury laws that put a limit on the amount of interest charged on a loan. Points are permitted but must be disclosed under the Truth-in-Lending Act. Refusing to loan in ghetto areas may be the illegal practice of redlining.

86. **D.** RESPA prohibits rebates, tie-ins, kickbacks, and referral fees in connection with the closing of a real estate transaction.

87. **D.** Legal title does not pass at the first closing; only equitable title passes when the vendee receives the agreement of sale. At the second closing, when the vendee satisfies the terms of the agreement of sale, the deed will pass the legal title.

88. **B.** Institutional lenders are heavily regulated by federal and state agencies. Pension funds are private lenders.

89. **A.** At first, Fannie Mae was a federal agency, but later it became a private corporation.

90. **A.** A mortgage *banker* could be a lender as well as an arranger.

91. **D.** Each deposit is insured up to $100,000 by the Savings Association Insurance Fund (SAIF). Banks pay insurance premiums to the Bank Insurance Fund (BIF). The Federal Deposit Insurance Corporation (FDIC) regulates both of these insurance funds.

92. **B.** Under a land contract, the buyer has equitable ownership, but the seller keeps record title.

93. **D.** Choice (A) insures deposits, (B) operates in the secondary mortgage market, and (C) regulates savings associations.

94. **A.** Savings associations have been key participants in the residential real estate marketplace.

95. **D.** Credit unions are rising fast in popularity as a source of residential financing. While life insurance companies seldom make individual residential loans, they do operate in the secondary market, thus providing mortgage funds. Mortgage *bankers* lend money but mortgage *brokers* don't; mortgage brokers act as conduits, locating available funds to put together a transaction.

96. **C.** How the individual carries the property on his books has little relevance to current value. Book value is the price paid, plus any improvements, less tax depreciation taken.

97. **D.** Fannie Mae operates only in the secondary mortgage market.

98. **B.** Anyone, including the borrower (not necessarily the seller), may pay the discount points. The purchaser may pay an origination fee not to exceed 1 percent.

99. **B.** Because many lenders immediately sell their loans in the secondary mortgage market, they make their profit on the origination and service charges.

100. **A.** VA will allow up to four units, provided the veteran occupies one of the units.

101. **C.** The FHA may give its approval to a project developer, subject to obtaining qualified buyers within the time limit. This is known as a *conditional commitment.*

102. **A.** The seller would be debited the amount of the discount points.

103. **D.** If the buyer obtains financing, the seller will get cashed out and can pay off the existing mortgage. The seller would not be primarily liable if the buyer assumed the note, although he or she would remain secondarily liable.

104. **C.** In states using the trust deed, the borrower is called the *trustor* (mortgagor), the lender is called the *beneficiary,* and the third party holding title is called the *trustee.*

105. **D.** The existing second mortgage will be paid off, so a release or satisfaction piece must be recorded. Nothing need be recorded concerning the assumption because the obligation to assume will be stated in the deed. This is recorded an instant before the purchase-money second mortgage.

106. **A.** A 90 percent loan would be $70,200. $70,200 × 0.02 (2%) = $1,404.

107. **B.** The conveyance tax (transfer tax) is paid when the agreement of sale is recorded. When the vendee pays in full and satisfies all the terms and conditions of the contract, then legal title will be transferred. Until then, the vendee has equitable title.

108. **C.** With an FHA conditional loan, the property is appraised and loan values are approved, subject to the qualification of buyers.

109. **D.** Conventional loans do not involve government insurance (FHA) or guarantee (VA). Depending on the loan provisions, they may be prepaid and assumed or sold *subject to.* Nonconventional loans would be VA and FHA loans. Through use of an acceleration clause, a lender may decide to limit a borrower's ability to sell the property to a buyer who would assume the loan. (The lender could call the full amount of the loan.) VA and FHA loans can be freely prepaid with no penalty.

110. **B.** FHA insures only first mortgages given by approved lenders.

111. **A.** After the floods of 1993, the National Flood Insurance Reform Act of 1994 was created to impose certain mandatory obligations on lenders to escrow insurance funds on new loans in flood hazard zones. Special Flood Hazard Areas (SFHA) for inland zones are initially identified with the letter A. An A zone is subject to inundation by the 100-year flood, and if a lender is used, flood insurance must be purchased.

112. **C.** The VA requires that the veteran certify eligibility for its guaranteed nonconventional loans. The eligibility remains with the property until the loan is paid off or another veteran assumes the loan and substitutes his or her own eligibility.

113. **C.** During borrowing periods of high interest, FHA's 245 graduated payment mortgage is attractive. With this program, by deferring some of the interest, the monthly payments (in the loan's early years) are artificially lower, but such payments gradually increase each year for five years. After the fifth year, the deferred interest is added to principal and the remaining balance is amortized over the remaining 25 years. These loans appeal to borrowers who anticipate an increase in their earning power, especially younger married couples.

114. **C.** Unlike the broker, the mortgage *banker* is capable of originating loans as well as servicing the loans arranged for others. The mortgage banker operates in the primary mortgage market (originating loans) as well as in the secondary mortgage market (selling loans, especially to Fannie Mae).

115. **D.** As each monthly $600 is paid, a portion is applied to reduce the principal balance of the debt. This results in a lower interest payment for the next month because interest is now calculated on a lower balance.

116. **D.** FHA loan payments are typically all-inclusive payments, which include a payment after taxes and insurance are paid (as in a budget mortgage). The FHA interest rates are fixed.

117. **D.** Private mortgage insurance (PMI) is frequently used to insure a portion of a conventional loan. FHA does insure certain nonconventional loans under its Mutual Mortgage Insurance Plan.

118. **D.** To assume a VA loan committed after March 1, 1988, a purchaser must be able to qualify based on VA guidelines.

119. **D.** Choices (A), (B), and (C) do regulate certain loan transactions on a national level, but interest rate ceilings are typically controlled by individual state usury statutes.

120. **D.** Freddie Mac is most active in the secondary mortgage market for savings association financing. Its requirements have caused considerable standardization of loan documents throughout the country.

121. **D.** If the seller were to sue the buyer for the full contract price and also repossession of the property, it would be a windfall. The seller is attempting to cancel the contract on one hand and enforce the contract on the other hand.

122. **D.** Note that FHA discontinued its investor loan program in 1989.

123. **D.** The FHA 245 is the graduated payment loan program in which monthly payments start low but then increase as the loan matures, while the borrower's income is expected to increase as well. The 203(b) program is the most popular level-payment home loan insurance program.

124. **D.** Most contracts for deed contain a forfeiture clause permitting the seller to either repossess the property or elect to seek money damages. Usually the seller cannot get both the property and damages. The recent trend, however, in cases where the buyer has built up a large equity, is to force a foreclosure sale and return any excess monies to the buyer. Because the deed has been placed in escrow, the death of the seller would normally have no effect on the deed. The principal determination to be made by the probate court is who is entitled to the payments of the balance due.

125. **B.** The FHA gives the buyer a choice to back out if the appraisal value (CRV) exceeds the sales price.

CHAPTER 10

Mortgages and Foreclosures

Nearly all real estate transactions involve some form of financing. Even when the buyer has adequate funds to purchase in cash, the buyer often prefers to advance only part of the purchase price, borrowing the balance and repaying it over a period of years—thus leveraging the investment.

The parties to a mortgage are the mortgagor/borrower and the mortgagee/lender. The mortgagor is required to sign a mortgage and a promissory note—the note makes the borrower personally liable for the debt, while the mortgage pledges (hypothecates) the property as security to guarantee repayment of the note. Thus, even if the mortgagor decides to abandon the property, the mortgagor is still personally liable for the debt, and the mortgagee can obtain a personal judgment against the mortgagor for any deficiency between the foreclosure sale price and the amount of the debt.

When the secured property is sold, the debt is typically paid and the mortgagee releases the lien of its mortgage from the records. In some cases, the loan remains on the property, and the new buyer assumes the mortgage or takes subject to the mortgage, the principal difference being that the new buyer becomes personally liable for the debt in an assumption.

The questions in this chapter test your comprehension of the following topics:

- Clauses commonly found in mortgages

- Different classifications of mortgages

- Consequences of a default under a note and mortgage

- Assumptions and sales subject to a mortgage

KEY WORDS

Amortization: The gradual repayment of a debt by means of systematic payments of principal and interest over a set period, where at the end of the period there is a zero balance.

Assumption of mortgage: The act of acquiring title to property that has an existing mortgage on it and agreeing to be personally liable for the terms and conditions of the mortgage, including payments.

Balloon payment: The final payment of a note or obligation that is substantially larger than the previous installment payments and that repays the debt in full; the remaining balance that is due at the maturity of a note or obligation.

Blanket mortgage: A mortgage that is secured by several structures or a number of lots. A blanket mortgage is often used to finance proposed subdivisions or development projects, especially cooperatives.

Deficiency judgment: A judgment against a borrower, endorser, or guarantor for the balance of the debt issued when the security for a loan is insufficient to satisfy the debt.

Due-on-sale clause: A form of acceleration clause found in some mortgages, requiring that the mortgagor pay off the mortgage debt when selling the secured property, thus resulting in automatic maturity of the note at the lender's option.

Foreclosure: A legal procedure whereby property used as security for debt is sold to satisfy the debt in the event of default in payment of the mortgage note or default of other terms in the mortgage document.

Hypothecate: To pledge something as collateral without giving up possession of it (i.e., a borrower pledges real property as collateral but doesn't give up possession of the property pledged).

Lien: A charge or claim that one person (lienor) has upon the property of another (lienee) as security for a debt or obligation. Liens can be created by agreement of the parties (mortgage) or by operation of law (tax liens).

Mortgage: A legal document used to secure the performance of an obligation. In effect, the mortgage states that the lender can look to the property in the event the borrower defaults in payment of the note.

Mortgagee: The one that receives and holds a mortgage as security for a debt; the lender; a lender or creditor that holds a mortgage as security for payment of an obligation.

Mortgagor: The one who gives a mortgage as security for a debt; the borrower; usually the landowner; the borrower or debtor who hypothecates or puts up his property as security for an obligation.

Partial release: A clause found in a mortgage that directs the mortgagee to release certain parcels from the lien of the blanket mortgage on the payment of a certain sum of money.

Prepayment penalty: The amount set by the creditor as a penalty to the debtor for paying off the debt prior to its maturity. The prepayment penalty is charged by the lender to recoup a portion of interest that it had planned to earn when it made the loan.

Purchase-money mortgage: A mortgage given to the seller as part of the buyer's consideration for the purchase of real property and delivered at the same time that the real property is transferred as a simultaneous part of the transaction.

Redemption, equitable right of: The right of a mortgagor who has defaulted on the mortgage note to redeem or get back his or her title to the property by paying off the entire mortgage note prior to the foreclosure sale.

Second mortgage: A mortgage that is junior or subordinate to a first mortgage; typically, an additional loan imposed on top of the first mortgage, which is taken out when the borrower needs more money.

Straight note: A promissory note evidencing a loan in which "interest only" payments are made periodically during the term of the note, with the principal payment due in one lump sum on maturity.

Trust deed: A real property security device (also called a *deed of trust*) very similar to a mortgage, except that there are three parties: the trustor, the trustee, and the beneficiary (the lender).

MISTAKEN IDENTITY

The following words are often confused with one another. Note the difference in meaning of these mistaken identity words and phrases.

Mortgagor/Mortgagee: The *mortgagor* (borrower) gives the mortgage to the *mortgagee* (lender). The mortgage thus pledges (hypothecates) the property as collateral for the loan, and promises the repayment of money (note).

Acceleration/Alienation: An *alienation clause* (due on sale or restraint on alienation) triggers the acceleration of the full debt upon a transfer of title; it is a specific type of *acceleration clause.*

Subordination/Subrogation: *Subordination* means to give up priority to an anticipated future mortgage or lien, whereas *subrogation* means to substitute a creditor who succeeds to the rights of another.

Trustor/Trustee/Beneficiary: Under a deed of trust, the *trustor* (borrower) transfers title to a *trustee* for the benefit of the *beneficiary* (lender).

Estoppel certificate/Reduction certificate: The *estoppel certificate* is issued by the mortgagor to establish the amount of the debt and whether any defenses exist, whereas the *reduction certificate* is issued by the lender to someone who is about to assume the loan and states the remaining loan balance.

Foreclosure/Forfeiture: A *foreclosure* action extinguishes any claim the mortgagor may have to the real property securing a defaulted loan, whereas a *forfeiture* refers generally to the loss of a right to something as a result of nonperformance of an obligation or condition.

Subject to/Assumption: Both involve the sale of a property without paying off the underlying mortgage. With an *assumption* the buyer agrees to become personally liable for any deficiency judgment upon default; *subject to* means the seller remains primarily liable for the note and the mortgage.

QUESTIONS

1. On the closing of the sale of mortgaged property, the seller *MUST* in every case
   A. pay off the mortgage.
   B. deliver the deed to the grantee.
   C. obtain the approval of the mortgagee.
   D. obtain a new mortgage.

2. A mortgage is usually released by a
   A. reversion.
   B. reconveyance.
   C. quitclaim deed.
   D. satisfaction piece.

3. A clause in a mortgage or lease, stating that the rights of the holder shall be secondary to a subsequent lien, is called a(n)
   A. subordination clause.
   B. habendum clause.
   C. escalation clause.
   D. recapture clause.

4. If the mortgagee has the property sold at a foreclosure sale and it brings an amount inadequate to pay off the loan, what can the mortgagee do?
   A. Sue the mortgagor for the deficiency
   B. Cancel the sale
   C. Appeal to the Supreme Court
   D. Attach all other properties owned by the debtor

5. ◎ What will happen on the sale of a mortgaged property by foreclosure?
   A. Any existing listing of the property with the broker is terminated.
   B. Foreclosure requires the payment of a commission to the listing broker.
   C. Any tenant may remain in occupancy until his or her lease is ended.
   D. The owner is forbidden from bidding at the foreclosure sale.

6. Mortgage satisfaction is evidenced by which of the following?
   A. Estoppel certificate
   B. Release of lien
   C. Reduction certificate
   D. Certificate of no defense

7. An *acceleration clause* found in a promissory note or mortgage means that
   A. on the happening of a certain event, the entire amount of the unpaid balance becomes due.
   B. payments must be made more frequently at a future specified date.
   C. the interest rate can increase.
   D. payments may not be made more frequently than specified.

8. ◎ Which of the following occurs when the mortgagor is declared bankrupt?
   A. The mortgagor retains equitable title to the property but forfeits legal title.
   B. The mortgagor no longer owes any money under the mortgage note.
   C. The mortgagee will give the mortgagor one year to pay back the debt.
   D. Title will pass to the receiver in bankruptcy.

9. An individual, partnership, or corporation to whom title to or an interest in a property is conditionally conveyed as security for a loan is known as the
   A. mortgagor.
   B. borrower.
   C. mortgagee.
   D. lessee.

10. Which of the following must sign the mortgage and the note?
    A. Mortgagor
    B. Mortgagee
    C. Trustee
    D. Beneficiary

11. Of the following, who is benefited by an acceleration clause in a mortgage or trust deed note?
    A. The borrower
    B. The lender
    C. A future purchaser on resale of property
    D. The trustee

12. The mortgagor's right to reestablish ownership after default is known as
    A. redemption.
    B. reestablishment.
    C. acceleration.
    D. subordination.

13. A trust deed must be signed by the
    A. beneficiary.
    B. trustor.
    C. lender.
    D. trustee.

14. The main advantage of a wraparound mortgage is that the
    A. borrower gains additional financing at a higher rate than the market interest rate.
    B. originator of a wraparound mortgage is the primary mortgage holder.
    C. wraparound mortgage specifically finances subdivisions.
    D. effective interest rate is typically lower than the prevailing rate on new mortgages.

15. All of the following likely would be classified as second mortgages *EXCEPT* a
    A. wraparound mortgage.
    B. construction loan.
    C. seller-assisted loan.
    D. junior loan.

16. All of the following statements are true of the promissory note used to finance real property *EXCEPT* that it is
    A. the written promise of the borrower to repay the loan.
    B. the fundamental loan document.
    C. typically recorded.
    D. signed by the mortgagor.

17. The certificate executed and acknowledged by the mortgagee, stating the amount due on the mortgage, is known as the
    A. estoppel certificate.
    B. reduction certificate.
    C. deed of trust.
    D. novation certificate.

18. Which of the following is *TRUE* when the seller takes back a mortgage from the buyer as part payment for the sale?
    A. The seller is entitled to possession of the property until the debt is paid.
    B. The seller retains legal title.
    C. No second mortgages may be placed on the property by the buyer.
    D. The mortgage is a purchase-money mortgage.

19. The use of an acceleration clause in a mortgage or a deed of trust is to
    A. require that the mortgagor make more payments per month.
    B. increase the amount of the monthly payments.
    C. require that the entire balance be paid at once when exercised.
    D. pressure the mortgagor into making payments.

20. A written acknowledgment that a mortgage has been satisfied is *BEST* called a(n)
    A. subordination.
    B. promissory note.
    C. release of lien.
    D. estoppel certificate.

21. In the event a first mortgagee fails to record his or her mortgage and a good-faith second mortgagee records his or her mortgage first, all of the following would be true *EXCEPT* that
    A. the second mortgagee has priority.
    B. the borrower is personally liable to both lenders.
    C. the first lender will still be able to collect the money owed.
    D. an unrecorded mortgage cannot be enforced and collected on.

22. What type of mortgage may permit a builder to obtain the release of lots, one at a time, as they are developed?
    A. Blanket mortgage
    B. Package mortgage
    C. Open-end mortgage
    D. Conventional mortgage

23. Which of the following events results in the release of a mortgage lien?
    A. Foreclosure sale
    B. Sale by mortgagor
    C. Lease of property
    D. Further encumbrance

24. A promissory note creates which of the following?
    A. Secured mortgage
    B. Personal obligation
    C. Specific lien
    D. General lien

25. A conditional conveyance of land designed as security for the payment of money or the performance of some act that will become void on such payment or performance is a(n)
    A. lien.
    B. deed of trust.
    C. general warranty deed.
    D. option.

26. If mortgaged property is sold and the buyer assumes and agrees to pay the mortgage debt
    A. the lender can recover the balance from either the seller or the buyer or both.
    B. the seller no longer has any liability for the debt.
    C. only the buyer has any liability.
    D. the property cannot be sold at foreclosure if the buyer defaults.

27. In researching records at the office of public records, you can usually distinguish between a first and a second mortgage by
    A. the date of instrument.
    B. the words *first* or *second* preceding the phrase *this indenture.*
    C. notations made by the recorder.
    D. the date of recording.

28. ◎ Which of the following *BEST* describes a reduction certificate?
    A. It shows the balance due on a mortgage.
    B. It shows the sales price has been reduced on the listing.
    C. It shows the property has gone down in value since it was last appraised.
    D. It shows the interest rate has been reduced from the original loan rate.

29. By which means could a deed of trust be discharged?
    A. By default
    B. By reconveyance to the trustor
    C. By refusal of the beneficiary to release control
    D. When the seller can prove clear title to the property

30. A $150,000, interest-only loan at 10 percent in which the entire principal is due at the end of the term is *BEST* described as which type of loan?
    A. Graduated
    B. Term
    C. Amortized
    D. Declining balance

31. A clause that advances the time for payment of a debt is a(n)
    A. acceleration clause.
    B. balloon payment clause.
    C. prepayment clause.
    D. escalation clause.

32. When you use real property as security for a loan, you do which one of the following?
    A. Pledge it
    B. Hypothecate it
    C. Assign it
    D. Devise it

33. A second mortgage is
    A. greater in value than a first mortgage.
    B. a junior lien on real estate that has a prior mortgage.
    C. always made by the seller.
    D. used in practically all real estate purchases.

34. A promissory note that provides for payment of interest only during the term of the note is a(n)
   A. installment note.
   B. straight note.
   C. amortized note.
   D. nonnegotiable note.

35. In real estate financing, the debt is evidenced by a
   A. mortgage.
   B. promissory note.
   C. chattel mortgage.
   D. financing statement.

36. The clause in a mortgage note that permits the loan to be paid off at any time without a penalty is called a(n)
   A. subordination clause.
   B. acceleration clause.
   C. "or more" clause.
   D. nonresponsibility clause.

37. A partial release clause is used commonly in a(n)
   A. lease.
   B. blanket mortgage.
   C. attachment.
   D. judgment lien.

38. When the seller finances the buyer's purchase of a home, it is *MOST* precisely described as
   A. a conventional mortgage.
   B. a chattel mortgage.
   C. a purchase-money mortgage.
   D. home financing.

39. The words *balloon payment* on a mortgage refer to the
   A. first payment.
   B. last payment.
   C. middle payment.
   D. total payments.

40. In the absence of an agreement to the contrary, the mortgage that normally has priority is the
   A. mortgage for the largest amount.
   B. first mortgage executed and delivered.
   C. mortgage recorded first.
   D. construction loan mortgage.

41. ◎ Which is an example of involuntary alienation?
   A. Trust deed
   B. Tax sale
   C. The first mortgage
   D. The construction mortgage

42. Which one of the following is *TRUE* about a promissory note?
   A. It may not be executed in connection with a loan on real property.
   B. It is an agreement to do or not to do a certain thing.
   C. It is the primary evidence of a loan.
   D. It is a note that is guaranteed or insured by a government agency.

43. The party to whom a mortgage is made is the lender, also called the
   A. mortgagor.
   B. mortgagee.
   C. lessor.
   D. trustee.

44. Buying real property "subject to the mortgage" is
   A. a type of conditional loan.
   B. a mortgage bought by Fannie Mae and sold to Ginnie Mae.
   C. the taking of title to property by a grantee with no personal responsibility to the lender for paying the mortgage loan.
   D. the right to foreclose without going to court.

45. The party who is similar to a mortgagor in a transaction involving a deed of trust is *BEST* called the
   A. lender.
   B. trustor.
   C. beneficiary.
   D. trustee.

46. ◎ The seller has a 20-year amortized first mortgage, which the buyer is to assume. Which of the following statements is *TRUE?*
   A. The loan must be a conventional loan to be assumable.
   B. The buyer's loan will be an amortized loan.
   C. Amortized loans are not assumable.
   D. Upon assumption the terms of the loan are usually changed.

47. What accompanies the mortgage document in a real estate loan transaction?
    A. Promissory note
    B. Deed
    C. Abstract
    D. Appraisal

48. The difference between the value of the property and the amount of the outstanding mortgage balance is *BEST* described as which of the following?
    A. Mortgagee's statutory equity
    B. Mortgagor's equity
    C. Value owing
    D. Debt service

49. An escalation clause in a mortgage usually provides for
    A. an adjustment of the interest rate under specified conditions.
    B. immediate payment of the full debt upon any default.
    C. a method of speeding up the payment to pay off the loan sooner.
    D. a locked-in interest rate in the event that interest rates increase.

50. Which statement can be made concerning a secured real estate loan?
    A. Charging a rate of interest higher than the legal maximum is called *points*.
    B. A subordination clause is a clause by which a prior lienholder permits a subsequent lien(s) to step ahead in priority.
    C. Prepayment is the lender's charge for making a loan.
    D. Each point is equivalent to 2 percent of the loan amount.

51. A mortgage that covers several parcels of land and may contain a provision for sale of an individual parcel, thereby reducing mortgage payments, is a(n)
    A. direct reduction mortgage.
    B. amortized mortgage.
    C. blanket mortgage.
    D. declining balance mortgage.

52. If a buyer of real property agrees in the contract of purchase to assume an existing loan, the
    A. seller is entirely relieved of all responsibility to pay the note in full.
    B. seller remains solely responsible for repayment of the note.
    C. buyer can lose the property only through foreclosure but cannot be sued for a deficiency judgment.
    D. buyer can be held liable if loan payments are not made.

53. Where there is a default on a mortgage, which of the following can occur?
    A. The lender can foreclose without the need of going through judicial proceedings if there is a power-of-sale clause in the mortgage.
    B. After the foreclosure sale, the borrower has a ten-year statutory right to redeem the property by paying all cash.
    C. The mortgagor can pay up all of the back payments at any time and thus remain in good standing with the lender.
    D. Only if there is an escalation clause in the mortgage can the lender foreclose.

54. An *equitable period of redemption* refers to a time within which
    A. a lender can foreclose on a borrower who is in default.
    B. the debtor can reclaim the property by payment.
    C. a prospective purchaser can bid on the property.
    D. the court may take possession of the secured property.

55. When the foreclosure sale of mortgaged property does *NOT* yield enough to pay off the mortgage, the lender
    A. must pay for the expenses of collection.
    B. may pursue other assets of the borrower for the deficiency.
    C. may cancel the sale and repossess the property.
    D. accepts debt that stays with the property and transfers to the new buyer.

56. In preparing the mortgage document, one should note that the
    A. mortgagor is not named in the mortgage.
    B. mortgagee is not named in the mortgage.
    C. mortgagor does not sign the mortgage.
    D. mortgagee does not sign the mortgage.

57. If foreclosure sale proceeds are less than the outstanding debt and foreclosure expenses, which of the following remedies is available?
    A. There is no remedy.
    B. The mortgagee must absorb the loss, because the mortgagor is liable only for foreclosure expenses.
    C. The owner has the statutory right of redemption.
    D. The mortgagee may obtain a deficiency judgment against the mortgagor.

58. The monthly payment on a loan remains the same, yet the amount applied to interest decreases and the amount applied to principal increases as the loan gets older. This is an illustration of which of the following?
    A. Amortization
    B. Depreciation
    C. Subrogation
    D. Inflation

59. In the mortgage, the lender can establish which of the following?
    A. The right of redemption
    B. The length of the redemption period
    C. A usurious rate of interest
    D. The terms of repayment

60. What advantage to the borrower does a 20-year amortization loan have over a 15-year amortization loan?
    A. A lower amount of interest
    B. Lower monthly payments
    C. Higher monthly payments
    D. Lower down payment

61. Which of the following is *TRUE?*
    A. The acceleration clause is placed in a mortgage document for the benefit of the mortgagor.
    B. The escalation clause is placed in the mortgage contract to facilitate foreclosure.
    C. The defeasance clause tells when the payments are due and defines any late charges.
    D. Charging more than the legal rate of interest is called *usury.*

62. A deed that conveys title to a mortgagee from a mortgagor and prevents legal action to recover the lender's collateral is known as a deed
    A. of surrender.
    B. in lieu of foreclosure.
    C. of release.
    D. of reconveyance.

63. All of the following statements are true concerning a purchase-money mortgage *EXCEPT*
    A. it can be given by the purchaser to the seller to secure partial payment.
    B. it allows the buyer to obtain title to the property.
    C. any mortgage that is part of the purchase price of the property is a purchase-money mortgage.
    D. it is only used for second mortgages.

64. A mortgage that allows for advances to a mortgagor up to a certain maximum is a(n)
    A. package mortgage.
    B. open-end mortgage.
    C. purchase-money mortgage.
    D. wraparound mortgage.

65. On the satisfaction of a debt secured by a deed of trust, the title is reconveyed to the borrower by the
    A. trustor.
    B. beneficiary.
    C. lender.
    D. trustee.

66. An example of written evidence of a promise to repay borrowed money is a(n)
    A. abstract.
    B. acknowledgment.
    C. covenant.
    D. promissory note.

67. A deed of trust is used to do which of the following?
    A. Convey land to a trustworthy friend
    B. Secure a loan of money by real property
    C. Convey land to a trustee for a minor
    D. Secure a loan of money by trade fixtures

68. A mortgagor's right, in some states, to reclaim the foreclosed property from the successful bidder after the foreclosure sale is
    A. satisfaction of mortgage.
    B. equitable right of redemption.
    C. an action for judgment.
    D. statutory right of redemption.

69. A blanket mortgage does which of the following?
    A. Covers several parcels of land
    B. Finances the furniture and appliances in a dwelling
    C. Covers any property being financed, whether real or personal
    D. Covers the total payment of principal, interest, taxes, insurance, and so on

70. A buyer purchased a furnished, fee simple home and is going to assume the existing mortgage. The settlement company will arrange to have drawn up all the following with the exception of the
    A. bill of sale.
    B. note and mortgage.
    C. assumption agreement.
    D. warranty deed.

71. A statement from a borrower setting forth the amount of the balance unpaid, the interest rate, and any claims she may have against the lender is called a(n)
    A. lender's certificate.
    B. title certificate.
    C. estoppel certificate.
    D. financial certificate.

72. A clause in a mortgage that may permit the lender to call the entire balance due if the property is sold or otherwise conveyed by the mortgagor is called a(n)
    A. defeasance clause.
    B. alienation clause.
    C. subordination clause.
    D. escalation clause.

73. A mortgage may be discharged by all of the following EXCEPT
    A. satisfaction.
    B. power of sale.
    C. death.
    D. release.

74. The points of conventional loans are computed and based on
    A. sales price.
    B. listing price.
    C. loan amount.
    D. closing costs.

75. A secured loan with a payback based on 25 years but which is to be paid in full in ten years may be any of the following EXCEPT a(n)
    A. balloon mortgage.
    B. installment contract.
    C. amortized loan.
    D. graduated payment mortgage.

76. A mortgage that permits the interest charge to range up and down according to the money market is called a(n)
    A. escalation mortgage.
    B. net mortgage.
    C. open mortgage.
    D. variable-rate mortgage.

77. Which is *TRUE* concerning the typical purchase-money mortgage?
   A. The seller takes back a mortgage as part of the purchase price.
   B. The seller is disposing of a mortgage loan.
   C. The buyer is denied the prepayment privilege.
   D. The seller is denied the prepayment penalty.

78. When a buyer "assumes and agrees to pay" an existing loan on the property, which of the following is *TRUE?*
   A. The seller is relieved from liability.
   B. The buyer and the seller are liable for the loan.
   C. Only the seller is liable.
   D. Only the buyer is liable.

79. Which of the following terms *BEST* describes the right to pay off a mortgage debt after default?
   A. Foreclosure
   B. Prepayment
   C. Redemption
   D. Escalation

80. All of the following persons in a real estate purchase transaction using a purchase-money trust deed sign the deed of trust *EXCEPT* the
   A. borrower.
   B. trustor.
   C. trustee.
   D. purchaser.

81. A mortgage contains a clause providing for the assignment of rents. Who benefits from this clause?
   A. Mortgagor
   B. Mortgagee
   C. Purchaser
   D. Trustee

82. ◎ Which of the following parties to a real estate sales transaction would have the *MOST* exposure to liability?
   A. Grantor of a quitclaim deed
   B. Grantor in a loan assumption
   C. Grantee taking subject to the loan
   D. Grantor selling subject to the loan

83. A house is owned subject to a first mortgage. This property is said to be
   A. restricted.
   B. subordinated.
   C. executed.
   D. encumbered.

84. Under an adjustable-rate mortgage, which of the following may occur?
   A. The term of the loan may not be extended.
   B. The interest rate may decrease one percentage point.
   C. The number of lenders involved changes each year.
   D. No prepayment is allowed.

85. When is a mortgagor released from liability under a mortgage?
   A. On a sale subject to the mortgage
   B. On an assumption of the mortgage
   C. On a sale under a land contract
   D. On an assumption and novation

86. ◎ Which of the following statements regarding the interest on a long-term amortized mortgage loan is *TRUE?*
   A. Unless otherwise provided, interest is usually charged in arrears, meaning at the end of each period for which interest is due.
   B. The interest portion of each payment remains the same throughout the entire term of the loan.
   C. The monthly payment will remain the same, and out of each monthly payment, the same amount will be applied to principal and toward interest.
   D. Amortized loans must have a floating interest rate.

87. ◎ A borrower obtains a home improvement loan secured by her house that is neither insured nor guaranteed by a government agency. She has obtained which type of loan?
    A. Wraparound
    B. Purchase-money
    C. Subordinated
    D. Conventional

88. The mortgage clause that permits the borrower to pay off the entire debt ahead of schedule without being charged a penalty is called a(n)
    A. acceleration clause.
    B. escalation clause.
    C. level-off-payment clause.
    D. prepayment clause.

89. ◎ A borrower goes to a savings association to obtain a $39,000 second mortgage on his home. Which of the following statements is *TRUE?*
    A. To create a valid mortgage loan, the borrower must sign two separate instruments, a mortgage and a note.
    B. A service charge of three points on this loan would be $300.
    C. This would be called a purchase-money mortgage.
    D. There would be a subordination clause in the second mortgage.

90. Mortgaged real property is generally conveyed by
    A. refinancing the loan.
    B. written approval of the mortgagee.
    C. delivery of a deed.
    D. satisfaction of the mortgage.

91. Which one of the following illustrates a voluntary transfer of legal title?
    A. Eminent domain
    B. Adverse possession
    C. Deed of trust
    D. Foreclosure

92. All of the following are true about a recorded mortgage instrument *EXCEPT* that it
    A. creates a specific lien.
    B. is a security device for a promissory note.
    C. secures the loan with the property.
    D. is a debenture.

93. Which of the following statements is *TRUE* concerning an amortized mortgage?
    A. There is a gradual decline in the monthly payments.
    B. The amount of the borrower's equity in the property is gradually reduced.
    C. It creates an unsecured loan.
    D. The last payment is equal to the third payment.

94. All of the following statements regarding a loan assumption are true *EXCEPT* that
    A. the grantee becomes liable for the original promissory note.
    B. both grantee and grantor are liable for repayment of the loan.
    C. if the grantee defaults, the grantor is secondarily liable.
    D. the grantor is released from liability.

95. Which of the following *BEST* describes the upset price?
    A. The lowest price offered in a foreclosure sale
    B. The price below which the property will not be sold
    C. The price that is the final bidding price
    D. A concealed price that beats out all others

96. ◎ In a real estate purchase, the buyer assumes the mortgage. On the closing statement, such assumption would appear as a
    A. debit to seller, credit to buyer.
    B. credit to seller, debit to buyer.
    C. credit to buyer and seller.
    D. debit to buyer and seller.

97. The buyers purchased a vacant lot under a 15-year mortgage, where they intend to build a residence in five years. From the buyer's point of view, the mortgage should contain which type of clause?
    A. Subrogation
    B. Release
    C. Subordination
    D. Escalation

98. ◎ Which of the following is directly involved in a nonjudicial foreclosure of real property?
    A. The public advertising and sale of mortgaged property
    B. The appointment of a commissioner
    C. Summons and complaint
    D. Court approval to sell

99. A buyer buys an older home for renovation that he or she expects to begin when he or she moves into the house in several years. The *BEST* mortgage to obtain would be a(n)
    A. open-end.
    B. blanket.
    C. package.
    D. piggyback.

100. A clause in a blanket mortgage that permits mortgagors to assign parcels of property covered by the mortgage on payment of a specific amount is *BEST* termed a
    A. partial assignment.
    B. release.
    C. novation.
    D. due-on-sale.

101. Which of the following statements is *TRUE* regarding similarities of a mortgage to a trust deed?
    A. They have the same number of parties.
    B. They have similar foreclosure processes.
    C. They transfer the same interest to the lender.
    D. They involve a promissory note.

102. Why would a seller *MOST* likely lend money to a buyer on a purchase-money mortgage?
    A. To obtain a secure investment
    B. To provide long-term income
    C. To facilitate the sale
    D. To obtain a high rate of interest

103. In an assumption-of-mortgage transaction, the seller typically pays for which one of the following?
    A. Deed
    B. Promissory note
    C. Mortgage
    D. All closing costs

104. A construction lender might require the lessor/owner to do what in order to borrow the money?
    A. Refinance
    B. Subordinate the fee
    C. Accelerate the loan
    D. Depreciate the fee

105. ◎ There is a $50,000 mortgage at 14 percent for 15 years; monthly payments are $664.80. The loan principal is reduced by 3.7 percent during the fifth year. How much interest is paid during the fifth year?
    A. $6,128
    B. $7,000
    C. $7,658
    D. $7,977

106. A loan in which the mortgagor receives monthly payments for life with the balance of the mortgage to be paid at death is called a(n)
    A. index mortgage.
    B. rollover mortgage.
    C. wraparound mortgage.
    D. reverse annuity mortgage.

107. Which of the following is *LEAST* likely to contain a partial amortization clause?
    A. Agreement of sale
    B. Wraparound mortgage
    C. Straight note
    D. Balloon mortgage

108. Which type of mortgage financing is designed for elderly homeowners?
    A. Growing equity mortgage
    B. Reverse annuity mortgage
    C. Interim loan
    D. Graduated payment mortgage

109. Which of the following would *MOST* likely trigger a due-on-sale or alienation clause in a mortgage?
    A. A one-year lease
    B. A transfer into trust
    C. A transfer to a spouse
    D. A foreclosure sale

110. A buyer has $120,000 equity in a duplex home. If the buyer buys a new home before the duplex sells, what type of loan would *MOST* likely be obtained?
    A. Package loan
    B. Blanket loan
    C. Swing loan
    D. Take-out loan

111. ◎ In comparing a growing equity mortgage (GEM) with a 30-year amortized loan, all of the following are true of the GEM loan *EXCEPT* that the GEM
    A. amortizes over a shorter period.
    B. total interest paid is less.
    C. equity grows more slowly.
    D. payments increase over term of loan.

112. On a foreclosure, which is *TRUE?*
    A. The mortgagor gets the balance of sale proceeds after all debts are paid.
    B. The mortgagor's attorney will get paid out of sales proceeds.
    C. The mortgagee will not recover attorney fees out of sales proceeds.
    D. The mortgagor has a two-year right of redemption.

113. A loan in which the lender cannot obtain a deficiency judgment on foreclosure is called
    A. nonrecourse.
    B. satisfaction.
    C. balloon.
    D. straight.

114. All of the following appear in a promissory note *EXCEPT*
    A. interest.
    B. points.
    C. term of lease.
    D. purchase price of property.

115. Under what type of program can a financial institution underwrite an FHA loan?
    A. Direct establishment
    B. Direct endorsement
    C. Direct capitalization
    D. Direct programming

116. All of the following are features of a reverse annuity mortgage *EXCEPT*
    A. negative amortization.
    B. the elderly borrower owns property free and clear.
    C. the lender pays out money each month.
    D. the property is security for repayment.

117. ◎ A secured loan in which the borrower can lose the property but is *NOT* personally liable for any deficiency judgment is called a(n)
    A. nonrecourse loan.
    B. adjustable loan.
    C. assumable loan.
    D. judgment loan.

ANSWERS

1. **B.** Without delivery of the deed, there would be no transfer. The existing mortgage could be paid off, assumed, or taken subject to.

2. **D.** This is also called a *release.* A reconveyance is used in a trust deed. Though a quitclaim deed would be possible, a satisfaction piece is more usual.

3. **A.** This clause is frequently found in second mortgages that allow the mortgagor to refinance the first mortgage. A recapture clause is found in shopping center percentage leases; a habendum clause is likely in a deed; and an escalation clause covers increases or decreases in payments.

4. **A.** Most states allow a deficiency judgment, but some states (such as California) have antideficiency laws that limit the recovery to the property itself.

5. **A.** Because foreclosure sale is an involuntary sale, the broker is not the procuring cause of the sale.

6. **B.** Another name for a release is a *satisfaction piece*. The estoppel certificate (also called *certificate of no defense*) is used when assigning a mortgage. It confirms the terms of the mortgagor's debt to prevent later dispute over any of the terms.

7. **A.** The note will accelerate on default. It is called a *due-on-sale* or *alienation clause* if the note will accelerate on a *transfer* of the property. This clause is also found in installment land contracts.

8. **D.** The title passes to the receiver in bankruptcy. The mortgagor still owes the debt, but lenders usually rely on the sale of the secured property to obtain reimbursement for the loan. As a secured creditor, the mortgagee would receive preference in the bankruptcy distribution.

9. **C.** This is especially true in a title-theory state. On full payment, the mortgagee will lose its conditional title in the secured property as a result of the defeasance clause.

10. **A.** The note evidences the debt and the mortgage transfers an interest in the secured property; thus the borrower, not the lender, must sign.

11. **B.** The lender can declare the entire amount due on default and then sue to foreclose.

12. **A.** After foreclosure, some states provide for a statutory right of redemption within one year after the foreclosure sale; other states provide for an equitable right of redemption only up to the actual foreclosure sale.

13. **B.** The trustor is the borrower who must sign; the beneficiary is the lender; and the holder of naked title is the trustee.

14. **D.** A wraparound is a junior mortgage; but because the lender puts out only the cash difference between the existing mortgage and the total loan, the interest rate tends to be lower than the prevailing rate (but is usually higher than the existing mortgage's rate). The wraparound mortgage is actually a junior mortgage that overstates its principal by the amount of the surviving, underlying prior mortgages (i.e., the principal balance of the wraparound loan includes the principal balances of all existing mortgages). For example, a buyer gets a mortgage for $140,000 at 9 percent, which wraps around the seller's existing mortgage of $100,000 at 7 percent, even though the current rate of interest is 11 percent. The wraparound lender puts up only $40,000 in cash and uses the buyer's monthly 9 percent payments to pay both the existing first mortgage ($100,000) and the wraparound loan ($40,000). It is like a consolidation loan, with the wraparound lender disbursing all the monthly payments.

15. **B.** The construction lender typically insists on being in first lien position. Choices (A) and (D) by definition are not first mortgages, and most seller loans are designed to help finance the difference between the buyer's first mortgage and the balance due on the purchase price.

16. **C.** The mortgage, not the note, is recorded because the note does not create an interest in real estate; also, lenders often do not want the terms of the loan made public.

17. **B.** The reduction certificate is used when a buyer assumes or takes title subject to a mortgage. The estoppel certificate is executed by the mortgagor to assist the mortgagee in assigning the loan.

18. **D.** Possession and title pass to the buyer but the seller retains a security interest pending full payment of the debt. Sellers usually do not restrict the buyer's right to seek junior financing.

19. **C.** Such a clause does make the borrower think twice about defaulting. Without this clause, the lender would have to bring suit each month that a scheduled payment was missed.

20. **C.** Another name for this is *satisfaction piece.*

21. **D.** Recordation determines priority of mortgage liens (in the absence of a subordination clause). Even if a mortgage is not recorded, the mortgagor is obligated under the note, for the debt is still effective between the borrower and the lender. An unrecorded mortgage is still valid against the mortgagor; it is just *not* valid against the claim of a good-faith second mortgagee who records first.

22. **A.** Blanket mortgages are often used in developing subdivisions. These mortgages should contain carefully worded partial release clauses to release individual lots from under the umbrella of the mortgage as they are sold.

23. **A.** The foreclosure sale would extinguish the security interest in the property but not necessarily the debt (there could be a deficiency judgment).

24. **B.** The mortgage creates the secured obligation; the note is evidence of the debt.

25. **B.** A deed of trust, like a mortgage, is a specific type of lien that involves a conditional conveyance of real property to a trustee to secure a debt.

26. **A.** Unless released, the seller (original mortgagor) is secondarily liable for payment of the debt; in a sense, the seller is a surety or guarantor. If the seller is released, this is called a *novation.*

27. **D.** Date of recordation determines priority. Here is an exception: If the earlier recorded mortgage contained a subordination clause, the latter mortgage would take priority.

28. **A.** A reduction certificate is signed by the mortgagee to show the terms of the loan to a buyer who is assuming or taking title subject to the loan.

29. **B.** Default would trigger the foreclosure process. When the debt is paid, the trustee conveys back to the borrower (trustor) by a reconveyance deed.

30. **B.** A term or a straight note is an interest-only note with the full principal balance due in one lump sum at maturity. Under choices (A), (C), and (D), there are payments to principal during the loan.

31. **A.** A balloon payment is the final payment in an amount that exceeds the regular monthly payment; it is not found in a fully amortized loan.

32. **B.** To hypothecate is to put up as security *without* surrendering possession (in a pledge there is a surrender of possession). To devise is to transfer real property by will.

33. **B.** It is subordinate to earlier mortgages and may be taken by the seller or any other lender.

34. **B.** Amortized notes include payments of principal and interest; notes are typically negotiable and thus easily transferable.

35. **B.** To secure the note, the lender obtains a mortgage. A financing statement is used in financing personal property under the Uniform Commercial Code.

36. **C.** Also called the *prepayment privilege clause,* prepayment is allowed if, for example, the monthly payment is listed as "$600 or more."

37. **B.** Release clauses enable the borrower to sell off subdivision parcels free and clear of the underlying blanket mortgage; these releases also are used in some condominium sales.

38. **C.** Conventional mortgages are usually considered by lending institutions to be non-government-assisted loans. Chattel mortgages involve a personal property loan transaction. There are many types of home financing alternatives.

39. **B.** Balloon payments are popular in installment land contracts and nonamortized purchase-money second financing.

40. **C.** Recordation determines priority, lacking a subordination agreement.

41. **B.** A tax sale is not voluntary; it results from failure to pay taxes. A deed of trust, like a mortgage, is a voluntary alienation (transfer) of real property to secure a loan.

42. **C.** The note evidences the debt and the mortgage secures it. Choice (B) defines any contract.

43. **B.** The lender is the mortgagee; the borrower is the mortgagor. Note the two *e*'s in *lender* and the two *o*'s in *borrower*.

44. **C.** On default, the buyer would lose the property but would not be obligated for the seller's loan (as he or she would if the loan had been "assumed").

45. **B.** The best answer is the trustor, who is also the borrower.

46. **B.** VA or FHA loans are also assumable with approval. Unless the parties agree otherwise, the terms of the assumed loan remain the same. The word *recasting* refers to changing the terms.

47. **A.** Without the note, the mortgage is not an effective lien. An appraisal report usually precedes the decision to make a loan. In the case of a home improvement loan, there would be no deed involved (choice (B)).

48. **B.** Any excess over the balance due the lender after a foreclosure sale belongs to the mortgagor after other expenses have been paid.

49. **A.** The modern version of the escalation clause is the variable-rate (or adjustable-rate) mortgage. Choice (B) is the acceleration clause.

50. **B.** An owner selling vacant land to a developer might take back a purchase-money mortgage and subordinate it to a construction loan so the developer can complete the project, and thus begin to repay the owner. Choice (A) is usury.

51. **C.** Popular in subdivision developments, blanket mortgages must be carefully checked for definite and unambiguous partial release provisions.

52. **D.** Both buyer and seller are personally liable, unlike in a "subject to" loan, choice (C). Seller is not relieved unless there is a novation, as there frequently is under "modern" assumptions.

53. **A.** Nonjudicial foreclosure is often permitted, provided the mortgage contains a power-of-sale clause. Statutory redemption periods, if any, usually do not exceed one year. There is, however, an equitable right of redemption up to the time of the foreclosure sale. As to choice (C), not all mortgages contain the right of "reinstatement."

54. **B.** In many states, to redeem the property, the borrower must pay back the entire debt, not just the overdue payments. The purpose of foreclosure is to cut off this right to redeem.

55. **B.** Unless it is a nonrecourse loan or there is antideficiency legislation, the mortgagee can seek a deficiency judgment, which could act as a general judgment lien when it is filed. The expenses are typically applied against the mortgagor's debt.

56. **D.** The mortgage transfers a security interest; thus, the transferee need not sign (just as a grantee usually does not need to sign the deed).

57. **D.** The mortgagee will not be able to obtain a deficiency judgment, however, if there is state antideficiency legislation or if the loan is a nonrecourse loan.

58. **A.** Note that in the early years of the loan most of the monthly payment is applied to interest and very little to principal.

59. **D.** The right and period of redemption are controlled by state law and cannot be waived by contract.

60. **B.** Although the principal amount and the rate of interest are the same, the fact that the payments are spread over five more years results in lower monthly payments. For example, on a $100,000 loan at 12 percent, the monthly payment on a 15-year amortization is $1,200.22. Each payment is $1,101.12 based on 20 years.

61. **D.** The acceleration clause benefits the lender; the escalation clause permits fluctuations in the interest rate to reflect changes in the money market.

62. **B.** The lender must check to see if there are any other liens on the property, because this

type of deed will not cut off the rights of other lienholders as does a foreclosure action.

63. **D.** Compare this with seller-assisted financing by means of an installment sales contract, in which the buyer gets equitable, not legal, title.

64. **B.** Such mortgages are not very popular today, especially because of the frequent transfer of mortgages in the secondary mortgage market. They usually can't exceed the original amount of the loan.

65. **D.** A deed of reconveyance goes back to the trustor from the trustee.

66. **D.** If secured by real property, a mortgage is also involved.

67. **B.** Choice (C) is a deed *in* trust.

68. **D.** The equitable right of redemption is that period up to the foreclosure sale. Many states allow a redemption period after a tax sale.

69. **A.** Choice (B) is a package mortgage.

70. **B.** The deed usually contains an assumption clause obligating the grantee to take on the grantor's obligations under the existing note and mortgage. There would be a new note and mortgage (or novation) if the seller were to be relieved of all liability.

71. **C.** It is important that purchasers of a mortgage in the secondary mortgage market obtain this estoppel certificate. Most mortgages have provisions requiring that the mortgagor execute an estoppel certificate on request of the mortgagee. The mortgagor states that he or she has no claims, set-offs, or defenses to assert against the debt.

72. **B.** An alienation clause is a specific type of acceleration clause (also called a *due-on-sale clause*). The defeasance clause terminates the lender's interest in the property upon full payment.

73. **C.** The estate of the deceased mortgagor is responsible for existing contracts and debts. Some mortgagors obtain a term life insurance policy to cover this situation.

74. **C.** Each point equals 1 percent of the loan amount. If the lender charged three points on a $60,000 loan involved in the purchase of an $80,000 property with $2,000 in closing costs, the charge for the points would be $1,800.

75. **D.** The loan is paid in installments, which are computed using a 25-year amortization with a balloon payment in ten years. A graduated payment mortgage is a loan for the full term.

76. **D.** Also called an *adjustable-rate mortgage.* A similar effect can be obtained by an escalation clause in a mortgage.

77. **A.** Technically, any loan to acquire the property is a purchase-money mortgage, although the term is most commonly treated as a seller-assisted loan.

78. **B.** The buyer is primarily liable, and the seller is secondarily liable. In a sale "subject to" the mortgage, the buyer is not liable to the lender.

79. **C.** The right to pay off a mortgage debt at any time up to the foreclosure sale is called the *equitable right of redemption.* Some states give an additional time after the foreclosure sale—this is called the *statutory right of redemption.*

80. **C.** The trustee merely holds the legal title as security for payment of the debt by the trustor/purchaser/borrower.

81. **B.** The lender is the mortgagee and usually would seek an assignment of rents as additional security when lending money secured by rental property.

82. **D.** The grantor selling subject to a loan remains primarily liable for the debt and secondarily liable as a surety in a loan assumption. The grantor of a quitclaim deed has the least exposure.

83. **D.** The mortgage lien is an encumbrance on the title. The facts given do not indicate any public or private restrictions on the property.

84. **B.** The interest rate on an adjustable-rate mortgage may increase or decrease, depending on the terms of the loan. If there is an increase, the monthly payments could stay the same but the term might be extended.

85. **D.** With a novation, there is a substitution of the new buyer for the seller, and the lender agrees to the release of liability of the seller.

86. **A.** Interest is paid in arrears; therefore, the payment due September 1 covers interest for the August period. The amount of the monthly payment applied to interest gradually decreases as the principal on the loan is slowly paid off.

87. **D.** The borrower has obtained a conventional home improvement loan. It is not a purchase-money loan because the funds are not used to purchase or acquire the property.

88. **D.** This is a prepayment privilege clause.

89. **A.** The mortgage, not the note, would be recorded. In choice (B), the charge would be $1,170.

90. **C.** Mortgaged property may be sold by assumption, subject to refinancing satisfaction, but in these cases, there must be transfer of legal title, as shown by delivery of a deed.

91. **C.** In a deed of trust, the borrower transfers legal title to a trustee as security for a loan from the beneficiary.

92. **D.** The mortgage is a lien on the property and is security for payment of the note (which is evidence of the debt). Debentures are unsecured notes.

93. **D.** Monthly payments are equal, but as the loan matures, the amount applied to principal increases (thus increasing the buyer's equity), and the amount applied to interest decreases.

94. **D.** The grantee is primarily liable, with the grantor being secondarily liable for the debt. A novation results in a full release.

95. **B.** In some foreclosure actions, the court determines an upset price (a bottom price) below which offers to buy will not be considered.

96. **A.** The buyer's assumption represents money the seller will not receive at closing (thus, a debit); it is how the buyer will pay a portion of the purchase price (thus, a credit).

97. **C.** To obtain a construction loan, the lender usually will require that the existing first mortgagee subordinate his or her loan position (i.e., to be junior) to the construction lender.

98. **A.** Some states permit a form of foreclosure in which the mortgaged property is sold at a public auction after proper notice of sale has been given in newspaper ads if the mortgage contains a power-of-sale clause. By statute, states may permit a period of redemption after the foreclosure sale (statutory right of redemption) or up to the time of the sale (equitable right of redemption).

99. **A.** Under an open-end mortgage the buyer can obtain additional monies for renovation later on—up to the amount of the original loan—without having to renegotiate a new mortgage.

100. **B.** A release clause, or partial release clause, will remove a specific parcel from the lien of the blanket mortgage. Partial assignments typically involve the transfer of all of the lease term as it applies to a portion of the leased premises.

101. **D.** The trust deed and mortgage are devices used to secure the repayment of a debt. The trust deed uses a trustee to hold title and has a more expeditious foreclosure mechanism.

102. **C.** While (A), (B), and (D) may all be factors the seller considers, the most popular reason for carryback financing is to facilitate the sale because this opens up the market to more potential buyers.

103. **A.** Seller usually pays for the deed. There is no need to prepare a new mortgage and note.

104. **B.** The security is more valuable if the lender has an interest in the fee simple as well as in the leasehold estate.

105. **A.** $664.80 \times 12 = \$7,977.60$. $\$50,000 \times 3.7\% = \$1,850$ principal reduction, less $\$7,977.60 = \$6,128$.

106. **D.** These have not proved to be very popular.

107. **C.** A straight note is for interest only.

108. **B.** The lender pays the borrower a monthly annuity secured by the equity in the home (ideal for elderly persons looking for monthly income). In a growing equity mortgage (A), the monthly payment amount gradually increases, which results in a faster paydown of the principal due (and thus an increase of growth in the equity).

109. **B.** Transfer into a trust is a *voluntary* movement of title.

110. **C.** A swing or bridge loan uses the equity in the unsold home as a part of the security for the new loan.

111. **C.** Monthly payments gradually increase, with more going to reduce principal and increase equity.

112. **A.** Any equity goes to the borrower/mortgagor.

113. **A.** The lender must look to the property to satisfy any default on the loan.

114. **D.** The purchase price is found in the sales contract; the note states the amount of the loan.

115. **B.** In 1983 the FHA set up a direct endorsement program to enable certain recognized lenders to handle the evaluation and loan qualification process, thus helping to reduce the red tape typically found in the FHA loan process.

116. **A.** The reverse annuity mortgage gives elderly homeowners a chance to borrow money against the equity in their homes even though they may have insufficient income to otherwise qualify for a loan. The loan is repaid either as of a specified date or upon the death of the borrower. A graduated payment mortgage is characterized by negative amortization.

117. **A.** A nonrecourse loan means the lender's only recourse in the event of default is to force a sale of the property. If there is a shortfall between the sales proceeds and the amount owed, the lender cannot seek recourse against the borrower. In some states, antideficiency legislation produces the same result (i.e., restricting the lender to the proceeds from the sale of the security).

Transfer of Property Ownership

This part contains questions on the topics of

- different ways of transferring title to real property;

- types of deeds;

- elements of adverse possession;

- the function of escrow to close a transaction;

- types of evidence of title; and

- recordation of documents in the public records

Expect 10 percent to 15 percent of the national portion of the examination to contain questions on the topics covered in Part D.

Acquisition of Title: Deeds

The most common way to acquire real property is voluntary alienation—transfer by way of a deed following the signing of a contract to purchase. The major types of deeds are the warranty deed and the quitclaim deed.

For a deed to effectively convey valid title to the grantee, the deed must be in writing, name a living grantee, contain an adequate description of the property, and be properly delivered during the lifetime of a competent grantor.

Questions in this chapter will test your comprehension of the following topics:

- Warranty and quitclaim deeds

- The importance of delivery and recording of deeds

- The essential elements of a valid deed

- Covenants found in a warranty deed

- Use of adverse possession to transfer title

KEY WORDS

Adverse possession: The acquiring of title to real property owned by someone else, by means of open, notorious, and continuous possession for the statutory period of time.

Bargain and sale deed: A deed that recites a consideration and conveys all of the grantor's interest in the property to the grantee.

Conveyance: The transfer of title to real property by means of a written instrument such as a deed or an assignment of lease.

Deed: A written instrument by which a property owner "grantor" transfers to a "grantee" an ownership in real property.

Grantee: The person who receives from the grantor a grant of real property.

Grantor: The person transferring title to, or an interest in, real property. A grantor must be competent to convey; thus, for example, an insane person cannot convey title to real property.

Habendum clause: That part of the deed beginning with the words "to have and to hold" following the granting clause and reaffirming the extent of ownership that the grantor is transferring.

Quitclaim deed: A deed of conveyance that operates, in effect, as a release of whatever interest the grantor has in the property; sometimes called a *release deed*.

Special warranty deed: A deed in which the grantor warrants or guarantees the title against only those defects arising during the period of his or her tenure and ownership of the property and not against defects existing before the time of his or her ownership.

Warranty deed: A deed in which the grantor fully warrants good clear title to the premises. Also called a *general warranty deed*.

MISTAKEN IDENTITY

The following words are often confused with one another. Note the difference in meaning of these mistaken identity words and phrases.

Grantor/Grantee: The *grantor* (seller) transfers legal title to the *grantee* (buyer) using a deed.

Covenant/Condition: A *covenant* is a promise to do something (as in a covenant of quiet enjoyment in a deed), whereas a *condition* is a contingency that must be met, otherwise a particular property right could be gained or lost.

Deed/Bill of sale: A *deed* transfers legal title to real property, whereas a *bill of sale* transfers legal title to personal property.

QUESTIONS

1. ◎ A quitclaim deed *ALWAYS* will convey good legal title to real property in which of the following cases?
   A. The grantor is living on the property at the time of the conveyance.
   B. The grantor has good legal title to the real property.
   C. The grantee has received a certificate of title from a licensed title company.
   D. The grantor acquired title under a forged deed.

2. The grantor delivers a signed deed to her attorney, but the grantee's name is omitted. The grantor dies before any name is inserted. The deed is
   A. invalid when made but valid when the grantee fills in his or her name.
   B. invalid when made but valid when recorded.
   C. valid if the deed is delivered to the grantee.
   D. invalid.

3. Hank executes a deed of his farm to Seth. Hank keeps the deed in his safe-deposit box. On his death, the box is opened, and attached to the deed is a note to give the deed to Seth. Who has title to the farm?
   A. Seth
   B. Hank's heirs
   C. The state
   D. Seth's heirs

4. A quitclaim deed is frequently used to
   A. remove a cloud on a title.
   B. remove an escrow.
   C. terminate a power of attorney.
   D. evict a tenant.

5. Following the execution of a sales contract, a deed usually is executed. To be valid, the deed must contain which of the following?
   A. Seller's name but no signature
   B. Buyer's name and signature
   C. Names of buyer and seller
   D. Date

6. When does legal title to real property pass from the seller to the buyer?
   A. On the date the deed is recorded
   B. When the closing statement has been signed
   C. When the deed is placed in escrow
   D. When the deed is delivered

7. A quitclaim deed transfers the interest of the
   A. grantee.
   B. mortgagor.
   C. grantor.
   D. lessee.

8. Which of the following is covered by the covenant against encumbrances in a general warranty deed?
   A. Undisclosed subsurface waterpipe easement
   B. Restrictive zoning ordinance
   C. Public restrictions
   D. Riparian rights of neighboring owners

9. For a deed to be valid, which of the following must be *TRUE?*
   A. The grantee must execute the deed.
   B. The deed must be delivered during the lifetime of the grantor.
   C. The deed must be dated.
   D. The grantee must have legal capacity to contract.

10. Effective delivery of a deed depends on
    A. the knowledge of its existence by the grantee.
    B. mere physical transfer of the deed to the grantee.
    C. the intention of the grantor.
    D. prior acknowledgment of the grantor's signature.

11. To be admissible to record in the appropriate public record office, a deed must be
    A. signed by grantor and grantee.
    B. a printed form.
    C. signed by the grantee.
    D. signed by the grantor.

12. ◎ A quitclaim deed may be used to accomplish all of the following *EXCEPT*
    A. transferring an interest to a cotenant in common.
    B. removing a cloud from title, such as a possible dower interest.
    C. warranty title forever.
    D. correcting record title.

13. For a deed to be valid, which of the following must be included in the deed?
    A. The exact consideration paid for the property
    B. The amount of the loan
    C. The grantor's age
    D. The grantee's name

14. A person to whom real estate is conveyed, the buyer, is also called the
    A. assignee.
    B. offeror.
    C. grantee.
    D. optionee.

15. ◎ Which one of the following situations would make a deed void?
    A. The grantor has signed under a power of attorney.
    B. The deed is made to a fictitious grantee.
    C. The grantee is not named but is sufficiently described in other terms.
    D. The signature of the grantor is spelled differently from the typed spelling on the deed.

16. For adverse possession, all of the following elements are required *EXCEPT*
    A. hostile.
    B. notorious.
    C. continuous.
    D. tacking.

17. ◎ A deed prepared and signed but *NOT* delivered is
    A. invalid as between the parties, but valid as to subsequent recorded interests.
    B. valid as between the parties.
    C. valid as between the parties, but invalid as to subsequent recorded interests.
    D. invalid as between the parties.

18. The word *hostile* as applied to adverse possession means that the
    A. tenant hates the landlord.
    B. possessor claims ownership, rejecting other claims.
    C. possessor will defend land by force if necessary.
    D. possessor has fenced off the land.

19. Deeds that limit the liability of the grantors to their own acts and all persons claiming by, through, and under them are known as
    A. special warranty deeds.
    B. general warranty deeds.
    C. quitclaim deeds.
    D. trust deeds.

20. In a valid deed, which of the following statements about the grantee is *CORRECT?*
    A. A deed may be used to convey title to a person with an assumed name.
    B. The grantee in a deed may be a fictitious person.
    C. The grantee must be of legal age.
    D. The grantee's name may be omitted from the body of the deed, just as long as his or her signature is present.

21. A private individual could acquire fee title by all of the following *EXCEPT*
    A. devise.
    B. adverse possession.
    C. demise.
    D. voluntary conveyance.

22. ◎ The presence of a corporate seal on a deed
    A. means that consideration was paid.
    B. implies that the proper or authorized person signed the deed.
    C. indicates that title is being conveyed to a corporation.
    D. indicates there has been a valid delivery.

23. A quitclaim deed provides which of the following warranties?
    A. Covenant of further assurance
    B. Covenant of quiet enjoyment
    C. Quiet title
    D. No warranties

24. All of the following are necessary to the validity of a deed *EXCEPT*
    A. grantor execution.
    B. delivery to grantee.
    C. recording the deed.
    D. designating the grantee.

25. The clause that defines or limits the quantity of the estate being conveyed is the
    A. partition clause.
    B. revocation clause.
    C. habendum clause.
    D. reversion clause.

26. For a deed to be valid, which of the following must occur?
    A. There must be manual delivery of the deed.
    B. The deed must be signed by the grantor and grantee and then recorded.
    C. The deed must have a habendum clause.
    D. The deed must be in writing.

27. To ascertain if title to private property can be acquired by adverse possession, one must check
    A. state law.
    B. clouds on the title.
    C. with a previous owner.
    D. any previously recorded deeds.

28. ◎ Hanna hands Connie a deed with the intent to pass title and asks Connie not to record the deed until Hanna dies. When is the deed valid?
    A. The deed is valid on Hanna's death.
    B. The deed is valid immediately.
    C. It is void.
    D. The deed is valid when Connie records the deed.

29. Which of the following deeds offers the *LEAST* protection to the grantee?
    A. Bargain and sale
    B. Special warranty
    C. General warranty
    D. Quitclaim

30. All of the following are necessary to acquire title by adverse possession *EXCEPT*
    A. hostile use.
    B. continuous use against the will of the owner for the statutory period.
    C. payment of just compensation.
    D. having claim or color of title.

31. A declaration made by a person to an official stating that a deed has been freely and voluntarily executed is called an
    A. acknowledgment.
    B. authorization.
    C. authentication.
    D. execution.

32. Which of the following parties is in the weakest position against a claim of title by a stranger?
    A. A nonoccupant holder of a warranty deed
    B. A nonoccupant holder of an unrecorded quitclaim deed
    C. One who holds an unrecorded deed
    D. One who holds a recorded quitclaim deed to the property

33. If the grantor delivers a deed to the grantee in which the name of the grantee has been left out inadvertently, the deed is
    A. invalid.
    B. voidable.
    C. valid.
    D. forged.

34. Deeds may be prepared by which of the following?
    A. A licensed appraiser
    B. A lawyer or the owner of the property
    C. A licensed salesperson
    D. The principal's broker only

35. When buyers use a quitclaim deed to extinguish their interest in a recorded agreement of sale, the quitclaim deed should be signed by the
    A. vendor.
    B. vendee.
    C. original notary.
    D. broker.

36. The recording of a warranty deed
    A. guarantees title.
    B. insures ownership.
    C. verifies title.
    D. constitutes constructive notice of ownership.

37. ◉ Samantha signs a deed of her property to Polly and delivers it to a neutral escrow company with irrevocable instructions to deliver it to Polly on Samantha's death. On Samantha's death, what is the status of the property's title?
    A. The property passes to Samantha's heirs.
    B. The property passes to Polly.
    C. It escheats to the state because there was no will.
    D. Polly will receive only a life estate in the property.

38. In the transfer of real property by deed, ownership changes hands when the deed has been
    A. signed.
    B. delivered.
    C. recorded.
    D. notarized.

39. If a deed to a property were drawn to a grantee and he died prior to the date of the deed's delivery, which of the following statements would be *TRUE?*
    A. The property would revert to government ownership by escheat.
    B. The property would become part of the grantee's estate and be passed on to his heirs.
    C. The deed would be considered invalid.
    D. The deed would be considered valid.

40. Of the following, which statute or act creates the need for a deed to be in writing?
    A. Statute of descent
    B. Recording Act
    C. Statute of frauds
    D. Statute of limitations

41. The covenant in a deed that states that the grantor has full possession of the premises in fee simple (or any other estate the grantor purports to convey) is called the covenant of
    A. seisin.
    B. habendum.
    C. quiet enjoyment.
    D. further assurance.

42. ◉ The covenant against encumbrances in a deed of conveyance warrants against the existence of all of the following undisclosed matters *EXCEPT*
    A. mortgages against the land.
    B. judgment liens against the land.
    C. easements that adversely affect the land.
    D. zoning ordinances that limit the use of the land.

43. Which of the following is *TRUE* relating to a conveyance of real property?
    A. An illiterate grantor is incompetent.
    B. A conveyance by an unmarried minor transfers absolute title.
    C. A grantor cannot sign with an "X."
    D. A grantee can be a minor.

44. To convey title to real property, a deed must contain which of the following?
    A. Words of conveyance
    B. An offer and acceptance
    C. Grantor's marital status
    D. Acknowledgments of grantor and grantee

45. Which of the following persons must sign a deed for it to be valid?
    A. Grantor (seller) or transferor
    B. Grantee or transferee
    C. Broker handling the transaction
    D. Lender if there is financing involved

46. Which of the following statements regarding the recording of deeds is *TRUE* in most states?
    A. An unrecorded deed is not enforceable between grantor and grantee.
    B. A deed must be signed by the grantor to be recorded.
    C. A deed with the grantee's name omitted is acceptable for recording.
    D. An unacknowledged deed is void.

47. As far as its validity between grantor and grantee is concerned, a deed that is *NOT* dated, acknowledged, or recorded is
    A. invalid because of these omissions.
    B. void.
    C. revocable by the grantor.
    D. valid despite these omissions.

48. A claim for adverse possession is *MOST* nearly valid if the
    A. occupant makes improvements, fences the area, and cultivates the land.
    B. claim is under the mistake of right.
    C. person occupies the premises for the statutory period with or without the owner's consent.
    D. possession is hostile against the owner.

49. Which of the following is an essential element of a valid deed?
    A. Legal description of the property
    B. Grantee who is of age and of sound mind
    C. Recording
    D. Acknowledgment

50. Marketable title to real property is *LEAST* likely to be conveyed
    A. to a minor.
    B. by a quitclaim deed.
    C. by a minor.
    D. by a special warranty deed.

51. A valid deed in completion of a sales contract must be signed by the
    A. buyer.
    B. seller.
    C. buyer and seller.
    D. seller and listing agent.

52. ◎ A valid deed must contain which of the following groups of elements?
    A. Competent grantor, valuable consideration, habendum clause
    B. Property description, words of conveyance, covenants of title, execution
    C. Habendum clause, grantor's signature, delivery, and acceptance
    D. Named grantee, competent grantor, delivery, grantor's signature

53. A deed signed only by the grantor is
    A. invalid until recorded.
    B. valid, and title will pass when the deed is delivered.
    C. valid only when recorded.
    D. invalid as far as subsequent purchasers are concerned.

54. A document in which legal title to real property is transferred from one person to another is a
    A. contract of sale.
    B. lease.
    C. deed.
    D. listing.

55. In a deed the grantee must
    A. be of sound mind and memory.
    B. be of legal age.
    C. be named.
    D. sign the deed.

56. A deed whereby the grantor makes certain covenants and warrants to defend against certain claims that arose only during the period of the grantor's ownership is a
    A. quitclaim deed.
    B. general warranty deed.
    C. nominal deed.
    D. special warranty deed.

57. Deeds that purport to convey an interest but make no warranty of good title are called
    A. bargain and sale deeds.
    B. quitclaim deeds.
    C. habendum deeds.
    D. release deeds.

58. All of the following deeds are valid *EXCEPT* a deed to a(n)
    A. partnership.
    B. actual person under an assumed name.
    C. fictitious human person.
    D. foreign corporation.

59. Which of the following statements is *TRUE* concerning a general warranty deed?
    A. It must be signed by the grantee if he or she is a trust beneficiary.
    B. It insures title.
    C. The grantor's warranty is limited to his or her own acts only during the time he or she was in possession of the title.
    D. It is the most protective deed a grantee can receive.

60. All of the following may affect the validity of a deed *EXCEPT*
    A. proper signature.
    B. lack of money consideration.
    C. delivery.
    D. competent grantor.

61. At which point in a real estate transaction does legal title to real property pass?
    A. Execution of option
    B. Exercise of option
    C. Delivery of agreement of sale
    D. Delivery of deed

62. Which of the following statements is *TRUE* concerning recording a deed?
    A. A forged deed is made valid by recording.
    B. A delivered deed is not valid until it is recorded.
    C. A deed must be signed by grantor and grantee to be recorded.
    D. Recording is not needed to make a deed valid.

63. A warranty deed would be used to convey all the following *EXCEPT* a
    A. fee simple estate.
    B. life estate.
    C. less-than-freehold estate.
    D. fee conditional estate.

64. ◎ Clarence delivers a valid deed to Benjamin, who fails to record the deed. Benjamin then loses the deed and dies with Clarence in an accident before it is found. Who owns the property?
    A. Clarence
    B. Benjamin's heirs
    C. The government
    D. Clarence's heirs

65. The buyer should keep the original recorded deed because
    A. it is the only evidence of title.
    B. if lost, the buyer loses title.
    C. it is needed to transfer title.
    D. it is proof of title.

66. The two parties involved are most likely to sign all of the following documents *EXCEPT* the
    A. purchase contract.
    B. listing.
    C. lease.
    D. warranty deed.

67. ◎ Which of the following statements regarding a bargain and sale deed is *TRUE?*
    A. It transfers possession but not legal title.
    B. It is used when the grantor is unsure whether he or she has good title.
    C. It contains a covenant of seisin.
    D. It has no covenants, but it does have an implication that the grantor has good title.

68. ◎ For which of the following reasons would a grantor decide to use a special rather than a general warranty deed?
    A. The grantor is unsure whether there are any encumbrances on the title.
    B. The grantor wants to limit liability to defects occurring during ownership.
    C. The grantor wants to give as many warranties as possible.
    D. The grantor is aware of recent defects in the title.

69. Which of these statements about deeds is *TRUE?*
    A. The special warranty deed contains the most covenants.
    B. The quitclaim deed is no different from a bargain and sale deed.
    C. The quitclaim deed gives the least protection to the grantee.
    D. The general warranty deed offers the least liability to the grantor.

70. ◎ One tenant in common attempts to convey the entire fee simple interest in the property to a grantee by using a general warranty deed. Which covenant in the deed would be violated?
    A. Covenant of further assurance
    B. Covenant of seisin
    C. Covenant of quiet enjoyment
    D. No covenants violated

71. On examination of the public records, the examiner discovers a deed with an assumption of mortgage. Which of the following would *MOST* likely not be found in the deed?
    A. A granting clause
    B. Grantor's signature
    C. Grantor's age
    D. Grantee's signature

72. All of the following are true regarding a transfer of title by adverse possession *EXCEPT*
    A. the transfer of title is governed by state law.
    B. the transfer is involuntary.
    C. the transfer is voluntary.
    D. a prescriptive period is involved.

73. A deed is signed by a grantor on Sunday and delivered to the grantee on Tuesday. Which of the following statements is *TRUE?*
    A. The deed is invalid.
    B. The deed is not acceptable for recordation.
    C. The deed is voidable.
    D. The deed is effective to transfer title.

74. A grantor is willing to make the standard covenants of good title, but wants to limit her liability to claims arising during the ownership term. The grantor should execute which type of deed?
    A. General warranty
    B. Gift
    C. Quitclaim
    D. Special warranty

75. All of the following are likely to contain a legal description of a parcel of real property *EXCEPT* a
    A. deed.
    B. tax statement.
    C. mortgage.
    D. preliminary title report.

76. Which of the following documents is *MOST* likely to be incorporated by reference in a warranty deed?
    A. Power of attorney
    B. Bill of sale
    C. Declaration of restrictions
    D. Assignment of lease

77. Of the following terms, which does *NOT* describe the type of occupancy needed for adverse possession?
    A. Open and notorious
    B. Continuous
    C. Exclusive
    D. Lawful

78. Which of the following statements *BEST* describes the covenant of quiet enjoyment in a general warranty deed?
    A. Grantee will not be disturbed by unnecessary noise.
    B. Guarantor will not enter the property without prior notice.
    C. Guarantor has the rights, title, and ownership that he or she claims to have.
    D. Guarantor will pay for any damages caused by improper drafting of the deed.

79. For adverse possession to be effective, all of the following must be present *EXCEPT*
    A. uninterrupted and continuous possession.
    B. open and notorious possession.
    C. occupied by original adverse possessor.
    D. exclusive and hostile possession.

80. ◎ A deed has been properly escrowed with an attorney, and closing is scheduled for 13 days later. If the seller dies before closing, when does legal title pass?
    A. Title passed when the deed was placed into escrow.
    B. Title passes when and if the estate provides another deed.
    C. Because the escrow dies with the seller, no deed or legal title will pass at closing.
    D. Title passes on closing.

81. ◎ A property is sold at an execution sale by way of a sheriff's deed. What type of warranties does the grantee receive?
    A. Covenant of further assurance
    B. None, because the sheriff has no grant of authority
    C. General warranties of title
    D. Implied warranty of good title and quiet enjoyment

ANSWERS

1. **B.** Quitclaim deeds transfer the interest of the grantor, *if any*. For example, a trespasser living on the property could not convey good title, but the real owner could. The title company could be mistaken.

2. **D.** A valid deed must contain the names of the grantor and the grantee; the grantee's name should be filled in by the grantor or her agent. The attorney does not have authority to fill in the deed after the grantor's death. Recording does not make an invalid deed valid. Delivery must occur during the life of the grantor.

3. **B.** There is no delivery; that is, Hank did not give up *control* over the deed during his lifetime as he would have if he had handed it to Seth or put it into an escrow. To accomplish his purpose, Hank should have prepared a will that, unless revoked, would have the effect of transferring title on Hank's death.

4. **A.** A quitclaim deed might be used if there is doubt as to whether some distant heirs of a grantor have a valid claim. To clear the title, the heirs might be asked to execute quitclaim deeds. Other uses would be to remove possible dower or encroachment claims.

5. **C.** These are both essential elements to a valid deed, as are delivery and acceptance and legal description. Also, it must be in writing and signed by the grantor.

6. **D.** Delivery is the key; recording is not necessary, though it is strongly recommended.

7. **C.** The title of the grantor is transferred to the grantee, regardless of the type of deed.

8. **A.** Because the easement was not disclosed, the grantee could recover for the loss in value caused by this easement (an encumbrance). Zoning laws, public restrictions, and riparian rights are matters of public knowledge and therefore are not covered under the covenant against encumbrances.

9. **B.** Only the grantor need sign unless the grantee assumes some obligation, as in a loan assumption. Only the grantor need be competent.

10. **C.** The grantor can hand it to the grantee with instructions to have it reviewed by an attorney—thus, (B) is false. The grantee's acceptance is often presumed when the grantee had no knowledge about the deed (before the grantor's death)—thus, (A) is false. Acknowledgment is generally necessary for recording, but deeds do not have to be recorded to be valid, just delivered—thus, (D) is false. In all cases, the grantor must possess the mental intention to transfer legal title to the grantee for a valid delivery to have been accomplished.

11. **D.** Only the grantor need sign a deed.

12. **C.** A quitclaim deed contains no warranties. One cotenant often transfers his or her entire interest to another cotenant by way of a quitclaim deed. A title report may reveal the lack of a wife's release of dower in some conveyance in the chain of title—a quitclaim deed signed by the spouse can cure this title defect.

13. **D.** Only sales contracts *require* the actual consideration, although fiduciary deeds do state the actual consideration. Often, deeds just state a nominal consideration. While marital status may be required by state law to record a valid deed, it is not needed to make the deed valid. A deed is not valid unless a grantee is named, although a deed to someone's "youngest sister" is adequate to identify the grantee.

14. **C.** The buyer may be the offeror in a sales contract. As far as a conveyance is concerned, the buyer is the grantee. One who receives real property by gift (donee) or by devise (devisee) also is called the *grantee*.

15. **B.** There must be a grantee in existence (e.g., a properly formed corporation). Grantors sometimes use assumed names for business purposes; such use may cause title searching problems, but delivery depends on the grantor's intention, not the name used. A deed to "John Smith and wife" would be adequate, even though the wife's name hasn't been given.

16. **D.** *Tacking* refers to meeting the continuous time element by linking together successive periods of possession by different occupants, such as a father's four years added to his son's succeeding ten years.

17. **D.** Without delivery, there is no valid deed. The undelivered deed is invalid as between the parties and invalid as to any other interests in the property.

18. **B.** A person who occupies the property with the consent of the landowner could not assert an adverse possession claim. This explains why tenants in common usually cannot claim adverse possession against each other unless there is a clear ouster by one tenant.

19. **A.** Special warranty deeds are frequently used by fiduciaries such as guardians and trustees. In a general warranty deed, the warranties extend to defects arising even before the grantor acquired title—fiduciaries will not usually assume this risk.

20. **A.** While the grantee can use a fictitious name, it must be a person in existence (i.e., you could not convey your property to Mickey Mouse or your pet poodle). One could, however, transfer property to a trust with directions to the trustee to allow the poodle to live there in regal splendor.

21. **C.** Demise is a conveyance for years, as in a lease. Devise is a gift of real property by a decedent's last will and testament. Adverse possession requirements vary according to state law but involve a hostile claim to land of another for a definite minimum period of time.

22. **B.** A corporate grantor may use a seal, although a seal is usually no longer a legal requirement. In ancient times, deeds were sealed and not signed.

23. **D.** There are no warranties in a quitclaim deed. These warranties are found in the general warranty deed.

24. **C.** Although recording is not necessary for the validity of a deed, prudent grantees will record to give constructive notice to third parties and thus protect their interest.

25. **C.** Also called the *to have and to hold clause,* the habendum clause is customarily included in a deed. It indicates that the grantor is conveying, for example, a fee simple or life estate.

26. **D.** Delivery in escrow could be sufficient; deeds need not be signed by the grantee or recorded to be valid.

27. **A.** Each state has different rules concerning adverse possession. For example, California requires 5 years of continuous, hostile possession, whereas Hawaii requires 20 years. Also, one may acquire title even though there are clouds on the title.

28. **B.** Delivery is effected by the grantor's intention, not by recording. Here, Connie received title but simply did not record it. Recording is not necessary to validate a deed.

29. **D.** The correct choice (D) is followed in order of increasing protection by (A), then (B), then (C). In a bargain and sale deed, there are no warranties, but the grantor does assert ownership of title.

30. **C.** Just compensation is involved in cases of eminent domain. "Color of title" would pertain to a situation where one is in possession under a defective deed, such as a forged or an improperly delivered deed.

31. **A.** Acknowledgments are usually taken by a notary public and are partially designed to eliminate forgery of documents. Therefore, notaries should require proper identification. Acknowledgments also are evidence that the document is authentic.

32. **B.** This grantee has given no constructive notice of the rights of recording or possession and has no warranties to assert against the grantor in the event the stranger proves to have a superior title.

33. **A.** Only the grantor or the grantor's authorized agent can fill in the essential element of the grantee's name. Until such time, the deed is void (not voidable), because it is missing an essential element.

34. **B.** Preparing a deed *for another* can be done only by a lawyer in most states. However, a few states do allow the use of standard forms for deeds that can be completed by title companies.

35. **B.** This quitclaim deed will release from the record title any trace of the buyer's (vendee's) equitable title.

36. **D.** The whole world now is charged with notice of the grantee's rights and the contents of the deed. A title insurance policy is used to ensure good title.

37. **B.** Most courts will relate delivery back to the date when the deed was first put into escrow, and they will hold that there was a valid delivery during Samantha's life. In effect, this legal fiction of the courts holds that Polly had title but Samantha kept a life estate.

38. **B.** Execution is not enough, and recording and acknowledgment are not required to make a deed effective. Delivery is the key. Delivery by a properly appointed escrow agent acting for the grantor is effective.

39. **C.** Delivery must take place within the grantee's lifetime; otherwise the deed is invalid. Proper delivery includes acceptance by the named grantee.

40. **C.** An old English statute (1677) adopted in differing forms in all jurisdictions requires that to be enforceable, the transfer of any interest in real property must be in writing and signed by the party to be charged.

41. **A.** Thus, if a grantor asserts ownership of a fee simple yet owns only a life estate, there would be a breach of the covenant of seisin (also spelled seizin).

42. **D.** Zoning ordinances are matters of public knowledge that are not covered by the covenant against encumbrances.

43. **D.** The *grantee* can be incompetent or a minor. An illiterate *grantor* may sign by a "mark" that should be witnessed. Although some states treat a minor's deed as being voidable, most treat it as being void.

44. **A.** Sales contracts (not deeds) need to contain a meeting of the minds, as evidenced by an offer and acceptance. (C) and (D) may be required to *record* a deed.

45. **A.** Only the grantor need sign, unless the grantee is assuming the mortgage.

46. **B.** The unrecorded deed is valid between the parties but may be unenforceable against a subsequent purchaser for value who records first. The acknowledged signature of the grantor is a requirement for recordation.

47. **D.** The date is useful to prove when it was delivered, but it is not required, nor is recording or acknowledgment.

48. **D.** Hostile claim is the key. The occupant under (A) could be a lessee, and (C) is wrong because adverse possession cannot be with the owner's consent.

49. **A.** A street address is usually insufficient as a legal description; thus, a metes-and-bounds, a subdivision lot and block number, or a government survey system description should be used. The grantor must be of age and of sound mind. The grantee could be a mentally deficient minor when title is passed but would need a guardian appointed to later transfer the interest.

50. **C.** Provided the grantor of the quitclaim deed had good title, that good title could be transferred, although a grantee would be wise to inquire why the grantor is not giving any warranties of title. If there is any doubt of a clear title, obtaining a title insurance policy is recommended. A deed by a minor is voidable. A guardian must be appointed and empowered by the court to convey.

51. **B.** The seller is the grantor; the grantee (buyer) need not sign.

52. **D.** Deeds need not contain a valuable consideration (it could be good consideration, such as love and affection), a habendum clause, or covenants of title (quitclaim).

53. **B.** The grantee need not sign, but there must be delivery; recording is not necessary, but is recommended.

54. **C.** A contract of sale transfers equitable interest; a lease transfers possession; a listing employs a broker to solicit prospective buyers for the seller's property.

55. **C.** It is the grantor who must be competent and who must sign. The grantee merely must be identified and in existence.

56. **D.** The quitclaim deed contains no specific covenants; the general warranty deed covers claims arising from defects that existed even before the grantor acquired title.

57. **A.** A bargain and sale deed may be used by a grantor who has good title but does not want to make any warranties with respect to title. In this sense, it is slightly more beneficial to the grantee than a quitclaim deed (which is often used when grantees are unsure whether they have any title to a property).

58. **C.** The grantee must exist at the time of delivery. Thus, a deed to a grantor's grandchildren is not valid if the grantor is only ten years old at delivery.

59. **D.** Trust beneficiaries do not have the power to sign contracts or other documents involving the trust; only the trustee has that power. Trustees sign a special warranty deed, not a general warranty deed. Title insurance, not the deed, would insure the title.

60. **B.** It could be a gift deed involving only good consideration. Only contracts need valuable consideration; deeds are conveyances.

61. **D.** In (A), (B), and (C) the buyer may receive some equitable title, but the buyer will receive legal title only when the deed is delivered.

62. **D.** While deeds should be recorded, recording is not legally required to make them valid. Note that recording will not validate an otherwise invalid deed.

63. **C.** The deed should state in the granting clause or the habendum clause which type of estate is being conveyed. This is important because a life estate terminates on death. Choice (C) is a lease.

64. **B.** In most states, once delivery has taken place, Clarence no longer would have an interest in Benjamin's property. In any dispute with Clarence's heirs, Benjamin's heirs would have the burden of proving delivery was made (a difficult but not impossible burden).

65. **D.** While a courthouse record is usually adequate evidence, the production of the deed is one way to prove title. While recording is not usually mandatory, a recorded copy will aid the grantee in proving title if the original or the courthouse record is lost or destroyed.

66. **D.** A deed is a conveyance that must be signed by the grantor. The listing is signed by both seller and broker; the lease by a landlord and tenant; and the purchase contract by a buyer and seller.

67. **D.** A bargain and sale deed transfers legal title. If the grantor is unsure of the title, a bargain and sale deed should not be used. The grantor should use a quitclaim deed, because there is an implication of good title when a bargain and sale deed is used.

68. **B.** The special warranty deed restricts liability to defects occurring after the seller acquired title, whereas the general warranty deed is a warranty "forever" that covers prior defects as well.

69. **C.** As far as the grantor's liability is concerned, the general warranty deed gives the most exposure; then the special warranty deed (covers only the time the grantor owned the property); then the quitclaim deed (with no liability).

70. **B.** Because the grantor does not have the complete estate, the other tenants in common would have to join in the deed. Here the grantor would be liable under the covenant of seisin, because the grantor is not well seised of the *whole* estate.

71. **C.** A granting clause would distinguish the deed from a mortgage. The grantee signs the deed, promising to pay the loan obligation.

72. **C.** Each jurisdiction has its own particular time requirements, but most agree on the essential elements of open, notorious, continuous (tacking is allowed), and, most important, hostile possession.

73. **D.** Deeds signed on Sunday are just as valid as those signed on any other day of the week and will be accepted for recordation on any day the public record office is open for business.

74. **D.** The general warranty covers claims arising prior to as well as during the grantor's ownership, whereas a special warranty deed covers only claims arising by, through, or under the actions of the grantor. The quitclaim deed makes no covenants of title, and the gift deed usually does not contain all the standard covenants of title.

75. **B.** Deeds and mortgages are conveyances of real property; therefore, they must contain a legal description of the property. The title report must describe the particular property it covers. The tax statement generally lists just the address or tax identification number.

76. **C.** It is common practice among subdividers to record a master declaration of restrictions on the permitted uses in the subdivision. They then refer to this declaration rather than retyping all the restrictions on each deed.

77. **D.** The occupancy is technically a trespass, and if it is continuous for the statutory period, title is acquired by way of adverse possession. If the occupant were on the property with the owner's permission, then the "hostile" element would be missing.

78. **C.** If, for example, the guarantor (grantor) did not have good title because the prior deed was forged, then the grantee could sue the guarantor for breach of the covenant of quiet enjoyment. Choice (D) describes the covenant of further assurances.

79. **C.** The possession must be open, actual, continuous, and hostile (POACH), as well as exclusive (or continuous, actual, notorious, open, and exclusive (CANOE)). A successor in interest to the original adverse possessor (for example, through a purchase agreement or will) can "tack on" his or her possession to the original period of possession to meet the statutory period.

80. **D.** The rule is that a deed is valid only if the grantor is alive at the time of delivery. When death occurs during escrow, most courts will create the legal fiction that delivery occurred when the deed was first deposited in escrow, at which time the grantor was alive. Although delivery relates back, actual passing of legal title does not take place until closing.

81. **B.** The sheriff's deed is effective to transfer title to satisfy a court judgment. The sheriff has no authority to issue any warranties. The property is transferred in "as is" condition.

Settlement Procedures: Escrow, Evidence of Title, and Recording

The fact that a seller can produce a deed to the property is not always adequate proof of ownership, and it clearly is not enough to satisfy a lender. The best practice is to require a preliminary title policy to ascertain the degree of ownership and the existence of any encumbrances in the recorded chain of title. At closing, the buyer should acquire a title insurance policy.

Recording is the act of entering into the public records the written instruments affecting the title to real property, such as deeds, mortgages, options, and assignments. State recording laws give legal priority to those interests that are recorded first. Proper recordation gives constructive notice to the world of the existence of the recorded document and its contents. Recording permits, rather than requires, that documents be recorded—remember, "first to record is first in right."

Recording does not make valid an otherwise invalid document, nor does failure to record make invalid an otherwise valid document. Possession gives constructive notice, so it is important to check whether a person is occupying under a lease or some claim of ownership.

The questions in this chapter test your comprehension of the following topics:

■ The purpose and effect of the state recording law

■ The different types of evidence of title

■ Key features of a title insurance policy

■ The role of an escrow in real estate transactions

■ The federal Real Estate Settlement Procedures Act (RESPA)

K E Y   W O R D S

Abstract of title: A concise, summarized history of the title to a specific parcel of real property, together with a statement of all liens and encumbrances affecting the property. The abstract of title does not guarantee or ensure the validity of the title of the property. It merely discloses those items about the property that are of public record and thus does not reveal such things as encroachments, forgeries, and the like.

Chain of title: The recorded history of matters that affect the title to a specific parcel of real property, such as ownership, encumbrances, and liens, usually beginning with the original recorded source of the title.

Clear title: Title to property that is free from liens, defects, or other encumbrances, except those that the buyer has agreed to accept, such as mortgage to be assumed, the ground lease of record, and the like; established title; title without clouds.

Cloud on title: Any document, claim, unreleased lien, or encumbrance that may impair or injure the title to property or make the title doubtful because of its apparent or possible validity.

Constructive notice: Notice of certain facts that is implied by law to a person because he or she could have discovered the fact by reasonable diligence or by inquiry into public records.

Escrow: The process by which money and/or documents are held by a disinterested third person (a "stakeholder") until the satisfaction of the terms and conditions of the escrow instructions (as prepared by the parties to the escrow).

Marketable title: Good or clear title reasonably free from risk of litigation over possible defects; also referred to as *merchantable title*. Marketable title need not, however, be perfect title.

Quiet title action: A circuit court action intended to establish or settle the title to a particular property, especially where there is a cloud on the title.

Recording: The act of entering into the book of public records the written instruments affecting the title to real property, such as deeds, mortgages, contracts of sale, options, assignments, and the like. Proper recordation imparts constructive notice to all the world of the existence of the recorded document and its contents.

Settlement: The act of adjusting and prorating the various credits, charges, and settlement costs to conclude a real estate transaction.

Title insurance: A comprehensive contract of indemnity under which the title company agrees to reimburse the insured for any loss if title is not as represented in the policy.

Title search: An examination of the public records to determine what, if any, defects there are in the chain of title.

MISTAKEN IDENTITY

The following words are often confused with one another. Note the difference in meaning of these mistaken identity words and phrases.

Chain of title/Cloud on title: The *chain of title* reveals the succession of owners in the history of a property, whereas a *cloud on title* is a defect or impairment in the title.

Quiet enjoyment/Quiet title: *Quiet enjoyment* is the right to uninterrupted use of the property, whereas *quiet title* is the name of a legal action to prove valid title to real property.

Acknowledgment/Affidavit: An *acknowledgment* is a formal declaration by the signer of a document, whereas an *affidavit* is a sworn statement that the facts contained in the affidavit are true and correct.

QUESTIONS

1. The chronological record of all conveyances and encumbrances affecting the recorded title to real property is known as a
   A. title insurance policy.
   B. chain of title.
   C. cloud on title.
   D. title report.

2. Which of the following statements regarding title insurance is *TRUE?*
   A. When a lender requires an American Land Title Association (ALTA) extended policy of title insurance to cover its interest, the policy is not assignable.
   B. When a buyer acquires title insurance to protect his or her equity, the policy may be passed on to the next buyer when the property is later sold.
   C. It protects the seller from negligence by the title or abstract company doing the search.
   D. It protects against losses suffered owing to defects in the title.

3. The standard form title insurance policy insures against
   A. governmental actions.
   B. forgery of a deed.
   C. rights of parties in possession.
   D. water and mineral rights.

4. When a title search reveals that there is a broken chain of title, this is *BEST* cured by
   A. a quitclaim deed.
   B. a general warranty deed.
   C. partition.
   D. a quiet title proceeding.

5. A system of land title registration in which the state guarantees title is the
   A. Pennsylvania system.
   B. Torrens title system.
   C. Colorado system.
   D. regular system.

6. The *BEST* way to discover a flaw in the recorded title to a piece of real property is by
   A. calling the county surveyor.
   B. taking out property insurance.
   C. undertaking a search of title.
   D. hiring a lawyer.

7. For a prospective buyer of real estate to investigate the validity of the title, the buyer should request a(n)
   A. survey.
   B. title search.
   C. estoppel certificate.
   D. warranty deed.

8. A broker finds a prospective buyer for a single-family dwelling, and the subject of title insurance has come up. The buyer wants the greatest owner protection available. Which of the following should the broker recommend?
   A. Certificate of title
   B. Standard coverage policy of title insurance
   C. Abstract of title
   D. Extended coverage policy of title insurance

9. When a title insurance company issues an ALTA extended policy, such a policy usually extends beyond the risks normally insured under the standard policy to include all of the following *EXCEPT*
   A. unrecorded mechanics' liens.
   B. unrecorded physical easements.
   C. the effect of zoning regulations.
   D. the rights of parties in possession.

10. Which of the following types of evidence of title gives the *LEAST* protection to a buyer?
    A. Abstract of title
    B. Title search
    C. Certificate of title
    D. Policy of title insurance

11. Which of the following functions does an abstract of title perform?
    A. Guarantees a clear title
    B. Insures the title
    C. Gives the abstracter's opinion of the title
    D. Offers a condensed history of all recorded documents

12. Tracing the conveyances and encumbrances of real property is known as a
    A. chain of title.
    B. title search.
    C. cloud on title.
    D. recordation of title.

13. ◎ A property on which a mortgage will be recorded is likely to have an on-site inspection under which of the following?
    A. An ALTA extended policy
    B. A standard coverage policy
    C. Only on request by a mortgagor
    D. An inspection is necessary for any type of title insurance policy

14. A standard policy of title insurance insures against all of the following *EXCEPT*
    A. matters of record.
    B. forgery.
    C. mining claims.
    D. contractual capacity.

15. When transactions involving the sale of real estate are placed in escrow, this means
    A. a designated agent agreed to by the parties holds the necessary documents until the terms are met.
    B. they are completed in secrecy.
    C. the broker holds the papers until the registration of title is completed.
    D. the broker is no longer involved.

16. Which of the following provides the *BEST* surety of good title?
    A. Certificate of title
    B. Title insurance
    C. Quitclaim deed
    D. Color of title

17. If escrow instructions differ from the deposit receipt or sales contract and the escrow instructions have been signed by both the buyer and seller, which of the following is correct?
    A. A new deposit receipt must be written.
    B. Escrow instructions take precedence.
    C. The deposit receipt takes precedence.
    D. Everything is void; the parties must start over.

18. A proper escrow, once established, should be
    A. managed by a licensed broker.
    B. void at the seller's option.
    C. voidable at the option of either buyer or seller.
    D. not subject to the control of any one interested party.

19. A standard form policy of title insurance protects against loss resulting from all of the following *EXCEPT*
    A. encroachments on the property.
    B. failure to deliver an earlier recorded deed.
    C. lack of capacity of the grantor.
    D. forgery in the chain of title.

20. In an escrow transaction, the escrow officer is a(n)
    A. representative of the title company, to ensure title validity.
    B. officer of the land court.
    C. agent for the broker.
    D. agent for the buyer and seller and holder of all pertinent papers.

21. To what does the term *chain of title* refer?
    A. Recording law
    B. Will beneficiaries
    C. Title companies
    D. Succession of property owners

22. When handling an escrow for both parties, the escrow holder is acting as a(n)
    A. agent of the seller.
    B. employee of the buyer.
    C. independent contractor.
    D. beneficiary.

23. A valid escrow is likely to be created in connection with all of the following *EXCEPT*
    A. sale of property.
    B. mortgage loans.
    C. bankruptcy.
    D. real property exchange.

24. Earnest money deposits are most likely to be held in escrow by all of the following *EXCEPT* a(n)
    A. broker.
    B. licensed escrow company.
    C. attorney.
    D. salesperson.

25. An abstract of title is *BEST* described as a(n)
    A. brief digest of the title to a particular property.
    B. summary of each deed in a title search.
    C. appraisal of the lands and the improvements.
    D. summary of all improvements and encroachments on the property.

26. ◉ Which of the following concerning escrow is *TRUE?*
    A. An escrow cannot be altered by either party except with the consent of both parties.
    B. The escrow company is the agent of the grantor.
    C. A salesperson may perform the escrow function.
    D. An escrow may be canceled by a dissatisfied buyer.

27. An owner's title insurance policy protects the owner against
    A. loss of property due to mortgage foreclosure.
    B. loss of title to a claimant with superior right of title.
    C. losses due to fire damage.
    D. monetary loss resulting from personal judgment liens against the owner.

28. ◉ Which of the following statements about evidence of title is *TRUE?*
    A. Title insurance insures the lender against loss in case of a default and foreclosure.
    B. An abstract of title insures the buyer against loss due to any matters that could be disclosed in a title search and also against losses due to "off-record" risks.
    C. An abstract of title is the most secure evidence a buyer can receive.
    D. An abstract of title offers no guarantee of title.

29. The records assembled in chronological order that document the chain of title are called a(n)
    A. cloud on title.
    B. affidavit of title.
    C. title insurance policy.
    D. abstract of title.

30. When money in a pending purchase of real property is held in escrow, the broker can obtain out of escrow an advance on earned commission
    A. if only the buyer gives written consent.
    B. if only the seller gives written consent.
    C. without the need for consent.
    D. only when both buyer and seller give their written consent.

31. Which of the following statements about title insurance is *CORRECT?*
    A. Dollar coverage under a mortgagee's policy of title insurance remains constant.
    B. Dollar coverage under an owner's policy of title insurance declines as the loan declines.
    C. The buyer pays annually for coverage as long as the policy is in effect.
    D. The insurance coverage on a mortgagee's policy is based on the declining balance of the loan.

32. Where is the *BEST* place to find a cloud on title?
    A. Application for title insurance
    B. Appraisal
    C. Warranty deed
    D. Title search

33. ◎ When a mortgagee requires a title insurance policy on the secured property, the
    A. policy protects the interests of the lender and the owner.
    B. policy is assignable.
    C. policy is for the life of the mortgagor.
    D. mortgagee will require both an owner's and a lender's policy.

34. After signing a contract for the sale of real estate, the deed is delivered to the buyer or held by a third person designated as the
    A. principal.
    B. assignor.
    C. grantor.
    D. escrow.

35. An abstract of title accomplishes which of the following?
    A. Insures the title
    B. Gives a history of the title, including the recorded encumbrances against the property
    C. Guarantees validity of title
    D. Protects the purchaser against any forgeries in the record

36. ◎ An owner's title insurance policy terminates all coverage of the owner
    A. whenever the owner becomes a grantor under a deed of conveyance.
    B. when the mortgage is paid off.
    C. when the grantor buys a new property.
    D. on written mutual cancellation.

37. The only daughter in a large family inherited a condominium apartment from her father after a lengthy probate proceeding in which there were many conflicting claims to the apartment. Before selling the property she would be *BEST* advised to obtain a
    A. termite report.
    B. new mortgage.
    C. title opinion.
    D. survey.

38. The usual standard policy of title insurance insures against loss due to
    A. forgery in the chain of recorded title.
    B. encumbrances not disclosed by official public records.
    C. rights of parties in possession.
    D. actions of government agencies.

39. Which type of evidence of title requires the *LEAST* amount of search through the records?
    A. Abstract of title
    B. Torrens certificate
    C. Title insurance
    D. Regular certificate of title

40. If a title policy reveals the existence of numerous liens not disclosed in the sales contracts, the title is said to be all of the following *EXCEPT*
    A. clouded.
    B. unmerchantable.
    C. unenforceable.
    D. unmarketable.

41. There are several requirements in a valid escrow concerning the sale of real property. One of them is
    A. a claim of marketable title.
    B. the services of a real estate licensee.
    C. a valid and enforceable written contract for the sale of the land.
    D. that the escrow holder have an interest in the subject matter.

42. Escrow is often used for all of the following purposes *EXCEPT* to
    A. determine that outstanding and unpaid liens will be satisfied.
    B. see that the purchase price is paid and all checks have cleared the bank.
    C. offer properties for sale to prospective buyers.
    D. disburse funds from a sale to the appropriate people.

43. A written instrument of value is deposited with a disinterested third party who will deliver it on the fulfillment of some condition. This *BEST* describes which of the following?
    A. Bill of sale
    B. Promissory note
    C. Escrow
    D. Hypothecation

44. Against which of the following risks does a standard owner's policy of title insurance normally afford protection?
    A. Encroachments
    B. Rights of parties in possession
    C. Zoning ordinance
    D. Minor's deed

45. Recording a deed is for the greatest benefit of the
    A. grantor.
    B. public trustee.
    C. attorney.
    D. grantee.

46. In real estate transactions, all of the following documents are usually recorded *EXCEPT* the
    A. deed.
    B. offer to purchase.
    C. second mortgage.
    D. purchase-money mortgage.

47. It is common procedure to record all of the following instruments *EXCEPT* a(n)
    A. land contract.
    B. quitclaim deed.
    C. assignment of a mortgage.
    D. promissory note secured by a mortgage.

48. For a deed to be validly recorded in most states, all of the following are true *EXCEPT* that it must be
    A. acknowledged.
    B. recorded in the proper sequence of the chain of title.
    C. signed by the grantee.
    D. signed by the grantor.

49. An unrecorded deed is valid and binding
    A. between parties to the deed.
    B. on a later bona fide purchaser for value who first records the deed.
    C. even if not delivered.
    D. when signed by the grantee.

50. Constructive notice of a fact is established by
    A. entering it in the public record.
    B. acting openly in accordance with the fact.
    C. communicating the fact directly to each interested party.
    D. testifying to the existence of the fact under oath in open court.

51. Deeds are recorded to provide
    A. actual notice.
    B. constructive notice.
    C. proof of validity.
    D. evidence against forgery.

52. A deed made and delivered but *NOT* recorded is
    A. valid between the parties and valid as to third parties with notice.
    B. valid between the parties and valid as to subsequent recorded interests.
    C. valid between the parties and invalid as to subsequent donees (recipient by gift) of the property.
    D. invalid between the parties.

53. ◎ Arnold sells Blackacre Farm to Bradley, who does not record the deed. Arnold then makes a gift of Blackacre to Conrad by way of a deed, which Conrad records. Which of the following is *TRUE?*
    A. Because Conrad recorded his deed before Bradley, Conrad has better title to Blackacre than Bradley.
    B. Bradley has better title than Conrad, because Conrad is not a bona fide purchaser for value.
    C. Bradley has superior title to Conrad because the deed was given to Bradley first.
    D. A recorded deed takes priority over all others, regardless of how the grantee acquires title.

54. Which of the following persons is protected by the recording laws?
    A. A person who acquires title by will
    B. A person who acquires title by gift
    C. A person who acquires title in good faith and for value
    D. A person who acquires property free of title defects

55. A buyer is interested in buying property in another state without an inspection. The buyer should obtain a(n)
    A. quitclaim deed.
    B. abstract of title.
    C. bargain and sale deed.
    D. extended coverage title insurance policy.

56. Someone who *CANNOT* act as a notary on a deed is a(n)
    A. attorney at law.
    B. real estate broker.
    C. interested person.
    D. employee in the recording office.

57. Which of the following is *TRUE?*
    A. Recording a deed guarantees its validity.
    B. The venue shows the place where property has been purchased.
    C. Recording protects against defects in the deed.
    D. Recording gives constructive notice.

58. Which of the following statements is *FALSE?*
    A. An acknowledgment is a formal declaration made before some public officer, usually a notary public, by a person who has signed a real estate document or other instrument stating that the signature is genuine and given freely.
    B. To give constructive notice to the public, a document affecting a piece of real estate should be recorded.
    C. Recording is the best security against an unmarketable title.
    D. The recording laws protect those who rely on what is contained in the public records.

59. A bona fide purchaser for value who records his or her deed will take precedence over a grantee with a prior unrecorded deed
    A. if the purchaser for value has actual knowledge of the prior unrecorded deed.
    B. if the prior unrecorded deed's grantee has taken possession of the property and is living in a house on the property.
    C. because the prior deed comes first in time.
    D. because the purchaser for value has a right to rely on what is found in the records.

60. The recording system performs which of the following functions?
    A. Insures title against loss due to third-party claims
    B. Cures major defects in title
    C. Protects against fraud and forgeries
    D. Gives notice to all of the existence of documents

61. Deeds are recorded for which of the following purposes?
    A. To provide constructive notice of their existence
    B. Because the law requires it
    C. Because an unrecorded deed is not valid
    D. To make title marketable

62. An acknowledgment may be void if
    A. made before an officer who did not witness the signature.
    B. made before an officer who has an interest, such as a lessor.
    C. not made at the time the instrument was signed.
    D. not made on oath or affirmation.

63. A person must record an instrument within what period of time after it is signed and delivered?
    A. 30 days
    B. 90 days
    C. One year
    D. No time limit

64. All of the following are insurance policies against losses suffered due to defects in the chain of title to a specific parcel of real estate *EXCEPT* a(n)
    A. mortgagee's policy.
    B. insurer's policy.
    C. owner's policy.
    D. joint owner-lender policy.

65. How frequently are title insurance premiums paid?
    A. Semiannually during ownership
    B. Bimonthly during ownership
    C. Only at the time of issuance
    D. At the start and end of the policy term

66. ◎ A standard title insurance policy offers protection to an owner against which of the following?
    A. Defects arising after the date of the policy
    B. Encroachments
    C. Costs of defending a lawsuit challenging the title
    D. Unrecorded mechanics' liens

67. The Real Estate Settlement Procedures Act (RESPA) is designed to regulate which of the following?
    A. Disclosures of closing information
    B. Procedures for recording titles to real estate
    C. Ceilings on interest rates charged
    D. Those who are qualified to prepare a settlement statement

68. In closing a real estate transaction, various expenses and carrying charges are apportioned between the buyer and seller. These apportionments appear on the settlement statement as
    A. profits and losses.
    B. debits and credits.
    C. debits only.
    D. those that always have an offsetting entry.

69. ◎ Which of the following statements about escrow officers is *TRUE?*
    A. They can disburse money and documents when all conditions of the escrow have been satisfactorily met.
    B. They must be individually licensed by the real estate licensing agency.
    C. Anyone can perform the escrow function.
    D. They are used only when the property involves financing.

70. Under the rules and regulations of RESPA, which is *TRUE?*
    A. Buyers may not use their attorneys at a closing.
    B. Lenders can require the use of a designated closing agent.
    C. Lenders cannot charge points on a loan.
    D. Borrowers receive an explanation of settlement charges.

71. Which of the following documents serves as the *BEST* evidence of good title to a property?
    A. Warranty deed
    B. Bill of sale
    C. Abstract of title
    D. Mortgage

72. A properly established escrow is voidable at the option of
    A. the seller.
    B. the buyer.
    C. the buyer's or seller's broker.
    D. both buyer and seller acting together.

73. ◎ When a property is sold subject to an existing lease that has nine months before it expires, all of the following statements regarding the settlement statement are true *EXCEPT* that the
    A. security deposit is a credit to the buyer.
    B. prepaid rent is a credit to the buyer.
    C. security deposit is a debit to the seller.
    D. prepaid rent is a credit to the seller.

74. An escrow company performs which of the following functions?
    A. Collects all monies and pertinent documents for distribution
    B. Determines that title is marketable
    C. Represents either the buyer or the seller
    D. Performs the title search

75. All of the following documents will most likely be recorded *EXCEPT* the
    A. quitclaim deed.
    B. satisfaction of mortgage.
    C. power of attorney.
    D. offer and acceptance.

76. Carlos deeds a property to Julio, who fails to record. Carlos subsequently deeds the same property to Augusto. Which one of these statements is *TRUE?*
    A. Julio owns the property based on his having the first deed.
    B. Augusto is the owner if he first records without notice of Julio's rights.
    C. Augusto and Julio are now tenants in common.
    D. Carlos remains the owner because both deeds are void.

77. All of the following can act as an escrow agent to close a transaction *EXCEPT* the
    A. lender.
    B. attorney.
    C. real estate broker.
    D. home inspection company.

78. An escrow agent will prepare all of the following *EXCEPT* the
    A. deed.
    B. escrow instructions.
    C. closing statements.
    D. conveyance tax certificate.

79. ◎ A seller sells a five-unit rental building. How are the tenants' security deposits treated on the closing statement?
    A. Credit seller
    B. Debit buyer
    C. Debit seller, credit buyer
    D. Credit seller, debit buyer

80. ◎ On the closing statement, the earnest money deposit is
    A. a double entry.
    B. prorated.
    C. a credit to buyer.
    D. a debit to seller.

81. All of the following are requirements of RESPA *EXCEPT* that the lender
    A. collects three months' reserves for tax and insurance.
    B. provides a good-faith estimate of settlement charges.
    C. gives the borrower an information booklet upfront.
    D. must use a HUD-1 Settlement Statement and allow the borrower time to inspect it.

82. Which of the following events must happen on the closing of a real estate purchase transaction?
    A. The conveyance document must be recorded at the county recording office.
    B. The buyer must be given occupancy of the property.
    C. The buyer must pay the entire purchase price in cash at that time.
    D. The deed must be delivered.

83. ◎ How would a purchase-money second mortgage given by the purchaser to the seller appear on the settlement statement on closing a real estate sale?
    A. Credit to purchaser and debit to seller
    B. Debit to purchaser and credit to seller
    C. Only as a debit to the buyer
    D. Only as a credit to the seller

84. For which of the following is the escrow agent responsible?
    A. To make certain that all encumbrances on the title are removed prior to closing
    B. To make certain that the buyer is in possession of the property prior to closing
    C. To conduct a search of public records
    D. To disburse all funds according to the agreement of the parties

85. All of the following would be covered in a standard title insurance policy *EXCEPT*
    A. special assessments.
    B. prescriptive easements.
    C. recorded mortgages.
    D. competency of parties.

86. At closing the settlement agent is responsible for making payments for all of the following *EXCEPT* the
   A. balance due on the seller's mortgage.
   B. title insurance premiums.
   C. recording fee.
   D. salesperson's commissions.

87. Which of the following is *NOT* a requirement of RESPA?
   A. A specific closing statement form must be used for all settlements on one-family to four-family dwellings.
   B. An information booklet must be provided to the borrower by the lender.
   C. A limit is placed on the fees a lender can charge a borrower.
   D. An estimate of settlement charges must be provided by the lender.

ANSWERS

1. **B.** Usually a title company or licensed abstracter conducts a title search of the chain of title in the public records to see what, if any, clouds on title there may be. A title insurance policy insures against losses suffered owing to certain undisclosed title defects.

2. **D.** A lender's extended title insurance policy is assignable to facilitate the commercial transfer of mortgages in the secondary mortgage market. Because the owner's policy is not assignable, a new buyer has to pay a one-time fee to cover any defects up to the time of purchasing a personal policy. (ALTA is the American Land Title Association.)

3. **B.** All title insurance policies cover hidden risks, such as forgery in the chain of title. An extended policy, such as an ALTA policy, would cover against (C) and (D), but few policies would extend to (A).

4. **D.** A lawsuit to quiet the title will clearly establish the rights of parties after a gap in the title is found. In a few cases where the gap is obvious, a quitclaim deed from the interested party or heir could be helpful.

5. **B.** The Torrens system of title registration was designed from ship registration procedures in which title can be transferred or encumbered only by notation on the proper registration of title (certificate of title).

6. **C.** A title search would be needed to discover the flaw. Assuming a reputable title company gives its opinion, it is not usually necessary to hire an attorney.

7. **B.** The survey would reveal physical defects such as encroachments. The warranty deed would give only a right to sue the grantor in the event there was a title defect.

8. **D.** An extended coverage title policy will insure against hidden risks and matters that an inspection of the property would reveal, such as mechanics' liens, undisclosed easements, or rights of parties in possession.

9. **C.** It would be an unusual endorsement even on an extended coverage policy that would cover matters of zoning and governmental regulation.

10. **B.** The title search is the actual process of tracing the chain of title. At least with (A), (C), and (D), some protection would be given to the buyer in the event of improper or negligent searching through the title.

11. **D.** An abstract is a document that summarizes (digests) the various recorded instruments found in the chain of title. It neither insures nor guarantees the title, although the abstractor would be liable for negligence in conducting the search if something such as a recorded second mortgage were overlooked.

12. **B.** In a title search, one runs through the chain of title to discover any clouds on title.

13. **A.** A standard policy generally confines itself to insuring against defects in the records such as forgery, whereas ALTA policies extend to physical defects (such as encroachments) because many lenders want this extra protection (which the borrower pays for anyway).

14. **C.** Mining and water claims are more likely to be excluded from the standard title insurance policy than any of the other choices.

15. **A.** Escrow acts as the stakeholder, an intermediary between buyer and seller to make sure the parties perform their respective obligations before title and money pass.

16. **B.** In the event of loss due to a title defect, the title insurance carrier most likely would make good the insured's loss in the same way a surety company would. There are no warranties with a quitclaim deed. For there to be liability under a certificate of title, there needs to be some title company negligence.

17. **B.** Because the conflicting matter in the mutually agreed-on subsequent escrow instruction is a modification of the original contract, the escrow agreement usually takes precedence. In a counteroffer, it is the offer that is modified.

18. **D.** Escrow does not take individual "change orders" from either party; both parties must consent to any change in the original contract or escrow instructions.

19. **A.** Encroachments are physical matters not on the public records, such as overhanging trees, which would be covered only in an extended title insurance policy.

20. **D.** The escrow officer is a neutral party but is the agent for the seller as far as holding title and the agent for the buyer as far as holding money. Escrow is a fiduciary relationship.

21. **D.** Each *link* in the chain of title refers to a successive ownership of that particular property. There must be no gap in the chain of ownership.

22. **C.** Escrow is really a neutral third party hired by both buyer and seller to achieve a certain result.

23. **C.** Transfers of a bankrupt's property are usually handled through the federal court and are subject to court approval.

24. **D.** A salesperson can act only as a subagent of the broker's principal.

25. **A.** An abstract of title summarizes not only deeds but also all recorded documents affecting the title, such as leases, options, and mortgages.

26. **A.** The escrow company is the agent of both grantor and grantee. Once the transaction is in escrow, it is placed out of the unilateral control of either party.

27. **B.** Mortgage foreclosures would occur if the owner defaulted on the mortgage. Title insurance is concerned with title losses.

28. **D.** Title insurance would protect the lender against a title defect or challenge to title to the secured property. An abstract neither guarantees nor insures title. Off-record risks include forgery and incapacity.

29. **D.** The abstract tends to be a long document because it is the actual summary of documents found in the chain of title and not just the title company's opinion of title.

30. **D.** Both parties must consent before the broker can draw from escrow against earned commission. Otherwise, there could be a problem in a case where the buyer is entitled to the return of his or her deposit. In some states, advance fees are regulated.

31. **D.** Coverage is steady for an owner, but it declines for the lender as the loan decreases (like a term life insurance policy). There is a one-time payment.

32. **D.** The application for title insurance won't reveal anything.

33. **B.** The mortgagee policy protects only the lender and is assignable when the loan is sold. For a small premium the owner can and should get protection under a joint lender-owner policy, which is not assignable by the owner.

34. **D.** Escrow will hold the deed until both parties have fully performed their obligations under the existing contract of sale.

35. **B.** The abstract will reveal such recorded encumbrances as judgment liens, easements, or mortgages.

36. **D.** The policy is not assignable to any buyer of the property. If, however, the grantee later sues the grantor for breach of warranty of title, the title company will defend the suit and protect the grantor based on the policy. Mutual cancellation would result from a settlement dispute.

37. **C.** Because the probate proceeding might not effectively settle all the claims of heirs to the property, the daughter should be advised to obtain a title policy insuring her title. This will make her property more marketable.

38. **A.** The standard policy limits its coverage to matters of public record, including hidden risks such as forgery, nondelivery of a deed, or incapacity.

39. **B.** In a Torrens search, there is only one major document to check—the certificate of title registration.

40. **C.** A buyer might agree in the sales contract to take the property subject to all the disclosed liens. The key is disclosure.

41. **C.** Escrow, which is a disinterested stakeholder, cannot carry out the terms of an unenforceable agreement.

42. **C.** Escrow often uses the funds generated by the buyer to pay off unpaid taxes and mortgages so that the buyer will get the free and clear title promised by the seller in the sales contract.

43. **C.** Escrow might, for example, hold the buyer's funds pending delivery of the seller's deed. Hypothecation refers to mortgaging.

44. **D.** The title policy usually protects against recorded conveyances that are ineffective owing to incapacity.

45. **D.** The grantee puts the world on notice of his or her rights in the property when the deed is recorded.

46. **B.** Most sales contracts involve a short-lived transaction and are not recorded.

47. **D.** A note does not involve an interest in real property. Also, most lenders do not want the details of loans to be made public.

48. **C.** Acknowledgment is usually required to lessen the risk of forgery. If, for example, the document is recorded before the transferor gets title, it will not be found in a regular chain of title search of the grantor-grantee index; therefore, it is not constructive notice of the rights of the parties.

49. **A.** The validity of the deed between the parties is not affected by failure to record. Most states rule that a good-faith purchaser for value who first records, without notice of the earlier unrecorded deed, will have title superior to that of a prior grantee under an unrecorded deed.

50. **A.** The law presumes that people have notice of matters published in the public record even though a person may not have actual notice.

51. **B.** Anyone who deals with a property without first checking the public records does so at his or her own risk. Actual notice means direct knowledge of a fact.

52. **A.** If the deed is not recorded, a subsequent purchaser for value (from the original grantor), without notice of the first unrecorded deed, could get superior title by recording the subsequent deed first. Donees are not protected under the recording law (nor are devisees).

53. **B.** The recording laws do not protect a subsequent donee who gets property as a gift after an earlier unrecorded deed, even though the donee first records. In this case, the first in time, first in right rule would apply.

54. **C.** Recording laws are designed to protect subsequent good-faith purchasers for value (i.e., money, not a gift) who first record. (In certain "notice" jurisdictions, it is not necessary that the prevailing party record first.)

55. **D.** In this situation the buyer should obtain an extended title insurance policy to cover against matters that would be revealed by an inspection, such as encroachments, adverse possession, and mechanics' liens.

56. **C.** An interested person such as a grantee could not notarize the grantor's signature, even though properly licensed as a notary. Should be an "arm's-length transaction."

57. **D.** Recording an invalid deed will not make it valid. The venue refers to the jurisdiction where the notary is authorized to take acknowledgments of signatures.

58. **C.** To lessen the chances of forgery, most states require that a document be acknowledged by a notary public as a prerequisite for recording. Recording will not cure a defective title.

59. **D.** Recording laws will protect subsequent purchasers for value only without actual or constructive notice. Possession can give constructive notice of the rights of the person in possession, thus illustrating the importance of a property inspection.

60. **D.** The recording system neither insures nor corrects title defects; it merely gives constructive notice of the rights of people as to certain property.

61. **A.** Recording laws are voluntary, not required. In Torrens system property, however, registration of title is required.

62. **B.** The signature need not take place before the notary, but a disinterested notary must identify the person as the one who signed of his or her own free will. Choice (D) is an affidavit.

63. **D.** By not recording, however, the person risks losing the property.

64. **B.** The insurance company is the insurer. The mortgagee has an insurable interest, as does the owner. The borrower is often required by the lender to obtain a mortgagee (lender) policy. Because this policy protects only the lender, the owner should, for a slight extra charge, obtain a combined policy that will protect both the borrower and the lender in the event of a loss.

65. **C.** The premium is paid once at the beginning of the coverage and covers defects occurring up to the date of the policy.

66. **C.** The title policy covers defects of record that occurred up to the date of the policy, including costs to defend even an unfounded lawsuit. Choices (B) and (D) are covered under an extended policy.

67. **A.** RESPA is a federal law requiring disclosures of certain closing data, such as estimated closing costs, to consumers.

68. **B.** Profits and losses appear on an income statement, whereas debits (or charges) and credits are accounting terms used in a closing statement.

69. **A.** Most states require licensing of escrow companies but not individual escrow agents.

70. **D.** The buyer is free to use an attorney and the lender can use any settlement agent, but RESPA prohibits the lender from dictating the use of one particular agent.

71. **C.** As abstract of title is a summary of those documents found in the chain of title after a title search has been run. The warranty deed, like the bill of sale, does not prove the title; it merely promises that title is as represented and conveyed.

72. **D.** A proper escrow is beyond the control or unilateral action of any one party, although both may agree to cancel or modify.

73. **D.** Prepaid rent is a debit to the seller and a credit to the buyer, because the seller has already received this income for the unused period. The seller who has this money must return it to the buyer, who will eventually return it to the tenant, provided there are no damages at the time of lease termination.

74. **A.** Escrow is a neutral stakeholder that holds the deed pending payment by buyer and clearing of any checks. A title company renders the opinion as to the marketability of title.

75. **D.** Most contracts of sale are not recorded because there is a relatively short time between signing and closing. If an attorney-in-fact is to sign a document that will be

recorded, then the power of attorney must first be recorded (under the "equal dignities rule").

76. **B.** The recording laws will protect Augusto if he is a bona fide purchaser for value who first records.

77. **D.** Also, a salesperson cannot act as escrow agent.

78. **A.** An attorney usually prepares the deed.

79. **C.** The seller keeps the security deposit money, yet the buyer will have to return it to tenants at end of their leases. The buyer should confirm amounts with tenants.

80. **C.** It is a single-entry item.

81. **A.** The lender is permitted to collect up to two months of reserves or impounds. Within three days of application the lender needs to provide a good-faith estimate of the settlement charges (not exact amount of total charges).

82. **D.** While recording is recommended, it is not required. Delivery is a prerequisite to transfer of legal title at closing. The seller may be given a period of time after settlement in which to relocate—the buyer then would be wise to obtain a rental agreement.

83. **A.** The loan is credited against the purchase price owed by the purchaser. It represents cash the seller will not receive at the time of settlement. This is a broker-level question.

84. **D.** Escrow is responsible for making certain that the parties have performed their respective contractual obligations prior to closing—the buyer may have agreed to take title subject to certain encumbrances or to delay taking possession.

85. **B.** The standard title insurance policy covers matters of public record, questions of delivery, and competency. Only an extended policy covers matters that an inspection would reveal, such as a prescriptive easement.

86. **D.** The proper person to pay the salesperson is the broker.

87. **C.** There are no limits on fees. What RESPA requires is the disclosure of fees and expenses to close the transaction.

Real Estate Settlement Exercises

On the broker examination, there will be several questions requiring a general knowledge of how to prepare a settlement or closing statement, including the mathematics of prorations. Salesperson candidates should be able to complete the proration problems in this chapter. You will not have to complete a settlement statement on the exam. In all prorations, you should use a 360-day year and a 30-day month.

To assist the broker candidate in knowing how to prepare the settlement statements, a settlement statement guide has been provided. It shows most of the possible areas that may be encountered in a problem and whether these items are to be shown as a debit or credit to the buyer or seller.

There is no definite order in which these entries appear on a settlement statement, although purchase price is typically first, and the last entries are the balance due from buyer and net proceeds due to seller. Note that a few of these entries may differ from custom and practice in your area (especially items such as title insurance). Also, few closing statements will contain *all* these entries, but they are listed here for study purposes. A properly prepared sales agreement will expressly state which party is to pay which expenses. Using this guide and the Student Settlement Statement Worksheet, you should have no difficulty answering questions about the settlement statement. Special emphasis should be given to learning what items are typically debits and credits to the buyer and seller.

KEY WORDS

Closing statement: Detailed cash accounting of a real estate transaction showing all the money that was received and disbursed by the brokerage firm.

Commingling: An unlawful act of mixing the broker's personal funds with those of customers and clients. State laws regulate trust accounts and mandate that brokers maintain a trust or escrow account for the protection of their customer's and client's funds.

General ledgers: A chronological, state-regulated journal of all receipts and disbursements of client funds that pass through a brokerage's trust account.

Individual ledgers: A chronological, state-regulated journal that records the entry of all receipts and disbursements for each real estate or rental transaction that passes through the broker's trust account.

Prorations: When closing a real estate transaction, it is often necessary to divide the costs between the seller and the buyer for property taxes, fuel costs, and rent. Proration provides for the equitable distribution of prepaid income and expenses.

Reconciliation: An accounting procedure that balances a trust account by comparing the combined individual ledger balances with the balance of the general ledger.

Trust accounts: State regulated accounts that contain, except for the maintenance charge of the account, only earnest money, rents, and management funds that belong to customers and clients.

STUDENT SETTLEMENT STATEMENT WORKSHEET				
SETTLEMENT DATE:	**BUYER'S STATEMENT**		**SELLER'S STATEMENT**	
CLOSING DATE	**DEBIT**	**CREDIT**	**DEBIT**	**CREDIT**
1. Consideration (purchase price)	X			X
2. Initial deposit (earnest money)		X		
3. New first or second mortgage (deed of trust)		X		
4. Existing mortgage payoff (deed of trust)			X	
5. First or second purchase-money mortgage (deed of trust) with seller		X	X	
6. Mortgage assumed (deed of trust)		X	X	
7. Land contract (agreement of sale)		X	X	
8. Interest arrears (assumption)		X	X	
9. Interest on new loan	X			
10. Interest on mortgage payoff			X	
11. Taxes in arrears		X	X	
12. Taxes in advance	X			X
13. Delinquent taxes			X	
14. Insurance assumed/advance	X			X
15. Rent collected in advance		X	X	
16. Rent owed	X			X
17. Preparation of deed			X	
18 Abstract or certificate of title			X	
19. Title search			X	
20. Title insurance	X			
21. Appraisal fee (requested by lender)	X			
22. New conventional mortgage (loan fee)	X			
23. Discount points (VA) (FHA) (Conventional)		Negotiable		
24. Loan origination fee (VA) (FHA)		Negotiable		
25. Prepayment penalty			X	
26. Mortgage assumption fee	X			
27. Conveyance tax			X	
28. Mortgage release			X	
29. Recording mortgage release			X	
30. Recording deed	X			
31. Recording mortgages	X			
32. Escrow fees	X		X	
33. Commission			X	
34. Survey		Negotiable		
35. Inventory (separate bill of sale)	X			X
SUBTOTALS	X	X	X	X
36. Balance due from buyer		X		
37. Net proceeds due to seller			X	

SETTLEMENT STATEMENT GUIDE

1. *Consideration (purchase price).* The full amount is credited to the seller and the full amount is debited to the buyer.

2. *Initial deposit (earnest money).* The amount of the earnest money deposit is credited to the buyer.

3. *New first or second mortgage (deed of trust).* The full amount of the mortgage will be shown as a credit to the buyer because it is the means by which the buyer will pay the purchase price.

4. *Existing mortgage payoff (deed of trust).* Will show as a debit to the seller.

5. *First or second purchase-money mortgage (deed of trust) with seller.* Enter the full amount as a credit to the buyer and a debit to the seller (the mortgagee).

6. *Mortgage assumed (deed of trust).* The full amount will show as a credit to the buyer and a debit to the seller because the seller will be receiving less cash at closing.

7. *Land contract (agreement of sale).* The full amount will show as a credit to the buyer and a debit to the seller because the seller does not receive it in cash at the closing.

8. *Interest arrears (assumption).* When buyer assumes existing mortgage, prorate the interest and enter this amount as a credit to buyer and debit to the seller.

9. *Interest on new loan.* This amount will be shown only as a debit to the buyer because the buyer has to pay interest from the date of closing until the first loan payment date, which is usually the first day of the following month.

10. *Interest on mortgage payoff.* This amount will be shown only as a debit to the seller.

11. *Taxes in arrears.* Prorate the taxes and enter the amount as a credit to the buyer and a debit to the seller.

12. *Taxes in advance.* Prorate the taxes and enter the amount as a debit to the buyer and a credit to the seller.

13. *Delinquent taxes.* If taxes are delinquent, enter this amount only as a debit to the seller.

14. *Insurance assumed/advance.* If paid in advance, prorate the insurance and enter it as a debit to the buyer and a credit to the seller.

15. *Rent collected in advance.* If the property being purchased is presently being rented, the rent collected in advance from the tenant will show as a credit to the buyer and a debit to the seller.

16. *Rent owed.* If the property being purchased is being rented and the rent has not yet been collected from the tenant, the amount will be shown as a debit to the buyer and a credit to the seller.

17. *Preparation of deed.* This most commonly will be a debit to the seller. In a few jurisdictions, this is negotiable.

18. *Abstract or certificate of title.* Debit this amount to the seller.

19. *Title search.* Debit this amount to the seller.

20. *Title insurance.* Debit full amount to the buyer.

21. *Appraisal fee (requested by lender).* Charged to buyer if requested by lender.

22. *New conventional mortgage (loan fee).* Debit to the buyer.

23. *Discount points (VA) (FHA) (Conventional).* Can be paid by buyer or seller except in FHA-negotiated interest rate loan programs.

24. *Loan origination fee (VA) (FHA).* Negotiable.

25. *Prepayment penalty.* Debit this amount to the seller.

26. *Mortgage assumption fee.* If there is a charge for assuming the existing mortgage, debit this amount to the buyer.

27. *Conveyance tax.* This will show as a debit to the seller.

28. *Mortgage release.* A mortgage release from the lender will be shown as a debit to the seller.

29. *Recording mortgage release.* Seller will want the lender's release recorded; therefore, it will show as a debit to the seller.

30. *Recording deed.* This will be a debit to the buyer.

31. *Recording mortgages.* The recording of any mortgages will show as a debit to the buyer.

32. *Escrow fees.* Escrow fees are usually split in half; therefore, they will show as a debit to both buyer and seller.

33. *Commission.* The commission, which is a percentage of the sales price, will show as a debit to the seller. If it were a buyer's agency agreement, then it might in some cases be charged to the buyer.

34. *Survey.* Who pays for surveying and staking varies from state to state; the payment is therefore negotiable and to be determined between the parties.

35. *Inventory (separate bill of sale).* If the buyer is to purchase inventory, which is on a separate bill of sale, this will show as a debit to the buyer and a credit to the seller.

36. *Balance due from buyer.* This is the amount shown after subtracting the buyer's credits from his or her debits. It will be entered as a credit if it is needed to balance a double entry system.

37. *Net proceeds due to seller.* This is the amount the seller will receive from the buyer and may be determined by subtracting the seller's debits from his or her credits. It will be entered in the seller's debit column.

QUESTIONS

Closing Statement Preparation—Part 1

Indicate where the following entries would be entered on a closing statement as a debit or credit for buyer and seller.

1. Purchase price:
2. Earnest money deposit:
3. New first mortgage:
4. Second purchase-money mortgage (with seller):
5. Taxes arrears:
6. Insurance assumed:
7. Preparation of deed:
8. Title insurance:
9. Recording deed:
10. Commission:

Settlement Statement Prorations—Part 2

1. The tax year is January 1 to December 31. Taxes for the first half of the tax year have been paid. Closing is September 1 of the same year. Taxes are $432 per annum. What is the actual entry?

2. A fire insurance policy has an unused portion of six months, ten days. The policy costs $151.20 for three years. What is the actual entry?

3. Annual taxes are $3,600 paid in advance on January 1. Closing is September 1. What is the tax proration?

4. Closing date is December 15. Fire insurance is $720 for three years, paid in advance on February 15 of the same year. What is the actual entry?

5. The balance of the mortgage assumed is $40,000 at 11 percent interest. Payments are due on the tenth of the month. Closing date is March 1. What is the actual interest proration?

6. A property for sale has a rental cottage. Rent of $600 is payable in advance on the tenth of the month. Settlement date is July 20. What is the actual entry shown for the buyer and seller?

7. Taxes are $648 yearly. Closing is December 15. The last half of the calendar year is unpaid. What is the actual entry?

8. An old mortgage of $50,000 at 8 percent is being paid off. There also will be a new mortgage of $60,000 at 12 percent. The old mortgage is due on the 1st of the month, the new mortgage on the 15th. The settlement date is July 15. What is the actual entry, if any, for both mortgages and interest?

9. Closing date is March 15. Taxes, $480 per year, are unpaid. What is the actual entry for the unpaid portion?

10. Closing date is October 10. Mortgage assumed is $21,400 at 9 percent. Mortgage payments are paid on the 20th of each month. What is the actual entry?

11. One-year insurance policy for $900 is paid through December 31 of this year. Closing will be December 15 of the same year. What will be the amount of the proration?

12. Annual taxes of $441.60 are due semiannually on January 1 and July 1. The second semiannual portion had not been paid when the house sold on August 1. What is the proration?
    A. Debit seller $184
    B. Debit seller $37
    C. Credit buyer $73
    D. Credit seller $184

13. Prorate the prepaid taxes as of the June 15 settlement date, if a $120,000 property is assessed at 55 percent value with a tax rate of $3.20 per $100 valuation on a calendar year basis.
    A. Credit seller $1,144, debit buyer $1,144
    B. Debit both $968
    C. Credit buyer $1,144, debit seller $968
    D. Credit both $968

14. The seller sold his home on August 20. He prepaid the taxes of $3,060 on January 1 for this calendar year. What was the prorated tax owed to the seller?
   A. $1,955
   B. $849
   C. $1,105
   D. $2,210

15. A house is sold on May 15. The yearly taxes are $760, and the water costs $80 a year. The seller prepaid the taxes and water on January 1. At closing what does the buyer pay the seller?
   A. $525
   B. $385
   C. $455
   D. $595

16. On January 1, the seller paid $130 for a three-year insurance policy. On April 1, the beginning of the tax year, she also paid the annual property taxes of $625. The property sold on August 15. What prorated amount does the seller receive?
   A. $261
   B. $337
   C. $418
   D. $494

17. A condo sold for $95,000. The mortgage balance was $33,000, escrow fees were $450, deed preparation was $90, and a 6 percent commission was paid. The seller received a $750 tax credit and gave a $15,000 second mortgage to the buyer. What did the seller receive at closing?
   A. $41,510
   B. $43,522
   C. $55,010
   D. $71,510

18. The buyer deposited $2,500 on a $47,000 house. He has a 90 percent loan, receives a $250 proration credit, and pays a $950 attorney fee and 4 points on the mortgage. How much money does the buyer bring to closing?
   A. $4,342
   B. $4,592
   C. $4,842
   D. $5,850

19. A sales transaction closes on August 15. Rent of $900 has been paid for the month. What is the proration?
   A. Debit buyer $450
   B. Credit seller $450
   C. Debit buyer $480
   D. Credit buyer $480

ANSWERS

Closing Statement Preparation—Part 1

1. Purchase price: Debit buyer, credit seller

2. Earnest money deposit: Credit buyer

3. New first mortgage: Credit buyer

4. Second purchase-money mortgage: Credit buyer, debit seller

5. Taxes arrears: Credit buyer, debit seller

6. Insurance assumed: Debit buyer, credit seller

7. Preparation of deed: Debit seller

8. Title insurance: Debit buyer

9. Recording deed: Debit buyer

10. Commission: Debit seller

Settlement Statement Prorations—Part 2

1. Credit buyer, debit seller $72 each. $36 per month × 2 months = $72.

2. Debit buyer, credit seller $26.60 each. $4.20 per month × 6⅓ months.

3. Debit buyer, credit seller $1,200 each. $300 per month × 4 months.

4. Debit buyer, credit seller $520 each. $20 per month × 26 months.

5. Credit buyer, debit seller $244.44 each. $4,400 per year equals $366.66 per month × ⅔ month. (Interest paid in arrears, due on 10th. Thus owed from February 10 to March 1.)

6.   Credit buyer, debit seller $400. Tenant paid entire amount in advance, thus seller must be charged ⅔ month, which is also credited to the buyer.

7.   Credit buyer, debit seller $297 each. $54 per month × 5½ months.

8.   Debit seller $50,000 for mortgage payoff and $166.66 for interest in arrears. New mortgage will be shown as $60,000 credit to the buyer. There will be no interest proration on the new mortgage at this time. $333.33 per month × ½ month.

9.   Credit buyer, debit seller $100. $40 per month × 2½ months.

10.   Credit buyer, debit seller $107. $1,926 annual interest. $160.50 per month × ⅔ month.

11.   Credit seller, debit buyer $40. $2.50 per day × 16 days.

12. **B.** July 1 to August 1 = 1 month of taxes owed (debit) by seller.
$441.60 ÷ 12 = $36.80.
Debit seller $37.

13. **A.** $120,000 market value × 55% = $66,000 assessed value.
$66,000 ÷ 100 = 660 × $3.20 = $2,112 annual taxes.
$2,112 ÷ 12 = $176 per month × 6.5 months (June 15 through December 31) = $1,144 prepaid by seller, owed by buyer.
Credit seller $1,144, debit buyer $1,144.

14. **C.** $3,060 ÷ 12 = $255 per month.
$255 ÷ 30 = $8.50 per day.
Seller prepaid 4 months and 10 days.
$255 × 4 = $1,020 + ($8.50 × 10)
$85 = $1,105.

15. **A.** $760 + $80 = $840 ÷ 12 = $70 per month; seller prepaid May 15 through December 31, or 7.5 months.
$70 × 7.5 = $525.

16. **D.** 3 years = 36 months.
$130 ÷ 36 = $3.61 per month.
The unused portion of the insurance policy is 28.5 months × $3.61 = $102.92.
Property taxes are $625 ÷ 12 = $52.08 per month.
The unused portion of taxes (August 15 through March 31) is 7.5 months × $52.08 = $390.62.
$102.92 + $390.62 = $493.54.

17. **A.** Seller's credits of $95,750 minus the debits of $54,240 equals $41,510.

18. **B.**

Buyer's Credits		Buyer's Debits	
Deposit	$2,500	$4,700	down payment
Proration	250	1,692	points
	$2,750	950	attorney
		$7,342	

$47,000 × 90% = $42,300 loan.
$47,000 − $42,300 = $4,700 down payment.
$42,300 × 4% = $1,692 loan points.
Debits of $7,342 less credits of $2,750 equals $4,592 needed at closing.

19. **D.** Seller has been paid rent for the last 16 days of the month. $900 ÷ 30 = $30 per day × 16 = $480. Credit buyer $480. Note also that with expenses like taxes, the seller pays up to the day of closing and the buyer takes over on the day of closing.

Real Estate Brokerage

This part contains questions on the topics of

- law of agency and business ethics;

- fiduciary relationships;

- listing agreements;

- elements of a valid sales contract;

- provisions in a sales contract;

- option contracts;

- antidiscrimination: federal Fair Housing, Americans with Disabilities acts;

- Truth-in-Lending disclosures;

- lease agreements;

- property management;

- securities; and

- ethics

Expect 35 percent to 40 percent of the national portion of the examination to contain questions on the topics covered in Part E.

Agency and Business Ethics

When a principal delegates authority and an agent agrees to act on the principal's behalf, an agency relationship is created. Most state laws require that agency relationships be written in order to protect both the principal and the agent.

The agent owes the principal the fiduciary duties of good faith, full disclosure, confidentiality, obedience, accounting, and the exercise of reasonable skill and care. Expiration of the term, death of either party, mutual rescission, or revocation can terminate any agency relationship. Generally, the principal has the power to revoke the agency contract at any time, but if breached, may be liable for the payment of a commission if the agent has done nothing wrong.

Consumers have the right to expect real estate agents to be trustworthy and responsible. Those agents that adhere to the standards established by the National Association of REALTORS® Code of Ethics meet this challenge of professionalism. Those members that adhere to these principles are called REALTORS®. Business ethics are vital because every day real estate agents face dilemmas in areas of agency law, discrimination, dealing with stigmatized properties, environmental disclosures, and daily interaction with each other.

Questions in this chapter will test your comprehension of the following topics:

- Fiduciary obligations of agent to principal

- Difference among listing agent, subagent, and buyer's agent

- Real estate commissions

- Disclosure of material facts

- Use of power of attorney

KEY WORDS

Agency: A relationship created when one person, the principal, delegates to another, the agent, the right to act on the principal's behalf in business transactions and to exercise some degree of discretion while so acting. An agency gives rise to a fiduciary relationship and imposes on the agent, as the fiduciary of the principal, certain duties, obligations, and high standards of good faith and loyalty.

Agency disclosure: State requirement that real estate agents disclose in writing the type of agency relationship that will be performed (i.e., single or appointed agency, consensual dual agency, non-client, and so on).

Agent: One who is authorized to represent and to act on behalf of another person (called the *principal*). Real estate brokers are the agents of their clients, whether seller's or buyer's, to whom brokers owe a fiduciary obligation. Salespersons are the agents of their brokers and do not have a direct personal contractual relationship with either sellers or buyers.

Appointed agency: A single agency relationship where a broker assigns one agent to singularly represent either a buyer or seller to the exclusion of every other agent in the broker's office.

Attorney-in-fact: One who is authorized by another to act in his or her place under a power of attorney.

Broker: One who acts as an intermediary between parties to a transaction. A real estate broker is a properly licensed person who, for a valuable consideration, serves as an agent to others to facilitate the sale or lease of real property.

Client: Someone for whom an agent works and who is called the principal. The client could be a seller, a buyer, a landlord, or a tenant.

Commingling: To mingle or mix; for example, to deposit client funds in the broker's personal or general account. Licensees found guilty of commingling can have their licenses suspended or revoked by the state's Real Estate Commission.

Cooperating broker: An outside broker who joins with another broker in the sale of real property.

Consensual dual agency: Representing both principals (buyer and seller) in a single transaction. Here a single agent coordinates the sale, keeping both parties' business confidential.

Customer: Someone with whom an agent works and to whom the agent must be honest.

Fiduciary: A relationship that implies a position of trust or confidence wherein one is usually entrusted to hold or manage property or money for another. Among the obligations a fiduciary owes to the principal are duties of loyalty; obedience; full disclosure; the duty to use skill, care, and diligence; and the duty to account for all monies.

General agent: One who is authorized to perform any and all acts associated with the continued operation of a particular job or a certain business. A property manager would be a good example of a general agent.

Independent contractor: One who is retained to perform a certain act, but who is subject to the control and direction of another only as to the end result and not as to how he or she performs the act. The critical feature, and what distinguishes an independent contractor from an employee or agent, is the right to control.

Power of attorney: A written instrument authorizing a person (the attorney-in-fact) to act as the agent on behalf of another to the extent indicated in the instrument.

Principal broker: The licensed broker directly in charge of and responsible for the real estate operations conducted by a brokerage company.

Procuring cause: The effort that brings about the desired result, as in producing the buyer for the listed property.

Property disclosure reports: State laws requiring property owners to disclose everything they know about their property to prospective buyers. This legislation places the burden of disclosing latent defects on the seller. However, although an agent doesn't have a *duty to discover* these defects, an agent still has a *duty to disclose* those they do know.

Special agent: An agent authorized by a principal to perform a single act like procuring a buyer or finding a house and negotiating an offer.

Subagent: An agent assigned to represent the same principal (seller) as the broker. In offices that practice subagency, all of the sales agents (in that office), on every company listing, represent the seller. Accordingly, all buyers working with these agents would have to be told that the seller is being represented but not them as a buyer. However, should both parties agree, a consensual dual agency agreement could be signed authorizing the same agent to conduct both sides of the transaction.

Undisclosed dual agency: An illegal practice of representing both sides of a transaction without the prior written consent of the parties being represented.

MISTAKEN IDENTITY

The following words are often confused with one another. Note the difference in meaning of these mistaken identity words and phrases.

Selling agent/Seller's agent: The *selling agent* works with a buyer making an offer and making the sale, whereas the *seller's agent* is the listing agent.

Cooperating agent/Subagent: The selling agent from another firm is called the *cooperating agent,* and may be either a buyer's agent or a *subagent* of the seller. If a subagent, then the cooperating agent owes fiduciary duties to the seller.

Principal/Principle: 1. The client is the *principal* in an agency relationship. 2. The original amount of a loan. (Sometimes principal is misspelled as *principle,* which is *a rule* or *doctrine.*)

QUESTIONS

1. The responsibilities of a real estate sales agent in a listing agency relationship include all of the following *EXCEPT*
   A. exercise of due care.
   B. accountability.
   C. obedience.
   D. repair of defects.

2. After showing a property a number of times and not securing an acceptable offer, the broker decides to buy the property himself. He must do which of the following?
   A. Wait until the listing expires and then make an offer to purchase
   B. Make his true position known to the seller
   C. Wait until he receives an offer and then offer a higher price
   D. Wait for at least 30 days and then offer the full asking price

3. The listing broker owes a direct fiduciary responsibility to whom?
   A. The listing salesperson
   B. The buyer
   C. The buyer's broker
   D. The seller

4. A subagent of a seller would *BEST* be described as which of the following?
   A. Special agent
   B. General agent
   C. Buyer's broker
   D. Universal agent

5. The *BEST* description of a special agent would be a person who
   A. is an attorney.
   B. is a property manager.
   C. has limited authority.
   D. has universal authority.

6. All of the following are fiduciaries *EXCEPT* the
   A. principal.
   B. trustee.
   C. guardian.
   D. receiver.

7. A salesperson employed by a real estate broker to show and sell property listed with the broker is *BEST* described as a(n)
   A. agent of the broker, who is an agent for the principal.
   B. agent for the principal.
   C. principal party to the transaction.
   D. independent contractor, not an agent.

8. An agency agreement to sell a specific piece of real property will be terminated by all of the following *EXCEPT*
   A. the death of the broker.
   B. bankruptcy of the seller.
   C. revocation of the listing salesperson's license.
   D. insanity of the broker.

9. When a salesperson makes a misrepresentation of a fact, the salesperson is liable only
   A. when the statement was made with malicious intent.
   B. if the salesperson is licensed.
   C. when the statement is a material fact.
   D. if the salesperson has a listing agreement.

10. An owner requests that a broker list a property for sale at $70,000. On inspection, the broker believes the property is worth $80,000. The broker should
    A. get a listing for the property at $70,000.
    B. buy the property for $70,000.
    C. suggest that the owner list the property for $75,000, so there will be room for bargaining.
    D. inform the seller that the property is worth $80,000.

11. The broker's responsibilities in presenting to the seller a written offer to purchase include all of the following *EXCEPT*
    A. making known to the seller all written offers before the seller accepts an offer.
    B. making known the ramifications and practical effects of an offer.
    C. presenting only the offers that are within 10 percent of the asking price.
    D. presenting all offers as rapidly as they are received.

12. When a property is advertised "principals only," which of the following groups is *EXCLUDED?*
    A. Agents
    B. People who are willing and able
    C. Persons wanting to live on the property
    D. Financially capable brokers interested as buyers

13. The position of trust assumed by the broker as an agent for the principal is described *MOST* accurately as a
    A. trustee relationship.
    B. trustor relationship.
    C. confidential relationship.
    D. fiduciary relationship.

14. As agent of the seller, a real estate broker is usually authorized to do all of the following *EXCEPT*
    A. bind the principal under a sales contract.
    B. advertise the listed property.
    C. place a For Sale sign on the listed property.
    D. cooperate with other brokers to effect a sale.

15. A seller tells her broker that termites have destroyed the floor and that the swimming pool is in violation of the city setback requirements. Which of the following must the broker's salesperson disclose to a prospective buyer?
    A. The condition of the floor only
    B. The pool violation only
    C. Both
    D. Neither, if the seller asks that it be done that way

16. ◎ In handling a real estate transaction, a broker should
    A. provide the client with a statement of the receipts and disbursements of the client's money.
    B. not reveal building code violations to the client.
    C. reveal only those things that are part of the public record.
    D. reveal only the items requested by the seller.

17. A fiduciary relationship usually exists between a principal and all of the following *EXCEPT* a(n)
    A. trustee.
    B. administrator.
    C. appraiser.
    D. receiver.

18. Regarding financial agreements made by the client, the broker
    A. need not see that those agreements are put in writing.
    B. is limited to setting the sales price and brokerage fee.
    C. may delegate this responsibility to the sales manager.
    D. is ethically bound to see that all contracts express the specific written agreement of parties concerning the details of the transaction.

19. A broker usually pays a salesperson a share of the commission received by the broker from a sale when
    A. the salesperson submits a sufficient earnest money deposit to the broker.
    B. the sale is consummated and title is transferred to the purchaser.
    C. there is a valid and binding offer and acceptance.
    D. the contract and earnest money are placed in escrow.

20. Which is *TRUE* about a fiduciary?
    A. Is a disinterested third party
    B. Looks after the principal's best interests
    C. Must be an employee of the broker
    D. Must be paid a fee

21. ◎ According to the laws of agency
    A. a broker must always charge a commission and put the amount on the listing form.
    B. a broker may sue and collect a commission even though he had a forfeited license when the commission was earned.
    C. the commission will be based on the listed price.
    D. the principal and the client are the same person.

22. Bernie works as a salesperson for Reginald. Bernie lists Yancey's house. What is the *BEST* way to classify Bernie's agency relationship?
    A. Agent of listing broker Reginald
    B. Agent of seller Yancey
    C. Subagent of cooperating broker
    D. Independent contractor

23. ◎ The seller's broker negotiating a difficult sales contract between an experienced seller of real estate and a novice purchaser should do which of the following?
    A. Not be concerned about the buyer's lack of experience
    B. Refuse to continue negotiating with the purchaser
    C. Insist that the purchaser employ an attorney
    D. Suggest that the purchaser consider employing another broker or an attorney

24. An agent will usually be entitled to receive a commission if the agent
    A. presents a written offer to purchase during the term of a valid listing.
    B. is the procuring cause of the sale.
    C. has an open listing and the property is sold by another broker with an open listing.
    D. holds an exclusive-agency listing contract and the property is sold by the seller.

25. The commission rate for the sale of real estate is determined by
    A. silent agreement among brokers in a local area.
    B. fixed schedules approved by the state licensing commission.
    C. scarcity of real estate for sale.
    D. negotiation between the broker and the seller.

26. The relationship between property owner and broker is that of
    A. seller and purchaser.
    B. attorney and client.
    C. principal and agent.
    D. optionor and optionee.

27. A salesperson responds to an ad in the paper of a "For Sale by Owner." The owner gives the salesperson a key to inspect the property being sold. What type of agency is *MOST* likely created?
    A. Fiduciary
    B. Implied agency
    C. Contractual
    D. No agency

28. The cooperating broker in a real estate transaction may be any of the following *EXCEPT* a
    A. listing broker.
    B. subagent.
    C. selling agent.
    D. buyer's agent.

29. A broker who signs a contract to manage an owner's property becomes a
    A. lessor.
    B. trustee.
    C. receiver.
    D. fiduciary.

30. Salespeople may accept compensation of their predetermined share of the commission from
    A. the multiple-listing service.
    B. the owner of the property.
    C. their employing broker.
    D. a cooperating broker.

31. It is an unethical practice for a broker representing a seller to do which of the following?
    A. Advise the seller of the highest price a prospective purchaser may be willing to pay
    B. Advise a prospective purchaser of the lowest price the seller is willing to accept
    C. Suggest to the buyer that the full asking price is an appropriate offer
    D. Encourage a broker from another company to try to sell the property

32. An attorney-in-fact, in executing the powers given to her under the provisions of a general power of attorney, usually has the right to do all of the following *EXCEPT*
    A. encumber the principal's property with the attorney-in-fact as beneficiary.
    B. sign the principal's name.
    C. record the power of attorney in the county where the principal's property is located.
    D. collect money for the principal.

33. A real estate broker may recover a commission in all of the following cases *EXCEPT*
    A. charging a 13 percent commission on raw land.
    B. failing to give the owner a copy of the listing at the time it is signed.
    C. charging more than 6 percent commission on residential land.
    D. while holding an inactive license.

34. A licensee who holds a bona fide option to buy a property is all of the following with respect to the property owner *EXCEPT* a(n)
    A. principal.
    B. agent.
    C. optionee.
    D. prospective buyer.

35. An agent with a valid listing is generally considered to have earned a commission
    A. only if title is transferred.
    B. when an offer has been secured from a prospective buyer.
    C. when a ready, willing, and able buyer who offers to buy on the principal's listing terms has been produced.
    D. only when the principal signs a contract of sale.

36. Any person, partnership, association, or corporation who authorizes or employs another, called the *agent,* to perform certain acts on his, her, or its behalf is *BEST* called the
    A. seller.
    B. broker.
    C. principal.
    D. assignor.

37. A real estate salesperson might lawfully accept an extra commission in a difficult sale from a(n)
    A. appreciative seller.
    B. thankful buyer.
    C. broker-employer.
    D. mortgage lender.

38. A broker must open a separate account
    A. for each condominium project handled.
    B. for each separate earnest money deposit handled.
    C. into which he may place both the client's money and his personal money.
    D. into which he may place all clients' monies and nothing more.

39. All of the following terminate an agency relationship *EXCEPT*
    A. the destruction of the subject matter.
    B. making an offer.
    C. death of the owner.
    D. bankruptcy of the principal broker.

40. One who has the right to sign the name of the principal to a contract of sale is a(n)
    A. real estate broker.
    B. special agent.
    C. attorney-in-fact.
    D. paralegal.

41. ◎ When money is deposited in a client trust account, part of which will be used to pay the broker's commission,
    A. the broker can withdraw her rightful share of the money before the real estate transaction is consummated or terminated.
    B. accurate records must be kept on the account.
    C. all interest belongs to the broker.
    D. the broker can recover the advertising expenses of the sale out of this account before closing.

42. An agency has been breached. The court may declare the remedy to be any of the following *EXCEPT*
    A. rescission.
    B. damages.
    C. specific performance.
    D. forfeiture.

43. The prime obligation of an agent to the principal is
    A. mutual trust.
    B. reverence.
    C. loyalty.
    D. thrift.

44. All of the following describe a fiduciary relationship *EXCEPT*
    A. lawyer to a client.
    B. trustor to beneficiary.
    C. listing broker to seller.
    D. property manager to owner.

45. If a salesperson uses undue influence in a real estate transaction, all of the following would be true *EXCEPT* that
    A. his license could be subject to suspension.
    B. his license could be subject to revocation.
    C. the broker of the salesperson would automatically lose her license.
    D. the contract could be voidable.

46. All of the following describe a fiduciary relationship *EXCEPT*
    A. agent to seller.
    B. mortgagor to mortgagee.
    C. attorney to client.
    D. attorney-in-fact to principal.

47. ◎ Which of the following facts about a listed property can a broker conceal?
    A. That the property is located within a 100-year floodplain zone
    B. That the family den was built without a building permit
    C. The type of neighbors who live in the surrounding area
    D. The results of an engineer's report regarding the environmental hazards

48. As a broker for a 30-unit condominium project, you discover that the exterior walls are 13½ inches from where they should be according to the building plans. You should do which of the following?
    A. Disregard it as being insignificant
    B. Seek an amendment to the plans
    C. Retain an architect
    D. Inform the client

49. A real estate broker who has entered into an agency contract with a seller may delegate responsibilities under the contract to one or more salespeople because
    A. all agency contracts are assignable.
    B. the contract always contains this specific authority.
    C. this is an implied authority arising out of custom.
    D. the real estate licensing agency permits this.

50. A broker inspected the seller's house and discovered it was 600 square feet larger than the tax records had indicated. The extra area is an addition built without a building permit. The broker should tell the client all of the following *EXCEPT* that
    A. the government could force the seller to remove the 600-square-foot addition.
    B. the seller should disclose this fact to any prospective buyer to avoid any claim of misrepresentation.
    C. the addition is no longer relevant because it has already been completed.
    D. the new buyers should be informed that they could be forced to tear down the illegal improvement.

51. The owner wants to sell property without the aid of a real estate broker. The owner may legally do all of the following *EXCEPT*
    A. evaluate the purchasing power of the buyer.
    B. write up the sales contract between seller and buyer.
    C. require that the buyer assume the present mortgage.
    D. state preference for a buyer of the same color.

52. When a buyer is about to buy a property, which of the following statements is *TRUE?*
    A. The listing broker can request that the earnest money check be made payable to her.
    B. The salesperson can request the check be made payable to him.
    C. The salesperson should accept only cash for earnest money.
    D. It is mandatory for the validity of a contract to take earnest money.

53. A power of attorney for a real estate sales contract is effective when
    A. it is not in writing.
    B. either party dies.
    C. it is signed by the principal.
    D. it is signed only by the attorney-in-fact.

54. A real estate office has a listing for $90,000. A buyer makes an offer for $105,000. Without the knowledge of the seller, the listing office can do which of the following?
    A. Offer to buy the property through a nominee for $90,000
    B. Suggest that the broker reduce the offer to $90,000
    C. Buy directly from the seller for $95,000 and the next day resell to that original buyer for $105,000
    D. Present the $105,000 offer to the seller

55. All of the following describe a special agent *EXCEPT* one who has
    A. authority to find a buyer for a seller.
    B. power of attorney to sell a property
    C. authority to represent a principal in all matters.
    D. authority to represent a buyer to find a property.

56. The broker for the seller owes an obligation to do which of the following?
    A. Divide the commission with another broker chosen or preferred by the buyer
    B. Divulge to the buyer the lowest price at which the seller will sell
    C. Present to the principal all written offers the broker receives, including all of the terms and conditions of each offer signed by a prospective buyer
    D. Keep the property in top condition

57. As commission for negotiating the sale of a $1 million hotel, a broker received title to a parcel of land valued at $30,000. The same day that the escrow on the hotel closed, the broker sold the land for $40,000. Which of the following is *TRUE* about the broker's actions in selling the land?
    A. Such action violates the licensing law because of the secret profit.
    B. Such action violates the licensing law if the broker does not give written notice to the hotel client of the sale.
    C. It is illegal to receive land as a commission.
    D. It is proper behavior because the broker did not resell the land until after title to it was received.

58. The relationship between a real estate agent and a principal is *MOST* similar to which of the following?
    A. Optionee and optionor
    B. Vendee and vendor
    C. Trustee and beneficiary
    D. Mortgagee and mortgagor

59. ◎ All of the following actions by a real estate agent are considered fraud *EXCEPT*
    A. not disclosing that a septic tank overflows into the stream and the county has issued a citation.
    B. telling the buyer that this is one of the best town houses in the county.
    C. providing estimates of income potential based on past figures much higher than actual income.
    D. concealing a cracked foundation with spray paint.

60. ◎ What is the appropriate remedy for a broker against a seller who wrongfully refuses to pay an earned commission?
    A. File an attachment
    B. File a lawsuit
    C. File a lien against the property
    D. File a lis pendens

61. All but which one of the following are proper responsibilities of a real estate agent?
    A. Loyalty
    B. Skill
    C. Financing
    D. Accountability

62. Under which of the following circumstances might a broker be liable for misrepresentation for negotiations with a prospective buyer?
    A. The broker states the land area is approximately one acre, when it is actually 44,000 square feet.
    B. The broker fails to mention that a structurally unsound grocery store is a non-conforming use.
    C. The broker passes on accurate information to the buyer that was given to him by the seller.
    D. The broker fails to disclose the height of the building.

63. Which of the following statements is *TRUE?*
    A. A listing broker can tell a prospective buyer that the seller will accept less than the asking price if the seller will, in fact, accept the lower figure.
    B. A listing broker can refuse to transmit an offer to the seller if she thinks it is too low.
    C. The broker should present the first offer, then wait until that is accepted or rejected before presenting the next one.
    D. The broker must present all offers as soon as she receives them.

64. ◎ All of the following statements concerning the principal-agent disclosure are true *EXCEPT*
    A. as long as a broker discloses that he is acting for a named principal, the broker usually is not liable if the principal defaults.
    B. a broker is personally liable for the principal's default on a contract that the broker negotiated without naming the principal.
    C. the broker may work for either the buyer or seller but not for both.
    D. the broker can act for both the buyer and seller in the same transaction as long as his or her position is disclosed and agreed to in writing by both of the parties.

65. To establish a firm legal contract between a broker and a seller, the prudent broker should
    A. obtain an oral listing agreement from the seller.
    B. file a suit in a court of law.
    C. wait until a buyer is found and then seek to put the listing in written form.
    D. have her employment contract (the listing) in writing.

66. A real estate broker may lose the right to a commission in all cases, *EXCEPT* if she
    A. is guilty of a misstatement of known facts.
    B. is not licensed when hired as an agent.
    C. can show she had a written exclusive-right-to-sell contract in force at the time of the sale.
    D. quotes information to a buyer not authorized by a seller.

67. A listing broker receives an offer that fully matches the listing terms. Before presenting the offer, the broker receives two more offers, one for less than the listing price but for cash and one for more than the listing price but where the seller has to take back a mortgage. What is the *BEST* approach for the listing broker?
    A. Present the offer for the highest price
    B. Present all offers at the same time
    C. Present the cash offer first
    D. Present the offers in the order received, one at a time

68. A real estate licensee should advise the use of legal counsel in which of the following cases?
    A. In determining the value of a property before taking a listing
    B. In comparing interest rates and discounts offered by several lenders
    C. In determining the effect of a due-on-sale clause
    D. In presenting an offer from a potential purchaser

69. Before obtaining a listing on a property that shares a driveway with the adjacent house, the owner insists that the broker not mention this fact to any prospective purchaser. Regarding this problem, the broker should
    A. inform a prospective buyer in spite of the seller's insistence.
    B. not mention this fact unless a buyer asks.
    C. refuse the listing if he can't persuade the owner to disclose.
    D. do as the seller asks.

70. A broker has a listing on a house that contains a provision that the house is to be sold in an "as is" condition. The broker learns of a major hidden defect in the property. When showing the house to a prospective purchaser, the broker should
    A. advise the buyer of the defect.
    B. point out only that the house will be sold in an "as is" condition.
    C. mention the defect to the buyer only if asked.
    D. inform the buyer that the seller has disclosed no defects.

71. Concerning a sale between a buyer and seller, the real estate licensee should
    A. advise them to have the title searched.
    B. tell them the legal effect of the liens contained in the title commitment.
    C. recommend the method of holding title.
    D. advise the buyer against the use of a buyer's agent.

72. A broker can accept commissions from both buyer and seller under which one of the following conditions?
    A. Only if there is a written listing from both
    B. Under no circumstances
    C. Only if both consent after full disclosure
    D. Only if the total amount is under $10,000

73. Which of the following is *MOST* likely treated as an independent contractor?
    A. Principal broker
    B. Salesperson
    C. Broker in charge
    D. Secretary

74. Because the broker is in a hurry, she or he persuades the seller to sign a blank listing agreement so she or he can fill it out in a few days. This is a
    A. violation of the labor laws.
    B. commonly accepted business practice.
    C. highly unprofessional business practice.
    D. valid contract.

75. The fiduciary relationship between real estate broker and seller is most likely terminated at which point?
    A. On listing the property in the MLS
    B. On finding a ready, willing, and able buyer
    C. On close of escrow (settlement)
    D. When the seller retains an attorney to handle the closing

76. A power of attorney that is effective even after the principal's subsequent disability or incapacity is called which one of the following?
    A. Unilateral
    B. Durable
    C. Continuous
    D. Fixed

77. All of the following are material facts that need to be disclosed by the real estate broker *EXCEPT* that
    A. the prior tenant had AIDS.
    B. the roof leaks.
    C. there is a drainage problem.
    D. the house is not connected to a sewer.

78. ◎ A buyer client asks the broker about the value of a particular property. The broker should
   A. provide an appraisal estimate of the property value based on comparable sales in the neighborhood.
   B. indicate that she is not an appraiser but can provide information on prices that other properties have sold for recently.
   C. provide an appraisal estimate based on a statistical analysis of MLS listing prices.
   D. provide an appraisal estimate of the property value based on her best judgment.

79. A licensed broker who represents both the buyer and the seller as clients in the same transaction is *MOST* commonly known as a
   A. cooperating broker.
   B. designated agent.
   C. middleman.
   D. consensual dual agent.

ANSWERS

1. **D.** The usual special agency involved between broker and seller normally does not include the repair of the listed property.

2. **B.** It is not necessary that the listing first expire, but the agent must be extremely careful to disclose his or her interest in writing and avoid any possibility of self-dealing or secret profiting.

3. **D.** The listing broker owes fiduciary duties to the seller, although he or she also has an ethical duty to treat fairly all parties to the transaction, including the buyer. The broker has a master-servant relationship with the salesperson (whether employee or independent contractor).

4. **A.** The salespeople of the broker would be agents of the broker and subagents of the seller assigned to a special task and cloaked with limited authority—finding a ready, willing, and able buyer to buy on the listing terms.

5. **C.** A real estate agent has limited authority and is a special agent. A property manager whose duties include many tasks would most likely be a general agent. One who has complete authority is known as a universal agent.

6. **A.** The principal is the one to whom the fiduciary duties are owed; for example, fiduciary duties are owed by a receiver to a bankrupt estate, by a guardian to his or her ward's estate, and by a trustee to the beneficiary of the trust.

7. **A.** The salesperson is a subagent of the seller and is authorized to carry out many of the duties of the broker. This is true regardless of whether the salesperson claims to be an employee or an independent contractor for tax purposes.

8. **C.** An agency agreement is a personal service contract and will terminate on death of either the agent or the principal. Bankruptcy results in the involuntary transfer of title to the receiver, so this will terminate the listing. Because the listing is a contract between the agent (broker) and the principal, what happens to the salesperson who obtained the listing will have no effect.

9. **C.** For example, the fact the buyer is a veteran is usually not a material fact, except if the buyer is assuming a VA loan. The salesperson is also liable for innocent misrepresentations (false statements made either in ignorance or in good faith). Usually the salesperson is not a principal party to a transaction, such as buyer or seller.

10. **D.** The broker has a fiduciary duty to protect the best interests of the client, which, in this case, would be to inform the owner of the true worth of the property and then discuss an appropriate listing price.

11. **C.** Regardless of the order in which offers are received by the broker, the broker should present all written offers—even after one

offer is accepted, because it should be left up to the owner whether to accept a backup contract. The broker plays a critical role in explaining the effect of an offer's contingencies, financing provisions, or a "time is of the essence" clause.

12. **A.** The owner does not want to deal with intermediaries such as real estate agents.

13. **D.** The broker has the fiduciary duties of loyalty, care, obedience, skill, accountability, and confidentiality.

14. **A.** Under the limited authority received in the standard listing contract, the broker cannot normally commit the principal to a sales contract (absent a power of attorney).

15. **C.** Failure to disclose material defects in property for sale could be grounds for a charge of misrepresentation by the agent (concealment of material fact), especially in view of the present consumer-favoring trend of the courts away from the former caveat emptor (let the buyer beware) doctrine.

16. **A.** One of the fiduciary duties is to account for client monies. The agent can be liable for failure to reveal any pertinent fact about the property.

17. **C.** The appraiser is hired to render an independent evaluation of the property and generally is not entrusted with the client's properties or authorized to act as an agent.

18. **D.** Practically speaking, in most states the parties rely on the broker, not an attorney, to protect them in their contract negotiations, especially regarding the financial commitments of the transaction (purchase contract terms, such as price, financing, and contingencies).

19. **B.** Although the broker and salesperson usually earn their commission when the contract is signed, payment of the commission typically is deferred until the sale is closed.

20. **B.** The fiduciary is a very interested party who is held to a high standard of trust and confidence toward the principal's property.

21. **D.** The broker may waive any commission but cannot sue for a commission unless able to prove that he or she was licensed and had a written employment agreement.

22. **A.** As a salesperson, Bernie is the agent of the listing broker. This is true even if Bernie is an independent contractor for tax purposes. Reginald is the primary agent of the seller. Bernie also represents Yancey but not as the primary agent, more in the capacity of Reginald's agent (technically a subagent, although in common terminology *subagency* usually refers to a cooperating broker working with the listing broker on behalf of the seller).

23. **D.** The broker has a duty to treat all parties fairly yet owes first and undivided loyalty to the seller. The seller's broker should recommend that the buyer get assistance, so the buyer will be in an equal bargaining position. Otherwise, the buyer may try to cancel the contract later for alleged undue influence.

24. **B.** The written offer must be either on the listing terms or acceptable to the seller. Note, however, that it is less important for an agent to be the procuring cause in an exclusive-right-to-sell listing than in an open listing.

25. **D.** Any attempt to fix the rates by the commission, local board, or groups of brokers would be in violation of state and federal antitrust laws.

26. **C.** It is a fiduciary relationship.

27. **D.** The salesperson has not been employed by the owner to sell the property. The owner has merely allowed the salesperson to arrange a convenient showing to a prospect.

28. **A.** The listing broker is the seller's agent. The licensed cooperating broker may represent either the seller as a subagent or the buyer as a buyer's agent; also called the *selling agent*.

29. **D.** The broker is placed in a special position of trust and confidence in this fiduciary management relationship.

30. **C.** Salespersons can receive money only from their employing brokers; they can't take even a special bonus directly from a principal.

31. **B.** The broker would be breaching the duties of loyalty and confidentiality to reveal a price to a buyer other than that agreed on by the owner in the listing or addendum. Rather than saying, "The property is listed at $100,000, but I know the owner will take $90,000," the broker should say, "The property is listed at $100,000 and if you are going to submit an offer of less than that, I'll take the offer to the seller and see what he or she says."

32. **A.** Such self-dealing action would violate fiduciary duty because the agent-lender would have a conflict of interest.

33. **D.** There is no limit on the amount of commission. Under most state license laws, the broker must give the owner a copy of the listing at the time it is signed—failure to do so usually won't affect the right to a commission, but it might result in suspension or revocation of the license.

34. **B.** Brokers can be principals for their own accounts. In such cases, they must disclose their license status.

35. **C.** Even if the principal decided not to sign, the broker who was the procuring cause may have earned a commission if the offer matched the listing terms.

36. **C.** Certain principal-agent relationships are fiduciary relationships. A seller is but one common example of a principal.

37. **C.** A salesperson cannot receive compensation directly from anyone other than her broker.

38. **D.** Many brokers use one client trust account but have separate ledgers for each transaction.

39. **B.** When the property is destroyed or when the purpose of the agency is accomplished, the listing terminates. This could be when a ready, willing, and able buyer is produced with an offer at the listing terms or when the buyer's offer is accepted.

40. **C.** An attorney-in-fact operates under a power of attorney. Under the equal dignities rule, this power should be in recordable form if the attorney is to sign the name of the principal to a recordable document such as a deed.

41. **B.** The broker cannot withdraw money even though the commission has been earned.

42. **C.** Courts will not force someone to perform a personal service agency contract; money damages will suffice to compensate for the breach.

43. **C.** Undivided loyalty is the essence of the agency relationship.

44. **B.** Trustor to beneficiary in a deed of trust is the relationship of debtor to creditor or borrower to lender.

45. **C.** The contract may be voidable because of the actions of the principal's agents. For this reason it is important to select a competent and ethical agent. It must be proved that a broker failed to supervise (not an automatic assumption).

46. **B.** This is a debtor-creditor relationship.

47. **C.** The broker must disclose material facts to the buyer. Choice (A) is a material fact because the lender will require that the buyer (borrower) obtain federal flood insurance. Choice (B) is material because the concealment of a known building code violation amounts to fraud. Choice (C), however, could involve a discrimination complaint based on steering.

48. **D.** Because many legal questions are raised, this is an example of a situation in which the client or builder should be notified. The building discrepancy is a material fact that should not be disregarded.

49. **C.** It is customary for a broker to delegate to the sales staff (as subagents of the principal) the performance of certain tasks, such as showing property or finding buyers.

50. **C.** The seller should be told that the building department may have the power to force a removal of an illegal addition. Such a material fact must be disclosed to the buyer. If the seller orders the broker not to reveal this information, the broker may have to withdraw from the listing to avoid becoming a party to the concealment.

51. **D.** An owner cannot violate federal and state antidiscrimination laws. Preparing one's own legal documents is permissible.

52. **A.** The broker then must deposit the check into a client trust account or into escrow. Deposit checks cannot be made payable to the salesperson, who has no authority in this matter.

53. **C.** Death terminates the agency power of attorney. Because the statute of frauds requires that real estate sales contracts be in writing, then, under the "equal dignities rule," the power of attorney must also be of the same dignity, that is, be in writing.

54. **D.** If a broker decides to purchase property that is listed with the firm, it is essential to disclose in writing his or her true position. A straw man or intermediary cannot be used to buy for the broker in secret. The broker could lose his or her license for such self-dealing in obtaining secret profits.

55. **C.** All of these are examples of a special agency except (C), which is an example of a universal agency.

56. **C.** The broker may not decide which offer would be the best to present to the seller.

57. **D.** It is proper for the broker to accept land as a commission, and there is no obligation to disclose to the client what becomes of the commission.

58. **C.** The trustee in a deed of trust is a fiduciary who holds title to the secured property for the benefit of the beneficiary (lender). The trustor is the borrower.

59. **B.** Agents are liable for concealing or intentionally falsifying material facts. Statements such as "the best town houses" are classified as puffery or matters of judgment. If facts such as property condition or income statistics are misrepresented with intent to deceive, then the agent is guilty of fraud and subject to punitive as well as actual damages.

60. **B.** A broker can seek a money judgment against the seller but usually does not qualify as a laborer under the mechanic's lien law.

61. **C.** Agents are not responsible for arranging financing, although they often use their skills to help their buyer-customer obtain needed financing on the best terms available.

62. **B.** The use of the word *approximately* in citing land areas gives leeway for slight differences in square feet. The broker must disclose pertinent facts, such as the fact that because of zoning regulations the new buyer probably would not be able to make needed structural changes to the grocery store without risking loss of nonconforming use status. The building height is an obvious fact.

63. **D.** A broker cannot quote a price less than the price authorized by the seller (usually the listing price), even though the broker knows the seller will accept. The broker has a duty of undivided loyalty and should encourage the buyer to make an offer, which the broker will transmit to the seller. The broker must transmit *all* written offers (not just the high ones) and let the seller make the final decision.

64. **C.** The broker is not liable on the principal's contracts unless there are special facts involving misrepresentation. But if the broker fails to reveal his position as agent, then responsibility would fall to the broker for the contracts he signs. The broker then may seek damages against the undisclosed principal. Dual agency is permitted, provided full disclosure is given and consent is obtained from both buyer and seller.

65. **D.** Even in those states that permit oral listings, it is good practice to obtain such an employment agreement in writing to avoid disputes. A lawsuit is only necessary in those cases where a seller breaches the terms of an enforceable listing agreement.

66. **C.** If a broker is guilty of misrepresentation, she may lose the right to a commission, especially where the principal is an innocent party who suffers damage. To be entitled to a commission, the broker must be licensed at the time of the hiring and at the time of performance under the terms of the listing.

67. **B.** The broker must try to locate the seller immediately to present offers as they are received. Because this is not always possi-

ble, the broker should keep the seller apprised of all offers received (or even ones that may be in the works). It would be improper practice to urge a seller to decide whether to accept or reject an offer before presenting other offers known to the broker.

68. **C.** An attorney could best advise on the legal consequences of clauses such as prepayment, subordination, or due on sale. Although (A) might best be done by an appraiser and (B) by a mortgage broker, both of these overlap into typical work (D) done by the broker.

69. **C.** A shared driveway could involve an encroachment or an easement and is the type of material fact that must be disclosed to the buyer, otherwise there could be a problem with unmarketable title or with misrepresentation. If a broker can't persuade the principal of the need to make this disclosure, the broker may have to refuse the listing so that he is not a party to a fraud. The broker must inform the seller of all knowledge and offer recommendations. If the broker *already* has the listing, then choice (A) is a possibility.

70. **A.** The use of the words "as is" does not protect the seller or broker from liability for misrepresentations owing to concealment of material defects that can't be easily observed. In essence, this phrase informs the buyer that the seller intends to make no repairs to the *obvious* problems with the structure.

71. **A.** It is sound advice to have the title searched to discover any defects. If the broker sees there are defects or if the client seeks information on the legal effect of various liens, the broker should refer the client to an attorney because only an attorney is qualified to give legal advice. The listing broker should not discourage the buyer from seeking independent advice.

72. **C.** Dual agency is permitted, *provided* both buyer and seller give their informed consent in writing after full disclosure.

73. **B.** The salesperson must not be compensated on a hourly basis. The principal broker and the broker in charge act in a supervisory capacity. The secretary is an employee.

74. **C.** The proper practice is to complete the essential portions of the agreement before the seller signs it. Not doing so is highly unprofessional if not illegal.

75. **C.** The special relationship terminates on the completion of the purpose of the agency, that is, the closing of the sale. This is true even though the broker has earned the commission on procuring the buyer. Note that the fiduciary duty of confidentiality continues even after the agency ends.

76. **B.** The written power of attorney must clearly show the intent to be *durable*.

77. **A.** Licensing laws specifically exempt AIDS from material fact disclosure.

78. **B.** The broker should not give professional advice unless she has the professional qualifications to do so and is willing to assume the risk.

79. **D.** A consensual dual agent has two clients, the buyer and the seller, both consenting to the common representation. A designated or appointed agent refers to a special classification (in certain states) that permit one person in an office to be appointed to represent the buyer and another agent appointed to represent the seller, without the broker being deemed a dual agent. The cooperating broker typically refers to the agent representing the buyer (and the listing broker agreeing to cooperate and compensate).

Listings

A listing is a written employment contract in which the owner authorizes a broker to deal with prospective buyers on behalf of the owner. The listing is a personal service contract that can neither be recorded nor assigned. The amount of commission is negotiable between the owner and the broker's agent.

The listing agent represents the seller; in some cases, the listing agent may offer to represent the buyer as well as the seller in what is called a *consensual dual agency*. In other cases, the buyer may decide to retain the services of a buyer's broker to represent the buyer exclusively—in most cases, the buyer's broker will be paid from an authorized commission split with the listing broker. Check state law for new classifications such as *designated agency* or *appointed agency* or *transaction broker.*

The main types of listings are the exclusive listings, open listings, and net listings. The multiple-listing service (MLS) is an organization of local or regional brokers who agree to share their listings by pooling them on a shared Web site.

The questions in this chapter test your comprehension of the following topics:

- Types of listing contracts

- The multiple-listing service

- Termination of listing agreements

- Responsibilities of the listing agent

- When a commission is earned

KEY WORDS

Commission: The compensation paid to a real estate broker (usually by the seller) for services rendered in connection with the sale or exchange of real property.

Exclusive agency: A written listing agreement giving one agent the right to sell property for a specified time but reserving to the owner the right to sell the property himself or herself without payment of any commission.

Exclusive listing: A written listing of real property in which the seller agrees to appoint only one broker to sell the property for a specified period of time. The two types of exclusive listings are the exclusive agency and the exclusive-right-to-sell.

Listing: A written employment agreement between a property owner and a broker authorizing the broker to find a buyer or a tenant for a certain real property.

Multiple-listing service (MLS): An organization created by REALTORS® to facilitate the sharing of listings among member brokers.

Net listings: A listing where the broker and client-seller agree that the client-seller will receive a net amount from the sale of the property. The broker then takes everything over the agreed net figure as commission. The taking of a net listing is a breach of the broker's fiduciary duty of reasonable care and in most states illegal because the listed price must be identified on the listing contract.

Open listing: A listing given to any number of brokers. The first broker who secures a buyer ready, willing, and able to purchase at the terms of the listing is the one who earns the commission.

Protection clause: A clause contained in a listing that provides protection for the broker. It states that a broker is still entitled to a commission (for a set period of time after the listing has expired) if the property is sold to a prospect that was introduced to the property during the listed period. In some states, before the expiration of the listing, the broker is required to give the owner a list of the names that protection is being sought for or no protection will be granted.

MISTAKEN IDENTITY

The following words are often confused with one another. Note the difference in meaning of these mistaken identity types of listings.

Exclusive right to sell/Exclusive agency: The *exclusive right to sell* gives the broker a commission no matter who sells the property (the owner or other brokers), whereas under an *exclusive agency,* no commission is due if the seller finds the buyer.

QUESTIONS

1. In a multiple listing, a salesperson who nego-
   tiates a sale is directly responsible to
   A. the listing broker.
   B. her employing broker.
   C. the multiple-listing service.
   D. the seller.

2. The listing broker brought a pre-approved
   buyer to the seller and obtained a $500 ear-
   nest money deposit. The two agreed on the
   purchase price and entered into a contract.
   Later the buyer and seller decide to mutually
   rescind the contract and did so. If the listing
   broker decided to pursue and sue the seller
   for a commission, how much commission is
   the broker entitled to earn?
   A. $500
   B. $1,250
   C. Full commission
   D. Nothing

3. A contract that provides for the payment of a
   commission to the listing broker, no matter
   who sells the property, is called a(n)
   A. net listing.
   B. open listing.
   C. exclusive-agency listing.
   D. exclusive-right-to-sell listing.

4. A listing contract will be terminated by any of
   the following *EXCEPT*
   A. destruction of the listed property.
   B. death of the listing broker.
   C. bankruptcy of the listing broker.
   D. a sudden increase in market value.

5. When a broker gets a listing
   A. the listing should be prepared in writing.
   B. any buyer must be furnished with a copy
      of the listing.
   C. the seller may lawfully cancel it any time
      the seller decides the broker is not doing a
      good job.
   D. there is no fiduciary relationship between
      a broker and the seller.

6. A property is listed with a broker at $65,000,
   although the broker is told that the owner
   will accept $62,000. A buyer prefers to sign
   an offer for $62,000, but indicates $65,000
   could be offered. The broker should
   A. refuse to submit the $62,000 offer.
   B. suggest a compromise of $63,500.
   C. persuade the buyer to make a $65,000
      offer.
   D. persuade the buyer to go to another broker.

7. Except under specific conditions, an agent
   may serve only one principal at a time; how-
   ever, a principal may contract to have more
   than one agent. Which of the following would
   BEST describe such a situation?
   A. Multiple listing
   B. Open listing
   C. Exclusive agency
   D. Exclusive right to sell

8. Under open listings, which of the following is
   TRUE?
   A. More than one broker may attempt to sell
      the listed property.
   B. All brokers with open listings on the
      property will split the commission when
      the property is sold.
   C. Each listing must be canceled in writing.
   D. The listing must be submitted to the mul-
      tiple-listing service.

9. A broker may provide for which of the fol-
   lowing in an exclusive listing contract?
   A. An automatic continuation of the term of
      the listing beyond the final termination
      date specified in the contract
   B. Permission to post a sign on the property
      being listed
   C. Permission for the salesperson to show
      the listing only to U.S. citizens
   D. Permission to conceal presence of radon

10. Which of the following is *TRUE?*
    A. A broker must get the signatures of all owners on the listing form to be entitled to any commission.
    B. A broker should not advertise without the written authorization of the owner.
    C. A broker should not place a sign on the property without written authority.
    D. All other brokers showing the property also must have written authority to do so.

11. ◎ All of the following terminate an agency created by a listing *EXCEPT*
    A. insolvency of the listing broker.
    B. fire destroying the listed property.
    C. mental disability of the listing salesperson.
    D. death of the owner.

12. The listing contract creates a(n)
    A. fiduciary agency relationship between broker and seller.
    B. special agency relationship between broker and salesperson.
    C. agency between the buyer and the seller.
    D. agency between the buyer and the broker showing the property.

13. Which of the following statements about listing brokers is *TRUE?*
    A. A listing broker can tell a prospective buyer that the seller will accept less than the asking price if the seller will, in fact, accept the lower figure.
    B. A listing broker can refuse to transmit a "too-low" offer to the seller.
    C. The broker needs to present only full price offers.
    D. If the offer is not going to be full price, the broker should still encourage the buyer to make a written offer.

14. An agent for the seller is considered to have earned a commission
    A. only if a sale is completed and title is transferred.
    B. if a purchaser is produced who is ready, willing, and able to buy on terms acceptable to the purchaser.
    C. when the agent presents a written offer if it is for full price, regardless of its terms.
    D. if a binding contract to purchase is signed, even if the seller later defaults.

15. ◎ A salesperson holds two listings—an open listing on one property and an exclusive listing on another. Neither one contains a safety clause, and one week after both listings expire, the two owners get together and exchange properties without previously being shown the properties. The salesperson
    A. may sue for full commissions on both.
    B. may sue for commission on the open listing.
    C. may demand full commission on the exclusive listing.
    D. will receive no commission from either listing.

16. Which type of listing gives a broker the greatest protection?
    A. Open listing
    B. Net listing
    C. Exclusive right to sell
    D. Exclusive agency

17. When a broker has an exclusive-right-to-sell listing
    A. the seller may sell the property independently without the obligation to pay a commission.
    B. the broker is entitled to a commission if a sale does not close owing to the seller's fault.
    C. only the broker is allowed to show or sell the property.
    D. anything over the asking price is considered to be the broker's commission.

18. Under federal law, which of the following is prohibited?
    A. Taking a net listing
    B. Taking a listing in which the broker will receive all of the purchase price that exceeds an agreed amount
    C. Signing a listing with more than one broker
    D. Taking a listing that excludes sales to parents with children

19. ◎ After showing a listed property to a prospect, the broker with an exclusive-agency listing, to protect his commission, should
    A. make a record of it in the broker's files.
    B. notify the seller of the prospect's identity.
    C. send an office memo to the prospective buyer.
    D. wait until the prospect makes a deal with seller.

20. To a listing broker, the property owner is known as a(n)
    A. agent.
    B. fiduciary.
    C. prospect.
    D. principal.

21. A copy of a listing agreement must
    A. be presented to the person signing the agreement.
    B. include all the terms and conditions of the sale.
    C. be given to the purchaser.
    D. be given to the broker representing the purchaser.

22. An exclusive listing is terminated with no further liability by
    A. mutual agreement.
    B. the principal's default.
    C. election of the seller.
    D. election of the broker.

23. In listing and marketing real property, it is important for the salesperson to do all of the following *EXCEPT*
    A. check the survey stakes and boundaries.
    B. determine who is in actual possession of the property.
    C. select an escrow company to handle the closing.
    D. obtain the signature of the seller(s).

24. To be enforceable, an open listing must
    A. have a specific termination date and be in writing.
    B. be signed by both buyer and seller.
    C. be canceled in writing by all listing brokers.
    D. state a specific asking price.

25. The owner of a property who signed a 60-day listing with a broker was killed in an accident before the broker procured a buyer. This listing is
    A. binding on the owner's heirs to carry out the promises.
    B. no good as an authorization, but binding if a buyer is secured later.
    C. terminated immediately on death.
    D. still in effect because the owner's intent was clearly stated.

26. Death of either the principal or agent terminates the
    A. listing contract.
    B. contract for sale.
    C. deed.
    D. mortgage.

27. A broker can take part of the commission out of the client's trust account prior to closing
    A. on seller's permission.
    B. provided there are enough funds left over to complete the closing.
    C. at any time after the deposit is placed in escrow.
    D. only on written consent of the buyer and seller.

28. When a salesperson enters into a listing contract as agent of a broker, the salesperson must do all of the following *EXCEPT*
    A. execute the contract by signing the broker's name.
    B. give a copy of the listing contract to the owner.
    C. carefully explain all of the terms of the contract to the seller.
    D. give a copy of the listing contract to the broker with whom the salesperson is associated.

29. ◎ A listing broker can do which of the following without written approval of the seller?
    A. Buy the property directly from the seller/client, then resell it immediately to a buyer for a higher price
    B. Have a friend buy the property directly from the seller/client and resell it immediately to a buyer and split the profit with the friend
    C. Quote a price considerably lower than that specified by the listing
    D. Encourage a buyer to submit a written offer even if it doesn't match the asking price

30. In a typical real estate listing contract, the broker would be *BEST* described as
    A. a dual agent.
    B. a special agent.
    C. the principal for the agent.
    D. the principal for the subagent.

31. If the real property owner is a corporation, then the individual authorized to sign the listing agreement is the
    A. president.
    B. secretary.
    C. person named by corporate resolution.
    D. treasurer.

32. The seller misrepresented the zoning of the property. The listing broker then unintentionally placed incorrect information into the multiple-listing service. Which one of the following is *LEAST* likely to be liable for the misrepresentation?
    A. The MLS
    B. The listing salesperson
    C. The seller
    D. The listing broker

33. Which of the following statements about exclusive listings is *TRUE?*
    A. An exclusive-right-to-sell listing should be in writing.
    B. An exclusive-agency contract can be terminated prior to the expiration date only by the sale of the property by the listing broker.
    C. Death of the owner will not terminate the listing.
    D. If the property is destroyed, the listing will still remain active.

34. When a broker has an exclusive-right-to-sell listing
    A. the seller may sell through his or her own efforts without obligation to pay a commission.
    B. the broker who procures a cash buyer on the listing terms is entitled to a commission, regardless of whether the sale of the property is closed.
    C. any money above the listed price goes to the broker.
    D. the listing is given to more than one broker.

35. The type of listing in which the broker and seller are *LEAST* likely to know the amount of money that will be received as commission for the sale of the property is a(n)
    A. open listing.
    B. exclusive-authorization-to-sell.
    C. multiple listing.
    D. net listing.

36. A broker obtains an oral exclusive-right-to-sell listing for 13 months. The listing is usually
    A. valid.
    B. binding.
    C. unenforceable.
    D. enforceable.

37. A broker has *MOST* likely earned a commission in which of the following cases?
    A. The broker has communicated the acceptance of the seller to the buyer.
    B. The broker has obtained a substantial deposit with an offer.
    C. The broker presents a written offer to the seller.
    D. The broker finds a buyer who communicates an interest to pay the full asking price.

38. All of the following are valid reasons to terminate an exclusive listing *EXCEPT*
    A. the listing person transfers to another brokerage company.
    B. broker and seller agree to terminate.
    C. the seller refuses to sell to minorities.
    D. the property is destroyed by natural cause.

39. The phrase *procuring cause* is *MOST* significant to a seller in relation to a(n)
    A. exclusive agency.
    B. open listing.
    C. exclusive-right-to-sell listing.
    D. net listing.

40. The seller's broker was working with a buyer under an exclusive-authorization-to-sell listing and presented an offer at less than the listed price. At the same time, the owner was dealing with another buyer who offered more money for the property and all in cash. The owner sold to the buyer who paid all in cash at the higher price. The broker is entitled to
    A. a reasonable commission based on the offer.
    B. stop the sale of the property.
    C. void the sale.
    D. a commission based on the higher selling price.

41. In the absence of a prior agreement as to when the broker's commission is earned, such commission is earned
    A. on consummation of the deal.
    B. on a meeting of the minds of buyer and seller.
    C. at the time the broker introduces the buyer to the seller.
    D. when the deed is delivered.

42. An exclusive-right-to-sell listing contract does which of the following?
    A. Provides that if the owner sells the property independently, the broker does not receive a commission
    B. Terminates on the death of the seller
    C. Continues even if the owner or the broker goes through bankruptcy
    D. Allows for verbal cancellation

43. After the sale, the listing broker refused to split the commission with the buyer's broker as agreed. Who is responsible for paying the buyer's broker?
    A. Listing salesperson
    B. Listing broker
    C. Seller
    D. Escrow service

44. The principal in the fiduciary relationship created by a listing agreement is the
    A. seller.
    B. salesperson who got the listing.
    C. broker.
    D. buyer.

45. A broker secured a signed offer with a $5,000 deposit on the exact terms of a listing, but the seller refused to accept it. Which of the following statements is *TRUE?*
    A. The broker could maintain a suit for commission in court.
    B. The buyer could maintain a suit to force the seller to sell because there was compliance with the listing.
    C. The broker should tell the seller that the seller must accept.
    D. The broker cannot collect a commission in excess of $5,000.

46. A broker can obtain a commission from both the buyer and seller in which case?
    A. With written permission of buyer and seller
    B. Under no circumstances
    C. When the broker holds the listing and then acts on behalf of the buyer in negotiating the purchase
    D. When the broker is working with a buyer who eventually buys a property listed in-house

47. ◎ A broker is holding an earnest money deposit, equal to the amount of the commission. The seller, at the closing, not only refuses to pay the broker a commission but also demands the broker pay him the entire deposit. The broker should
    A. refuse to permit the closing of the deal.
    B. retain the earnest money as commission.
    C. file a complaint with the real estate licensing agency.
    D. pay the earnest money to the seller and then sue for the commission.

48. The listing broker usually can show the buyer all of the following EXCEPT
    A. a subdivision map of the property.
    B. a copy of the seller's recorded deed.
    C. the listing contract.
    D. tax office data.

49. ◎ During the listing period under an exclusive-right-to-sell listing, the seller and buyer execute an option to purchase. If the option is not exercised until four months after the listing has expired, which is TRUE?
    A. The broker has earned a commission based on the consideration paid for the option.
    B. The broker has earned a commission based on the purchase price.
    C. There is no commission earned for the option, only for the listing.
    D. The commission will be two full commissions earned for the listing and the sale on the option.

50. Two months prior to the expiration date of an exclusive-right-to-sell listing agreement, the owner decides not to sell the property and orders the broker to stop marketing the property. Which statement is CORRECT?
    A. The broker can elect to sue the owner for breach of contract.
    B. The broker can keep showing the property to interested buyers.
    C. The broker is the procuring cause of any sale.
    D. The listing remains valid during any protection period.

51. ◎ Which is TRUE concerning the printed words in a form listing contract?
    A. The parties may not cross out any of the printed words.
    B. Handwritten words take precedence over printed words if there is a conflict or inconsistency.
    C. Nothing may be added to the printed form except in those spaces that provide for such additions.
    D. If handwritten items are added, signatures must be acknowledged before a notary public.

52. The owner of a property gives a broker an exclusive-right-to-sell listing. The broker produces a buyer who makes a full-price cash offer without any contingencies. Which is TRUE?
    A. The broker has earned a commission even if the owner refuses to accept the offer.
    B. The owner cannot refuse the offer.
    C. The broker earns the commission only if the offer is accepted.
    D. If the owner refuses the offer, the buyer can sue for specific performance.

53. If a buyer presents a broker with an offer at the full listing price contingent on financing
    A. the broker has earned commission.
    B. the broker, provided so authorized in writing by the seller, could accept the offer and bind the principal.
    C. the buyer is obligated to buy even if the contingency is not satisfied.
    D. contingencies have no effect on the potential of the broker's earning a commission.

54. Before visiting an owner of property to obtain a listing, a real estate licensee should do which of the following?
    A. Perform a competitive market analysis
    B. Order a formal appraisal from a bank
    C. Have a completely signed contract
    D. Obtain a title insurance policy

55. When a broker prepares to take a listing on a residential house, he will find it helpful to do all of the following *EXCEPT*
    A. gather recent data on sales in the area.
    B. consider the availability of mortgage funds.
    C. obtain any relevant data from the available public records.
    D. consider the seller's religious preference.

56. A listing broker inspects the property and discovers a shared driveway. The listing broker should reveal this fact on all of the following contracts *EXCEPT*
    A. the listing.
    B. the offer to purchase.
    C. the broker's agreement to split commission.
    D. an option to buy the property.

57. In an exclusive listing with a 120-day expiration period, the owner sells the property to one of the broker's previous referrals on the 121st day. What commission is the broker entitled to receive?
    A. None
    B. 50 percent
    C. 75 percent
    D. Full

58. ◎ A person gives an option to sell while an exclusive-right-to-sell listing contract is still in effect. The optionee exercises her option four months after the listing expires. Which one of the following regarding the broker's commission is *CORRECT?*
    A. The broker is not entitled to his or her commission because the sale takes place after the listing expires.
    B. The broker is not entitled to his or her commission because he or she is given only an exclusive right to sell and not an option.
    C. The broker is entitled to his or her commission because the option to sell was signed during the term of the listing.
    D. The broker is entitled to his or her commission only if he or she had shown the property to the person who exercised the option.

ANSWERS

1. **B.** Salespeople, as subagents, are always directly responsible to the broker who holds their licenses, whether their broker is the listing or the selling broker.

2. **C.** Because the broker produced a ready, willing, and able buyer, the commission established in the listing agreement has been earned.

3. **D.** "The commission is owed if I produce the sale for you or by anyone else." Under an exclusive-agency listing, no commission is owed if the seller finds the buyer. Under an open listing, the broker must be the procuring cause.

4. **D.** While the sudden increase won't terminate the listing, a prudent broker should discuss with the owner the benefits of increasing the listing price and extending the term of the listing.

5. **A.** It is good business practice to get the listing in writing even in those states where this is not required under either the statute of frauds or the licensing law. In choice (B), the listing is a private contract between broker and seller.

6. **C.** The broker has a fiduciary duty to the principal (seller) to obtain the best possible price. Although the broker is ethically bound to treat all parties fairly, this does not mean the broker must make sure the buyer gets outside advice or representation.

7. **B.** Only the agent under an open listing who is the "procuring cause" will be entitled to the commission. Under a multiple listing, there is only one listing contract and only one agent; the cooperating broker would be a subagent working with the listing broker.

8. **A.** The agent with an open listing who proves to be the "procuring cause" of the sale will be entitled to the full commission; the others will get nothing. Disputes often arise as to who is the real procuring cause. An MLS generally does not take open listings.

9. **B.** Courts do not favor automatic extension provisions in listings, especially because many unsophisticated sellers end up having to pay two commissions. For example, an owner thinks the 90-day listing has expired and so signs a new listing with Broker 2. When Broker 2 finds the buyer, Broker 1 also claims a commission under the earlier exclusive listing that had never been canceled in writing by the owner. Radon is a material fact the broker must disclose to the buyer.

10. **B.** If one cotenant signed the listing, most courts will imply a promise by the signing tenant to obtain the authorization of the other cotenant. Later, if the broker produces a buyer and the tenant can't get the authorization, the broker can still get a commission from the signing cotenant. Prudent brokers, however, should take extra steps to protect themselves in these situations. Many states require written authorization for the broker to advertise, and it is good business practice to obtain this written permission in the listing.

11. **C.** Because the agency agreement is between the owner and the broker, the death or mental disability of the salesperson would not affect the listing.

12. **A.** The listing contract is between the seller and broker; the salesperson is a subagent under the broker and is authorized to perform certain tasks in accomplishing the purposes of the listing.

13. **D.** Unless authorized by the seller, the broker may not quote a price other than that authorized in writing, even if the broker knows the seller will accept the lower price. The broker should encourage the buyer to submit an offer, which can then be discussed with the seller. The broker must submit all written offers for the seller's consideration.

14. **D.** If the agent produces an acceptable buyer and the buyer and seller later decide to cancel the agreement, the broker has still earned commission. Choice (B) is false because the offer must match the listing or be on terms acceptable to the seller, not just to the purchaser.

15. **D.** Because the listings had terminated and there is no mention of any safety clause (which would extend the term to cover any buyers registered with the owner), the salesperson is entitled to nothing.

16. **C.** Under an exclusive-right-to-sell listing, the broker gets a commission regardless of who is the procuring cause, even if it is the seller who finds the buyer during the listing term.

17. **B.** Only under an exclusive-agency listing (or an open listing) would the seller not be obligated to pay a commission. If the seller is at fault (delivering an unmarketable title), then the broker has the right to sue. (Some brokers elect not to sue because of potential bad publicity.)

18. **D.** Net listings are not prohibited by federal law; however, they are illegal in some

states. They are generally frowned on (it would be easy to take advantage of unsophisticated sellers). Choice (D) violates federal fair housing law.

19. **B.** The broker often will send a registered or certified letter to the seller to prove the broker found the buyer. A memo in the broker's files does little good in establishing the fact that the seller knew this buyer had worked with the broker. This method helps prevent sellers from asserting that they found a buyer.

20. **D.** The buyer is the prospect or customer, and the broker is the agent or fiduciary.

21. **A.** The broker must give a copy at the time the signature is obtained. While the general limits of the acceptable terms of sale may be outlined, it is usually the offer that details the actual terms and conditions of the sale.

22. **A.** The parties to a contract usually may terminate it by mutual agreement, but default will trigger the remedy provisions of the contract.

23. **C.** By locating the stakes, the salesperson might discover any obvious encroachment problems. The salesperson also should ascertain if parties in possession, if any, are just tenants or if they might be claiming some superior title to the premises. Selecting an escrow company or settlement agent should be left to the buyer and/or seller.

24. **D.** The open listing is an employment agreement between broker and seller. Unlike exclusive listings, it does not need a specific termination date.

25. **C.** Under general agency principles, death terminates an executory listing agreement.

26. **A.** Death does not usually discharge contractual rights or obligations, except for personal service contracts such as listings.

27. **D.** The broker cannot touch the monies in the client trust account for a transaction unless both buyer and seller consent in writing to such a draw on the commission earned. This rule is designed to protect the parties in the event the deal is not consummated.

28. **A.** The salesperson should not use the broker's name unless authorized in writing.

29. **D.** The actions in (A), (B), and (C) appear to violate the agent's duty to avoid secret profits in the real estate transactions of the principal. The fact that the resale in choice (B) was immediate leaves little room for the broker to argue that the best interests of the principal were being served.

30. **B.** The broker has limited authority, specifically to find a ready, willing, and able buyer on the listing terms. The broker does not have the authority to sign contracts binding the principal unless a power of attorney is held. The listing agent can become a dual agent by also representing the buyer with written consent of both buyer and seller.

31. **C.** The corporate resolution will reflect the fact that the board of directors has authorized the transaction and has designated the person(s) authorized to sign.

32. **A.** The MLS acts as a conduit of information. Like a newspaper, the MLS is not liable for misinformation contained in the MLS listings. Clearly, the seller is liable. The listing broker and salesperson also are culpable, especially if the true information was easy to verify.

33. **A.** Many states require that exclusive-right-to-sell listings be in writing to avoid disputes. Mutual agreement, death, or sale can terminate an exclusive agency contract by the owner.

34. **B.** The broker is entitled to a commission, even if the seller is the procuring cause. Unless expressed or implied otherwise, earning the commission is not dependent on closing (especially if the seller is at fault in failing to close).

35. **D.** In a net listing, the broker will receive any amount in excess of an agreed-on sales price; it could be nothing or it could be substantial.

36. **C.** If the state's statute of frauds requires that the listing be in writing, then an oral listing is unenforceable. Also, contracts that may not be performed within one year often must be in writing.

37. **A.** Under choice (A), there is now an accepted contract, so it would not matter even if the sales price were less than the listing price, as it could be in choice (B).

38. **A.** The listing belongs to the broker, even if the seller prefers to move the listing to a salesperson's new firm. Termination is proper if the parties agree, if the property is destroyed, if the listing expires, or if the seller breaches the listing by requiring that the broker participate in unlawful acts.

39. **B.** The only broker entitled to the commission under an open listing is the one who is the procuring cause of the sale; this is not a requirement under exclusive listings, which also might be net listings.

40. **D.** Under the exclusive-authorization-to-sell listing, the broker earns a commission based on the sales price, regardless of who is the procuring cause of the sale.

41. **B.** The broker earns the commission by procuring a buyer on the listing terms or on terms acceptable to the seller. In this case, the buyer and seller would have reached a mutually agreeable contract on the meeting of the minds. Even if the deal were not consummated because of the seller, the broker has already earned the stated commission.

42. **B.** If it were an exclusive-agency listing, the owner could sell and pay no commission. Death terminates personal service agency contracts such as listings.

43. **B.** The agreement to split any commission is between the listing broker and the buyer's broker. While the statute of frauds does not typically require that this agreement be in writing, a prudent broker will be sure it is in written form.

44. **A.** The principals to the listing agreement are the seller and the salesperson's broker, but the principal in the *fiduciary* relationship is the seller. The broker is the agent, and the salesperson is the subagent. The salesperson works for the broker.

45. **A.** The listing broker, based on the agreed percentage of the listing price, can sue the seller because there was full performance. The seller is under no obligation to accept any offer, but is obligated to compensate a performing broker.

46. **A.** The broker must be careful to give both parties full written disclosure of a double compensation and obtain their approval. Such a practice is common in tax-deferred exchanges.

47. **D.** The broker has a fiduciary duty of obedience and a duty to account for all the client's money. The broker cannot use client monies to set off or satisfy personal claims. A lawsuit may be the only answer.

48. **C.** The listing agreement is a confidential contract between the seller and the broker. Because it may contain some inaccurate information, the best procedure is to verify all material data and present them to the buyer in a separate fact sheet.

49. **B.** Most listings entitle a broker to a full commission on the exercise of an option that was entered into during the term of the listing. There will be one commission, which will be paid when the property is sold (to the buyer under the option). This will be split if there are two brokers, one representing the seller on the listing and the other representing the buyer under the option. If there is only one broker acting for both parties, he or she will retain the entire commission but will receive no more than that.

50. **A.** The owner can terminate the agency at any time but remains liable for any damages incurred by the broker due to the breach of contract (i.e., withdrawal prior to expiration date or any valid protection period). Damages could be expenses incurred in showing and advertising the property.

51. **B.** The parties frequently cross out inappropriate form language and initial any changes that are made. Handwritten terms supersede printed words on the theory that the parties have modified the form.

52. **A.** The broker has performed under the terms of the listing. The owner is under no obligation to the buyer to accept the offer, although he or she still is liable for the broker's commission. An owner may decide it would be better to reject the offer if the property has dramatically increased in value or if he or she is now unsure about selling. The buyer has no legal right to demand that the seller accept the offer. Only the broker can sue, and only for the amount of the commission.

53. **B.** On a contingent offer, the broker has not earned commission until the contingency is satisfied or waived. Although the usual listing gives the broker only limited authority, some sellers may add authority for their brokers to bind them to contracts (e.g., under a power of attorney).

54. **A.** Bank appraisals are not needed at the time of listing, especially if an experienced licensee can prepare an accurate comparable analysis using the market comparison approach.

55. **D.** Recent sales data will help determine a comparable price for listing, and mortgage availability information is useful to foresee whether the seller might have to negotiate seller carryback financing with the buyer. Public information—such as tax assessments, recorded zoning, setbacks, and so on—is useful and may be needed by the buyer to make his or her decision to buy. A survey at that time would be premature and perhaps unnecessary.

56. **C.** The listing contract should detail all material facts concerning the property—the time of listing is the time to discover if there are any encumbrances or defects. Naturally, this fact should be disclosed in writing to the buyer because the shared driveway could either be an encroachment or involve an easement. Material facts should also be disclosed on the offer to purchase and the option to buy.

57. **A.** Unless the listing has a "protection clause," the broker gets nothing because the listing has terminated. Most protection clauses allow the broker to collect a commission (within a set, written period of time) if the property is sold to a prospective buyer that was introduced to the property during the originally listed period of time.

58. **C.** The buyer was found during the listing period. Note that there would be no full commission if the option were not exercised.

Sales Contracts and Options

The real estate purchase contract is one of the most important documents in the real estate transaction. Typically, there is a time span of several weeks between the time the buyer and seller reach agreement and the time the transaction is closed. If the parties are not bound to a legally enforceable contract, they may try to change their minds when either buyer's or seller's remorse sets in. The sales contract also serves as the blueprint for the rest of the transaction—financing, prorations, expenses, and closing. Once the contract is signed, the deal is set and the parties cannot modify their agreement without the other side's approval.

A contract is an enforceable promise to do or not to do a certain thing. To be a binding promise, the contract must be supported by consideration; the parties must have legal capacity and mutually consent; and the object of the contract must be lawful. Contracts are classified as express or implied; unilateral or bilateral; executory or executed; valid, void, or voidable; unenforceable under the statute of frauds or barred under the statute of limitations. If the buyer breaches the contract, the seller sometimes retains the earnest money deposit as liquidated damages. If the seller defaults, the buyer could sue for specific performance to obtain title to the property.

An option is an agreement to keep open, for a set period, an offer to sell or lease real property—often used to give the buyer time to resolve questions of financing, title, zoning, and feasibility before committing the buyer to purchase. An option merely creates a contractual right; it does not give the optionee (buyer) any estate in the property. Under an option, the optionor must sell the property if the optionee gives notice of exercise of the option, but the optionor cannot force the optionee to buy.

The questions in this chapter test your comprehension of the following topics:

- The essential elements of a valid contract

- The enforceability of contracts

- Default and remedies

- Use of options in real estate transactions

- Typical provisions in sales contracts

- Use of an earnest money deposit

KEY WORDS

Acceptance: The expression of the intention of the person receiving an offer (offeree, usually the seller) to be bound by the terms of the offer.

Addendum: An agreement that adds terms and conditions and incorporates them into the legal document.

Assignment: The written transfer of interest in a mortgage, lease, or contract.

Breach of contract: Violation of any of the terms or conditions of a contract without legal excuse; default, nonperformance, such as failure to make payment when due.

Consideration: An act or forbearance, or the promise thereof, that is offered by one party to induce another to enter into a contract; that which is given in exchange for something from another.

Contingency: A provision placed in a contract that requires the completion of a certain act or the happening of a particular event before a contract is binding.

Contract: A legal agreement between competent parties who agree to perform or refrain from performing certain acts for a consideration. In real estate, there are many different types of contracts, including listings, contracts of sale, options, mortgages, assignments, leases, deeds, escrow agreements, and loan commitments, among others.

Contract sale: A financial agreement between the contract holder (vendor) and the contract purchaser (vendee) for the purchase of real property.

Counteroffer: A new offer made as a reply to an offer received from another; this has the effect of rejecting the original offer, which cannot thereafter be accepted unless revived by the offeror's repeating it.

Default: Failure to fulfill a duty or promise or failure to perform any obligation or required act. The most common occurrence of default on the part of a buyer or lessee is nonpayment of money.

Deposit: Money offered by a prospective buyer as an indication of good faith in entering into a contract to purchase; earnest money; security for the buyer's performance of a contract.

Duress: Unlawful constraint or action exercised on a person whereby that person is forced to perform some act against his or her will. A contract entered into under duress is void.

Executory contract: A contract in which one or both of the parties has not yet performed.

Offer: A promise by one party to act or perform in a specified manner provided the other party will act or perform in the manner requested.

Offer and acceptance: The two components of a valid contract; a "meeting of the minds."

Option: An agreement to keep open, over a set period, an offer to sell or purchase property.

Rescission: The legal remedy of canceling, terminating, or annulling a contract and restoring the parties to their original positions; a return to the status quo.

Specific performance: A legal action brought in a court of equity to compel a party to carry out the terms of a contract.

Statute of frauds: The law that requires that certain contracts be in writing and signed by the party to be charged therewith in order to be legally enforceable.

Statute of limitations: That law pertaining to the period of time within which certain actions must be brought to court.

Time is of the essence: The clause in a contract that emphasizes that punctual performance is an essential requirement of the contract.

Unilateral contract: A contract in which one party makes an obligation to perform without receiving in return any express promise of performance from the other party, such as an open listing contract, where the seller agrees to pay a commission to the first broker who brings in a ready, willing, and able buyer.

MISTAKEN IDENTITY

The following words are often confused with one another. Note the difference in meaning of these mistaken identity words and phrases.

Down payment/Deposit: The amount of cash offered by a buyer—as an indication of good faith in entering into a contract to purchase—or purchaser at the time of purchase. Even though a down payment usually includes the earnest money deposit, the terms are not synonymous. (Earnest money is applied toward the total amount of cash down payment due at the closing.) If the buyer completes the purchase, the deposit money is applied toward the purchase price.

Executed/Executory: An *executory* contract is one that still needs to be performed, whereas an *executed* contract has been completed.

Option/Right of first refusal: An *option* is a right to purchase property at a set price for a fixed period of time, whereas a *right of first refusal* is a right to purchase property only if it is offered for sale in the future.

Rescission/Restriction: *Rescission* is the remedy on breach of contract in which the parties return to their respective positions before the contract (return to the status quo), whereas *restriction* is some limitation placed on the use of the property.

Unilateral/Bilateral: A *unilateral* contract involves one promise to perform (option contract), whereas a *bilateral* contract involves mutual promises to perform (as in a sales contract).

Void/Voidable: A *void* contract lacks the essential elements to be valid, whereas a *voidable* contract is valid, except one of the parties has the ability to void it because of some wrongdoing.

Optionor/Optionee: The seller (*optionor*) gives the buyer (*optionee*) the right to purchase the property in return for the buyer's paying option money. The buyer then has the option to buy or not for a set price during the option period.

Statute of frauds/Statute of limitations: The *statute of frauds* requires that certain contracts be in writing to be enforceable, whereas the *statute of limitations* sets time limits on the ability to file a lawsuit to enforce a right.

QUESTIONS

1. When withdrawing an offer to purchase before it is accepted by the seller, the offeror is first entitled to a refund of the deposit at which of the following times?
   A. After the buyer obtains a court order
   B. Immediately
   C. After the seller has had an opportunity to accept the agreement and declines
   D. After the broker deducts earned commission

2. Certain elements must be present in a real estate sales contract involving a single-family residence if the contract is to be valid. Although the following elements are recommended, which one is *NOT* an absolute necessity?
   A. Description of land
   B. Type of deed
   C. Names of the parties
   D. Sales price

3. A builder agrees to build a house and sell it to a buyer in 180 days. The buyer agrees to pay the negotiated price within 45 days after completion. The contract, before completion of the house, may be referred to as a(n)
   A. executory contract.
   B. implied contract.
   C. voidable contract.
   D. executed contract.

4. Each of the following is an essential element of every real estate sales contract *EXCEPT*
   A. acknowledgment.
   B. legality of object.
   C. consideration.
   D. reality of consent.

5. To be enforceable in court, a sales contract must have
   A. an earnest money deposit.
   B. competent parties.
   C. an acknowledgment.
   D. a witness.

6. The listing broker can do all of the following with the earnest money deposit *EXCEPT*
   A. place it in a client trust account until closing.
   B. deposit the money in the broker's general operating account.
   C. apply it as liquidated damages on buyer's default.
   D. return the money to the buyer if the seller is unable to provide marketable title.

7. A sales agreement must contain which of the following?
   A. Mortgage loan
   B. Offer and acceptance
   C. Date of the offer
   D. Legal description of the property

8. Which term *BEST* describes a court order to carry out the terms of a signed real estate sales contract?
   A. Specific performance
   B. Lis pendens
   C. Attachment
   D. Subpoena

9. A vendee is *BEST* described as one who
   A. sells or offers to sell.
   B. buys or offers to buy.
   C. loans money.
   D. borrows money.

10. When a seller sold his home, he removed his built-in hot tub prior to closing. Nothing was said about the hot tub in either the listing or the sales contract. Which is a *TRUE* statement?
    A. The hot tub was a trade fixture and belongs to the seller.
    B. The hot tub remained personal property after attachment to the home plumbing system.
    C. The sales contract should have excepted specifically the hot tub.
    D. The hot tub becomes real property on severance.

11. After the seller accepts an offer and the buyer's agent telephones the buyer to say "congratulations," when is the accepted offer binding?
    A. When the seller signed the offer.
    B. When the buyer's agent telephoned the buyer(s).
    C. When the buyer receives a copy of the accepted offer.
    D. When the buyer's agent received the seller's signed acceptance.

12. A real estate contract signed by an unmarried minor is
    A. void.
    B. voidable.
    C. unenforceable.
    D. indefeasible.

13. ◎ A novation is *BEST* defined as
    A. the substitution of one party for another in a contract wherein both the original parties remain liable.
    B. the substitution of one party for another in a contract wherein the original contract is extinguished and the undertaking of the new party is a new obligation.
    C. the same as an assignment.
    D. a means of acquiring title by adverse possession.

14. A buyer and a seller agree to the purchase of a house for $200,000, in which the buyer will make a $30,000 down payment and the seller will take back a ten-year purchase-money mortgage for the balance. The sales contract is likely to be held valid even though the parties fail to provide which of the following?
    A. Closing date
    B. Interest rate
    C. Sales price
    D. Signature of buyer and seller

15. On the seller's default, what should happen to the earnest money?
    A. It belongs to the broker.
    B. It should be returned to the buyer.
    C. It should be placed in an escrow fund.
    D. It should be retained by the seller.

16. Which of the following statements about certain provisions in a purchase agreement is *TRUE?*
    A. "Time is of the essence" means there is a periodic tenancy.
    B. The agreement is voidable if the closing date is omitted.
    C. To accept the property "as is" means to accept obvious as well as hidden defects.
    D. If the sale is contingent on the happening or nonhappening of some event, it must be stated in writing in the contract.

17. Which of the following constitutes a rejection of an offer?
    A. Mistake of law
    B. Lapse of time
    C. Counteroffer
    D. Mistake of fact

18. Which of the following phrases does *NOT* pertain to a real estate contract?
    A. Valuable consideration
    B. Offer and acceptance
    C. Words of conveyance
    D. Reality of consent

19. A buyer makes an offer at less than the asking price. The seller then makes a counteroffer. The buyer refuses the counteroffer. If the seller then accepts the first offer, which of the following statements about the transaction is *TRUE?*
    A. The buyer is legally bound to complete the deal.
    B. The broker has earned a commission.
    C. The buyer is released from the offer when the seller makes a counteroffer.
    D. The broker is liable if the contract is unenforceable.

20. The law that bars legal claims after certain periods of time is known as the
    A. statute of frauds.
    B. statute of limitations.
    C. Administrative Procedures Act.
    D. real estate law.

21. An oral contract to lease real estate for a four-year period is
    A. voidable.
    B. unilateral.
    C. void.
    D. unenforceable.

22. A contract of sale *CANNOT* exist without an offer and which one of the following?
    A. An assignment
    B. A mortgage
    C. An assessment
    D. An acceptance

23. When a prospective buyer is in the locality and able to inspect the property, the prospect ordinarily has a right to rely on
    A. the broker's representations regarding future value of the property.
    B. nothing the broker says.
    C. everything the broker says.
    D. the broker's representations regarding concealed details of construction of the building.

24. An indefeasible contract is one that
    A. cannot be voided.
    B. is void.
    C. is voidable.
    D. is unenforceable.

25. A real estate sales contract usually will be terminated by
    A. death of either party.
    B. delivery of the deed.
    C. assignment.
    D. either party's changing his or her mind.

26. A written and signed real estate contract can be voided for which of the following reasons?
    A. One of the parties failed to read the instrument before signing it.
    B. One of the parties was an unmarried minor when the contract was signed.
    C. One of the parties became sick.
    D. The buyer failed to include a Social Security number.

27. The legal remedy *MOST* likely used by the seller on abandonment and default by the buyer under a recorded contract of sale is a
    A. trustee's sale.
    B. lis pendens action.
    C. partition action.
    D. quiet title suit.

28. A buyer withdraws a written offer before the seller has signed. What is the broker's position in the transaction?
    A. The broker splits earnest money with the seller.
    B. The broker charges commission later.
    C. The broker gets nothing.
    D. The broker is entitled to expenses.

29. An assignment of property rights in a real estate sales contract constitutes a(n)
    A. lease.
    B. encumbrance.
    C. lien.
    D. conveyance.

30. A clause in a sales contract or a mortgage that requires punctual performance is described as
    A. specific performance.
    B. time is of the essence.
    C. escalation.
    D. subrogation.

31. Which of the following is *TRUE* concerning an assignable option?
    A. It can be valid without a consideration.
    B. It can be passed on to another.
    C. It is binding only on the assignor.
    D. The assignment may be oral.

32. Which one of the following is required by the statute of frauds to be in writing?
    A. Notes and mortgages on real estate
    B. Commercial and residential leases for any period of time
    C. Licenses to use real property
    D. Agreements by one broker to split fees with another broker

33. Which of the following terms is out of place with the others?
    A. Vendor
    B. Grantor
    C. Lender
    D. Seller

34. Unless there are certain provisions to the contrary, the terms of the contract usually
    A. are not binding after closing because the terms of the contract are merged into the deed.
    B. are enforceable after closing.
    C. bind the lender as well as the buyer and seller.
    D. are voidable at closing.

35. ◎ If fire destroys a home after the contract of sale is signed by both parties but prior to closing, all of the following are true under the Uniform Vendors and Purchasers Risk Act *EXCEPT*
    A. the party in possession generally bears the risk of loss.
    B. the seller bears the risk of loss if in possession and holding legal title at the time of the loss.
    C. the buyer assumes responsibility on signing the sales contract.
    D. responsibility generally passes to the buyer on closing or occupancy, whichever occurs first.

36. Which of the following is an essential element of any contract?
    A. Written instrument
    B. Words of conveyance
    C. Consideration
    D. Acknowledgment

37. The phrase "time is of the essence" means
    A. the buyer is in a hurry to take possession.
    B. the closing must be held in a hurry.
    C. things required to be accomplished by dates set forth in the agreement must be done on or before those dates.
    D. time is unimportant.

38. If the seller dies after the signing of the contract for sale of land and before the closing, which of the following is *TRUE?*
    A. The contract is voidable at the option of the seller's representative.
    B. The contract is voidable at the option of the buyer.
    C. The deal is terminated by operation of law.
    D. The death of the seller normally does not terminate the contract.

39. When a contract's terms have *NOT* been fully performed, it is known as a(n)
    A. executed contract.
    B. executory contract.
    C. unilateral contract.
    D. bilateral contract.

40. The statute of frauds, as applied to real estate sales contracts, prescribes all of the following *EXCEPT* that
    A. all contracts for the sale of real property, to be enforceable, must be in writing.
    B. such contracts must be signed by the party to be charged thereby.
    C. oral contracts are valid and enforceable.
    D. leases for periods of more than three years must be in writing.

41. If an option contract is duly executed by seller and buyer, which of the following is *TRUE?*
    A. The owner may or may not sell.
    B. The buyer must buy.
    C. The owner must sell, but the buyer need not buy.
    D. It is specifically enforceable by both parties.

42. The term *merchantable title* (or *marketable title*) means
    A. the title has no defects.
    B. the seller can transfer interest by deed.
    C. an abstract certified to date can be prepared.
    D. the title appears to be reasonably free of unacceptable defects.

43. If the buyer withdraws an offer before it has been accepted, the deposit money goes
    A. one-half to the broker and one-half to the buyer.
    B. all to the buyer.
    C. all to the seller.
    D. all to the broker.

44. A portion of a printed form contract is changed by typing in contrary provisions, which are then initialed by both parties. Which takes precedence?
    A. Printing over typing
    B. Neither—the contract is voidable because of the changes
    C. Typing over printing
    D. Neither—the parties may void the contract because of the change

45. All of the following are considered contracts *EXCEPT* a(n)
    A. mortgage.
    B. net listing.
    C. lis pendens.
    D. escrow agreement.

46. Reality of consent in a contract means all of the following *EXCEPT* that
    A. the terms of the contract must express the true intention of the parties.
    B. the parties' consent to the contract must be genuinely given.
    C. both parties give their consent at closing.
    D. both parties are certain and clear about what is being offered and what is being accepted.

47. A contract for the sale of real estate is an
    A. executed agreement.
    B. expected agreement.
    C. executory agreement.
    D. anticipatory agreement.

48. In connection with a contract for the sale of real estate, a rider is a(n)
    A. addendum.
    B. subrogation.
    C. lien.
    D. contract.

49. The phrase "time is of the essence" is most likely to be stated or implied in which of the following contracts?
    A. Exclusive authorization and right to sell
    B. Real estate receipt for deposit
    C. Grant deed
    D. Option

50. In the usual home purchase transaction, the offeror is *MOST* likely to be the
    A. vendee.
    B. trustee.
    C. mortgagee.
    D. lienee.

51. ◎ Where a contract of sale fails to mention the existence of a mortgage on the land but there is such a mortgage, which of the following is *TRUE?*
    A. The seller can compel the buyer to complete the deal.
    B. The signing of the contract of sale automatically makes the mortgage void.
    C. The buyer has the right to demand a title free and clear of the mortgage.
    D. The buyer must take title subject to the mortgage.

52. Which of the following statements concerning the assignment of a sales contract is *CORRECT?*
    A. The assignment of rights may be made only by the original seller.
    B. Sales contracts generally may be assigned.
    C. The contract becomes binding only on the assignor.
    D. All contracts are assignable.

53. Prospective purchasers of property, as evidence of good faith, frequently make a deposit called
    A. consideration.
    B. earnest money.
    C. collateral security.
    D. deferred purchase money trust.

54. A buyer submits an offer to buy a building contingent on qualifying for a loan. If the seller accepts, which is a *CORRECT* statement about the sales contract?
    A. If the buyer qualifies for the loan, the buyer can extend the closing dates if interest rates are expected to drop.
    B. If the buyer fails to qualify, the buyer is entitled to a return of the deposit money less the seller's attorney's fees.
    C. If the buyer qualifies but decides to cancel and buy a better property, the seller can sue for money damages.
    D. If the buyer cannot obtain the loan, the seller must pay the buyer's expenses for a credit report.

55. In theory, if a real estate broker threatens to injure a buyer's relative unless the buyer signs the offer to purchase, the contract is voidable because of the broker's use of
    A. undue influence.
    B. duress.
    C. prejudice.
    D. deceptive trade practice.

56. When buyer and seller enter into a definite written purchase agreement with no special conditions except that no closing date is specified, the contract normally is
    A. void for vagueness.
    B. voidable.
    C. enforceable.
    D. not acceptable by law.

57. Usually the right to declare a forfeiture of deposit money for breach of contract belongs to the
    A. buyer.
    B. seller.
    C. lender.
    D. broker.

58. The withdrawal of an offer before acceptance is called
    A. reversion.
    B. rescission.
    C. rejection.
    D. revocation.

59. A licensed real estate broker who holds an option on a property must notify the prospective purchaser that she is the
    A. optionee.
    B. optionor.
    C. tenant.
    D. lessee.

60. Acceptance of a sales contract is accomplished when the
    A. salesperson signs the sales contract.
    B. offeree signs the sales contract.
    C. offeror signs the sales contract.
    D. broker signs the sales contract.

61. The granting of an option to purchase a farm requires all of the following *EXCEPT*
    A. the holding of a real estate license.
    B. a valuable consideration to the optionor.
    C. that the contract be in writing to be enforceable.
    D. that the optionor sell if the option is exercised.

62. Under the statute of frauds, all contracts for the sale of real estate must be in writing. The principal reason for this statute is to
    A. prevent the buyer from defrauding the seller.
    B. prevent perjury and fraudulent proof of a fictitious oral contract.
    C. protect the buyer from the broker.
    D. protect the general public from fraud due to unrecorded deeds.

63. A prospective purchaser has a legal right to demand which of the following?
    A. A copy of the broker's employment contract with the seller
    B. The return of the earnest money deposit prior to the seller's acceptance of the offer to purchase
    C. Copies of any offers from other interested buyers
    D. A copy of any appraisal that was previously done on the property

64. A contract to purchase for cash is signed by the unmarried seller and by only one of the married buyers. The tenancy is to be tenancy by the entirety. The contract is
    A. enforceable.
    B. void.
    C. voidable.
    D. unenforceable.

65. For there to be a valid contract to purchase real estate, which one of the following elements must be present?
    A. Valuable consideration between buyer and seller
    B. Both husband and wife must sign as buyers
    C. The contract must be acknowledged and recorded
    D. Either an attorney or an escrow must handle closing

66. All of the following are contracts *EXCEPT* the
    A. closing statement.
    B. trust deed.
    C. listing.
    D. mortgage.

67. When a seller rejects an offer
    A. such rejection should be noted on the offer by the seller or broker and a copy returned to the prospective buyer.
    B. it constitutes a counteroffer.
    C. the buyer will forfeit any deposit submitted with the offer.
    D. the broker is still entitled to a commission.

68. Undue influence on the part of a salesperson in obtaining a sales contract may result in all of the following *EXCEPT*
    A. the contract's being declared voidable by the injured party.
    B. revocation of the salesperson's license.
    C. automatic suspension of the broker's license.
    D. termination of employment of the salesperson with the broker.

69. All of the following statements are true regarding a buyer's deposit on an offer to purchase *EXCEPT* that
    A. the buyer can rightfully demand full repayment if she withdraws the offer prior to seller's acceptance.
    B. the deposit is subject to forfeiture to the seller in the event the buyer fails to consummate the accepted agreement.
    C. it must accompany an offer.
    D. it is recommended but not essential with a contract to purchase property.

70. In preparing an offer to purchase real estate, a broker should include provisions relating to all of the following *EXCEPT*
    A. existing leases on the property.
    B. methods of financing the purchase.
    C. household items to include in the sale.
    D. terms and provisions of the seller's existing mortgage.

71. Which is *TRUE* concerning an earnest money deposit?
    A. It serves as a source of payment of damages to the seller in case of a buyer's breach.
    B. It is essential to the contract for the sale of real property.
    C. It must equal 10 percent of the purchase price.
    D. It may be kept by the broker as compensation if the offer is accepted.

72. ◎ Where money is actually paid as consideration for an option to purchase real property, the option
    A. cannot be assigned by the optionee.
    B. must be in writing to be enforceable.
    C. is binding only on the optionee.
    D. may be withdrawn by the optionee.

73. In the typical real estate transaction, before a sales contract has been signed by the offeree, the earnest money belongs to the
    A. broker.
    B. offeree.
    C. escrow.
    D. offeror.

74. A nonnegotiable note used as an earnest money deposit with an offer to purchase is acceptable with the permission of whom?
    A. Broker
    B. Buyer
    C. Salesperson
    D. Seller

75. ◎ If an offer has been accepted and the settlement officer discovers a cloud on the title and notifies the parties, the buyer can do all of the following *EXCEPT*
    A. sue to quiet title.
    B. accept the title with the cloud.
    C. immediately refuse the deal and demand a refund of all monies.
    D. demand that the seller remove the cloud prior to closing.

76. When an offer is contingent on the buyer's procuring a certain mortgage, the offer should state all of the following *EXCEPT* the
    A. amount of the loan to be procured.
    B. time period within which the buyer can procure the mortgage.
    C. clauses to be included in the mortgage document.
    D. maximum interest of the loan.

77. Riders in a real estate sales contract are valid in all the following cases *EXCEPT*
    A. when incorporated with the original contract by reference.
    B. if signed or initialed by both parties.
    C. if obtained by fraud.
    D. if handwritten.

78. One of the principal purposes of the statute of frauds is to
    A. eliminate the perjury and fraud that may occur in trying to prove oral contracts.
    B. set a time limit within which a lawsuit may be filed or barred.
    C. regulate personal property transfers.
    D. control the sale of business opportunities.

79. If a buyer offers to purchase a seller's home subject to the sale of the buyer's present home, how would you describe the subject-to-sale clause?
    A. Contingency
    B. Cancellation
    C. Condition
    D. Cloud

80. A rescission of a contract is a(n)
    A. ratification.
    B. return to the status quo.
    C. amendment to the terms of a contract.
    D. escrow arrangement.

81. An optionee in the usual real estate transaction has which of the following rights?
    A. To collect rents during the option period
    B. To legally enforce the exercise of the options even if the optionor no longer wishes to do so
    C. To occupy the property during the option period
    D. To grant right-of-way easements across property

82. When there is a "meeting of the minds," which of the following has been accomplished?
    A. Offer and acceptance
    B. Satisfaction of the contract's major terms
    C. Settlement has been held
    D. Acknowledgment and delivery

83. Any of the following is a normal method to discharge a contract *EXCEPT*
    A. divorce of either party.
    B. operation of law.
    C. agreement.
    D. performance.

84. If an illiterate person signs a contract, the contract is
    A. void.
    B. presumed valid unless fraud can be proven.
    C. voidable at the illiterate's option unless it was fully read aloud.
    D. voidable at the illiterate's option if illiteracy can be established.

85. Hadley gives Byron a check for $4,000 when Hadley signs a contract to purchase Byron's real property. The terms of the purchase are the $95,000 sales price paid as follows: $30,000 in cash from Hadley and $65,000 by way of a first mortgage for 30 years at 10 percent interest. Which of the following terms *BEST* describes the $30,000?
    A. Down payment
    B. Hand money
    C. Earnest money deposit
    D. Binder

86. All of the following statements concerning a sales contract are true *EXCEPT* that
    A. it transfers legal title.
    B. both parties are legally bound by it.
    C. it states the conditions under which the property is transferred.
    D. it states the rights and duties of each party during the duration of the contract.

87. If an option is due to expire on July 15 and the owner of the property dies on July 5, the option is
    A. binding on the heirs.
    B. valid, but it must be exercised within the statutory period.
    C. void.
    D. voidable.

88. ◎ Who has the right to sign a binding sales contract?
    A. An attorney-in-fact
    B. A trust beneficiary selling trust property
    C. The sales agent for the buyer
    D. Any corporate officer of corporate-owned property

89. Any of the following terminates an offer to purchase real property *EXCEPT*
    A. marriage of the buyer.
    B. death of the buyer.
    C. destruction of the property.
    D. revocation of the offer.

90. All of the following can be assigned *EXCEPT* a(n)
    A. contract for deed.
    B. option.
    C. trust deed.
    D. warranty deed.

91. A broker promises to give a $20,000 bonus to the first salesperson who sells 20 houses. What type of contract is this?
    A. Unilateral
    B. Executed
    C. Bilateral
    D. Nominal

92. If no date of possession is mentioned in the sales contract, the buyer should receive possession
    A. on the signing of the contract.
    B. when the seller vacates the property.
    C. on signing the deed.
    D. on the transfer of title.

93. The usual offer to purchase provides for all of the following conditions *EXCEPT*
    A. seller to pay cost of deed preparation.
    B. conditions by which the buyers will purchase the property.
    C. a requirement of early occupancy.
    D. the closing date.

94. Which is *TRUE* concerning real estate sales contracts?
    A. A seller can be sued for "specific performance" if a contract is not performed.
    B. A seller must sign an agreement to sell if the offer's terms are exactly in accordance with the listing agreement.
    C. The sole remedy for default of the buyer is a suit for specific performance.
    D. They must be on a printed form to make them binding.

95. ◎ If an option to purchase is exercised, which is *TRUE?*
   A. The option money is automatically applied to the purchase price.
   B. The optionor can be forced to sell the property.
   C. It is binding on the optionee.
   D. The purchase price may be increased.

96. All of the following are true about liquidated damages *EXCEPT* that they are
   A. enforced unless excessive in amount.
   B. fixed and certain in amount.
   C. limited to 2 percent of purchase price.
   D. a discharge of the obligation.

97. ◎ A buyer makes a written offer to purchase a seller's real property, stating the offer is good until Tuesday. Which is *TRUE?*
   A. The seller can create a contract by accepting the offer on Wednesday.
   B. The buyer can revoke her offer on Monday, even though the seller has not been given a chance to decide.
   C. The buyer cannot withdraw her offer until Tuesday.
   D. If the buyer wishes to withdraw the offer, the withdrawal must be in writing.

98. A buyer offers to buy property by assuming a $75,000 first mortgage. If, at closing, it turns out the loan balance is only $70,000, the
   A. buyer must pay the $5,000 in cash.
   B. seller must accept a $5,000 note from the buyer.
   C. seller must give a second mortgage.
   D. buyer can rescind the transaction.

99. All of the following are examples of real estate contracts *EXCEPT* a(n)
   A. exclusive-right-to-sell.
   B. agreement of sale.
   C. prospectus.
   D. lease.

100. A voidable contract is one that is
   A. legally insufficient and thus not recognized by law.
   B. not binding on either party.
   C. signed on a holiday.
   D. binding on one of the parties.

101. An executory contract is
   A. made by the executor of an estate for the sale of probate property.
   B. yet to be performed.
   C. performed completely.
   D. not yet accepted by either party.

102. When a purchaser signs an offer allowing the seller three days in which to accept the offer, the
   A. purchaser may not withdraw the offer before the expiration of the three days.
   B. purchaser may withdraw the offer only on written notice prior to the seller's acceptance.
   C. buyer puts up earnest money so that the seller may keep it if the buyer withdraws his offer.
   D. buyer can revoke at any time prior to acceptance.

103. The transfer of rights under a contract without the release from obligation by the transferor is known as
   A. assignment.
   B. novation.
   C. succession.
   D. supersedure.

104. If the sales contract does *NOT* specify otherwise, real estate sales contracts
   A. are assignable.
   B. can be assigned only with the consent of the seller.
   C. may be oral.
   D. may be valid at the option of the buyer.

105. An illiterate person is considered
   A. insane.
   B. incompetent to contract.
   C. one who can't speak.
   D. one who cannot read or write.

106. A binder given by a buyer in a real estate transaction
    A. must be monetary.
    B. may be withdrawn by the buyer any time before the seller accepts and signs.
    C. must be in the form of a check.
    D. must be cash.

107. The printed matter in a sales contract usually includes some mention or reference to all of the following *EXCEPT*
    A. evidence of title.
    B. assessment or liens.
    C. proration of taxes.
    D. amount of discount points.

108. Which is necessary for a valid contract for the sale of real estate?
    A. All of the essential terms and conditions of the sale
    B. The name of the broker representing the seller
    C. The tenancy of the buyer
    D. The name of the sales agent representing the purchaser

109. An offer that does *NOT* describe the method and terms of financing but does state the price is
    A. voidable.
    B. valid.
    C. one lacking a legal purpose.
    D. not binding.

110. Each of the following is an essential element for a real estate contract *EXCEPT*
    A. legality of object.
    B. valuable consideration.
    C. words of conveyance.
    D. offer and acceptance.

111. In a contract of sale, the buyer
    A. must make an earnest money deposit.
    B. will owe the broker a commission when the contract is accepted, even if the sale is never consummated.
    C. will lose the earnest money if she withdraws prior to acceptance.
    D. must give valuable consideration.

112. When a husband and wife desire to buy real property in both their names for cash and the husband is not available to sign the purchase contract, which of the following is *TRUE?*
    A. The purchase contract is voidable if only the wife signs.
    B. The contract is void unless both husband and wife sign the contract.
    C. The husband must sign prior to closing.
    D. It is only when they desire to sell the property that both signatures are required.

113. An optionee can do which one of the following?
    A. Divert water from the property during the option period
    B. Collect rents during the option period
    C. Build a residence on the property during the option period
    D. Legally enforce the exercise of the option if the optionor decides against performing

114. All of the following are true under a contract of sale in which the date of occupancy is later than the settlement date *EXCEPT* that the
    A. buyer acquires legal title on settlement.
    B. contract should provide whether the seller is to pay any rent.
    C. buyer has the risk of loss.
    D. buyer will withhold the down payment.

115. Which is *TRUE* about valid contracts?
    A. Money must be the consideration.
    B. If the date is left off the contract, the contract is void.
    C. Earnest money is an essential consideration.
    D. The consideration can be the mutual promises to perform.

116. ◎ Belinda offers to buy Charlene's house subject to the contingency that Belinda complete the sale of her current home by November 15. Assuming Charlene accepts, which one of the following statements about the contingency is *CORRECT?*
    A. If Belinda sells her home by November 1 but decides not to buy Charlene's house, Charlene can sue for breach of contract.
    B. If Belinda does not sell her home, she can cancel the contract but loses her deposit money.
    C. If Belinda needs more time to close the sale, she is entitled to a 30-day extension.
    D. Belinda is entitled to a return of her deposit money if she withdraws her home from the market.

117. Which of the following *BEST* describes a clause in a sales contract providing that unless the buyer is able to obtain a new first mortgage, the contract can be terminated?
    A. Defeasance clause
    B. Subordination clause
    C. Habendum clause
    D. Contingency clause

118. The interest that a purchaser acquires when the offer to purchase has been accepted is
    A. a freehold estate.
    B. an estate in fee simple.
    C. equitable title.
    D. legal title.

119. Reality of consent will be lacking in a contract by reason of all of the following *EXCEPT*
    A. duress.
    B. misrepresentation.
    C. mistake.
    D. illiteracy.

120. A person must be of the age of majority to do which of the following?
    A. Hold title to real property
    B. Pay federal income tax
    C. Appoint an agent
    D. Contract to buy necessities

121. Alfie agreed to purchase Breck's property, and the written agreement was placed in escrow. Alfie deposited the full purchase price, but Breck refused to sign the deed. Breck's action is an example of
    A. breach.
    B. tender.
    C. rejection.
    D. rescission.

122. Which of the following is the *MOST* essential element for an enforceable real estate purchase contract?
    A. Being in writing
    B. Witnessed
    C. Date of contract
    D. Time of closing

123. ◎ Jamie, 16 years old and unmarried, employs Rapid Broker under an exclusive-authorization-to-sell listing to sell an apartment building Jamie inherited from her father. Rapid finds Ready Buyer, who executes a sales contract on the complete listing terms, which Jamie accepts. Which of the following statements is *TRUE?*
    A. Jamie can void the contract with Ready Buyer.
    B. Jamie is liable to Rapid Broker for the full commission.
    C. The contract is voidable by the buyer.
    D. The contract is binding on both parties.

124. At what stage in the typical real estate transaction is the sales contract signed by buyer and seller?
    A. Prior to the issuance of the buyer's title insurance policy
    B. Immediately after the lender commits to the loan
    C. At the same time as recordation
    D. Before the listing contract

125. All of the following constitute a type of consideration required to enforce a real estate contract to purchase an $85,000 property *EXCEPT* a(n)
    A. $85,000 cashier's check.
    B. written promise to pay $85,000 over five years at 11 percent interest.
    C. oral offer to purchase.
    D. earnest money deposit with a written offer.

126. Which is *TRUE* of a right of first refusal given to a prospective buyer?
    A. The seller must sell if the buyer decides to buy.
    B. The seller must accept the buyer's offer.
    C. The buyer must buy if the seller decides to sell.
    D. The seller must offer the property to the prospective buyer if the seller decides to sell.

127. A broker reading that "time is of the essence" in the client's contract would know that it *MOST* nearly means
    A. the contract is a lease creating a tenancy for years.
    B. the contract refers to that time period over which a property can be profitably used.
    C. that the unity of "time" must be present.
    D. that performance must be on or before the dates specified in the contract, with no extensions.

128. The failure to meet an obligation when due, as specified in a real estate contract, is *BEST* described as
    A. damages.
    B. defect.
    C. default.
    D. distraint.

129. In a real estate sales contract, which party has the right, on default, to declare the earnest money deposit forfeited?
    A. Buyer
    B. Attorney
    C. Escrow
    D. Seller

130. All of the following are essential elements of a real estate contract *EXCEPT*
    A. consideration.
    B. performance.
    C. in writing.
    D. competent parties.

131. The provision in a real estate sales contract that provides for loss of the buyer's deposit money in the event of buyer default is known as
    A. liquidated damages.
    B. nominal damages.
    C. punitive damages.
    D. release damages.

132. Kyle accepted an offer by Harold to purchase Kyle's house for $98,000, contingent on Harold's obtaining a conventional loan for $88,000 at 12 percent interest. Harold tried four lenders, but the best he could do was an $85,000 loan. Which of the following is *TRUE* about this contract?
    A. Harold will forfeit his earnest money if he does not purchase the house.
    B. Harold is obligated to purchase if Kyle offers to take back a second mortgage at 12 percent for $3,000.
    C. Harold will have to continue to seek out another lender.
    D. Because Harold cannot obtain the specified financing, the contingency will allow him the return of his earnest money with no further obligation.

133. On whom is a unilateral listing contract binding once the requested act has been performed?
    A. Vendee
    B. Broker
    C. Promisor
    D. Creditor

134. A buyer will buy a particular property only if the zoning can be changed. The buyer could put in an offer with a $5,000 earnest money deposit contingent on obtaining the zoning or she could negotiate a $3,000 option. Which is *TRUE* if the zoning cannot be changed?
    A. Under an option, the buyer is entitled to all the option money.
    B. Under a contingency in a sales contract, the buyer forfeits all the earnest money deposit.
    C. The money will be returned no matter which method is chosen by the buyer.
    D. If the contingency in the offer is not met, the buyer will obtain a refund.

135. A farm was listed by a seller. An interested buyer paid $5,000 for a 60-day option to purchase the farm for $85,000. After 45 days, the buyer submitted an offer to purchase the farm for $75,000. Which is *TRUE?*
    A. The option is terminated.
    B. The seller must accept the subsequent offer.
    C. A commission became payable when the seller gave a written option to the buyer.
    D. Only if the seller accepts the offer will he owe a commission.

136. When an option states nothing to the contrary, which is ordinarily *TRUE* regarding the optionee's rights?
    A. The optionee can assign or sell the option.
    B. The optionee can obtain a mortgage on the property.
    C. The option gives the buyer legal title.
    D. Title insurance is usually obtained before the option is exercised.

137. For a contract of sale to be valid, which is essential?
    A. It must be in writing and signed by both buyer and seller.
    B. It must state an earnest money deposit.
    C. It must have the signature of the agents for the buyer and seller.
    D. It must state a purchase price.

138. A broker has a listing on a house to be sold, and the sales contract contains an "as is" clause. The broker discovers a major problem with the roof. When showing a prospective buyer the property, the broker should
    A. point out the problem to the buyer.
    B. wait until the buyer asks about the roof.
    C. limit her disclosure to the fact that the house is sold "as is."
    D. obey the seller's instruction to conceal the defect.

139. The closing date on a sales contract is March 1. On March 3, the seller declares a forfeiture of the earnest money deposit. What should be done with the deposit?
    A. Return it to the buyer.
    B. Give it to the seller.
    C. Place the deposit in the listing broker's general account.
    D. Obtain written instructions from buyer and seller.

ANSWERS

1. **B.** The offeror can withdraw the offer any time prior to the communication of acceptance. Because there is no contract, any earnest money deposit must be returned immediately.

2. **B.** The sales contract that omits the type of deed is still enforceable, although the seller might get away with delivering just a quit-claim deed. An adequate (not necessarily a legal) description, price, and names of both buyer and seller are essential.

3. **A.** An executory contract is one that is yet to be performed.

4. **A.** Acknowledgments are required only if the parties desire to record the sales contract.

Reality of consent means that there was a voluntary meeting of the minds and that no obstacles to consent, such as fraud, misrepresentation, duress, or undue influence, were present.

5. **B.** If one of the parties were incompetent, the contract might be void or voidable, depending on the type of incompetency. Earnest money is customary but not essential, because the mutual exchange of promises of performance by buyer and seller is the required valuable consideration.

6. **B.** It is "commingling" to place a client's money in the broker's general account. Earnest money deposit is not essential for a valid contract, but it is customary to show the buyer's good-faith intent to perform. Should the buyer default, the seller may keep the earnest money as liquidated damages. If the seller defaults, the money is returned to the buyer. If the buyer performs, it is applied toward the purchase price.

7. **B.** An offer and acceptance is required to evidence a meeting of the minds. The sales contract could be for all cash (a "cash-out"). The date of the offer, while desirable, is not necessary. A general description of property will suffice.

8. **A.** Should the seller default, a buyer could seek the equitable remedy of specific performance. A judgment for money damages may be insufficient to satisfy the buyer, because each piece of real property is unique and irreplaceable.

9. **B.** The vendee is the buyer under an agreement of sale or land contract.

10. **C.** On attachment to the home, the hot tub went from personal property to real property (it became a fixture). Unless excluded in the sales contract, the hot tub remains part of the real property and cannot be severed by the seller. A trade fixture refers to an item of personal property affixed to leased premises by a tenant. It is expected to be removed by the tenant at the end of the lease, otherwise it becomes the property of the landlord.

11. **C.** Contract law allows any offer or counteroffer to be withdrawn prior to acceptance. Offer and acceptance requires that the buyer be in receipt of the seller's signed acceptance. While a phone call may be customary, verbal notification of acceptance doesn't meet the legal requirement. Even though the buyer's agent received notice of the seller's acceptance, the buyer's agent cannot bind the buyer to acceptance. The signed agreement must be delivered or faxed to the buyer before it is legally accepted.

12. **B.** The minor is *able* to *void* the contract, but it is enforceable against the adult. An indefeasible contract cannot be voided.

13. **B.** Choice (A) is an example of a typical loan assumption agreement. However, if the lender elects to release the original borrower from liability, then there is a novation.

14. **A.** Most courts will be able to supply a reasonable closing date based on local custom and practice. The interest rate is such an essential element of the financing that no court will be able to imply a reasonable interest rate (not the same as the prevailing rate)—thus, the contract will fail for indefiniteness.

15. **B.** The earnest money is to protect the seller against the buyer's default. If the seller defaults, the money must be returned to the buyer. If the buyer elects to sue the seller for specific performance, the money will most likely be deposited in escrow.

16. **D.** "Time is of the essence" means there must be punctual performance of the parties' legal obligations. If time is not made of the essence, most courts will imply a reasonable closing date for the contract to be valid. In those courts that won't imply a closing date, the contract would be void, not voidable. "As is" covers only obvious defects, not hidden defects known to the seller. Contingencies must be stated clearly.

17. **C.** A counteroffer rejects the original offer, no matter how slight the change. Lapse of time would terminate an offer.

18. **C.** Words of conveyance are essential for a valid *deed*. Reality of consent (mutual

agreement), consideration, and offer and acceptance involve essential elements of a valid *contract.*

19. **C.** If the seller makes any change to the offer, the buyer is free to reconsider or reject the property.

20. **B.** Although the statute of limitations may be for, say, six years, that period may be extended even further for various legal reasons—the defendant is a minor, parties are out of the state, and so on.

21. **D.** Most statutes of frauds require that long-term lease contracts be in writing to be enforceable.

22. **D.** Offer and acceptance are the two elements needed to establish the required meeting of the minds to show mutual agreement.

23. **D.** The broker would definitely be liable for misstatements of material facts, including concealment of material defects. However, matters of opinion or value usually are not considered to be material facts; thus, some things the broker says are regarded as puffing and would not be held to be misrepresentation.

24. **A.** A defeasible contract would be a conditional contract, for example, "I promise to sell you my house, provided you don't marry my daughter." The marriage before closing would defeat the buyer's rights under the contract.

25. **B.** Death does not usually terminate a real estate sales contract; such contract is binding on the decedent's estate. Death would, however, terminate a personal services contract, such as an executory listing contract. On delivery of the deed, the contract is usually extinguished; only the deed survives as the controlling document.

26. **B.** Persons who sign a contract without reading it (or the fine print) do so at their risk. Most contracts of minors are voidable at the election of the minor. In some states, a minor who marries is treated as an adult. However, minors' contracts for necessities such as food or clothing are not voidable.

27. **D.** To clear the record of the recorded contract, court action may be necessary. An easier solution is to persuade the defaulting vendee to execute and record a quitclaim deed.

28. **C.** Because there is no ready, willing, and able buyer accepted by the seller, the broker gets nothing.

29. **D.** Either the buyer or the seller usually can convey rights in a sales contract, unless prohibited in the contract itself.

30. **B.** For example, if it were important that the seller close in a certain tax year, the seller would be advised to insert a "time is of the essence" clause so the buyer would not be able to delay even one day into the next tax year.

31. **B.** An option must be supported by its own consideration. Whether it is assignable (transferable to an assignee) should be covered in the option agreement itself.

32. **A.** The statute of frauds requires that certain contracts creating interests in real property be in writing and signed by the party to be held to the contract; examples are real estate sales contracts, deeds, mortgages, and long-term leases (e.g., more than one year). Licenses are revocable rights to use another's land but are not "interests" in the land. While listings usually must be in writing, commission split arrangements are not covered by the statute of frauds (still, it is a good idea to put them in writing).

33. **C.** Vendor, seller, and grantor all refer to the same person—the owner of real property who contracts to transfer title.

34. **A.** Under the doctrine of merger, the contract does not survive the deed. Therefore, any important contract provisions that the parties want to retain should be inserted into the deed, or the contract itself should state that certain clauses "survive the closing" of the contract.

35. **C.** Many states have adopted the rule that risk of loss does not pass to the buyer until either legal title or possession passes.

36. **C.** Not all contracts need to be in writing or acknowledged, but no contract is enforce-

able unless there is consideration to support the parties' obligations. Consideration may be the mutual exchange of promises or commitments to perform.

37. **C.** "Time is of the essence" requires punctual performance—delays are not excusable.

38. **D.** The contract is binding on the seller's estate, and the buyer could bring an action against the estate for specific performance of the contract. The estate would receive the proceeds of the sale, which then would be distributed to the heirs.

39. **B.** Until the contract is fully performed (executed), it is said to be *executory.* In this sense, the word *executed* does not mean signed and delivered.

40. **C.** An oral contract regarding real estate may be valid, but a court will not enforce it unless it satisfies the statute-of-frauds requirements. The parties to be charged are those who are to be held to the contract (the ones to be sued in the event of breach of contract).

41. **C.** Because an option is a unilateral contract, the optionee is not obliged (nor can he or she be ordered) to perform, but if the optionee does elect to purchase, then the seller is bound to sell.

42. **D.** If a title report or inspection reveals encumbrances *not disclosed* in the contract of sale, then the title is not as it was marketed by the seller. The buyer can therefore rescind or force the seller to clear those curable defects.

43. **B.** Because there is no contract and thus no default, the earnest money binder belongs to the buyer.

44. **C.** The typed-in changes are modifications to the contract and take priority because they were subsequently agreed to by both parties.

45. **C.** A lis pendens is a formal notice that a lawsuit is pending concerning a particular property.

46. **C.** If, for example, the buyer intended to buy Lot 1 and the seller intended to sell Lot 2, there would be no true meeting of the minds owing to mutual mistake of fact. There must

be no obstacle to genuine consent, such as fraud, duress, undue influence, or misrepresentation (refers to consent at the time of the sales contract, not at closing).

47. **C.** The contract of sale is yet to be performed, that is, the buyer still has to produce the purchase price and the seller must produce the deed.

48. **A.** A rider is an addendum to a contract, for example, when the parties agree to include the furniture in the sale after the contract is signed. An addendum or rider should reference the basic contract and be signed or initialed by all parties.

49. **D.** If the optionee fails to exercise the option by the date specified, the option is terminated. If the purchase contract does not state "time is of the essence," most courts will allow a reasonable time to perform after the expiration of the stated closing date.

50. **A.** Typically, the buyer makes the offer after the seller has listed the property. The listing is not an offer to sell, just an employment agreement with a broker who is to solicit offers from prospective buyers (offerors). An example of a lienee would be a person holding a mechanic's lien.

51. **C.** The seller marketed a free and clear title, and that is what he or she can be compelled to convey.

52. **B.** Both sellers and buyers may assign their rights in a sales contract unless prohibited by the explicit terms of the agreement. Because of the rule that any sales contract may be assigned, some contracts have provisions stipulating that this particular sales contract cannot be assigned without consent. Listing contracts are not assignable.

53. **B.** Earnest money is not essential to a valid sales contract, but it is prudent business practice to require it. It is not the consideration.

54. **C.** If, despite good-faith efforts, a buyer cannot meet a contingency, the buyer is entitled to a return of the deposit money. However, if the contingency occurs, the contract is enforceable and the seller can hold the

buyer to the terms of the contract. Note that an option is different in that the buyer cannot be forced to buy, although the optionee (buyer) would forfeit the option money.

55. **B.** The buyer would have the ability to void (*voidable*) the contract based on the threatening conduct. Technically, the threat of force is called *menace.* The contract is voidable when a buyer has been unduly influenced to sign a contract, usually by pressure from someone in a close or confidential relationship.

56. **C.** Most courts will imply a reasonable closing date unless the facts indicate the parties intended that a specific closing date was essential to the contract. The best practice is always to include a realistic closing date.

57. **B.** Sometimes the broker and the seller agree to a splitting of the deposit money as damages for the buyer's breach. The seller must elect which course to follow. For example, a seller who kept the deposit money could not sue for damages if the property were resold later at a loss.

58. **D.** *Rejection* is the refusal to accept an offer; *rescission* is terminating an accepted offer (a contract); *reversion* is the return to the original transferor (as in reversion of title to the grantor on the death of a life tenant).

59. **A.** Broker-optionees must be careful that all parties know they are licensed.

60. **B.** When the seller signs the contract, this is typically the acceptance of the buyer's offer. Be sure that the seller or agent then notifies the buyer of the acceptance in order to eliminate any chance the buyer may try to revoke the offer.

61. **A.** Most optionors (sellers) are nonlicensees.

62. **B.** Only certain important types of contracts need be in writing to be enforceable; they include real estate sales contracts.

63. **B.** The buyer can revoke prior to acceptance. The listing is a confidential employment agreement between the seller and the broker. It should not be shown to the buyer,

because there could be inaccurate or unverified information on the listing.

64. **A.** All cotenant buyers need not sign the contract of sale for it to be enforceable. It is good practice, however, to get all to sign. Note that the executory contract would not be enforceable against the other spouse, because he or she has not signed the contract.

65. **A.** Something more than love and affection is needed as consideration, although courts usually do not inquire into the adequacy of consideration. One spouse can sign as buyer, but the contract cannot be enforced against the nonsigning spouse. Note that if husband and wife are *selling* property, both spouses must sign. Typically, deeds are recorded but contracts of sale are not. Nor is escrow or an attorney required to close a transaction.

66. **A.** Closing statements are statistical summaries of the amounts paid, payable, received, and receivable in a real estate transaction. Choices (B) and (D) are used in loan transactions.

67. **A.** The buyer should at least be advised that the offer was considered by the seller and then rejected. The rejection is only a counteroffer if so intended. Note that a counteroffer is also a rejection of the original offer.

68. **C.** Undue influence on the part of the agent will make the contract voidable and is typically grounds for license revocation.

69. **C.** The earnest money is really security for the buyer's performance—once there is a contract. It may be paid after acceptance.

70. **D.** Because the buyer takes the property subject to existing leases, any leases should be noted. Financing methods should be clearly stated, as should any items not considered fixtures.

71. **A.** Use of earnest money is both customary and prudent. It is not essential, because the buyer's promise to perform is sufficient consideration to support the seller's promise to sell.

72. **B.** Options involve an interest in real property and thus, under the statute of frauds, must be in writing to be enforceable. Unless pro-

hibited by its terms, most options would be assignable.

73. **D.** Until acceptance, the deposit money belongs to the buyer (offeror). It is usually held in trust by the broker or escrow.

74. **D.** It is acceptable with the permission of the seller (vendor), because the seller will try to collect on it in the event of the buyer's default.

75. **C.** On discovery of a title defect, the seller must be given a reasonable opportunity to correct the problem. The buyer has an equitable interest in the property and thus has grounds to sue.

76. **C.** So that the contract does not fail for being indefinite, it is good practice to specify the limits of the loan, such as "a loan of not less than $100,000 for a term no less than 30 years at an interest rate not to exceed 10 percent." It is a good idea to set a time limit for the buyer to meet the contingency so that the seller's property will not be tied up unduly. The contract usually does not contain all the clauses found in the mortgage.

77. **C.** The riders must make reference to the basic contract, or the basic contract must make reference to the riders. All parties must sign or initial the rider. It is best to make reference in each document to the other document so that anyone looking at the contract alone will not think that is the total agreement. For example, "See Exhibit 'A' attached hereto and hereby incorporated by reference."

78. **A.** Choice (B) refers to the statute of limitations.

79. **A.** A contingency is any provision in a contract that requires a certain act to happen before the contract becomes binding. Examples include subject-to-sale, subject to a home inspection, subject to a termite inspection, subject to an appraisal, etc.

80. **B.** The concept of rescission is to return the parties to their relative positions that existed before they attempted to contract.

81. **B.** The optionee has no rights to occupancy or rents until the option is exercised and the

purchase is closed, provided it is not a lease option.

82. **A.** There is said to be mutual agreement when there is reality of consent, as evidenced by a valid offer properly accepted.

83. **A.** Despite divorce, the contract is still enforceable against those parties who signed the contract.

84. **B.** There are many illiterate people who are perfectly competent to understand their rights and obligations in a contract. They simply get someone to read it for them.

85. **A.** The down payment includes the earnest money deposit (also called *hand money* or *binder*).

86. **A.** The sales contract is an executory contract giving the buyer the right to acquire legal title on satisfying the conditions of the contract.

87. **A.** An option is a contract, and death does not discharge contracts. The optionee could seek specific performance against the seller's estate. There is no statutory period for exercising an option; there is just a stated contract period.

88. **A.** Only the trustee can effect a sale of the trust property. The beneficiary's interest is personalty. The corporate officer needs specific authorization to sign on behalf of the corporation.

89. **A.** Choices (B), (C), and (D) would have a different effect *after* acceptance.

90. **D.** Deeds cannot be assigned because they are not executory contracts; they are conveyances. There would have to be a new deed prepared to convey the legal title. A contract for deed is also known as a *land contract,* an *agreement of sale,* or an *installment contract,* as opposed to a sales contract.

91. **A.** None of the salespeople is bound or obligated to sell 20 houses, but if a salesperson does perform this act, the broker's promise to pay will become binding.

92. **D.** Possession usually takes place on delivery of the deed, which often is several days after signatures are obtained on the deed,

and a month or so after the sales contract is signed.

93. **C.** The usual *contract* provides who will pay customary closing costs and contains the essential conditions of purchase.

94. **A.** Specific performance is a powerful remedy given to the purchaser. Even if the buyer offers more than the listing price, the seller is under no obligation to accept, although the seller may be liable to the broker for breach of the listing contract to pay a commission. The seller can sue for money damages.

95. **B.** Whether the option money is to be applied toward the purchase price is a question that should be addressed in the option itself; if it is not, a court may have to decide what was the unexpressed intention of the parties. The optionor must sell if the optionee elects to buy.

96. **C.** In fact, they often exceed 2 percent, although if too high (e.g., 25 percent), they will be treated as a penalty and hence be unenforceable in many states.

97. **B.** After the time of the offer lapses, the seller cannot create a contract by accepting. In effect, the buyer's late acceptance is a counteroffer, and there is no contract unless it is accepted by the seller. An offeror can revoke the offer any time prior to being notified of the acceptance.

98. **D.** There has not been a meeting of the minds on the essential term of financing, and the buyer can rescind. The seller cannot force the buyer to pay the extra in cash or to take back a mortgage.

99. **C.** A prospectus is an announcement or brochure describing a particular real estate offering, such as a new condominium project.

100. **D.** A voidable contract is legally sufficient, but the law gives one of the parties the ability to void such contract where, for example, fraud, misrepresentation, or a minor is involved.

101. **B.** The contract of sale in which buyer and seller bind themselves to future perfor-

mance is a classic example of an executory contract.

102. **D.** Unless the seller pays consideration to make the buyer's offer irrevocable (this would then be an option to sell) the buyer can revoke at any time (even verbally) prior to being notified of the seller's acceptance.

103. **A.** With an assignment, the assignor remains secondarily liable. A novation involves a release of the transferor.

104. **A.** Real estate sales contracts are generally assignable, but some specify that the buyer must first obtain the seller's consent.

105. **D.** Illiterates are not incompetent to contract; they just cannot read or write.

106. **B.** The binder or earnest money can be cash, a note, personalty, or services rendered.

107. **D.** If discount points are involved, they probably will be covered in the special conditions or financing sections.

108. **A.** If the parties leave any essential term or condition for future agreement, the contract will be too indefinite to be enforceable. Tenancy usually can be provided later, if buyers are undecided.

109. **B.** A cash sale would fit this question.

110. **C.** A contract to build an illegal gambling casino would be void. "Good consideration" (love and affection) is not sufficient to support a contract, though it is permissible for a deed. Valuable consideration could be giving or promising something of value, such as money or services in return for the performance of another or forbearance of a legal right (like waiving a debt).

111. **D.** The consideration used to support most real estate contracts of sale is the mutual exchange of promises to perform by buyer and seller; therefore, earnest money is not legally required. Most buyers do not agree to pay the broker a commission on default and so recovery from the buyer is quite difficult, if not impossible, unless the buyer had employed the broker.

112. **D.** One buyer can sign the contract and request that title be conveyed to himself or herself and another. It is much more vital for all sellers to sign than it is for all buyers, although the best practice is to obtain the signatures of all parties. The broker should advise the seller as to why the husband is not signing.

113. **D.** Even if the seller would suffer a hardship by having to sell, the optionee could obtain specific performance of the option contract.

114. **D.** In a late occupancy, the seller gets to stay in possession after closing. Some provision should be made as to rent, and the rental agreement should be in writing.

115. **D.** Services rendered, rather than money, could be the valuable consideration. Usually a date is not an essential term of a sales contract, though it is good practice to date the contract.

116. **A.** If the contingency is met, the contract is enforceable. Belinda would be entitled to the return of her deposit money if the contingency were not met (through no action on Belinda's part, such as withdrawing her home from the market).

117. **D.** Clauses (A) and (B) are found in mortgages and leases and (C) in deeds.

118. **C.** The vendee (purchaser) has the right to obtain legal title, provided the condition is performed, mainly to pay the purchase price. This right is referred to as *equitable title* and involves the legal doctrine of equitable conversion.

119. **D.** An illiterate person still is competent to contract.

120. **C.** A minor cannot appoint an agent (attorney-in-fact) to enter into contracts that the minor is not competent to execute. The minor would need a court-appointed guardian to act as an agent. A grantee does not have to be of legal age to hold title (A). Minors' contracts for necessities (food, clothing) are valid (D).

121. **A.** Violation of Breck's obligation to convey title is a breach of contract, and Alfie would

be free to seek the remedies of damages, rescission, or specific performance.

122. **A.** The statute of frauds requires that real estate purchase contracts be in writing and signed by the party to be charged. Witnesses are not required in most states. While dates are helpful, they are not essential. Most courts will be able to imply a reasonable time to close based on custom and practice in the community. In exceptional cases, however, the contract may specify that it is important for tax purposes that the contract close on time. In such a case, a court could find that the omission of a closing date was fatal.

123. **A.** Contracts entered into with minors are usually voidable by the minor unless they are contracts for necessities of life such as food, clothing, or shelter. While the minor is *able to void* the contract, the adult is not.

124. **A.** The real estate contract is typically entered into before the title report and the loan commitment. It is therefore important that the contract contain language covering whether there are any major encumbrances on title and whether the offer is subject to loan approval (a contingency).

125. **C.** A bargained-for promise to perform as well as money is sufficient to support a promise to sell.

126. **D.** Regarding a right of first refusal, the seller cannot be forced to sell the property unless the decision has finally been made to sell and the price determined. An option price must be definite when the option is signed.

127. **D.** The contract merely indicates that punctual performance is required, as in an option. Choice (B) refers to the appraisal concept of economic life.

128. **C.** The most common default is failure to pay the amount when due, as specified in a purchase contract, promissory note, or lease. Distraint is a legal process brought by a lessor to seize a lessee's belongings for rent due.

129. **D.** One of the seller's remedies on buyer default is to retain the earnest money deposit as liquidated damages.

130. **B.** Failure to perform a valid contract will, however, give rise to certain legal remedies, such as money damages or specific performance.

131. **A.** A liquidated damage clause states, in essence, that because actual damages are difficult to estimate at the time of signing the contract, the parties agree on an amount to liquidate or settle the contract in the event of buyer default. If the amount decided on is excessive (say 20 percent of sales price), a court might not enforce such a penalty provision.

132. **D.** Because the contingency was for Harold's benefit, he is not obligated to purchase unless the condition is met. The seller could not force him to accept an alternative method of financing.

133. **C.** Once a broker finds a ready, willing, and able buyer on the terms of a unilateral listing agreement, the seller-promisor's promise to pay a commission becomes enforceable. Many listing contracts today are worded as bilateral contracts.

134. **D.** On failure to exercise an option, the optionee usually forfeits all the option money. When the contingent event of zoning does not occur, the buyer is entitled to the return of all her deposit money.

135. **D.** An option is an enforceable contract and gives this buyer the *right* of election to purchase the farm for $85,000. The offer, only if accepted, would bind the seller to a separate contract, in which case the buyer would "lose" the $5,000 option money but would, under the accepted contract, be able to buy the farm for a lower price, thus saving $5,000 on the deal.

136. **A.** Like sales contracts, options are assignable unless prohibited by the terms of the option itself. The optionee does not have a mortgageable estate until the option is exercised. Until then, the optionee has a mere contract right, and this is not the most attractive security to a lender.

137. **D.** Technically, it need be signed only by the party to be charged (i.e., the party to be held to the contract), although it is best to get all to sign. For example, the seller could sign a letter confirming a prior oral agreement.

138. **A.** The "as is" clause means the property is sold in its present condition with obvious and disclosed defects. The seller cannot use the "as is" clause to defraud a buyer; therefore, if sellers or agents know of hidden defects, they must disclose such problems to the buyer. It is no defense to a fraud action that the broker was obeying the seller's instruction; brokers have to obey their client's *lawful* instructions.

139. **D.** Whoever holds the deposit money will be reluctant to give the money to the seller unless the buyer consents. Perhaps the reason the buyer has not performed is because of an alleged misrepresentation or a claim that the seller's title is defective.

CHAPTER 17

Federal Fair Housing, Truth-in-Lending, the Do Not Call Registry, and Environmental Disclosures

Two major federal laws affect discrimination in housing. These are the Civil Rights Act of 1866, which makes racial discrimination illegal anywhere in the United States, and the Fair Housing Act of 1968, as amended, which makes discrimination based on race, color, sex, religion, handicap, familial status, or national origin illegal in connection with the sale or rental of most housing and any vacant land offered for residential construction or use. Regulations cover the types of discriminatory advertising that are prohibited.

The Americans with Disabilities Act (ADA) is intended to protect individuals with disabilities from various forms of discrimination in employment, public services, and public accommodations. It affects real estate licensees in four ways: (1) employment practices, (2) design of real estate offices, (3) disclosure whether a building is in compliance with ADA standards, and (4) providing service to disabled buyers and sellers.

The federal Truth-in-Lending Act, nicknamed Regulation Z, is intended to ensure that borrowers in need of consumer credit are given meaningful information with respect to the cost of credit. In this way, consumers can more readily compare the various credit terms available to them and thus avoid the uninformed use of credit.

The Do Not Call Registry legislation went into effect October 1, 2003. The law makes telephone solicitation to any household number on the list illegal unless one has prior written permission; an established business relationship; or a personal relationship with the homeowner. Written permission is obtained by taking a listing or getting a signed buyer's or seller's agency agreement. These business relationships last 18 months after the termination of a transaction. If someone leaves a message to return their call, the law allows 90 days to play "phone tag." Personal relationships include calls to relatives, friends, close acquaintances, and those found on active client lists. Rulings state also that real estate referrals are not deemed "acquaintances" based solely on the referral. The penalty for violating the Do Not Call legislation is $11,000 per call.

Federal and state regulations require the disclosure of certain environmental risks such as radon, lead-based paint, underground storage tanks, mold, and asbestos. Since June 28, 2004, the purchase of HUD-owned (repossessed) property requires the use of a disclosure form, HUD-9548-E. This Radon Gas and Mold Notice and Release Agreement must be used to notify prospective purchasers that radon and mold have the potential to cause serious health problems. Brownfields Revitalization legislation is utilized to rejuvenate deserted toxic industrial sites into viable real estate projects. Often these sites are clustered near prime real estate opportunities and already enjoy easy access to existing infrastructure, labor markets, and other resources. Real estate agents should disclose the potential of such risks and recommend that qualified experts inspect the property before sale.

The questions in this chapter will test your comprehension of the following topics:

■ Grounds for discrimination

■ Exemptions under the fair housing law

■ Procedures for filing complaints

■ Examples of discriminating practices

■ Grounds for discrimination under the Americans with Disabilities Act

■ Types of transactions covered or exempt under the Truth-in-Lending Act

■ The Do Not Call List legislation

■ Federal environmental legislation and disclosure

Note: In addition to the federal rules covered in this chapter, students should consult state law covering these same issues.

KEY WORDS

ADA: Americans with Disability Act addresses the rights of disabled Americans in employment and public accommodations.

Asbestos: A mineral used to insulate pipes that can cause respiratory disease if it deteriorates and becomes airborne or friable.

Blockbusting: The illegal practice of inducing homeowners to list their homes by making prejudiced representations regarding the entry of minorities into a neighborhood.

Brownfields: Abandoned commercial or industrial sites that have contaminated soil. With current Brownfields legislation, the federal government is providing funds to clean up these sites and put them on the tax rolls.

Equal Credit Opportunity Act (ECOA): Federal legislation that was passed in 1974 and made it illegal for lenders to discriminate on the basis of a person's sex, marital status, or age in the granting of credit. In addition, the ECOA prohibited lending discrimination based on a person's race, color, religion, or national origin. Also, the ECOA prevents lenders from discriminating against borrowers of public assistance programs such as Social Security and food stamps. Therefore, credit applications are considered solely on the basis of net worth, income, job stability, and credit score.

EHO poster: The Equal Housing Opportunity poster. It is required to be posted in a conspicuous place at all real estate, appraisal, and lending institutions.

LUST: Federal legislation known as (Leaking) Underground Storage Tanks. In 1976 the Resource Conservation and Recovery Act (RCRA) was created to regulate the generation, transportation, storage, treatment, and disposal of hazardous wastes at active facilities such as landfills and businesses that stored petroleum-based product in underground storage tanks. RCRA was amended in 1984 to regulate the use of Underground Storage Tanks (UST) including design, construction, and operation of them from installation to closure. Also, it regulated the cleanup of leaks and spills, imposed record-keeping and reporting guidelines, and regulated financial responsibility for liability insurance on both owners and operators. Today the EPA oversees the federal (Leaking) UST programs known as LUST. The primary purpose of this federal legislation is to protect America's groundwater.

Redlining: The illegal practice by a lender denying loans or restricting the number of loans made in a certain area of town.

SARA: The Superfund Amendments and Reauthorization Act established cleanup standards for contaminated real estate sites; increased federal funding; and clarified lender liability and innocent landowner immunity for those that did some due diligence.

Title VIII: Another name for the Fair Housing Act of 1978; prohibits discrimination in housing based on one's race, color, religion, sex, handicap, familial status, or national origin.

Truth-In-Lending: Nicknamed Regulation Z, ensures that borrowers in need of consumer credit are given meaningful information in regard to the cost of credit including the Annual Percentage Rate (APR).

Wetlands: An area of habitat land affected by groundwater, such as a marsh. State and federal agencies like the U.S. Corps of Engineers regulate the development of wetlands.

QUESTIONS

1. The federal Fair Housing Act exempts from its requirements which of the following?
   - A. Discriminating in the rental of rooms or units in a four-family dwelling where the owner actually resides in one of the units
   - B. Denying a person access to a multiple-listing service on account of race
   - C. Steering
   - D. Blockbusting

2. The federal Fair Housing Act prohibits discrimination based on which of the following?
   - A. Race, national origin, or color
   - B. Religion, sex, or age
   - C. Religion, sex, or military status
   - D. Race, sex, or marital status

3. The federal Fair Housing Act makes discrimination in housing illegal if based on any of the following *EXCEPT*
   - A. marital status.
   - B. religion.
   - C. physical handicap.
   - D. sex.

4. ◎ In a large rental complex with several buildings, the landlord has developed a set of guidelines for the property manager to follow. Which one of the following guidelines is permitted under the federal Fair Housing Act?
   - A. Parents with small children must live in a separate building with windows specifically designed to protect children.
   - B. Do not disclose that a former tenant had AIDS.
   - C. Use an application form that asks what religious pastor or rabbi to contact in case of emergency.
   - D. Deny rentals to former drug addicts.

5. All of the following are covered under the federal Fair Housing Act because of the definition of *familial status EXCEPT*
   - A. condominiums that have a specific exemption defined under a "grandfathering" provision of state law.
   - B. one or more individuals under the age of 18 living with a parent.
   - C. families where one or more members are pregnant.
   - D. housing projects intended for occupancy solely by individuals 62 years of age or older.

6. Under the federal Fair Housing Act, which of the following is exempt?
   - A. Private clubs operating a commercial boarding house
   - B. Religious organizations giving preference to their members in renting church-owned housing
   - C. Nonresident owner of a duplex renting one unit
   - D. Real estate agent selling own home

7. ◎ Single-family housing privately owned by an individual owning fewer than three such houses may be sold or rented without being subject to the provisions of the federal Fair Housing Act if
   - A. no more than two houses, in which the owner was not the most recent occupant, are sold in any two-year period.
   - B. no more than one such house is sold in any two-year period.
   - C. discriminatory advertising is used.
   - D. the owner hires a real estate broker.

8. Which of the following is a protected person under the 1988 Fair Housing law as amended?
   - A. A person currently addicted to cocaine
   - B. An alcoholic seeking treatment
   - C. A person age 50 seeking to lease a unit in a qualified retirement home
   - D. A person with poor credit

9. The federal Fair Housing Act permits which of the following?
   A. Landlord must agree to the request of a handicapped renter to make reasonable modifications at the tenant's expense.
   B. Landlord can charge an extra security deposit to all tenants with pets.
   C. Landlord can deny housing to families if the building occupants are all over 60 years of age.
   D. If the landlord occupies one of the 12 rental units, the landlord can give preference to tenants of the same sex.

10. White persons are protected by the federal Fair Housing Act and have a right to bring suit under the act in all of the following cases *EXCEPT* if
    A. they receive threatening phone calls for having sold their home to a minority family.
    B. acts of discrimination deny them the opportunity to have neighbors who are members of minority groups.
    C. they are evicted by a landlord for having minority guests in their home.
    D. they are denied housing because they are Democrats.

11. ◎ Angela, a single parent with three children, applies to rent an apartment in a singles complex where her friend Bobbie lives. Angela is rejected because she has children. After Bobbie complains to the Secretary of HUD, Bobbie is evicted. Which is *FALSE?*
    A. The rejection of Angela violates the federal Fair Housing Act.
    B. Such reprisal action against Bobbie violates the act.
    C. The act applies to discrimination based on parental status.
    D. Bobbie can be held liable for filing a frivolous complaint.

12. Which of the following is probably a discriminatory practice under the 1988 Amendments to the federal Fair Housing Act?
    A. Not allowing a family with children to keep a small dog
    B. Requiring that a person with severe arthritis carry a small dog while riding in an elevator in a condominium project
    C. Requiring a partially deaf person to turn-down the noise from a television set after midnight
    D. Requiring prospective tenants to fill out a credit report

13. A real estate broker enters a neighborhood bordering a blighted area and, in good faith, offers owners a reduced commission rate if they list with the firm and the property is sold within 180 days. There is no mention of the blighted area. Such practice is
    A. blockbusting.
    B. steering.
    C. redlining.
    D. acceptable.

14. Under the federal Fair Housing Act, which of the following practices is prohibited?
    A. A live-in owner's refusal to rent a unit in a two-family dwelling to any member of a certain religious group
    B. A broker's refusal to show a listed dwelling to a prospective purchaser because of the latter's ethnic background
    C. Refusal to rent because the prospective renter is in military service
    D. Refusal to sell based on political preference

15. Authority under the federal Fair Housing Act rests with the
    A. Secretary of the Interior.
    B. Attorney General.
    C. Federal Housing Authority.
    D. Secretary of Housing and Urban Development.

16. Any of the following acts is forbidden by the federal Fair Housing Act *EXCEPT*
    A. racial discrimination in real estate board membership.
    B. discrimination on the basis of national origin.
    C. discrimination on the basis of age.
    D. racial discrimination in home repair financing.

17. Which of the following is a legal reason for offering a shorter than normal mortgage term?
    A. Physical frailty of borrower
    B. Pregnancy of borrower
    C. Short leasehold term
    D. Mental handicap of borrower

18. Under the federal Fair Housing Act, the aggrieved person
    A. must file within 280 days of the alleged discriminatory practice.
    B. must first file his or her verified complaint with HUD before commencing any action in a U.S. District Court.
    C. has one year to file.
    D. must retain an attorney.

19. A complainant under the federal Fair Housing Act must file a complaint
    A. directly with the governor's office.
    B. within 45 days of the alleged discriminatory act.
    C. within one year of the discriminatory act.
    D. directly to the state attorney general.

20. Under the federal Fair Housing Act, the burden to prove there was discrimination is on the
    A. court.
    B. complainant.
    C. respondent.
    D. Secretary of HUD.

21. Under the federal Fair Housing Act, it is permissible to
    A. approve a loan to a person who has stated the intention to rent the property only to members of a minority group.
    B. refuse to grant loans on the basis of the financial condition of an applicant who is a member of a minority group.
    C. refuse loans on properties because they are located in certain areas.
    D. give preference in approving loans to members of a certain race.

22. The federal Fair Housing Act does which of the following?
    A. Makes it illegal for a lender to deny for any reason a loan to an applicant who is a member of a minority group
    B. Exempts the owner of a private single-family residence if a real estate broker is not employed to sell the property and discriminatory ads are not used
    C. Prohibits loans to minority college students
    D. Exempts condominium owners from provisions of the act

23. Under what conditions can a homeowner refuse to sell a house to a person of another race?
    A. When no real estate broker is used.
    B. When the property owner has three or fewer homes and has not had another sales transaction within 24 months.
    C. The homeowner can never discriminate on the basis of race.
    D. When no discriminatory advertising is used.

24. The Civil Rights Act of 1866 prohibits discrimination in housing on the basis of
    A. race.
    B. religion.
    C. sex.
    D. marital status.

25. ◎ Which of the following is permitted under the federal Fair Housing Act?
    A. Charging a higher interest rate on a loan by a savings association on the grounds that the loan applicant intends to rent part of the subject property to members of a certain minority group
    B. Advertising property for sale only in publications primarily aimed at a particular ethnic group and using models only of that same ethnic group
    C. Giving preference to members of a certain sex in the selling of homes
    D. Giving preference to members of the same political party

26. The prohibitions of the 1968 Fair Housing Act apply to single-family housing in all of the following cases *EXCEPT* if
    A. it is single-family housing owned by a corporation.
    B. it is single-family housing privately owned by an individual who owns more than three such houses, or who sells, in any two-year period, more than one house in which he or she was not the most recent occupant.
    C. a real estate broker uses discriminatory advertising to attract buyers.
    D. the owner gives his or her home to his or her child.

27. In an effort to obtain more listings, a broker urges people in a certain neighborhood to sell because several minority types have recently moved in nearby and property values may decline. This is a violation of which law?
    A. Federal Fair Housing Act on blockbusting
    B. Federal Equal Credit Opportunity Act
    C. Federal Truth-in-Lending Act
    D. Federal Disclosure Act

28. The Americans with Disabilities Act (ADA) requires accessibility standards for the design of all of the following types of properties *EXCEPT*
    A. residential apartments.
    B. shopping centers.
    C. hotels and restaurants.
    D. commercial facilities.

29. A renter complained to HUD about his landlord's discriminatory practices in the building. A week later the landlord gave the renter an eviction notice. Under which of the following situations would there be a violation of the federal Fair Housing Act?
    A. The renter is two months behind in his rent.
    B. The landlord wants to get back at the "squealer."
    C. The renter has damaged the premises.
    D. The renter is conducting an illegal use on the premises.

30. A minority group is moving into an area immediately adjacent to an old subdivision. Xanadu Realty offers in good faith to list homes in the subdivision at a lower than usual rate if the owners list within 45 days. There is no mention of race. Which of the following is *TRUE?*
    A. The broker's license can be revoked.
    B. This is blockbusting.
    C. Such practice is not illegal.
    D. Brokers cannot lower their standard rate of commission.

31. An apartment rents only to singles. Refusal to rent to which of the following would result in a violation of the federal Fair Housing Act?
    A. Families
    B. Lawyers
    C. Military officers
    D. Married couples

32. ◎ After HUD has filed a *charge* that a violation of the Fair Housing Act has taken place, the complainant may elect which of the following forums for the case to be heard?
    A. Civil action in U.S. Bankruptcy Court
    B. An administrative law judge hearing
    C. Board of REALTORS® arbitration
    D. Binding mediation

33. A bank decides not to make real estate loans to the groups described below. Such refusal to which of the following groups would be a violation of the federal Fair Housing Act?
    A. Multiple groups seeking to live in one residence
    B. Three jazz musicians taking title as joint tenants
    C. Four university professors
    D. Three priests

34. A particular savings association has blocked out certain regions of the community where it will not place loans because of the ghetto conditions. Such a practice is called
    A. redlining.
    B. steering.
    C. warehousing.
    D. relocating.

35. The federal Fair Housing Act provides that a prima facie (at first view) case against a broker for discrimination will be established in a complaint against the broker if he or she fails to do which of the following?
    A. Display a HUD Equal Opportunity poster
    B. Join an affirmative marketing program
    C. Join the HUD antidiscriminatory task force
    D. Attend mandatory classes on fair housing

36. ◎ A broker is discussing a new listing with a prospective minority buyer. The buyer wants to inspect the property immediately, but the listing owner has instructed the broker not to show the house during the owner's three-week absence. The buyer insists on viewing the property. The broker should do which of the following?
    A. Show the property to avoid a violation of the federal Fair Housing Act
    B. Request that the Real Estate Commission arbitrate the problem
    C. Inform the buyer of the seller's instructions
    D. Notify the nearest HUD office

37. Several minority families recently moved into an all-white area. A broker advised her sales staff to try to obtain listings in this area but to avoid going to solicit these families because they were new purchasers and they probably would not yet be interested in selling. The broker's actions would violate which of the following laws?
    A. Federal Fair Housing Act
    B. Equal Credit Opportunity Act
    C. Truth-in-Lending Act
    D. Real Estate Settlement Procedures Act

38. All of the following acts on the part of a real estate broker would constitute steering and thus be prohibited under the Fair Housing Act *EXCEPT*
    A. directing a prospective buyer of one minority group to work only with a salesperson of the same minority group and to look at areas dominated by that minority group.
    B. directing a member of one minority group away from properties located in areas dominated by other races.
    C. referring a member of one minority group to properties located only in areas dominated by members of the same group.
    D. directing a minority buyer to an expensive subdivision.

39. Susan decides to use the services of OK Realty to locate a suitable home for her minority family. OK Realty assigns Tom, its only minority salesperson, who avoids showing Susan any properties outside her minority's neighborhoods despite the fact Susan had indicated an interest in houses in another district. OK Realty's discriminating action can *BEST* be described as
    A. redlining.
    B. blockbusting.
    C. steering.
    D. conciliation.

40. A religious group bought a house in a subdivision and organized it into a commune. A broker, eager to make some quick profits, began to canvass this neighborhood, soliciting listings by inquiring whether the owners knew who had just moved into the area and leaving the firm's business card. Which term *BEST* describes the broker's marketing program?
    A. Redlining
    B. Lawful solicitation
    C. Panic peddling
    D. Steering

41. Which of the following actions on the part of a federal credit union would violate the federal Fair Housing Act?
    A. Refusing to make loans on condominium conversion projects in a local neighborhood because of pending congressional hearings
    B. Refusing to make loans on apartment buildings in a local neighborhood because of a substantial increase in foreclosures over the past two years
    C. Refusing to make loans to minority applicants whose credit is substantial
    D. Refusing to make loans on commercial properties

42. All of the following are unlawful discrimination because of minority status and thus are prohibited under the federal Fair Housing Act *EXCEPT*
    A. using one set of credit standards for men and one for women.
    B. canceling the leases of white residents who entertain minority guests.
    C. referring minority prospects only to minority brokers or salespersons.
    D. refusing to loan money to a minority applicant because of a poor credit rating.

43. Which of the following practices is lawful under the federal Fair Housing Act?
    A. Requiring that all prospective residents have recommendations from current residents, if most or all of the current residents are white Catholics
    B. Selling lots only to builders approved by a realty company where no builder who is willing to sell to minority homeowners can get the necessary approval
    C. Requiring an applicant to sign a form noting the applicant's religious preference
    D. Requiring all applicants to submit a credit report

44. Which of the following practices is lawful under the federal Fair Housing Act?
    A. Requiring higher credit qualifications for minorities than whites
    B. Requiring higher down payments from minorities than from whites and prohibiting minorities from acquiring secondary financing
    C. Requiring greater security deposits from military enlisted men than from officers
    D. When marketing housing in a minority neighborhood, putting For Sale ads only in papers with a primarily minority readership to reduce the likelihood of integrating an area by selling to whites

45. Which of the following is considered discriminatory under the federal Fair Housing Act?
    A. Advertising in the "help wanted" section for a certain race
    B. Renting property to persons within certain income levels
    C. Advertising in rental section for "military only"
    D. Selling residential subdivision land only to Protestants

46. A landlord owns a multifamily dwelling near a hospital, and she occupies one of the units. She rents out the other units and says she prefers to rent to foreign doctors. Which of the following statements is *TRUE* under the federal Fair Housing Act?
   A. She is violating the act, assuming there are a total of three units in the dwelling.
   B. She is not in violation of the act, assuming there are four units.
   C. Indicating a preference for foreign doctors would not be grounds for a charge of discrimination under the act.
   D. She is in violation of the act because she is intentionally acting to discriminate.

47. ◎ If a complainant files a discrimination lawsuit in a federal district court, all of the following remedies are available to the complainant *EXCEPT*
   A. permanent injunction.
   B. actual money damages.
   C. temporary restraining order.
   D. triple damages.

48. A religious organization owns and operates a nonprofit condominium for its own members. It agrees to sell one of the units to a nonreligious group but to make an additional charge. Such action is
   A. lawful because the owners are a nonprofit religious organization.
   B. lawful because condominiums are exempt from fair housing laws.
   C. unlawful because HUD forbids surcharges of any kind.
   D. unlawful because the owner's action was a violation of fair housing laws.

49. When a broker is taking a listing on an owner-occupied single-family residence, if the owner states that he is *NOT* to show the property to anyone of Irish nationality, the broker should
   A. ignore the request and proceed with the listing.
   B. comply with the principal's request.
   C. make note of the fact in the listing and continue to list, hoping that no Irish want to see the property.
   D. refuse to take the listing.

50. A metropolitan transient home is owned and operated by a religious group as a nonprofit home for members of that group. Samantha wants to rent, and because she is not a member of that religious group, she is required to pay a large surcharge. Which of the following is *TRUE?*
   A. This action is legal because it is a nonprofit organization.
   B. This action is legal because she is only renting and not purchasing.
   C. This action is legal if membership is not based on color, race, sex, or national origin.
   D. This action is not legal.

51. Under Truth-in-Lending, it is permissible to advertise which of the following statements alone?
   A. $2,000 down
   B. 10 percent interest
   C. Reasonable monthly terms
   D. $125 per month

52. The federal Truth-in-Lending Act requires that the lender disclose which of the following when a purchase-money mortgage is made?
   A. Annual percentage rate
   B. Right of rescission
   C. Penalties for violating the act
   D. Total closing costs

53. The annual percentage rate must be revealed to which of the following consumers?
   A. Applicant for a residential first loan
   B. Applicant for a commercial first loan
   C. Applicant for an industrial first loan
   D. Applicant for a loan payable in three installments

54. Under Truth-in-Lending, a commercial bank lending on a first purchase-money mortgage must do which of the following?
   A. Disclose the total interest to be paid and the annual percentage rate
   B. Require that both mortgagee and mortgagor sign the documents before Truth-in-Lending disclosure requirements become effective
   C. Provide notice of a right of rescission
   D. Disclose the annual percentage rate

55. Under the Truth-in-Lending Act, disclosure of which of the following will trigger disclosure of other credit terms?
    A. 10 percent down payment
    B. 10 percent annual percentage rate
    C. No down payment
    D. Reasonable financing available

56. When computing an annual percentage rate for disclosure purposes under the Truth-in-Lending Act, the creditor would include as finance charges all of the following loan expenses *EXCEPT*
    A. the service charge for making the loan.
    B. loan finder fees.
    C. credit check.
    D. termite inspection fee.

57. The Truth-in-Lending Act is designed to do which of the following?
    A. Limit the amount of interest charged the borrower
    B. Limit the amount of closing costs
    C. Disclose total closing costs
    D. Disclose loan finance costs

58. The Truth-in-Lending Act limits which of the following?
    A. The number of discount points paid by the buyer
    B. The number of discount points that can be paid by a seller
    C. The amount of finance fees to be charged
    D. The kind of advertising about points

59. Under the Truth-in-Lending Act, the borrower (consumer), except in cases of a purchase-money mortgage to acquire or construct a home, has a right of rescission on notice for
    A. 24 hours.
    B. 3 business days.
    C. 2 calendar days.
    D. 72 hours.

60. The Truth-in-Lending Law applies to
    A. commercial loan transactions involving real property.
    B. residential real estate mortgages.
    C. all personal property transactions.
    D. unconscionable contracts.

61. Regulation Z provides a right of rescission
    A. to first mortgages to finance the purchase of a residential condominium unit.
    B. that expires three business days after the date of consummation of the transaction or the date on which the lender makes material disclosures, whichever is later.
    C. to all residential loans on real estate.
    D. that expires on default of the loan.

62. All of the following are included in the "finance charge" under the Truth-in-Lending provisions *EXCEPT*
    A. points.
    B. loan finder fee.
    C. attorney's fees.
    D. service charges.

63. Regulation Z controls which of the following?
    A. The amount of interest that can be charged in a credit transaction
    B. What can be included in advertisements of certain credit transactions
    C. The number of points that can be charged
    D. The length of the loan term

64. Under the advertising regulations of Regulation Z, all of the following are true *EXCEPT* that
    A. interest rates cannot be mentioned alone but, rather, the "annual percentage rate" must be stated.
    B. general terms such as "liberal terms available," "small down payments accepted," or "VA or FHA financing available" may be used.
    C. compliance is enforced by the Federal Trade Commission.
    D. real estate brokers are regulated as "arrangers of credit."

65. The primary purpose of the Truth-in-Lending Act is to
    A. save the general public money in installment purchases.
    B. establish a more uniform set of charges.
    C. disclose to the consumer the cost and conditions of the installment purchase.
    D. assist the federal government in controlling shady lending practices.

66. ◎ Which of the following is exempt from the right of rescission under the Truth-in-Lending Act?
    A. A conventional first purchase-money mortgage on the borrower's principal dwelling
    B. A land contract to purchase raw land from a developer on which to build a dwelling
    C. A home improvement loan
    D. A home equity loan

67. Who of the following is exempt from giving the rescission notice to a consumer purchasing a home, according to the Truth-in-Lending Act?
    A. Any second mortgagee
    B. A seller carrying back a purchase-money mortgage
    C. A broker arranging credit for a fee
    D. A home improvement lender taking a junior mortgage

68. Under Regulation Z, all of the following may be advertised alone *EXCEPT*
    A. 5 percent down payment.
    B. 9½ percent annual percentage rate.
    C. $73,600 cash price.
    D. very low monthly payments.

69. The Truth-in-Lending Act prohibits which of the following?
    A. Advertising credit terms
    B. Advertising in general terms such as "quick financing available"
    C. Advertising interest rates
    D. Advertising only the percentage of down payment

70. ◎ Regulation Z requires that lenders
    A. properly inform buyers and sellers of commercial property of all settlement costs in a real estate transaction.
    B. inform prospective home mortgage or trust deed borrowers of charges, fees, and interest involved in making a home mortgage or trust deed loan.
    C. disclose the lender's margin of profit in each loan.
    D. make loans to racial minority groups.

71. In accordance with the federal Equal Credit Opportunity Act of 1974, a lender discussing a home loan with a young couple who both work may consider all of the following factors *EXCEPT*
    A. verification of bank and savings accounts.
    B. age of either husband or wife.
    C. credit references supplied by the couple.
    D. verification of employment of husband and wife.

72. Under the federal Equal Credit Opportunity Act, the property manager who requires a credit report on a prospective tenant can do which of the following?
    A. Charge the tenant a fee for the cost of the report
    B. Disapprove of the creditworthiness of the tenant based on age
    C. Disapprove creditworthiness based on the tenant's sex
    D. Publish the report in the property manager association's monthly newsletter

73. A homeowner sells his house and takes back some financing. Under the Consumer Protection Act, what does Regulation Z require that the homeowner disclose to the buyer?
    A. Annual percentage rate
    B. Financing charge
    C. Three-day right of rescission
    D. Nothing

74. Which is *NOT* required in the Truth-in-Lending disclosure statement?
    A. Term of prepayment penalty
    B. Finance charge
    C. Annual percentage rate
    D. Amount of interest per installment

75. Which federal law requires that landowners be financially responsible for cleaning up hazardous wastes that have been leached from toxic wastes disposed of on a neighbor's property?
    A. The Resource Conservation and Recovery Act of 1976
    B. National Environmental Protection Act of 1969
    C. Superfund
    D. The Toxic Substances Control Act

76. ◎ Which of the following environmental hazards can be "friable"?
A. Asbestos
B. Formaldehyde
C. Radon
D. Polychlorinated biphenyls (PCBs)

77. ◎ Which of the following environmental hazards is indicated by leakage near electrical equipment such as transformers?
A. Asbestos
B. Formaldehyde
C. Radon
D. Polychlorinated biphenyls (PCBs)

78. Which federal law requires that landowners be financially responsible for cleaning up hazardous wastes that have been dumped on their property by prior owners or tenants?
A. The Comprehensive Environmental Response, Compensation, and Liability Act
B. The National Environmental Protection Act
C. The Toxic Substances Control Act
D. The Clean Water Act

79. The Americans with Disabilities Act (ADA) requires all of the following *EXCEPT* that
A. lessors must offer discounts to disabled persons using places of public accommodation.
B. employers must pay for reasonable changes to the workplace to allow disabled individuals to have an equal opportunity to work.
C. places of public accommodation (hotels, banks, office buildings) must remove physical and communication barriers that discriminate against disabled persons.
D. state and federal public agencies must take steps to make existing facilities accessible to and usable by disabled persons.

80. In a civil action brought by the U.S. Attorney General, what is the maximum civil penalty that can be assessed against a respondent for a first violation of the federal Fair Housing Act?
A. $50,000
B. $10,000
C. $25,000
D. $100,000

81. The existence of all of the following environmental conditions must be disclosed to a prospective purchaser as hazardous *EXCEPT*
A. wetlands.
B. lead-based paint.
C. radon.
D. asbestos.

82. All of the following are requirements of the Real Estate Settlement Procedures Act *EXCEPT* that the lender
A. collect three months' reserves for tax and insurance.
B. provide a good-faith estimate of settlement charges.
C. give the borrower an information booklet upfront.
D. must use a HUD-1 Settlement Statement and allow the borrower time to inspect it.

83. The federal agency that has authority to regulate interstate commerce, including telephone calls, is the
A. Federal Communications Commission.
B. Federal Bureau of Commerce.
C. Department of Interstate Transportation.
D. Federal Trade Commission.

84. Which of the following is *NOT* exempt from the Do Not Call legislation?
A. Political calls
B. Nonprofit tax-exempt charities
C. Survey requests by news organizations
D. Real estate agents

85. If a real estate agent has a contractual relationship with a client listed on the Do Not Call Registry, the agent
A. is only allowed to contact the client during the time of the transaction because the client is listed on the Registry.
B. may contact the client up to 6 months after the termination of the transaction.
C. may contact the client up to 12 months after the termination of the transaction.
D. may contact the client up to 18 months after the termination of the transaction.

86. The Resource Conservation and Recovery Act (RCRA) was created to regulate the generation, transportation, storage, treatment, and disposal of hazardous wastes at active facilities. It was amended in 1984 to regulate the use of underground storage tanks including design, construction, and operation from installation to closure. Also, it regulates the cleanup of leaks and spills, imposes record-keeping and reporting guidelines, as well as regulates the financial responsibility for liability insurance on both owners and operators. What is the nickname used to describe this underground storage legislation?
    A. UST
    B. LUST
    C. LIST
    D. LOST

87. The Comprehensive Environmental Response, Compensation, and Liability Act of 1980 was amended in 1986 to protect innocent landowners from cleanup liability. What is the abbreviated name of this federal legislation?
    A. Title VIII
    B. Title X
    C. FIREEA
    D. SARA

88. Legislation that helps resurrect deserted, non-operational, and dilapidated toxic industrial sites into tax-paying property is known as
    A. greenfields.
    B. whitefields.
    C. grayfields.
    D. brownfields.

ANSWERS

1. **A.** A limited exemption is afforded to an occupant-lessor in a dwelling not to exceed a fourplex, under Sec. 806(b)(2). Choice (B) is specifically prohibited under Sec. 806.

2. **A.** Age is not yet a grounds for a discrimination violation under the federal Fair Housing Act (FFH). The present grounds are race, color, sex, religion, handicap, family, or national origin.

3. **A.** Marital status (the status of being single or married) is not yet covered under the federal Fair Housing Act.

4. **B.** AIDS is a protected class under civil rights law, so it is illegal to disclose such information to a prospective tenant, even if the tenant specifically asks. Other protected classes are religion (can't use a discriminatory form that might imply a religious preference), parental status (can't have different rules for people with children as this might tend to discourage them from renting), and physical or mental handicap (can't discrimi-

nate against a *former* drug addict, but can if a current drug addict).

5. **D.** Housing projects for those 62 or over can prohibit families. There is a limited exemption for projects specially designed for seniors age 55 and older.

6. **B.** Religious organizations and private clubs can give preferences or restrict occupancy, provided the establishment is not run for a commercial purpose (it must be for a non-profit purpose) under Sec. 807.

7. **B.** Frequent turnover of properties would put the owner in the broker classification, thereby losing exempt status [see Sec. 803(b)].

8. **B.** Alcoholism is a disease and fits within the physical and mental handicap provision. A current drug user is not protected, although a reformed drug addict would be protected.

9. **A.** If the tenant agrees to restore the premises to their original condition on vacating, the tenant can make modifications such as

installing grab bars in the bathroom, widening interior doorways, or installing ramps for wheelchairs. The law specifically prohibits increasing security deposits to cover pets or people with a handicap. The elderly housing exemption requires that all occupants be age 62 or older; in housing for people age 55 or older, at least 80 percent of the units must be occupied by at least one person age 55 or older. There is a limited exemption for a landlord occupying one of four rental units.

10. **D.** (A), (B), and (C) are covered under the FFH Act, but political affiliation is not covered.

11. **D.** FFH covers discrimination against families. The FFH Act prohibits intimidation and reprisal actions against complainants (see Sec. 817).

12. **B.** The handicap provision requires adjustment in the rules to accommodate the handicapped, as long as this does not threaten the health and safety of others.

13. **D.** Blockbusting or panic peddling is a broker's encouragement of owners to list before property values drop owing to the arrival of certain minorities in the area. Steering is directing specific ethnic groups into or away from certain areas. Here, there is no connection between the reduced commission and any discriminatory ground.

14. **B.** An owner is exempt, provided he or she occupies one of the units in the dwelling and there are no more than four units in the dwelling. It is no defense to the broker that he or she is obeying the owner's directions to discriminate. If this is true, then the broker should give up the listing.

15. **D.** The complainant can go directly to HUD or to court. One advantage of going to the Secretary of HUD is that the activities of HUD in reviewing the case will help reduce the costs of the investigation.

16. **C.** Age is not yet a ground for discrimination under FFH, although it is a ground under many *state* discrimination laws.

17. **C.** Lenders cannot discriminate based on handicap or familial status, but they can deny loans based on sound economic reasons.

18. **C.** The statute of limitations is one year, but the complainant has a choice of filing with HUD or in federal court. Both the complaint and the answer must be verified (made under oath).

19. **C.** The state attorney general conducts litigation when the Secretary of HUD acts as a party.

20. **B.** In actual practice, however, the respondent often feels the obligation to prove there was no discrimination.

21. **B.** Under choice (A) the borrower would be discriminating in the rental program, and the lender can't be a party to the discrimination. A lender can refuse a loan for valid credit reasons, but not to discriminate against minority groups. Choice (C) is redlining.

22. **B.** It is only illegal if a loan denial is based on discriminatory reasons. Also, under choice (B) the owner cannot use discriminatory advertising.

23. **C.** The original 1886 Civil Rights Act does not allow a homeowner to discriminate on the basis of race in real or personal property transactions. There are *no* exceptions. Under the 1968 federal Fair Housing Act as amended, certain exemptions exist to the discrimination provisions, such as those stated in (A), (B), and (D).

24. **A.** A single-family owner who discriminates in the sale of his or her home based on race would not violate the federal Fair Housing Act, but would violate the Civil Rights Act of 1866. The 1866 act prohibits all racial discrimination, private as well as public, in the sale of real property.

25. **D.** The loan decision cannot be based on ethnic reasons, only economic reasons. As to choice (B), the federal Fair Housing Act also prohibits discriminatory solicitation that would encompass this type of selected advertising owing to its indirect effect on discrimination—it is selected on ethnic grounds.

26. **D.** The exemption does not apply to commercial developers or to people deemed to be in the business of selling or renting dwellings (such as those who own more than three dwellings).

27. **A.** Blockbusting is defined as "for profit, to induce or attempt to induce any person to sell or rent any dwelling by representations regarding the entry or prospective entry into the neighborhood of a person or persons of a particular race, color, religion, sex, or national origin." (A criminal does not fit into any of these categories.)

28. **A.** The ADA applies to places of public accommodation (theaters, shopping centers, restaurants, hotels, etc.) and commercial facilities (warehouses, factories, office buildings). ADA requires that owners of these properties make them accessible to persons with disabilities (physical and mental). ADA does not apply to residential properties such as residential apartment buildings and condominiums.

29. **B.** Retaliatory evictions are prohibited under the federal Fair Housing Act.

30. **C.** For blockbusting to exist, there must be some actual or implied representation about the effect of the entry of minority groups into the area.

31. **A.** The federal Fair Housing Act does not prohibit discrimination based on military service, marital status, or profession, but it does cover families.

32. **B.** If both parties agree, the case can be decided by an administrative law judge rather than go to a U.S. District Court. Unlike arbitration, mediation is not binding.

33. **D.** Multiple groups might violate local zoning requirements but, like noisy people, they are not covered under the federal Fair Housing Act.

34. **A.** Redlining got its name from the alleged practice of outlining in red on a map those areas where loans would not be made by a lender. Because these areas are typically where minority groups are located, this practice has the indirect effect of discrimination.

35. **A.** HUD does not strictly require that brokers display this small poster that states the broker does not discriminate in housing based on race, color, religion, handicap, familial status, national origin, or sex. But failure to post it will result in switching the burden of proof from the complainant to the respondent in a federal Fair Housing Act discrimination case. Affirmative marketing programs are entirely optional but are encouraged by REALTORS®.

36. **C.** An agent must obey the instructions of the principal, except where an illegal intent or act is involved. Here, the owner is acting reasonably with no indication of any unlawful bias.

37. **A.** Although the broker is probably acting in good faith, the solicitation program nevertheless has the effect of skipping minority groups and soliciting only nonminority members of the neighborhood. Such action could create an indirect taint of discriminatory selection.

38. **D.** Steering is discouraging the sale or rental of a dwelling because of the presence or absence of minority neighbors, whether the intention is actual, alleged, or implied. Referring minority prospects to minority salespersons is treating people differently because of their minority status, and such action is unlawful even though there may be a valid business purpose.

39. **C.** Steering is the unlawful practice of discouraging the sale or rental of a dwelling because of the presence or absence of minority neighbors. Referring minority prospects to minority salespersons or directing people to or away from certain neighborhoods based on a discriminatory reason is unlawful. It is treating people differently because of their minority status, even though there may be some valid business purpose.

40. **C.** Vigorous solicitation of sellers in a rapidly changing neighborhood is called *panic peddling.* Panic peddling is defined as soliciting sales or rental listings, making written or oral statements creating fear or alarm, transmit-

ting written or oral warnings or threats, soliciting prospective minority renters or buyers, or acting in any other manner to induce or attempt to induce the sale or lease of residential property, either (a) through representations regarding the present or prospective entry of one or more minority residents into an area or (b) through representations that would convey to a reasonable person under the circumstances, whether or not overt reference to minority status is made, that one or more minority residents are or may be entering the area.

Note: The term *minority* means any group that can be distinguished because of race, sex, religion, color, or national origin.

41. **C.** If refusal is based on sound economic reasons and not on any discriminatory basis, there is no violation. However, if the credit union decided not to make loans in certain ghetto areas based on racial problems that existed, then this would be the unlawful practice of redlining. The law applies to credit unions (also banks and savings associations) and commercial loans on multi-family units.

42. **D.** While discriminatory financial practices are unlawful, it is lawful to refuse to loan money if refusal is based solely on sound business practice. Assigning salespersons on the basis of minority status is to discriminate in the provision of services in connection with a real estate transaction.

43. **D.** The law prohibits not only direct discrimination but also practices that may be fair in form but discriminatory in operation. Even if the discrimination is unintentional and done through ignorance, the effect is discriminatory, and the result is a violation.

44. **C.** There may be sound economic reasons for distinguishing between officers and enlisted men; discriminating against the military, though not encouraged or endorsed, is usually not a violation of the FFH. Cases have held that a solicitation policy, as in (D), directed at blacks and excluding whites is a violation of the act.

45. **D.** Choice (A) does not cover a real estate transaction, and (B) is a typical factor to consider in renting.

46. **B.** Expressing a preference based on national origin is contrary to the provisions of the act. There is, however, an exemption to the owner-occupant of a dwelling occupied or intended to be occupied by no more than four families (a fourplex).

47. **D.** The complainant can persuade the court to issue orders preventing the respondent from continuing the illegal practices. Money damages are allowed for actual losses, but punitive damages are limited in amount. In cases involving willful intimidation, there is a fine or time in jail.

48. **A.** While making a surcharge is a discriminatory act (giving preference to a religious group), religious organizations are exempt if they are open to all to join and if they are run on a not-for-profit basis.

49. **D.** It is illegal under the federal Fair Housing Act to accept a listing that involves a discriminatory act, such as denying access to people of a certain national origin.

50. **C.** To qualify for the religious exemption under the federal Fair Housing Act, it is necessary that the home be operated for other than commercial purposes and that membership in the religion be open to all. Choice (A) is wrong because not all nonprofit organizations are exempt—only religious organizations and private clubs.

51. **C.** Advertising general credit terms is permissible, but once the creditor starts to advertise specific terms, a full disclosure must be made of all credit terms.

52. **A.** While a purchase-money lien is exempt from the need to disclose the finance charge and the total of payments, it still must disclose the annual percentage rate, which is the relationship of the total finance charge to the total amount to be financed.

53. **A.** Truth-in-Lending does not apply to commercial loans; it applies only to consumer (not corporate) loans of the household or

family variety. A credit transaction requires payments in more than four installments.

54. **D.** Lenders need disclose only the annual percentage rate. A mortgagee does not sign the mortgage or the note.

55. **A.** The disclosure of the specific percentage of down payment requires disclosure of the terms of repayment and the annual percentage rate. Advertising of general terms of financing (or that there is no down payment) is not regulated by Truth-in-Lending (part of the Consumer Protection Act and Regulation Z).

56. **D.** Only charges directly or indirectly related to making the loan are included in the finance charge.

57. **D.** The law does not limit costs or charges; it merely requires their full disclosure. RESPA also regulates disclosure of closing costs.

58. **D.** The law requires disclosure of the points only, which, under VA loan requirements, must be paid by someone other than the borrower.

59. **B.** Note the difference between calendar and business days.

60. **B.** The law is designed to protect the ordinary consumer in credit transactions that affect household and family matters. It does not apply to commercial investments. Personal property transactions over specified amounts (presently $25,000) are exempt.

61. **B.** First liens to acquire or construct a principal residence are exempt. The right of rescission is designed to protect homeowners from losing their homes (this includes condominiums and mobile homes) because of credit transactions that used the principal residence as security. Note that there is now a three-year statute of limitations if no disclosures are made.

62. **C.** Attorney's fees are regularly incurred in closing real estate transactions, regardless of whether credit is involved. Choices (A), (B), and (D) directly relate to the lending of money.

63. **B.** While state usury laws regulate the amount of interest, Truth-In-Lending controls ads of credit transactions that fit under Regulation Z.

64. **D.** The interest rate can be no more prominent in the ad than the annual percentage rate. Specific terms trigger the mention of all credit terms. Real estate brokers do not have to make the disclosures required of an "arranger of credit."

65. **C.** So that the consumer can best shop around for the most appropriate loan, the Truth-In-Lending law requires full disclosure of credit terms and use of a barometer of credit, that is, the annual percentage rate.

66. **A.** Certain first liens are exempt (those to buy or build a home) if they are liens in connection with a "residential loan transaction" (i.e., a lien created on the consumer's principal dwelling to finance the acquisition or initial construction of that dwelling).

67. **B.** The lien to purchase is exempt.

68. **A.** Advertising that there is a 5 percent down payment requires disclosure of all the credit terms.

69. **D.** The advertising of credit terms is regulated, not prohibited.

70. **B.** Regulation Z (Truth-in-Lending) does not apply to commercial property transactions, just to residential transactions involving mortgages, trust deeds, or installment land contracts. Regulation Z does not pertain to discrimination.

71. **B.** Under ECOA, the lender cannot allow someone's age to influence the loan decision. To do so would be illegal discrimination.

72. **A.** While a charge for the report is fair, it is illegal discrimination to deny services related to credit based on someone's being too old.

73. **D.** Because there are no facts that indicate the homeowner is a "creditor" (one who in the ordinary course of business extends credit), the Truth-in-Lending Act does not apply.

74. **D.** The total amount of interest must be stated, not the amount per installment.

75. **C.** Superfund imposes strict liability on landowners for cleanup expenses.

76. **A.** Asbestos can be friable or nonfriable. *Friable* means that it can easily break up and be released as tiny fibers into the air that can be inhaled and cause lung damage.

77. **D.** PCBs.

78. **A.** Congress has imposed cleanup responsibility through "Superfund," or as it is also known, the Comprehensive Environmental Response, Compensation, and Liability Act of 1980 (CERCLA).

79. **A.** The intent of ADA is to ban discrimination against individuals with qualified physical and mental disabilities by requiring equal access to employment, public accommodations, and government services. It does not require special discounts. ADA applies to places of public accommodation and commercial facilities, but not to residential condominiums, private clubs, or religious organizations.

80. **A.** If the U.S. Attorney General (i.e., the Justice Department) files suit to prevent a pattern or practice of discrimination, the maximum award against a first-time offender is $50,000; it is $100,000 for subsequent violations. The maximum an administrative law judge can award is $50,000.

81. **A.** The term *wetlands* describes a land area affected by groundwater, such as a marsh. Sellers should disclose if the property is in a wetland area. It is not a hazardous condition that can cause harm to the public, as are asbestos, lead-based paint, and radon gas (a cause of lung cancer). Development of wetland areas is subject to intense regulation by state and federal agencies (U.S. Corps of Engineers).

82. **A.** The lender is permitted to collect up to two months of reserves or impounds. Within three days of application, the lender needs to provide a good-faith estimate of the settlement charges (not exact amount of total charges).

83. **D.** The Federal Trade Commission regulates trade among the states via the power of commerce clause found in the Constitution of the United States. The FCC is limited in its scope of authority to transmission of signals.

84. **D.** Real estate agents are prohibited from using the telephone to solicit the business of those registered under this legislation.

85. **D.** The law exempts agents who have contractual or agency relationships for up to 18 months after the termination of a transaction. However, if specifically asked, this window period may be terminated by the client's request. Real estate firms are required to keep specific logs of those who make such a request and distribute to all potential future callers.

86. **B.** LUST is the acronym used for Leaking Underground Storage Tanks.

87. **D.** SARA is the Superfund Amendments and Reauthorization Act designed to create an "innocent landowner" defense against the strict liability interpretation of CERCLA.

88. **D.** Brownfields legislation guidelines give individual states authority to clean up abandoned toxic sites. Legislation, titled the Small Business Liability Relief and Brownfields Revitalization Act, was signed into law in 2002 and recognizes the finality of successful state-directed hazardous cleanup efforts.

18

Property Management, Lease Agreements, and Securities

Property management constitutes a special branch of the real estate business that consists of the operation, supervision, and execution of management policies pertaining to a given property. A property manager's basic purpose is to provide the client-owner with the highest continuous net return from the property consistent with its highest and best use and, at the same time, provide the tenant with the best service and value for the rent.

As general agents, property managers are often hired to preside over condominium association meetings and manage the association's business affairs. Sometimes the property manager's firm is assigned the task of handling complaints too. Other delegated tasks that a property management firm can perform include administering the association's financial business like budgeting; establishing and reconciling reserve accounts; collecting monthly fees; reporting annual interest income (IRS Form 1120H); reviewing bank statements and cancelled checks; filing nonprofit status reports with the Secretary of State; and hiring accounting professionals to audit the books. They can be empowered to enforce the Covenants, Conditions, and Restrictions (CC&Rs) as well as administer the association's maintenance contracts, contracts with vendors, consultants, and contractors, as well as other third party providers of goods and services, and insurance contracts.

A lease is an agreement whereby the landlord/lessor gives the tenant/lessee the right to use specific real property for a definite period, with consideration being the payment of rent. The lease is both a conveyance and a contract—it sets forth the rights and duties of the parties, and it is a transfer of the exclusive right to the use and possession of the property for a certain period of time.

Unless prohibited by the terms of the lease, the lessee may assign or sublet the premises. An assignment transfers the entire interest of the tenant; a sublease transfers a portion of the property or the remaining term of the lease, with the sublessor retaining primary liability under the lease. Leases may be terminated by breach of conditions and promises—by the tenant for improper use or nonpayment of rent; by the landlord for failing to provide quiet enjoyment and habitable premises (constructive eviction).

The questions in this chapter test your comprehension of the following topics:

■   The role and responsibilities of a property manager

■   Property management agreements

■   Rights and obligations of landlord and tenant

■   Types of lease agreements

■   Use of security deposits

■   Common provisions found in lease agreements

■   Types of transactions involving sale of securities

K E Y   W O R D S

Actual eviction: The legal process of removing a tenant from possession of the premises for some breach of the lease contract.

"As is" condition: Premises accepted by a tenant in its existing condition at the time of the lease including all physical defects.

Assignment: The transfer of the right, title, and interest in the property of one person, the assignor, to another, the assignee. In real estate, there are assignments of mortgages, contracts, agreements of sale, leases, and options, among others.

Attorn: To turn over or transfer to another money or goods. An agreement that recognizes that if the property is sold during the lease period that rents due will be paid to the new owner.

Buffer: A strip of real estate that transitions distinct land uses. It may be an earth berm, planted shrubs or trees, walls, or even fencing.

Buildout: The cost of configuring and finishing space to meet the tenant's needs.

CAM: An add-on fee paid by the tenant for common area maintenance.

Concessions: Rent abatement, build-out allowance, or other payment credits given by landlords to prospective tenants to induce them to sign a lease.

Constructive eviction: Acts done by a landlord that so materially disturb or impair the tenant's enjoyment of the leased premises that a tenant is effectively forced to move out and terminate the lease without liability for any further rent.

Depreciation: An accounting procedure used to determine the loss in a property's value for income tax purposes.

Equitable title: The equitable right to obtain ownership in a property whose legal title is actually in another person's name. Simply stated, it is the interest held by a contract purchaser prior to the transfer of title. Sometimes it is known as an "insurable interest."

Equity kicker: This is a participation loan for risky investments. The investor expects the normal investment return and further conditions that an opportunity be given to buy part ownership.

First refusal, right of: The right of a person to have the first opportunity either to purchase or lease real property.

Force majeure: Found in a lease that notes that one cannot be liable for forces that cannot be controlled or resisted like riots, strikes, arson, floods, hurricanes, tornadoes, etc.

Gross lease: A lease of property under which the lessee pays a fixed rent and the lessor pays the taxes, insurance, and other charges regularly incurred through ownership.

Ground lease: A long-term lease of just the land (land lease) with improvements made by the tenant.

Holdover tenant: One who stays on the leased premises after his lease has expired. The landlord normally has the choice of evicting the holdover tenant or permitting him to remain and continue to pay rent.

Landlord: The lessor or the owner of leased premises. The landlord retains a reversionary interest in the property so that when the lease ends the property will revert to the landlord.

Lease: A lease is both a contract between a lessor (landlord) and a lessee (tenant) and a conveyance or demise of the premises by the lessor to the lessee. A lease is a contract, in that it embodies the agreement between the parties.

Leasehold: A less-than-freehold estate that a tenant possesses in real property.

Lessee: The person to whom property is rented or leased; called a tenant in most residential leases.

Lessor: The person who rents or leases property to another. In residential leasing, the lessor is often referred to as a *landlord.*

Net lease: A lease, usually commercial, whereby the lessee pays not only the rent for occupancy but also maintenance and operating expenses such as taxes, insurance, utilities, and repairs. Thus the rent paid is "net" to the lessor.

Percentage lease: A lease whose rental is based on a percentage of the monthly or annual gross sales made on the premises.

Periodic tenancy: A leasehold estate that continues from period to period, such as month to month or year to year. All conditions and terms of the tenancy are carried over from period to period and continue for an uncertain time until proper notice of termination is given.

Property management: That aspect of real estate devoted to the leasing, managing, marketing, and overall maintenance of the property of others.

Right of first refusal: A clause in a lease that gives the tenant the first opportunity to buy should the owner obtain a legitimate offer that the tenant can match or refuse.

Security deposit: Money deposited by or for the tenant with the landlord, to be held by the landlord for the following purposes: to remedy tenant defaults for damage to the premises (be it accidental or intentional), for failure to pay rent due, or for failure to return all keys at the end of the tenancy.

Step-up lease: A lease with fixed rent for an initial term and provision for predetermined rent increases at specified intervals and/or increases based upon periodic appraisals; sometimes called a *graduated lease.*

Summary possession: A legal process used by a landlord to regain possession of the leased premises if the tenant has breached the lease or is holding over after the termination of tenancy.

Surrender: A premature conveyance of a possessory estate to a person having a future interest, as when a lessee surrenders the leasehold interest to the owner of the reversionary interest, the lessor, before the normal expiration of the lease.

Tenant: In general, one who holds or possesses property, such as a life tenant or a tenant for years; commonly used to refer to a lessee under a lease.

Tenant at will: A tenant who holds possession by permission of the landowner without an agreement for any fixed period of time.

Trade fixtures: Personal property used in a tenant's business that is attached or adapted to the landlord's space but is removable upon termination of the lease.

Uniform Residential Landlord Tenant Act: Legislation in several states designed to both protect and provide remedies for landlords and tenants.

MISTAKEN IDENTITY

The following words are often confused with one another. Note the difference in meaning of these mistaken identity words and phrases.

Security deposit/Earnest money deposit: The *security deposit* is paid by a tenant up-front to cover any default in the lease, including damage, whereas a buyer puts up *earnest money* at the time of an offer, to be forfeited in the event the buyer does not perform.

Tenancy at will/Tenancy for years: The *tenancy for years* lasts for a fixed period, whereas the *tenancy at will* may be canceled at any time by either landlord or tenant.

Eviction (actual or constructive): In an *actual eviction* the landlord evicts the defaulting tenant, whereas in a *constructive eviction* the landlord fails to provide the necessary services so the tenant is legally entitled to cancel the lease.

Leasehold/Leased fee: The *leasehold* is the lessee's interest, whereas the *leased fee* is the landlord's interest represented by the value of the remaining rent plus the reversion.

Gross lease/Net lease: In a *gross lease* the tenant pays a single amount and the landlord pays the expenses, whereas in a *net lease* the tenant pays a net amount to the landlord and the tenant pays the expenses.

QUESTIONS

1. Among the major responsibilities of a property manager are all of the following *EXCEPT* to
   A. obtain the highest possible return for the investor.
   B. preserve the building.
   C. maintain high occupancy.
   D. obtain a listing for resale.

2. A broker acting as a property manager of a building was instructed by the owner to paint the building for $1,000. Without the owner's knowledge and consent, the broker could
   A. contract the job for $800 and keep the extra $200.
   B. accept a rebate from the painter.
   C. do the entire job and keep the $1,000.
   D. could do nothing that was not within the scope of the employment contract.

3. All of the following should be included as fixed operating expenses in the budget for property management *EXCEPT*
   A. property manager's fees.
   B. ceiling replacement.
   C. fuel costs.
   D. maintenance.

4. A property manager's duties typically include all of the following *EXCEPT*
   A. collecting rents.
   B. making minor repairs.
   C. marketing space.
   D. investing profits from clients' properties.

5. A properly drawn property management contract should contain all of the following *EXCEPT*
   A. a legal description of the property.
   B. the terms and conditions of the employment.
   C. an outline of the expected duties.
   D. the scope of the authority.

6. One of the most effective ways for a property manager to both provide income to the owner and advertise the manager's own abilities is through a well-run building that has
   A. as high or higher rents than other similar buildings.
   B. satisfied tenants served by competent employees.
   C. the most complete and up-to-date accounting reports.
   D. the lowest-paid employees.

7. All of the following should be a consideration in selecting a tenant *EXCEPT*
   A. size of the space versus the tenant's requirements.
   B. the tenant's ability to pay.
   C. racial and ethnic backgrounds of the tenants.
   D. compatibility of the business with those of other tenants.

8. Certified Property Manager (CPM) is a designation awarded to qualified applicants by
   A. the local board of REALTORS®.
   B. the National Association of Real Estate Boards.
   C. state associations of real estate boards.
   D. the Institute of Real Estate Management.

9. Included in the property management budget as fixed operating expenses are all of the following costs *EXCEPT*
   A. hazard insurance.
   B. the property management fee.
   C. repair of damaged carpeting.
   D. reserves for overhaul and maintenance of air-conditioning and heating equipment.

10. Property managers are responsible for all of the following *EXCEPT*
    A. protecting the condition of real estate.
    B. maximizing income from real property.
    C. handling rents.
    D. drafting original legal documents for leasing space in the building.

11. ◎ A property manager, to secure the *BEST* return on the investment, would establish rental income by
    A. long-term rentals in the upper range of present rents.
    B. long-term contracts at the midpoint of present-day rentals.
    C. long-term contracts with a built-in escalation clause.
    D. month-to-month rentals.

12. ◎ Which of the following is *TRUE?*
    A. The most common way of setting up a rent schedule for units of space in a building is to compare the space units with other similar units, in similar buildings, in similar neighborhoods, and then to set competitive rents.
    B. If the rent is not paid by the rental due date, the property manager should immediately evict the tenant.
    C. The property manager should handle the listing and sale of the property.
    D. The property manager should be well versed in all tax benefits of the property to the employer.

13. In negotiating a commercial lease for an absentee owner, a property manager may be permitted to do all of the following *EXCEPT*
    A. determine the limits of concessions, such as three months' free rent to be offered to prospective tenants.
    B. initiate legal action against a tenant whose rent is many months in arrears.
    C. require that a tenant list with the property manager other property for sale.
    D. assist in determining the leasing prices.

14. All of the following are valid operating expenses for a building manager to put into the budget *EXCEPT*
    A. heating oil.
    B. cleaning supplies.
    C. debt service.
    D. management fees.

15. Which is *TRUE* regarding the role of a property manager?
    A. The establishment of competitive rents is an important function of property management.
    B. It is not the function of property management to investigate a prospective tenant's credit rating.
    C. The quality of a tenant is of little concern to the property manager, just as long as the tenant pays the rent on time.
    D. The manager must evaluate the proper financing for the building.

16. A broker who signs a contract to manage an owner's property becomes a
    A. lessor.
    B. trustee.
    C. receiver.
    D. fiduciary.

17. A broker acting as a property manager should place which of the following into the broker's business account?
    A. Rents
    B. Security deposits
    C. Deposits for pets from tenants
    D. Broker's earned commissions

18. In management of real estate, a broker may
    A. personally accept and keep rebates from suppliers.
    B. commingle rents received with the broker's own funds.
    C. invest security deposits in an interest-bearing account for the broker's own benefit.
    D. not make a secret profit.

19. Assume that a property manager is able to buy merchandise needed for the property through a relative at a lower price than from any other source. The manager should
    A. proceed with the purchases.
    B. proceed with the purchases, charging the owner a portion of the costs saved for work done in securing a better price.
    C. proceed with the purchases but inform the owner in writing that a relative owns the company from which purchases were made.
    D. not purchase from a relative.

20. A properly drafted property management agreement should contain all of the following *EXCEPT*
    A. names of the owner and the manager.
    B. a requirement that the manager provide periodic reports to the owner.
    C. outlined duties of the property manager.
    D. names of tenants in occupancy.

21. With reference to the function of a property manager, all of the following are the responsibility of a property manager *EXCEPT*
    A. obtaining the best possible return on the owner's investment.
    B. preserving the owner's investment.
    C. maintaining the interior condition of rental units.
    D. interviewing prospective tenants.

22. Which is *TRUE* regarding most properly drawn property management agreements?
    A. The manager obtains an exclusive listing to sell at any time.
    B. They define the rights and obligations of owners and agents.
    C. The manager acts as the sales agent if the property is to be sold.
    D. The manager usually has an option on the property.

23. All *EXCEPT* which of the following are true regarding property managers hired to keep the property fully occupied?
    A. Their management agreements must be in writing to be enforceable in court.
    B. One of their main functions is to protect their principal's investment.
    C. They have a fiduciary relationship with the owner.
    D. Their fees should be clearly outlined in the property management agreement.

24. All of the following should be covered in a properly drawn property management agreement *EXCEPT*
    A. management fees.
    B. operating expenses.
    C. duration or term.
    D. manager's duties.

25. All of the following would be present in a typical property management agreement *EXCEPT*
    A. provision for monthly reports.
    B. long-term contract period.
    C. names of parties.
    D. amount of management fees.

26. When describing the premises to be rented in a short-term office lease, the contract should include all of the following *EXCEPT* the
    A. legal description of the building.
    B. floor plan for the office.
    C. street address of the building.
    D. dimensions of the space.

27. ◎ A long-term lease is generally to the owner's advantage in all of the following cases *EXCEPT*
    A. when negotiating a commercial lease with an escalation clause.
    B. when the owner has made significant alterations in the space to suit the tenant.
    C. when economic times cause excessively high demands for rental space.
    D. during predicted economic downturns and recessions.

28. Building rules and regulations generally do all of the following *EXCEPT*
    A. protect the owner's investment.
    B. provide for the peaceful enjoyment of all tenants.
    C. keep rent increases to a minimum.
    D. serve the owner and offer benefits to the tenant.

29. A lease clause sometimes negotiated by a property manager that provides for rent increases of predetermined amounts at specific times over the term of the lease is *BEST* described as a(n)
    A. index clause.
    B. step-up clause.
    C. percentage clause.
    D. escalation clause.

30. A property manager *MOST* likely would conduct a market survey to determine
    A. appropriate use of the building.
    B. appropriate rents to charge.
    C. required maintenance.
    D. the availability of money.

31. A property manager should know that there will be an increased demand for apartment rentals when there is an increase in
    A. money supply.
    B. vacancy rates.
    C. mortgage rates.
    D. disintermediation.

32. A property manager of a commercial condominium project normally performs all of the following functions *EXCEPT*
    A. maintaining the common elements.
    B. making repairs inside units.
    C. maintaining books and records.
    D. marketing space.

33. ◎ In inflationary times, a property manager would favor long-term leases with rents based on all of the following *EXCEPT*
    A. graduated amounts.
    B. the consumer price index.
    C. the cost-of-living index.
    D. a fixed rate.

34. In negotiating a property management agreement with the owner of an apartment building, the property manager would *MOST* likely base the fee on which one of the following?
    A. Percentage of gross collectible income
    B. Percentage of net income
    C. Flat rate
    D. Cost and expenses

35. In a lease, the right of first refusal most nearly means the tenant can
    A. cancel.
    B. extend.
    C. buy at foreclosure sale.
    D. match an offer to relet.

36. Which of the following events normally is grounds for terminating a lease?
    A. The death of either the landlord or tenant
    B. The sale of the property
    C. Abandonment by the tenant
    D. Foreclosure by a mortgagee with a prior recorded mortgage

37. A landlord and a tenant agree to terminate a lease. This is *MOST* specifically known as
    A. release.
    B. rejection.
    C. abandonment.
    D. surrender.

38. ◎ What could happen if a commercial tenant who has been occupying a store on a ten-year lease refuses to vacate the premises at the end of the rental period?
    A. A tenancy-at-sufferance exists.
    B. The landlord may hold the tenant liable for another ten-year period of rent payments.
    C. The tenant is entitled to one extension.
    D. The landlord can forcefully eject the tenant.

39. Which of the following statements is *TRUE* concerning a sublease?
    A. The sublessee pays rent directly to the lessor.
    B. The sublessor is liable for any damages caused to the premises by the sublessee.
    C. The sublessor is no longer liable to the lessor.
    D. A sublease transfers the entire remaining balance of the term.

40. The interest that a landlord has during a valid tenancy is known as a
    A. right to profits.
    B. reversionary interest.
    C. right of reentry.
    D. tenancy at sufferance.

41. In which case is the tenant relieved of the obligation to pay rent?
    A. On abandonment
    B. On constructive eviction
    C. On death of the landlord
    D. Because of external economic factors

42. The provisions of a lease may provide for all of the following *EXCEPT*
   A. introduction of a nonconforming use.
   B. a 75 percent rent increase.
   C. a rent increase based on periodic appraisal.
   D. the right of first refusal or option to renew.

43. All of the following are necessary parts of a lease *EXCEPT*
   A. parties to the lease.
   B. term of the lease.
   C. option to purchase.
   D. terms of the rental payment.

44. Which of the following statements is *TRUE* in respect to the assignment of a lease?
   A. The original lessee is the sole party liable for the payment of the rent.
   B. It is the same as a sublease.
   C. The original lessee retains a right to use the property for a limited time.
   D. The entire leasehold is transferred.

45. Under a net lease, the tenant usually pays for all of the following expenses *EXCEPT*
   A. utilities.
   B. depreciation.
   C. taxes.
   D. insurance.

46. The term that *BEST* describes a tenant's interest in the property is
   A. life estate.
   B. reversionary interest.
   C. remainder interest.
   D. leasehold estate.

47. Liability to a third person who sustains injuries on the leased premises normally
   A. belongs to the tenant.
   B. belongs to the landlord.
   C. is the mutual responsibility of landlord and tenant.
   D. belongs to the property manager.

48. A residential periodic lease will be terminated by
   A. mutual consent.
   B. death of the landlord.
   C. bankruptcy of the lessor.
   D. outside claimants such as a trespasser.

49. A lease under which the rent will increase under certain circumstances is known as a(n)
   A. upgrade lease.
   B. graduated lease.
   C. piggyback lease.
   D. sandwich lease.

50. On foreclosure against the landlord by the holder of a prior recorded mortgage, a subsequent tenant's lease
   A. remains unaffected.
   B. may be terminated at the election of the mortgagee.
   C. is affected even if the lease was signed before the mortgage.
   D. is binding on the mortgagee.

51. A lease that requires that the landlord pay operating expenses of the property is called a
   A. net lease.
   B. gross lease.
   C. graduated lease.
   D. percentage lease.

52. All but which one of the following provisions concerning the property should be included in a rental agreement for a residential condominium apartment?
   A. Appraised value
   B. Intended use
   C. Amount of rent
   D. Expiration date

53. ◎ Assume a mortgaged property is leased. Because of default in payment, the mortgagee forecloses on the mortgage. Which of the following statements is *TRUE* regarding rights under the lease?
   A. The lessee is automatically released from any further obligation on the lease.
   B. The lease continues in effect despite the foreclosure.
   C. The lease is void because the mortgagor has no right to give a lease on mortgaged property.
   D. The lease may be terminated by the mortgagee but not by the lessee.

54. A lease of land only, on which the tenant agrees to construct a residence within a certain period of time, is *BEST* called a
    A. ground lease.
    B. gross lease.
    C. net lease.
    D. percentage lease.

55. The sale of a property that is under a long-term lease has which of the following effects?
    A. It terminates the lease on 45 days' notice by the new owner.
    B. It has no effect on the term of the lease as far as the tenant is concerned.
    C. It cannot be made unless the present tenant is notified of the intention to sell and given an opportunity to terminate the lease.
    D. It terminates the lease, and the tenant must negotiate a new lease with the new owner.

56. In a straight percentage lease, which of the following statements is *TRUE?*
    A. The owner usually has the right to examine the lessee's books.
    B. There will be a minimum fixed rent in addition to percentage rent.
    C. The tenant must pay expenses of the property such as taxes.
    D. The tenant may choose any type of accounting system.

57. A recapture clause is frequently used in what type of lease?
    A. Net lease
    B. Gross lease
    C. Straight percentage lease
    D. Business lease

58. A lease that has a definite termination date is known as a
    A. tenancy for years.
    B. periodic tenancy.
    C. tenancy at will.
    D. tenancy at sufferance.

59. Albert leased a warehouse to Bryan, who agreed to pay $1,000 per month to Albert in rent and pay the real property taxes, maintenance, insurance, and utilities. What type of lease *MOST* likely was signed by Albert and Bryan?
    A. Net lease
    B. Gross lease
    C. Percentage lease
    D. Sandwich lease

60. The right of first refusal gives the tenant which of the following?
    A. The first choice to bid on the property on foreclosure
    B. The right to terminate the lease on 30 days' notice
    C. The right to rerent (is binding on the lessor)
    D. The right to get first choice to rerent or buy if the owner decides to rent or sell

61. A graduated lease can be *BEST* defined as a lease
    A. that includes an option to purchase.
    B. that provides for a possible increase in rent at a stated future time.
    C. under which the landlord pays all ownership charges such as taxes.
    D. that is passed intact from one owner to the next under terms of a contract.

62. A tenant rents a house at the beach from July 1 to August 31. This is known as a(n)
    A. periodic tenancy.
    B. estate for years.
    C. tenancy at sufferance.
    D. tenancy at will.

63. The normal shopping center lease is which type?
    A. Ground lease
    B. Percentage lease
    C. Gross lease
    D. Sublease

64. A holdover tenancy is *MOST* likely created at the end of a tenancy
    A. in common.
    B. for years.
    C. at will.
    D. in severalty.

65. A tenancy at will is a tenancy of
    A. definite duration that either landlord or tenant can terminate at will.
    B. indefinite duration that the landlord can terminate at will.
    C. indefinite duration that either landlord or tenant can terminate at will.
    D. definite duration that the tenant can terminate at will.

66. ◎ Which of the following statements concerning leases is *TRUE?*
    A. When a property with an existing lease is purchased, it is not necessary for the purchaser to honor the lease.
    B. It is advisable that the lessee obtain lease insurance against nonperformance of the lessor.
    C. Lease rent includes principal and interest.
    D. A lease may be terminated by surrender and acceptance.

67. By definition, an "estate for years"
    A. must last for a year or more.
    B. must be for at least two years.
    C. is for a fixed term, whether a week, a month, or a decade.
    D. requires a written lease.

68. ◎ If the lease does *NOT* cover the point, the
    A. lessee is responsible for maintaining the interior of the premises and for waste.
    B. lessee is required to take out fire insurance on the leased premises.
    C. lease may not be assigned.
    D. lessor has the right to extend.

69. A tenant's rights under a lease
    A. are terminated when the property is sold.
    B. usually are terminated when the lessor dies.
    C. are superior to those of the lessor.
    D. usually are binding, even if the property is later mortgaged.

70. An instrument that transfers a right to possess real property but does *NOT* transfer an ownership interest is a
    A. deed.
    B. mortgage.
    C. land contract.
    D. lease.

71. Which of the following statements about leases is *TRUE?*
    A. A gross lease is one in which the rent is based on an agreed percentage of the gross income.
    B. A net lease is one in which the rent is based on a fixed percentage of the net income.
    C. A percentage lease requires that the tenant pay a percentage of the property taxes on the property.
    D. A gross lease is one in which the landlord pays the expenses normally incurred with property ownership.

72. An escalation clause in a lease provides for
    A. adjustment of rental payments to cover contingencies.
    B. extension of the rental period.
    C. a shortened rental term.
    D. more frequent payments on the rent.

73. Which of the following creates a lessor-lessee relationship?
    A. Life estate
    B. Agreement to lease
    C. Deed
    D. Lease

74. ◎ A reversionary interest in a leasehold situation
    A. constitutes a breach of a lease.
    B. expires when a lease is executed.
    C. is a landlord's right to use of the property on expiration of a lease.
    D. allows land to escheat at the termination of a lease.

75. The buyer buys a small office building in which there are several existing two-year leases for commercial space. Which is *TRUE?*
    A. The lessees can now be forced to pay higher rents to the buyer.
    B. The buyer takes title to the property subject to the terms of the lease.
    C. The leases are terminated on the sale of the building.
    D. The buyer may renegotiate the lease at the buyer's option within the first 60 days.

76. All of the following types of leases typically require notice to quit *EXCEPT*
    A. month-to-month tenancy.
    B. tenancy at will.
    C. tenancy for years.
    D. tenancy for months.

77. The term *lessor* is *MOST* likely to be used to describe a(n)
    A. tenant.
    B. owner.
    C. vendor.
    D. optionor.

78. A leasehold interest lying between the primary lease and the sublease is known as a(n)
    A. percentage lease.
    B. sandwich lease.
    C. inactive lease.
    D. undercapitalized lease.

79. A tenant who is constructively evicted by a landlord may consider the lease as being
    A. renewed.
    B. terminated.
    C. assigned.
    D. sold.

80. All of the following statements in reference to a lease are true *EXCEPT* that
    A. rent is always payable in advance.
    B. unless a contrary agreement is in effect, the lessee may sublet.
    C. a security deposit remains the property of the lessee until actual damages occur.
    D. a written lease can be altered by way of a witnessed, oral agreement.

81. Which of the following is *TRUE* about the security deposit in most residential leasehold situations?
    A. It must consist of the first and last month's rent.
    B. It can be applied only to cover physical damage caused to the premises.
    C. It must be returned at any time within one year.
    D. It may be put in an interest-bearing account.

82. In assigning a lease, the lessee with a lease that contains no provision covering assignment
    A. remains liable for any unpaid rent.
    B. must obtain written consent to such assignment.
    C. may not assign.
    D. is not liable for unpaid rent.

83. When the lessor in a net lease dies, the
    A. lease terminates.
    B. lessee has the option to terminate the lease.
    C. lease is void.
    D. lease is not affected.

84. When leased premises reach a physical condition such that the tenant is unable to occupy them for the purpose intended, the situation is legally recognized as a(n)
    A. dispossess eviction.
    B. actual eviction.
    C. constructive eviction.
    D. passive eviction.

85. A leasehold estate at will is which of the following?
    A. Tenancy for years
    B. Tenancy at sufferance
    C. Tenancy for an indefinite period
    D. Life estate

86. The interest of a tenant who came rightly into possession by permission of the owner but continues to occupy the premises without permission is called a(n)
    A. sandwich lease.
    B. estate at sufferance.
    C. estate at will.
    D. estate in remainder.

87. Which of the following *BEST* applies to a landlord-tenant relationship?
    A. Tenancy in common
    B. Tenancy at sufferance
    C. Joint tenancy
    D. Tenancy by the entirety

88. In the absence of specific agreement, rent on a commercial lease is due
    A. on the first day of the rental period.
    B. on the last day of the month.
    C. whenever the tenant wants.
    D. at the end of the rental period.

89. Escalation clauses found in leases
    A. are reflective of changed market conditions.
    B. are usually held by the courts to be unconstitutional.
    C. demand that the lease be terminated in the event of late payment.
    D. allow the tenant to assign the lease.

90. A percentage lease is one
    A. that provides for the broker's percentage of commission.
    B. in which the usual rent is based on the net profits of the tenant.
    C. that always allows the tenant to cancel the lease if his or her income falls below a desired amount.
    D. in which the tenant's usual rent is based on gross receipts.

91. If the situation is *NOT* covered in the lease and the leased property is sold, the lease
    A. must be renewed.
    B. is binding on the new owner.
    C. creates a tenancy from month to month.
    D. is considered surrendered.

92. The lessor under a net lease pays the
    A. taxes.
    B. special assessments.
    C. maintenance.
    D. mortgage principal payments.

93. The deposit that a lessee must pay is
    A. called an earnest money deposit.
    B. considered to be the property of the lessor during the term of the lease.
    C. called a binder.
    D. called a security deposit.

94. A lessee is responsible for all of the following on the leased premises *EXCEPT*
    A. waste by a third party.
    B. injury to a third party.
    C. hazardous holes or cracks in the sidewalk.
    D. damage to the carpeting of the dwelling.

95. In which one of the following situations can the landlord take title to the tenant's bar stools, tables, and chandeliers?
    A. Commencement of the lease
    B. Tenant's default for two months
    C. Tenant's bankruptcy
    D. Failure of the tenant to remove these items after the lease is terminated

96. Which of the following statements is *FALSE* under the Uniform Residential Landlord and Tenant Act?
    A. A landlord cannot charge a security deposit equal to more than one month's rent.
    B. The landlord must return the deposit within a specified number of days of the tenant's vacating the premises or specify reasons for withholding all or part of the deposit.
    C. The landlord must make any requested repairs up to a maximum of $1,000.
    D. The security deposit is the property of the lessee, but under the control of the lessor.

97. If a lessee defaults on a lease and abandons the property in good condition, the lessee could be held liable for which of the following amounts?
    A. The balance of the rent plus forfeiture of the security deposit
    B. The balance of the rent plus the cost to find a new tenant
    C. The balance of the rent
    D. Overdue rent less legal fees

98. In a lease that contains an escalation clause, which of the following is *TRUE?*
    A. The rent could increase 100 percent.
    B. The lessee has an option to renew for another term.
    C. The lease payment remains fixed over the term.
    D. The term of the lease may be extended indefinitely.

99. All of the following are features of a tenancy at will *EXCEPT*
    A. it terminates with proper notice by either party.
    B. it has no definite duration.
    C. sale of the property will terminate it.
    D. death of the landlord will not affect it.

100. The conveyance of an estate by lease is *BEST* described as a
    A. devise.
    B. demise.
    C. deed.
    D. decree.

101. A landlord who wants to regain possession of the leased premises gives notice to
    A. enjoin.
    B. attach.
    C. quit.
    D. relinquish.

102. Which lease provides for certain adjustments in rent based on specific time intervals?
    A. Ground lease
    B. Net lease
    C. Graduated lease
    D. Long-term lease

103. A lease for an apartment in a residential apartment project is usually which type of lease?
    A. Ground lease
    B. Gross lease
    C. Net lease
    D. Percentage lease

104. A lease based on gross revenues is a
    A. gross lease.
    B. net lease.
    C. percentage lease.
    D. recapture lease.

105. Calvin orally leases a store to Bud for one year. The lease is
    A. a valid tenancy for years.
    B. unenforceable owing to the statute of frauds.
    C. a valid tenancy from year to year.
    D. unenforceable owing to the statute of limitations.

106. A lease is which of the following?
    A. A contract
    B. A conveyance
    C. Neither a contract nor a conveyance but a separate document in itself
    D. Both a contract and a conveyance

107. The basic title that the lessor holds during the term of a lease is *BEST* known as
    A. reversion.
    B. remainder.
    C. diversion.
    D. revision.

108. Which one of the following can assign a lease?
    A. Tenant at sufferance
    B. Tenant at will
    C. Holdover tenant
    D. Tenant for years

109. Ace leases a commercial warehouse to Brayden for nine months. Which is *TRUE?*
    A. The lease must be in writing.
    B. The rights and obligations of Ace and Brayden are regulated by the Uniform Residential Landlord and Tenant Act.
    C. Ace has the right to raise the rent after six months.
    D. Brayden has a less-than-freehold estate.

110. An escalation clause in a lease provides for
    A. increased rentals because of higher oper-
       ating expenses.
    B. term extensions.
    C. renewal options.
    D. distraint.

111. The tenant usually is responsible for all of
     the following under a net lease *EXCEPT*
    A. utilities.
    B. insurance.
    C. taxes.
    D. depreciation.

112. Which of the following estates indicates a les-
     sor-lessee relationship?
    A. Life estate
    B. Estate for years
    C. Fee estate
    D. Estate in common

113. ◎ Caroline leases a farm to Arvin for five
     years. When Caroline dies two years later, it
     is discovered that she had only a life estate.
     What is the status of Arvin's lease?
    A. Valid lease
    B. Tenancy at sufferance
    C. Freehold estate
    D. Tenancy for years

114. A three-year lease of a farm property from
     Anna to Betty is terminated by
    A. Anna's selling the farm to Cindy.
    B. destruction of the farm by fire.
    C. Anna's selling the farm to Betty.
    D. Anna's mortgaging the farm.

115. Which of the following parties to a long-
     term ground lease is the holder of the leased
     fee?
    A. Lessor
    B. Lessee
    C. Grantee
    D. Grantor

116. When a developer obtains a ground lease and
     intends to obtain a construction loan to build a
     condominium project, what type of provision
     regarding financing should be included in the
     lease?
    A. Acceleration clause
    B. Escalation clause
    C. Subordination clause
    D. Subrogation clause

117. ◎ In the event a lessee, without good reason,
     abandons leased premises, leaving it in good
     condition, to what degree is the lessee nor-
     mally liable to the lessor?
    A. For rent payable to the date lessee leaves
       the premises, plus security deposit
    B. For rent payable to the date lessee leaves,
       plus security deposit and a percentage of
       rent payable for balance of term
    C. For rent due and payable for the remain-
       ing period of the lease
    D. For rent due and payable for the remain-
       ing period of the lease, plus the expense
       of locating a new tenant

118. ◎ Under the provisions of the Uniform Res-
     idential Landlord and Tenant Act, which of
     the following is *TRUE?*
    A. The maximum amount of money the ten-
       ant is required to pay at the start of the
       lease is equal to three months' rent.
    B. The lessor can put in the lease a require-
       ment for lessor's consent prior to the les-
       see's subletting the premises.
    C. The lessee has a right of first refusal.
    D. The lessor must place security deposits in
       an interest-bearing account for the les-
       sor's account.

119. The clause in a lease that gives a tenant the
     right to purchase leased property at a specific
     price is a
    A. reversionary right.
    B. holdover tenancy.
    C. lease option.
    D. right of first refusal.

120. During the term of the lease, whose property is the security deposit?
    A. Lessor
    B. Mortgagee
    C. Lessee
    D. Property manager

121. Which of the following must be contained in a commercial lease agreement for it to be valid?
    A. Amount of taxes on the leased premises
    B. Name of institution in which the security deposit is held
    C. Assessed valuation of the property
    D. Amount of rent to be paid and the method of payment (monthly, quarterly, and so on)

122. Which of the following is *FALSE* about selling interests in a Real Estate Investment Trust (REIT)?
    A. The antifraud provisions of the Securities Act apply.
    B. Salespeople need to be licensed under the securities law.
    C. Violation of the law is a criminal offense.
    D. Brokers need to be licensed under the real estate licensing law.

123. State laws that regulate real estate securities are called
    A. sunset laws.
    B. blue-sky laws.
    C. SEC laws.
    D. RESPA laws.

124. A property manager asks a real estate broker to find partners for a venture that he will manage. The broker should do which of the following?
    A. Contact the attorney general
    B. Check out the application of state and federal securities laws
    C. Refuse to help
    D. Charge a flat fee

125. ◎ Which of the following is *FALSE* concerning entities that are classified as Direct Participation Programs (DPPs)?
    A. Taxes are paid by the members of the entity.
    B. People who sell these programs need a special securities license.
    C. Examples of DPP entities include partnerships and S corporations.
    D. They are limited to ten investors.

126. All of the following transactions involve the sale of a security *EXCEPT*
    A. an investment contract.
    B. a condominium apartment with mandatory rental pool.
    C. shares in a limited partnership.
    D. the site of a commercial warehouse.

127. ◎ Selling a real property security without a securities license violates which one of the following laws?
    A. 1933 Securities Act
    B. 1934 Securities Exchange Act
    C. 1935 Securities Act
    D. 1936 Securities Investment Act

128. Which of the following security offerings is subject to the registration requirements of the 1933 Securities Act?
    A. A private placement offering to fewer than ten investors
    B. A security offering only to bona fide residents in a single state
    C. Shares in a residential real estate investment limited partnership
    D. Interest in a profit-sharing retirement plan

129. ◎ The interstate sale of a subdivision could fall under the federal securities laws if the seller does which of the following?
    A. Provides an inspection tour
    B. Guarantees profits through a rental pool
    C. Finances the sale
    D. Covers the first year's property tax

130. Assume there is a five-year lease at $5,000 per year. The lessor in year three usually *CANNOT*
    A. mortgage.
    B. sell.
    C. raise rent.
    D. devise.

131. ◎ When buying an investment piece of real estate, the buyer should obtain which of the following?
    A. Flood insurance
    B. Estoppel letter from tenants
    C. Reduction certificate
    D. Tax withholding statement

132. In a triple net lease, the tenant usually pays for all of the following *EXCEPT*
    A. insurance.
    B. utilities.
    C. management fees.
    D. mortgage payments.

133. When a group of investors and one or more sponsors acquire real estate, this is best called a
    A. rental pool.
    B. time share.
    C. syndication.
    D. group investment.

134. ◎ If a person selling real property securities in the form of a REIT is guilty of fraud, all of the following could occur *EXCEPT*
    A. a criminal penalty.
    B. a civil penalty.
    C. rescission of contract.
    D. actual damages multiplied by five.

135. All of the following types of ownership are likely to be subject to regulation by the securities law *EXCEPT* a
    A. limited partnership.
    B. subchapter S corporation.
    C. syndication.
    D. joint tenancy.

136. The property management agreement typically authorizes the property manager to do which one of the following?
    A. Prepare operating budgets and review the credit rating of potential tenants
    B. List and sell the property
    C. Collect security deposits and place them in the manager's general account
    D. Deny rentals to former drug addicts

137. Property managers need to recognize economic conditions that give rise to an increase in demand for more expensive rental units. What economic condition will cause such an increase in demand?
    A. Decrease in mortgage interest rates
    B. Increase in disposable income
    C. Decrease in consumer price index
    D. Increase in supply of rental units

ANSWERS

1. **D.** The property manager is a fiduciary but is not responsible for listing the property. This is an entirely different function from management.

2. **D.** A property manager who is going to get a rebate must get the owner's permission, preferably in writing.

3. **B.** Ceiling replacement would be a capital expenditure, the money for which would come from either reserve funds for replacement or a special assessment.

4. **D.** Property managers handle rents, minor repairs, and marketing of leases. They are not responsible for making investment decisions, such as handling real estate profits for their clients.

5. **A.** While the property should be generally described, it need not be a legal description, such as a metes-and-bounds description.

6. **B.** High rents (A) may not be the best barometer of an effective management program if

there are excessive maintenance and other unnecessary costs.

7. **C.** Such practice would violate the federal Fair Housing Act and most state discrimination laws.

8. **D.** IREM is an organization of the National Association of REALTORS®, which limits its membership to individuals (not firms) who meet minimum education and experience requirements in the area of property management.

9. **C.** This is not a regularly occurring carrying charge.

10. **D.** The property and its income are valuable assets of the owner, and the property manager is a fiduciary charged with the duty to protect and maintain them. Attorneys draft leases; property managers obtain signatures.

11. **C.** Without an escalation clause, the landlord would suffer the effects of inflationary trends.

12. **A.** Choice (B) is true because the manager should first make contact with the tenant to find out the reasons for the late payment, rather than immediately commencing legal eviction proceedings.

13. **C.** Concessions are negotiable points in the lease that are determined in the lessee's favor. If managers negotiate the lease, they should be sure that their authority extends to granting concessions. Most owners do not wish to be bothered with the hassles involved in eviction proceedings.

14. **C.** Mortgage payments are not a regularly occurring expenditure in an operating budget.

15. **A.** The property manager plays a key role in establishing appropriate rents and screening prospective tenants.

16. **D.** As a fiduciary, the property manager owes duties of loyalty, obedience, accountability, care, and skill to the owner.

17. **D.** The broker should establish a client trust fund account for rental management funds and keep these separate from the general fund and the residential sales client trust fund account. Once earned, commissions must be kept in the broker's business account.

18. **D.** Brokers must fully disclose in writing any personal interest they may have in regard to managed property.

19. **C.** The point is to notify the owner of such a pertinent fact.

20. **D.** Because the property management agreement is a contract, the parties must be named. It is in the best interest of the owner to receive periodic reports. Although a list of tenants will be needed, it does not have to be incorporated in the property management agreement.

21. **C.** Protecting the investment in the property and maximizing the return are two major reasons why an owner hires a professional property manager. Interior work is usually the tenant's responsibility.

22. **B.** It is not the role of a property manager to handle the sale of the property; he or she markets the space in the building.

23. **A.** Although it is the best practice, the statute of frauds does not require that property management agreements be in writing to be enforceable. However, if the agent is authorized to lease real property for longer than the period called for in the statute of frauds, then such authority must be in writing to be enforceable.

24. **B.** These are contained in the budget.

25. **B.** Most owners do not want to get locked into a long-term property management agreement.

26. **A.** The lease often will contain an exhibit in which the space to be leased is outlined on a floor plan.

27. **C.** The escalation clause will aid in keeping the lease in line with inflationary trends and rising operating costs.

28. **C.** Properly prepared rules will help both owner and tenant.

29. **B.** Such a step-up clause is found in a graduated lease. An escalation clause allows for increases and decreases based on changes in a specified index, such as increased taxes or maintenance costs.

30. **B.** By comparison with similar buildings in the area, the manager will have better insight into the amount of rent to charge. Required maintenance is determined by inspection and observation; use or zoning and availability of money have little relevance.

31. **C.** As mortgage rates increase, fewer people can qualify to purchase homes and so must continue to rent. Disintermediation refers to savings account withdrawals.

32. **B.** The property manager works for the association of owners and would be unnecessarily exposing the association to liability for faulty work done within individual units.

33. **D.** Rental rates should allow for rising costs and expenses and should not be locked in for long periods of time.

34. **A.** Most property managers' fees are based on a percentage of gross income (after deducting for vacancies and other rent loss) without taking operating expenses into account. Percentage fees are generally preferred to flat rates because they give the manager an incentive to increase the income from the property. The flat fee is often disadvantageous to the manager because it can be increased only by further negotiation with the owner.

35. **D.** If the lessor decides to lease the premises to a new tenant, the lessor must give a lessee with a right of first refusal the first chance to lease on the new terms. Sometimes a right of first refusal is worded so the lessee has the first chance to match an offer to purchase the property if it is offered for sale.

36. **D.** A lease is a contract as well as a conveyance, and neither death nor sale will affect the contract rights. The decedent's estate is bound by the terms of the lease, and any purchaser takes the property subject to the lease. The tenant takes possession subject to the mortgage.

37. **D.** A surrender refers specifically to a lease terminated by mutual agreement—technically, a surrender and acceptance.

38. **A.** A tenant at sufferance is a tenant who remains on the property after lease expiration and before the landlord has consented to the continued occupancy. A landlord may elect to hold the tenant over to a new term, but because of the statute of frauds, most "holdover" tenancies are limited to one year (in some states, three-year oral leases are valid).

39. **B.** The sublessee pays the sublessor (original lessee), who is directly liable to the lessor for the rent and for full compliance with the provisions of the original lease. The sublessor does not avoid liability by transferring part of the interest to the sublessee.

40. **B.** The lessor has a reversionary interest; he or she is entitled to recover the property, plus improvements, at the termination of the lease. The value of the leased fee is usually the rent (discounted to present worth) plus an estimated value attributed to this reversionary interest. The grantor of a conditional fee estate has the right of reentry.

41. **B.** A tenant cannot avoid contractual obligations by abandoning the premises. However, if the landlord substantially interferes with the tenant's right to peaceful habitability (for example, failing to repair plumbing or creating health hazards), then the tenant can leave the premises and be excused from paying rent.

42. **A.** By contract, the parties can agree to any rent increase, but they cannot agree to do something illegal, such as *commencing* a use that does not conform to the law.

43. **C.** A valid lease may or may not contain an option provision.

44. **D.** An assignment is a transfer of the entire leasehold, whereas a sublease transfers a portion by way of a separate agreement (such as the transfer of one-half of a ten-year lease).

45. **B.** Under a net lease the tenant pays many of the carrying charges, such as utilities, insurance, or taxes. Depreciation of the building is not a carrying charge and is handled by the landlord in computing a recapture rate for the investment.

46. **D.** It might be noted, however, that a lessor has a reversionary interest in the leased fee (the lessor's interest).

47. **A.** Generally, the party with control over the leased property is liable for waste and injuries to third parties in those areas. The tenant typically has exclusive control over the leased premises, whereas the landlord would have control over areas such as hallways, stairwells, and grounds.

48. **A.** By agreement, the lessee and lessor can reach a friendly surrender of their rights and obligations. Death usually does not terminate a contract such as a lease (except an estate at will).

49. **B.** A graduated lease often is a long-term lease with increases (specified in a step-up clause) in the rent structured to take place at established intervals at set amounts or at amounts to be reached by subsequent appraisal and arbitration.

50. **B.** A tenant takes a leasehold estate subject to the rights of prior recorded interests. The tenant would be advised, in these situations, to obtain a nondisturbance agreement from the mortgagee prior to executing the lease.

51. **B.** Under triple net lease the tenant would pay for all expenses, whereas another net lease (called a *modified net lease*) might cover just taxes. Thus, it is important to review the exact requirements of each net lease.

52. **A.** Normally, the appraised value has little bearing on the lessor-lessee relationship. The appraised value might become important in a long-term lease. If rent increases in later years, it will be negotiated based on value increases.

53. **D.** The mortgagee has the choice of whether to terminate the lease, because the lessee acquired the leasehold estate subject to the existing mortgage.

54. **A.** Ground leases are often long-term, 55 or more years, graduated net leases.

55. **B.** The purchaser takes the property subject to the rights of the lessee under the existing lease. This explains why it is important to inspect the property to discover the rights of parties in possession.

56. **A.** Inspection of books is typical, but a straight percentage does not provide for any minimum fixed rent.

57. **C.** The recapture clause would be found in a straight percentage lease. A landlord could recapture the premises and terminate the lease of a tenant not meeting specified income quotas.

58. **A.** The tenancy for years is the only type of lease that has a specific termination date. No notice to quit is needed to terminate the expired lease.

59. **A.** The landlord nets a specific amount and the tenant must pay the carrying expenses.

60. **D.** Depending on the wording, the right could be to match the first purchase offer or relet offer.

61. **B.** Such a lease contains a step-up clause that details how and when the increases will occur (it could also have a step-down clause for decreases).

62. **B.** The specific termination date is the key to a "tenancy or estate for years," a sometimes misleading classification because the term can be for less than a year.

63. **B.** It could be a straight percentage lease, a lease with a fixed minimum rent plus a percentage, or one of many other varieties.

64. **B.** If a tenant under a lease for a set term stays on after the term, the landlord can elect to hold the tenant to another term (usually not more than a year).

65. **C.** Either party can elect to terminate the tenancy, although most states now require a minimum amount of prior notice.

66. **D.** Purchasers buy subject to the rights of existing lessees. Usually, commercial lessors can obtain insurance to protect against *lessee* defaults in failing to pay rent or damaging premises.

67. **C.** If the estate for years period is less than one year, it may not have to be in writing to be enforceable under most statutes of frauds.

68. **A.** The person in control usually has the responsibility for waste and injury. Unless required by the terms of the lease, the lessee need not take out insurance, although it is wise to be covered.

69. **D.** Neither death nor sale of the property will terminate the lease. The mortgagee takes subject to existing leases.

70. **D.** The lessee acquires exclusive possession, but not legal or equitable ownership. A land contract transfers possession and equitable title.

71. **D.** A percentage lease is based on a percentage of gross income.

72. **A.** Such contingencies might include increases in energy costs or the cost-of-living index beyond specified levels; if so, rent would increase correspondingly.

73. **D.** An agreement to lease does not transfer exclusive possession of the premises or establish the parties as landlord or tenant.

74. **C.** The landlord is entitled to obtain the possession of the fee plus any improvements on the property that the tenant either did not remove willingly or was not permitted to remove (by contract, the parties can deal otherwise with the improvements).

75. **B.** The purchaser takes the property subject to the terms of existing leases and will have to wait until the two-year leases expire before he or she is able to raise the rent.

76. **C.** Even a tenancy at will requires some notice by either party that the tenancy is over.

77. **B.** An optionor is usually the seller (vendor). Note that in a lease-option the owner would be a lessor and an optionor.

78. **B.** The sandwich lessor is the lessee under the master lease in the case where a ground lease is made between the owner and a developer, who then leases to the occupant. The developer is sandwiched between the fee owner on one side and the fee user on the other side.

79. **B.** Constructive eviction might occur if the landlord allows the premises to become uninhabitable.

80. **A.** Unless otherwise specified in the lease or state law, rent is payable in arrears, when the tenancy is at an end. Because of this ancient rule, most leases and most residential landlord-tenant codes provide for rent payments to be made in advance. Provided there are witnesses to prove the oral modification, most written leases can be orally modified, although the best business practice is to obtain such modification in writing to lessen the chance of dispute.

81. **D.** The security deposit should not be earmarked as the last month's rent, for then it would be taxable as prepaid rent. It belongs to the lessee and is held in trust as security against physical damage, failure to pay rent, failure to return any items on the premises, such as keys, or failure to meet any other lease conditions.

82. **A.** Written consent is required only if stipulated in the lease. The lessee (assignor) remains secondarily liable in the event the assignee defaults.

83. **D.** Death does not alter the lease contract. The lessor's estate receives the rent, and the property titleholder must uphold the lease.

84. **C.** The tenant is thereafter relieved of rent payments once premises are vacated.

85. **C.** The tenancy at will exists until either party terminates it or dies or the property is sold. In a tenancy at sufferance, there is no lessor approval of the lessor-lessee relationship.

86. **B.** An estate at sufferance is different from a trespass; thus the tenant, who has the lowest estate in real property, cannot acquire title to the premises by way of adverse possession.

87. **B.** Answers (A), (C), and (D) are methods of owning real property. A tenancy at sufferance indicates there once was a valid landlord-tenant lease relationship, which has now expired.

88. **D.** Unless the lease provides otherwise (and most leases do), rent is not due until the end of the lease term.

89. **A.** Escalation clauses are partially designed to keep rents in line with inflationary trends. It is a permissible constitutional exercise of one's freedom to contract for legitimate purposes.

90. **D.** Naturally, the definition of *gross receipts* is quite an important part of the percentage lease (does it include returned merchandise, credit sales, mail orders, and so on?). *Profit* is a more difficult term to precisely define.

91. **B.** The new owner takes the property subject to the lease unless the lease contains a cancellation clause that provides that on a sale of the property the new owner may cancel the lease.

92. **D.** The lessee pays the carrying charges but the lessor pays for the debt reduction.

93. **D.** It is called a *security deposit* and is held in trust by the lessor, but it is the money of the lessee and can be used only to cover losses due to breach of the lease.

94. **C.** Having exclusive control of the leased premises, the lessee is liable for damage caused by third parties (guests) and for physical injury to third persons. Waste could be removal of topsoil, for example.

95. **D.** These items are considered "trade fixtures" and remain the property of the tenant unless the tenant fails to remove them at the termination of the lease.

96. **C.** The security deposit is limited and must be returned within a certain number of days; otherwise, the landlord may lose the right to withhold it. There is no requirement to make *any* requested repairs.

97. **C.** The lessee is not responsible for more rent than would have been required if the lease had not been breached and the lessee had remained the full term. The key word here is *plus.* Costs are allowed only if the new tenant is found prior to the end of the full term.

98. **A.** An escalation clause deals with rent increases, not a renewal option.

99. **D.** In addition, the tenancy at will can be terminated by death of either party or sale of the property.

100. **B.** A devise (A) is a conveyance of real property by will.

101. **C.** To terminate a periodic tenancy, the landlord would give a notice to quit. Also, prior to bringing an eviction action against a defaulting tenant, the landlord must usually give a notice to quit.

102. **C.** The graduated lease contains step-up clauses that frequently adjust the rent upward.

103. **B.** The landlord (owner) gets a lump-sum payment each month, enough to pay carrying charges such as taxes, maintenance, and insurance. This is true even though the tenant usually pays for utilities.

104. **C.** Shopping center leases are typically percentage leases based on tenants' gross revenues.

105. **A.** Most statutes of frauds permit oral leases for one year or less, although it is good practice to commit all leases to writing to lessen disputes between the parties.

106. **D.** A lease is a demise or conveyance of exclusive possession to the premises, and it is also a contract stating the rights and obligations of lessor and lessee.

107. **A.** A right of reversion can be transferred or assigned.

108. **D.** Neither (A), (B), nor (C) has an interest capable of transfer.

109. **D.** Most landlord-tenant codes cover residential leases only, not commercial leases.

110. **A.** Also included would be coverage for increased taxes. *Distraint* is the legal right of the landlord, under a court order, to seize a tenant's belongings for overdue rent.

111. **D.** The landlord is responsible for any losses caused by depreciation to the building, such as normal wear and tear deteriorations.

112. **B.** This nonfreehold estate specifies a definite duration.

113. **B.** Arvin leased the property subject to the reversionary interest of Caroline's grantor. On the end of the life estate, Arvin's interest in the property ceases and he is, at most, a tenant at sufferance until the owner determines whether to allow the tenancy to continue.

114. **C.** The lease is terminated because of the merger of the leasehold estate and the leased fee into Betty's sole ownership. While the destruction of a residential apartment would terminate a lease, the destruction of a farm on leased property may not terminate the lease because many of the farming activities may continue. (This rule has a historical basis in our once agrarian society.)

115. **A.** The lessor holds the leased fee, which is valued as the discounted value of the rent plus the value of the reversionary interest. The lessee holds the leasehold estate.

116. **C.** Commercial interim lenders usually insist on being in a first position and thus would want ground lessors to subordinate or make junior their leased fee positions.

117. **C.** The lessor is entitled to the rent for the remaining term except when a replacement tenant is found, in which case the lessor is entitled to rent for the unoccupied period up to the new lease, plus the cost of finding that new tenant.

118. **B.** In the usual lease situation, the tenant pays the first month's rent in advance plus a security deposit (one month's rent). If the lessor does not put in a requirement for consent, the lessee could assign or sublet without first obtaining the lessor's approval. State law determines if interest-bearing accounts are required.

119. **C.** In a lease option the price is fixed, whereas in a right of first refusal the tenant is given the right to purchase the property at whatever price is set by the seller and *only* if the seller decides to sell. The lessor's reversionary right refers to the fact that the land and improvements revert to the lessor at the end of the lease term.

120. **C.** The lessor (or lessor's agent) holds the security deposit for the lessee pending full performance of the lessee's obligation under the lease.

121. **D.** Except in special commercial net leases, taxes aren't usually a relevant part of lease agreements. Though the lessee's property, the security deposit can be held by anyone and, in fact, is often spent by the lessor. Some states now require that security deposits in residential transactions be placed in interest-bearing trust accounts.

122. **D.** REITs are securities, not real property; thus, real estate licenses are not required.

123. **B.** Designed to prevent fraud such as "promoting the sky," federal securities laws are regulated by the Securities and Exchange Commission (SEC).

124. **B.** Selling interests in a partnership may be deemed to be selling securities and thus requires a special license.

125. **D.** There is no limit. A Direct Participation Program (DPP) is any entity in which the investors participate directly in the tax benefits (e.g., a partnership or S corporation in which the taxes and deductions are passed through to the investors and not paid or taken by the entity). The National Association of Securities Dealers (NASD), a self-regulatory organization that licenses securities dealers, has a new limited license for people who sell real estate securities or interests in DPPs (Series 22 license).

126. **D.** A security involves any investment contract in which there is investment in a common enterprise for a profit motive, the profit to be obtained through the efforts of a third party (the sponsor). Resort condominiums with rental pool management often fit the definition of an investment contract.

127. **B.** The 1934 Securities Exchange Act regulates people who sell securities, including real property securities and investment contracts. The 1933 Securities Act regulates the securities themselves and requires registration and disclosure. Note that states have their own securities laws, often called *blue-sky laws,* that often require that the offering be fair, just, and equitable.

128. **C.** The 1933 Securities Act requires registration of securities unless exempt. One exemption is an offering to a limited number of investors; another exemption is the intrastate offering, which involves only one state. Note that even when a security is exempt from registration, the disclosure and antifraud provisions of the 1933 Securities Act still apply.

129. **B.** The sale of an "investment contract" in which profits are guaranteed through the efforts of persons other than the investor constitutes a security.

130. **C.** The rent is fixed for five years. Remember that with a five-year lease, the lessor should have paid a conveyance tax. If the lessor mortgages, sells, or wills the property, it will be taken subject to the lease.

131. **B.** The letter will *estop* the tenant from later denying the amount of rent owed, security deposit, and length of lease term.

132. **D.** The tenant pays for the carrying costs in addition to the basic lease rent. The lessor still makes the mortgage payments.

133. **C.** The syndication frequently is structured as a limited partnership and may be subject to state and federal law regarding registration of securities.

134. **D.** The antifraud provisions of the *federal* securities laws provide for stiff penalties, but not multiplied by five. The law applies to the seller and the broker.

135. **D.** A security often involves stock or an investment contract, as when one invests in a venture with the expectation of making profits through the efforts of the promoter. The sale of an investment condo with a mandatory rental pool arrangement involves the sale of a security and thus requires registration with federal and state securities agencies.

136. **A.** The property manager is responsible for the efficient leasing and overall maintenance of the property. Budgets are important to manage the property's investment and income as well as maintain the physical structure. The manager's job is to manage, the broker's job is to list and sell. Managers must avoid commingling client funds with their own funds. *Former* drug addicts are protected from discrimination under the federal Fair Housing Act.

137. **B.** As renters increase their disposable income, they can afford more expensive rental lodging. As mortgage interest rates go down, some renters begin to consider buying property.

Real Estate Mathematics

In order to provide your customers and clients with the numbers necessary to make decisions, a fundamental knowledge of general math is required. Most agents use financial calculators and partner with loan originators to answer their client's arithmetic and financial questions. It important to realize that practitioners empowered with math's secrets add value to every real estate transaction.

Basic arithmetic is involved in somewhere between 5 to 8 questions on the national portion of the examination. Accordingly, most states permit the use of a pocket calculator. When licensed, a financial calculator is best because it can quickly compute principal and interest (P & I) payments without the necessity of an amortization table. When using a financial calculator to test, look for these four critical keys that symbolically represent

1. the number of payment periods N;
2. the percentage of interest % I;
3. the payment PMT; and
4. the loan amount or present value PV.

By entering three out of the four identified variables, the calculator solves for the unknown fourth variable. For example, if a test question asked you to figure the P & I payment for a $200,000 loan amortized over 30 years at 6 percent interest, you would enter (30 × 12 = 360) 360 into N; 6 into % I; 200,000 into PV; and then solve for PMT. (Some calculators require that a compute key be touched prior to touching the PMT key). The solution is $1,199.10.

The amortization factor for borrowing $1,000 amortized over 30 years at 6 percent interest is $6. Using this amortization factor for the same problem, multiply the $6 times the number of 1,000s borrowed, 200.000, or 6 × 200 = $1,200.

The principal areas covered by the arithmetic problems are

■ commission;

■ interest;

■ investment or income;

- profit and loss;

- depreciation and appreciation;

- taxes and insurance;

- prorations;

- ratio, proportion, and scale; and

- area.

QUESTIONS

Commission—To solve commission problems, multiply the selling price by the agreed rate of commission. For example, what is the commission on a $200,000 sale if the commission rate is 6 percent? Solution: $200,000 × 6% = $12,000.

1. A three-bedroom house sells for $124,000 and the broker's total commission is 6 percent of the selling price. The commission is
   A. $744.
   B. $6,000.
   C. $7,440.
   D. $20,667.

2. On a $78,000 sale of a house, the rate of commission is 6 percent: the salesperson gets 40 percent of the commission and the broker gets the remainder. How much does the broker get?
   A. $1,872
   B. $2,808
   C. $4,680
   D. $40,000

3. The commission on a house that sells for $96,000 is $4,800. What was the rate of commission?
   A. 2%
   B. 5%
   C. 20%
   D. 50%

4. A salesperson received $2,880 for selling a house. This was 40 percent of the total commission on the sale of a $120,000 house. What was the commission rate on the sale?
   A. 3%
   B. 4%
   C. 6%
   D. 12%

5. A house sold for $110,000 and the rate of commission was 6 percent. If the salesperson got $1,980, what percentage of the commission did the salesperson get?
   A. 3%
   B. 30%
   C. 66%
   D. 70%

6. A broker charges a rental management fee of one-third of the first month's rent and 2 percent of each month's rent thereafter. The broker must pay a $100 "finder's fee" to an agent. If the house rents for $600 per month, how much does that licensed broker make in one year?
   A. $100
   B. $232
   C. $332
   D. $432

7. A broker gets 6 percent of the first $100,000 and 3 percent of any amount over $100,000. What would be the loss to the broker if a house listed for $180,000 has to be reduced by 20 percent?
   A. $1,080
   B. $7,320
   C. $8,400
   D. $15,720

8. A salesperson receives 50 percent of all commissions. The salesperson sells 160 acres for $750 per acre. The commission rates are 10 percent on the first $50,000, 8 percent on the next $25,000, and 6 percent thereafter. What is the salesperson's commission?
   A. $9,700
   B. $4,850
   C. $752
   D. $7,700

9. An agent who works only for a residential developer receives a 6 percent commission on the first $100,000 of sales for the month and 8 percent for all sales over that amount. In July she sold houses for $62,000, $74,000, $68,000, and $71,200. Approximately how much less would she have earned if she were on a straight 7 percent commission?
   A. $379
   B. $2,757
   C. $752
   D. $0

10. A 2,000-sq.-ft. office leases for $1.50 per sq. ft. per month, plus $0.46 per sq. ft. CAM (common area maintenance). Leasing commission for the five-year lease is 5 percent of the first $20,000 net rent, 4 percent of the next $20,000 net rent, 3 percent of the next $20,000 net rent, and 1 percent of the balance. The leasing agent receives 60 percent of the commission. How much does his broker receive?
   A. $2,160
   B. $1,660
   C. $2,490
   D. $1,440

Interest—To determine interest, multiply the annual interest rate by the investment opportunity. Interest is computed on an annual basis and often has to be prorated. For example, what is the simple interest on an $80,000 loan if the interest for nine months is $7,200? First, we know that the $7,200 is 75 percent of an annual amount. And simply stated, *any number divided by its percentage of the whole determines the whole number.* Therefore, $7,200 divided by 75 percent = $9,600. Next, the $9,600 must be divided by the loan to determine the interest rate: $9,600 ÷ $80,000 = 0.12 or 12%. Double-check your work by working the problem backwards: $80,000 × 12% = $9,600 × 75% = $7,200. This confirms that the answer is correct.

An alternative method to solving this same problem is to divide the $7,200 by nine (months) in order to determine the monthly interest of $800. Then multiply the monthly interest of $800 by 12 to annualize the interest (12 × $800 = $9,600). To solve, divide the $9,600 by $80,000 ($9,600 ÷ $80,000 = 0.12 or 12%).

11. Find the interest on $32,000 at 12¼ percent per annum (year) for 6 months.
   A. $326
   B. $1,320
   C. $1,960
   D. $2,640

12. If the interest on a loan at 13 percent per annum for 8 months was $5,400, what was the amount of the loan?
   A. $62,300
   B. $67,500
   C. $72,900
   D. $81,000

13. If the interest for 9 months on a loan of $80,000 was $7,200, what was the rate of interest per annum?
   A. 9.6%
   B. 10.5%
   C. 12%
   D. 13.5%

14. A purchase-money mortgage carried back by the seller for $60,000 at 10¾ percent was made February 1 and paid November 1. What was the total outstanding amount due at the time of payment?
   A. $48,375.00
   B. $55,162.50
   C. $64,837.50
   D. $66,450.00

15. A loan is made for 90 percent of the $96,000 appraised value of a house. The annual rate of interest is 12 percent. What is the bimonthly (every two months) interest payment?
   A. $684
   B. $864
   C. $1,728
   D. $8,208

16. On a simple interest loan of $15,000 that has an interest rate of 13 percent per annum, what is the total interest payment for 2 years, 6 months, and 10 days?
   A. $2,403.30
   B. $2,433.30
   C. $3,033.33
   D. $4,929.20

17. A person receives a purchase-money $30,000 loan from the seller at a reduced rate of 9 percent. Assuming the loan interest is calculated on a declining balance, if the payment is $250 per month, including interest, what is the person's balance after three payments?
   A. $29,898.86
   B. $29,924.43
   C. $29,949.81
   D. $29,975.00

18. A property was purchased for $87,000. The buyers got an 80 percent loan-to-value first mortgage. They gave the sellers a 10 percent second mortgage at 11.5 percent interest only for 5 years. What was the balloon payment?
    A. $8,783
    B. $8,617
    C. $8,800
    D. $5,003

19. In question 18, what was the down payment?
    A. $17,400
    B. $8,783
    C. $8,700
    D. $5,003

20. A 12 percent, 25-year mortgage has monthly payments of $10.90 per thousand of loan value. What total amount of interest will be paid on a $94,000 mortgage?
    A. $307,380
    B. $213,380
    C. $282,000
    D. $293,750

21. Monthly principal and interest payments are $550 on a $68,000, 8.5 percent mortgage. What is the balance after the first month's payment?
    A. $67,500
    B. $67,450
    C. $67,863
    D. $67,932

Investment or Income—This is often computed by using the IRV Formula.

The letter I represents an investment's NET Income; the letter R represents the investment's RATE of Return; and the letter V represents the investment's VALUE.

The formula works like this: draw a circle and then (using a horizontal line) divide it in half. Next, in the bottom portion, draw a vertical line separating it in half. Then, place an I in the top portion, an R in the lower left-hand portion, and a V in the lower right-hand portion of the circle. Then all you have to do is remember that NET Income divided by the Investment RATE = VALUE, or I/V = R, and that NET Income divided by VALUE = RATE, or I/V = R, and that RATE × VALUE = NET Income or R × V = I.

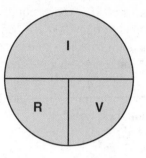

22. A property valued at $120,000 is earning an 8 percent return. What is the monthly return?
    A. $80
    B. $800
    C. $4,800
    D. $9,600

23. A property valued at $150,000 earns $750 per month. What is the annual percentage return?
    A. 6%
    B. 7.5%
    C. 9%
    D. 12%

24. A business shows a monthly profit of $1,050. If this is a 9 percent return, what is the value of the property?
    A. $9,450
    B. $14,000
    C. $94,500
    D. $140,000

25. A person owns a building with six apartments. Three of the apartments net the owner $200 each per month and the other three net $150 each per month. For what amount should the owner sell the building to net the same profit if he invests the money at 9 percent?
    A. $12,600
    B. $105,000
    C. $126,000
    D. $140,000

26. A person rents each of her five apartments for $600 per month and has a total amount of expenses of $1,000 per month. She has an investment of $50,000 at 8 percent a year in the bank. She decides to use the bank interest to pay for better and more frequent property maintenance. What percentage increase in rent per apartment must she obtain to offset this additional expense?
    A. 11.11%
    B. 20%
    C. 33.33%
    D. 66.67%

27. A store in a shopping center under a percentage lease pays a monthly rent of $600 plus 4 percent of the annual gross over $150,000. The gross yearly income was $250,000. If the lessor's interest in the store is valued at $150,000, what is the percentage return to the lessor?
    A. 7.5%
    B. 11.2%
    C. 14%
    D. 15%

28. A property is valued at $180,000 and is making an 8 percent annual net return on the investment. By what percentage must the monthly profit be increased to make a 10 percent annual return?
    A. 15%
    B. 20%
    C. 25%
    D. 30%

29. Bob wants to purchase a triplex where each unit rents for $750 a month. Taxes and insurance are $1,600 a year. What should he pay for it to earn himself 12 percent a year?
    A. $254,000
    B. $225,000
    C. $211,000
    D. $221,000

30. What is the "cap rate" for the comparable properties below?

Property	(A)	(B)	(C)
Gross Rents	$94,575	$104,620	$148,500
Interest Expense	$11,400	$14,620	$71,000
Net Income	$61,000	$68,000	$70,000
Sale Price	$554,500	$636,000	$618,000

    A. 15%
    B. 17%
    C. 11%
    D. 1.1%

31. A warehouse has a net annual income of $21,000. Appraiser Antonio estimates a 12 percent capitalization rate for this type of income property. Appraiser Bertolo thinks 11 percent is a more appropriate rate. Which appraiser has set a higher value for the warehouse?
    A. Appraiser Bertolo
    B. Both are equal
    C. Appraiser Antonio
    D. Not enough data

32. A 12-unit apartment building has a 9.5 percent return. What is the most an investor should pay if each unit rents for $395 a month?
    A. $600,000
    B. $603,736
    C. $598,700
    D. $682,000

Profit and Loss—These percentage problems are computed by using simple arithmetic and contain three elements. These elements are percentage, total, and part. To determine part, multiply the percent by the total. To find the total, divide the part by its percentage of the whole, and to discover the percentage, divide the part by the total.

Most calculators have a percent key (%) that converts percentages into decimals. Experiment a little with the calculator you are going to use at the test site and explore its boundaries. Some of the calculators do much more than simply multiplying percentages—they can add, subtract, and divide them too. For example, if a listing agent of a $200,000 home knows that buyers pay 52 percent more than the current value of their homes, what dollar range should be the agent's target market? The $200,000 listing price is 152 percent of the answer; therefore, we must divide the $200,000 by 152 percent to find the solution of $131,579. Divide $200,000 by 152 percent (use the percent key).

33. What percentage profit is made on a sale if the selling price is $90,000 and the purchase price is $75,000?
    A. 12%
    B. 15%
    C. 20%
    D. 120%

34. If the purchase price of a property was $50,000, what should the selling price be to realize a 5 percent profit?
    A. $47,500
    B. $51,500
    C. $52,500
    D. $53,750

35. A person buys a house for $50,000. He sells it for $60,000 with a 6 percent broker's fee and closing costs of $400. What was his percentage profit?
    A. 1.12%
    B. 5.6%
    C. 11.2%
    D. 12%

36. A house sells for $92,000, a 15 percent increase over the purchase price paid one year before. The seller paid the 9 percent interest on a 90 percent loan, taxes of $350, insurance of $150, and a 6 percent commission on the sale. What was the seller's return?
    A. Gain of $500
    B. Gain of $500
    C. Loss of $250
    D. Loss of $250 500

37. A house sells for $80,000. The seller pays 3 discount points to the lender on a 90 percent FHA loan and a 6 percent commission. If the seller bought the house for $50,000 five years ago, what was the annual rate of profit?
    A. 6%
    B. 9%
    C. 12%
    D. 18%

38. A person buys a house for $50,000 and wants to realize an 8 percent profit after paying a 6 percent real estate commission. What should the selling price be?
    A. $50,760
    B. $53,191
    C. $57,446
    D. $90,000

39. A house originally cost $30,000 to build. Over the next three years, costs went up 10 percent the first year, 20 percent the second year, and went down 3 percent the next year. What would the construction cost of the same house be if building had been postponed three years?
    A. $25,608
    B. $33,000
    C. $38,412
    D. $39,600

40. A property that sold for $80,000 was purchased for $70,800 three years earlier. What percentage profit did the owners receive?
    A. 11.5%
    B. 13%
    C. 15%
    D. 17%

41. A lot sold for $107,500. That represents a 14 percent loss on the property. What was the purchase price?
    A. $94,300
    B. $122,550
    C. $125,000
    D. $121,500

42. Mr. Kim netted $55,000 from the sale of his home. He paid off his $35,000 mortgage, $1,140 in closing costs, and a 7 percent commission. What was his sale price?
    A. $88,860
    B. $98,000
    C. $97,520
    D. $96,300

Depreciation and Appreciation—These problems are used to calculate the loss of value in a building or the increase in a property's value over a period of time. Straight-line depreciation allocates (in equal sums) the total depreciation over the useful life of a building. To calculate, divide the replacement cost by the number of years of useful life.

For example, an office building has a useful life of 50 years and is 14 years old. If it has an estimated replacement cost of $500,000, what is the current total depreciation of the building? $500,000 ÷ 50 years = $10,000 each year × 14 years = $140,000 in straight-line depreciation.

Appreciation is computed by adding a percentage increase to a property's original purchase price. For example, what is the current value of a home that was purchased for $200,000 if it has appreciated 20 percent?

One solution is to multiply the $200,000 × 20 percent to calculate the $40,000 increase and adding the increase to get $240,000. However, there is a shortcut method. By multiplying any number by 1, you get the same number. Therefore, by multiplying the $200,000 by 120 percent or 1.20 you can do both the multiplication and addition in one step. $200,000 × 120% = $240,000.

43. A $90,000 house depreciates an average 3 percent each year. What is the house's value after seven years?
    A. $60,000
    B. $61,100
    C. $71,100
    D. $81,100

44. A house depreciates 2½ percent per year for four years. If the house is now worth $108,000, what was it worth four years ago?
    A. $106,930.69
    B. $108,900.00
    C. $118,800.00
    D. $120,000.00

45. A house currently worth $153,000 was worth $180,000 five years ago. What was the depreciation per year?
    A. 2%
    B. 3%
    C. 5%
    D. 15%

46. A person has a $9,000 cottage that she depreciates using straight-line depreciation for 10 years. What is the dollar amount of depreciation each year?
    A. $900
    B. $1,000
    C. $1,100
    D. $1,800

47. It cost $40,000 to build a house on a $20,000 lot six years ago. If the house depreciates at 3 percent per year and the lot appreciates at 5 percent per year, what is the total value now?
    A. $6,800
    B. $26,000
    C. $32,800
    D. $58,800

48. If a $30,000 house depreciates at 3 percent per year for five years under straight-line depreciation, what is it worth now?
    A. $2,550
    B. $4,500
    C. $15,000
    D. $25,500

49. If 3 percent depreciation on a $30,000 house were computed each year on remaining value, what would it be worth after five years?
    A. $25,762
    B. $26,558
    C. $27,380
    D. $28,227

50. An office building has been appreciating 4 percent a year for 6 years. If it were built for $240,000, what is its value now?
    A. $297,600
    B. $300,000
    C. $303,700
    D. $340,000

51. A house originally cost $60,000 to build and the lot cost $40,000. Lot prices have increased 300 percent and building costs have doubled. What percentage did the whole property appreciate?
    A. 140%
    B. 240%
    C. 40%
    D. 280%

52. Today's reproduction cost for a rental unit is $180,000. The building has depreciated 15 percent and the land is worth $75,000. What is the present value of the property?
    A. $228,000
    B. $216,750
    C. $164,250
    D. $255,000

53. A house cost $44,000 and the lot $9,000 15 years ago. The lot has appreciated at 5 percent per year, and today the house and lot are worth $98,250. What average percentage per year has the house appreciated?
    A. 12.5%
    B. 6.4%
    C. 5.8%
    D. 87.5%

54. The tax assessment ratio for a house valued at $90,000 is 40 percent. If the tax rate is $3.50 per $1,000, what is the quarterly tax?
    A. $31.50
    B. $42.00
    C. $63.00
    D. $126.00

55. If a person's semiannual tax on a $120,000 home is $243 and the tax rate is $6.75 per $1,000 of assessed value, what is the tax assessment ratio?
    A. 4%
    B. 6%
    C. 40%
    D. 60%

Taxes and Insurance—Annual property taxes are determined by multiplying the assessed value by an assessment ratio or rollback in order to obtain the taxable value. The taxable value then is multiplied by a tax rate. Sometimes the tax rate is expressed in mills. An easy way to work these problems is to think of millage as a multiplication factor. For example, 40 mills in a problem could be converted to 4 percent of a property's taxable value. However, if a problem asks you to compute the problem per thousand, then the 40 mills should be thought of as $40 per thousand.

Example: What is the annual property tax, if a property is assessed at $200,000 and has a tax assessment ratio of 50 percent, and a tax rate of 40 mills? $200,000 × 50 percent = $100,000 × 4 percent = $4,000. Or $200,000 × 50 percent = $100,000 ÷ 1,000 = 100 × $40 = $4,000.

Be able to work the problem from the opposite view too. What is the value of a property that is taxed $4,000 and has a tax assessment ratio of 50 percent and a tax rate of 40 mills? Using your calculator, divide the $4,000 by 4 percent to arrive at $100,000. Then divide the $100,000 by 50 percent to arrive at the assessed value of $200,000. Or divide the $4,000 by $40 per thousand to determine the number of thousands (100) and then multiply the 100 by 1,000 to arrive at $100,000 and then divide the $100,000 by 50 percent to arrive at the solution of $200,000.

56. A person's semiannual tax on her $90,000 home is $78.75 and is based on a tax assessment ratio of 50 percent. What is the tax rate per $1,000 for her home?
    A. $1.57
    B. $3.14
    C. $3.50
    D. $35.00

57. A $120,000 home carries fire insurance on 80 percent of its value. If the rate is $3.50 per $1,000 of insured value for a three-year policy, what is the annual premium?
    A. $112
    B. $168
    C. $224
    D. $336

58. A person pays $168.75 each year for fire and home insurance. The rate is $3 per $1,000 of insured value for a two-year period. If the policyholder's house is worth $150,000, what percentage of that value is covered by insurance?
    A. 7.5%
    B. 25%
    C. 75%
    D. 85%

59. A property was conveyed for $60,000. If the conveyance tax rate was $0.07 per $100 value, what was the conveyance tax paid by the seller?
    A. $4.20
    B. $42.00
    C. $420.00
    D. $4,200.00

60. A property conveyed for $110,000 was charged a conveyance tax of $38.50. What is the tax rate per $100?
    A. $0.035
    B. $0.0385
    C. $0.385
    D. $3.50

61. Two years ago a property was assessed at $63,000. The tax rate was 90 mills. Last year the assessment was up to 10 percent, but the tax rate was down 10 percent. The taxes paid were
    A. up $56.70.
    B. down $56.70.
    C. the same.
    D. up $47.80.

62. The tax rate is $3.50 per $100 and the house is assessed at 65 percent of value for taxes. Ten years later the same rates are used, but the taxes had increased by $409.50. How much had the market value of the house increased?
    A. $117,000
    B. $180,000
    C. $11,700
    D. $18,000

63. A $60,000 home is assessed for 55 percent of its value. If the tax rate is $0.35/$10, what is the tax bill?
    A. $3,255
    B. $2,100
    C. $1,300
    D. $1,155

64. A 100' × 135' lot was assessed at $15 per front foot, and the house was assessed at $3,200. What is the total yearly tax if the rate is $4 per $100?
    A. $60
    B. $128
    C. $188
    D. $198

Prorations—Prorations are used to divide the financial responsibility of a sale. It is a mathematical means to deal fairly with property taxes, rental income, and prepaid items such as fuel. The seller pays for items owed by crediting the buyer and the buyer credits the seller for prepaid items. Unless identified to the contrary, proration figures generally include the day of closing. They may be calculated on either a 12-month, 30-day basis, or a 365-day year. In the absence of directions to the contrary, assume a 12-month, 30-day scenario.

65. The taxes of $390 have been paid for the entire calendar year. The seller sells on October 1. What is the amount of the remaining prepaid portion?
    A. $32.50
    B. $97.50
    C. $292.50
    D. $325.00

66. A house is sold on May 1. On January 1 of that year the three-year insurance was paid in an amount of $441 and the semiannual tax of $180 was paid. How much should be debited to buyer and credited to seller?
    A. $332
    B. $422
    C. $392
    D. $452

67. The taxes on a house for the fiscal year July 1 to June 30 are $900, to be paid in advance. If the house is sold February 15, what is the amount of the prepaid portion owed back to the seller?
    A. $56.25
    B. $100.00
    C. $337.50
    D. $562.50

68. A house sold March 15. The taxes for the first six months of the year are $195 and have not been paid. How much of this does the buyer pay?
    A. $32.50
    B. $81.25
    C. $113.75
    D. $195.00

69. The seller has made the October 1 payment on her mortgage at 8¾ percent, leaving a balance of $32,400. What is the amount of accrued interest as of the closing on October 20?
    A. $83.40
    B. $86.62
    C. $157.50
    D. $236.25

70. A property was sold on April 15, and the three-year insurance premium of $426 was paid on January 1 of the preceding year. How much does the buyer owe the seller?
    A. $11.83
    B. $24.26
    C. $118.30
    D. $242.52

71. On January 1, taxes of $600 are paid for the year and $120 is paid on the semiannual ground lease rent, both in advance. The house is sold April 10. How much is due the seller?
    A. $54.40
    B. $380.10
    C. $433.50
    D. $486.90

72. A house is sold on May 15. The yearly taxes are $760, and the water costs $80 a year. The sellers prepaid the taxes and water on January 1. At closing what does the buyer pay the sellers?
    A. $525
    B. $385
    C. $455
    D. $595

73. On January 1, a seller paid $130 for a 3-year insurance policy. On April 1, the beginning of the tax year, he also paid the annual property taxes of $625. The property sold on August 15. What prorated amount does the seller receive?
    A. $261
    B. $337
    C. $418
    D. $494

74. A seller sold her home on August 20. She prepaid the taxes of $3,060 on January 1 of this calendar year. What was the prorated tax owed to the seller?
    A. $1,955
    B. $849
    C. $1,105
    D. $2,210

75. Annual taxes of $441.60 are due semiannually on January 1 and July 1. The second semiannual portion had not been paid when the house sold on August 1. What is the proration?
    A. Debit seller $184
    B. Debit seller $37
    C. Credit buyer $73
    D. Credit seller $184

76. Prorate the prepaid taxes as of the June 15 settlement date if a $120,000 property is assessed at 55 percent value with a tax rate of $3.20 per $100 valuation on a calendar year basis.
    A. Credit seller $1,144, debit buyer $1,144
    B. Debit both $968
    C. Credit buyer $1,144, debit seller $968
    D. Credit both $968

Ratio, Proportion, and Scale—Work each problem in this section and then check your answers with the Answer Key before moving on to the next math section titled Area.

77. If 200 ft. of fence costs $900, what would 350 ft. of fence cost?
    A. $900
    B. $1,575
    C. $1,800
    D. $3,150

78. If a 9 × 12 ft. rug costs $1,500, what would a 14 × 16 ft. rug cost?
    A. $1,080.00
    B. $2,240.00
    C. $2,962.12
    D. $3,111.11

79. Lots A and B (see drawing below) have the same depth. Lot A is ¼ acre. How many acres are in Lot B?
    A. 0.031
    B. 0.31
    C. 3.1
    D. 31

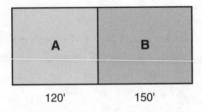

80. If 10 people take 8 hours to complete a job, how many hours would it take 15 people?
    A. 5.33
    B. 6.50
    C. 15
    D. 80

81. If a salesperson claims to sell 3 out of every 5 prospects, how many sales would result from 120 prospects?
    A. 18
    B. 36
    C. 72
    D. 120

82. In scale, if 2 in. represents a length of 6 ft., what would represent a length of 20 ft.?
    A. 2.67 in.
    B. 3.33 in.
    C. 6.00 in.
    D. 6.67 in.

83. A back yard is drawn on a plan 6½ by 3 in. If the scale is ½ in. = 5 ft. and sod costs $15 per square yard, how much would it cost to sod this lawn?
    A. $1,625
    B. $2,160
    C. $3,250
    D. $6,500

Area—Numbers and formulas for ready reference are as follows:

■ One Acre = 43,560 square feet.

■ One square yard = 9 square feet.

■ Rectangle: Area = Length × Width. For volume use V = L × W × H.

■ Triangle: Area = ½ of the Base × Height.

■ Circle: Area = π(3.14) × radius squared (that is, A = πr²). Circumference is figured by multiplying the diameter times π(3.14). Circumference of a circle = diameter × π(3.14).

■ Trapezoid: Area = (B1 + B2) × H divided by 2.

84. A lot is 70 × 120 ft. What fraction of an acre is this?
    A. ⅕
    B. ¼
    C. ⅓
    D. ½

85. What is the cost of the lot in the following illustration if the cost is $2.50 per sq. ft.?
    A. $562,500
    B. $1,125,000
    C. $2,500,000
    D. $4,500,000

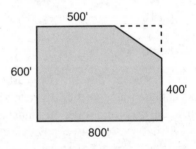

86. The house with the floor area shown below sells for $150,000. What is the cost per sq. ft.?
    A. $30
    B. $120
    C. $60
    D. $250

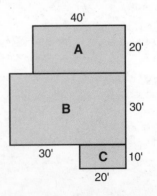

87. Compute the cost of ready-mixed concrete for a driveway of 70 ft. long, 10 ft. wide, and 3 inches deep at a cost of $30 per cubic yard.
    A. $44.80
    B. $54.80
    C. $82.20
    D. $194.40

88. A person buys the lot shown below for $12,000. To make way for the freeway, the state condemns the shaded area. What would be the market value of the shaded portion, assuming a 10 percent increase in value?
    A. $3,150
    B. $3,300
    C. $3,762
    D. $3,800

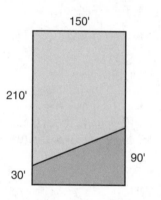

89. A property is for sale at $120,000. If the cost of the land is $15,000 per acre and the lot is rectangular with a 500 ft. frontage, what is the depth?
    A. 696.9 ft.
    B. 869.6 ft.
    C. 966.8 ft.
    D. 986.6 ft.

90. In your subdivision you are assessed $0.17 per sq. ft. for improvements. What is the charge if your lot is 60 ft. × 104 ft.?
    A. $1,080.60
    B. $530.40
    C. $1,060.80
    D. $624.00

91. A 90' × 120' lot sold for $75 a front foot. The adjacent lot sold for $0.75 a square foot. The second lot had 80' of frontage. If both lots sold for $12,750, how deep was the second lot?
    A. 100'
    B. 105'
    C. 120'
    D. 95'

92. A two-story house that is 42' × 45' is built at a cost of $45.20 per sq. ft. What is the value of the house?
    A. $85,428
    B. $121,142
    C. $149,000
    D. $170,856

Miscellaneous—The following questions review miscellaneous math commonly found in the real estate business.

93. The owner of an apartment house with 8 apartments spends $1,000 on improvements. How much should he increase each rent to recoup this expense in six months?
    A. $12.50
    B. $20.83
    C. $38.20
    D. $125.00

94. A person buys a parcel of land for $1 million. She then subdivides it into eight lots to sell for $150,000 each. What percentage of return on the money is this?
    A. 2%
    B. 4%
    C. 20%
    D. 40%

95. A person has six apartments that rent for $500 per month including utilities. If the utilities average $450 total per month, what would be the rent without the utilities?
    A. $75
    B. $85
    C. $415
    D. $425

96. A building with a net income of $10,000 was appraised at $100,000. What would be the value if the capitalization rate has decreased by one percentage point?
    A. $90,909
    B. $100,000
    C. $105,263
    D. $111,111

97. A salesperson is offered a straight salary of $2,000 per month or 40 percent of a 6 percent total commission. How much in monthly sales would make the two offers equal?
    A. $50,000
    B. $83,333
    C. $124,600
    D. $166,666

98. A salesperson gets $500 per month plus 40 percent of the 6 percent commission on sales. If she wants to earn $1,200 this month, how much must her sales be?
    A. $20,833
    B. $29,167
    C. $50,000
    D. $100,000

99. A house appreciates each year by 10 percent. This is equivalent to what percentage for five years?
    A. 50%
    B. 61%
    C. 71%
    D. 81%

100. Acme Savings and Loan Association suggests the buyer can buy a home valued at 3½ times her yearly income. What should her minimum weekly salary be to buy a home worth $120,000?
    A. $596.34
    B. $634.59
    C. $659.34
    D. $695.34

101. On a ¼-acre of land, approximately what percentage is occupied by a 2,500-sq.-ft. house?
    A. 23%
    B. 32%
    C. 34%
    D. 43%

102. A ¼-acre plot costs $5 per square foot. A house that is 60 × 40 ft. will cost $30 per square foot. What is the total cost?
    A. $87,120
    B. $126,450
    C. $130,680
    D. $174,240

103. The gross income on a property is $7,920. If this is a 6 percent return on cost, what is the cost?
    A. $47,520
    B. $74,448
    C. $83,952
    D. $132,000

104. On a 30-year mortgage in the sum of $110,000 at 11 percent, the monthly payment is $1,047.56. On the first payment, how much is applied to reduce the principal?
    A. $3.92
    B. $39.23
    C. $1,008.33
    D. $1,100.00

105. If the price of a house rises 10 percent the first year and 12 percent the second year, what is the percentage rise over the two years?
    A. 13.2%
    B. 22%
    C. 23.2%
    D. 120%

106. Find the cost of the lot below at $100 per square yard.
    A. $28,800
    B. $32,000
    C. $35,556
    D. $106,667

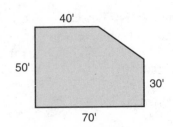

107. A 35 × 40 ft. house is on a ⅓-acre of land. What percentage is *NOT* taken up by the house?
   A. 10%
   B. 14%
   C. 86%
   D. 90%

108. A house originally cost $35,000 to build and the lot cost $20,000. Lot prices have increased by 300 percent and building costs have doubled. What percentage did the entire property appreciate?
   A. 36%
   B. 73%
   C. 136%
   D. 500%

109. A person owns a house with a $32,000 mortgage and his payment is $260 per month. He rents the house for $600 per month, paying 10 percent to a broker and saving $75 per month for repairs. The annual profit he makes is what percentage of his equity if the house would net $68,000 if he were to sell?
   A. 1.3%
   B. 3.6%
   C. 13%
   D. 36%

110. A house worth $90,000 is rented for a net profit of $400 per month. How much money invested at 12 percent would give the same net profit?
   A. $40,000
   B. $45,000
   C. $80,000
   D. $90,000

111. The mortgage payment on a house is $336 per month. How much money would have to be invested at 12.5 percent per annum to pay the monthly mortgage payment?
   A. $25,326
   B. $32,256
   C. $33,562
   D. $33,600

112. The buildings on a 150 × 220 ft. lot cover 30 percent of the lot. How many square feet are not covered by buildings?
   A. 7,000
   B. 10,900
   C. 23,100
   D. 33,000

113. A buyer applies at a bank for a loan to purchase a $60,000 home. The bank requires an 18 percent down payment on the first $30,000 and a 14 percent down payment on the remaining $30,000. What will be the bank's loan fee if they charge four points on the balance?
   A. $2,016
   B. $2,184
   C. $2,400
   D. $3,018

114. George earns $22,500 per year as a carpenter, and his spouse, Sarah, is a secretary earning $15,000. They are selling their present home for $70,000 and will receive their equity of $35,000 at closing. They contact a lender who uses a 2.5-times rule of thumb. The most expensive home they would be capable of purchasing would be
   A. $75,000.
   B. $89,750.
   C. $93,750.
   D. $128,750.

115. A buyer contracts to purchase a $75,000 home and puts up a good-faith deposit of $1,500. The commission is 6.5 percent paid by the seller. The buyer gets a $260 credit for real property taxes paid in arrears. If the buyer obtains an 80 percent conventional loan at 12 percent interest with three points, how much should she bring to the closing?
   A. $15,040
   B. $16,540
   C. $15,300
   D. $19,915

116. A home was purchased for $120,000. The bank gave a 75 percent LTV (loan to value) 30-year, 8½ percent mortgage. The monthly payment factor is 7.69. What is the down payment?
   A. $30,000
   B. $22,500
   C. $25,000
   D. $90,000

117. Refer to question 116. What is the principal balance on this mortgage after two monthly payments?
    A. $22,400
    B. $89,891
    C. $89,875
    D. $89,945

118. A $25,000 loan is paid off at the rate of $8.50 per $1,000. The owner has a 3-year insurance policy costing $540 and taxes are $405. What was the first month's payment?
    A. $212.50
    B. $261.25
    C. $291.25
    D. $238.75

119. The condominium sold for $95,000. The mortgage balance was $33,000, escrow fees were $450, deed preparation was $90, and a 6 percent commission was paid. The seller received a $750 tax credit and gave a $15,000 second mortgage to the buyer. What did the seller receive at closing?
    A. $41,510
    B. $43,522
    C. $55,010
    D. $71,510

120. The buyer deposited $2,500 on a $47,000 house. He has a 90 percent loan, receives a $250 proration credit, and pays a $950 attorney fee and 4 points on the mortgage. How much money does the buyer bring to closing?
    A. $4,342
    B. $4,592
    C. $4,842
    D. $5,850

121. A company insures houses for 85 percent of value at $1.10 per $100 for a 3-year policy. What does insurance cost for a $90,000 house?
    A. $842
    B. $990
    C. $2,525
    D. $2,805

122. A home has an economic life of 40 years. How old is the building when the depreciation has reached 27.5 percent?
    A. 11 years
    B. 27 years
    C. 14.5 years
    D. None of the above

123. FHA will insure a mortgage for 97 percent of the first $35,000 and 95 percent of the remainder up to $70,000. What are the buyer's loan costs on a $61,000 sale if the lender charges a 1 percent loan origination fee and 5 discount points?
    A. $587
    B. $3,050
    C. $3,519
    D. $610

ANSWERS

Note: Where appropriate, assume V = Value, R = Rate, I = Income.

Commission

1. **C.** $124,000 (V) × 0.06 (R) = $7,440 (I)

2. **B.** 78,000 (V) × 0.06 (R) = $4,680 (I). The commission is $4,680. Because the sales-person gets 40%, the broker gets 60%. $4,680 × 0.60 = $2,808.

3. **B.** $96,000 (V) × ? (R) = $4,800 (I). $4,800 ÷ 96,000 = 0.05 or 5%.

4. **C.** First determine the total commission: $2,880 is 40% of what?
    ? × 0.40 = $2,880
    $2,880 ÷ 0.40 = $7,200

The total commission was $7,200.
$120,000 (V) × ? (R) = $7,200 (I)
$7,200 ÷ $120,000 = 0.06 or 6%

5. **B.** First determine the total commission.
$110,000 (V) × 0.06 (R) = $6,600 (I)
$6,600 is the total commission.
Then the salesperson's commission was
what percent of $6,600?
$6,600 × ? = $1,980
$1,980 ÷ $6,600 = 0.30 or 30%

6. **B.** 1st month: 600 ÷ 3 = 200
$200 for the first month
Each month after: $600 × 0.02 = $12
For 11 months: $12 × 11 = $132
The total commission is $332 less $100
"Finder's fee" equals $232.

7. **A.** *Note:* These types of multiple-step prob-
lems are more prevalent in the broker's
exam than in the salesperson's exam.
Old Commission:
$100,000 × 0.06 = $6,000 plus
$80,000 × 0.03 = $2,400
Total: $6,000 + $2,400 = $8,400
Sales price:
Old price: $180,000 × 0.20 = $36,000
New price: $180,000 − $36,000 = $144,000
New Commission:
$100,000 × 0.06 = $6,000 plus
$44,000 × 0.03 = $1,320
Total: $6,000 + $1,320 = $7,320
Difference: $8,400 − $7,320 = $1,080

8. **B.** 160 × $750 = $120,000
$50,000 × 0.10 = $5,000
$25,000 × 0.08 = $2,000
$120,000 − $75,000 = $45,000
$45,000 × 0.06 = $2,700
$5,000 + $2,000 + $2,700 = $9,700
$9,700 × 0.50 = $4,850 is the commission
due to salesperson

9. **C.** $62,000 + $74,000 + $68,000 + $71,200 =
$275,200 total of all sales for the month
$100,000 × 0.06 = $6,000
$275,200 − $100,000 = $175,200
$175,200 × 0.08 = $14,016
$6,000 + $14,016 = $20,016 total commis-
sion: variable rates
$275,200 × 0.07 = $19,264 total commission: straight rate

$20,016 − $19,264 = $752 variable rate less
straight rate

10. **D.** $2,000 × $1.50 = $3,000 lease price per
month

Note: Do not include the common area
maintenance price because it is not
commissionable.
$3,000 × 12 = $36,000
$36,000 × 5 = $180,000
$20,000 × 0.05 = $1,000
$20,000 × 0.04 = $800
$20,000 × 0.03 = $600
$180,000 − $60,000 = $120,000 remaining
balance from 5-year lease
$120,000 × 0.01 = $1,200 commission:
remaining balance
$1,000 + $800 + $600 + $1,200 = $3,600
total commission
$3,600 × 0.60 = $2,160
$3,600 × 0.40 = $1,440

Interest

11. **C.** $32,000 (V) × 0.1225 (R) = $3,920 (I)
$3,920 ÷ 12 = $326.67 per month
$326.67 × 6 = $1,960

12. **A.** $5,400 for 8 months is $675 per month × 12
is $8,100 for the year.
Then:
? (V) × 0.13 (R) = $8,100 (I)
$8,100 ÷ 0.13 = $62,307.69

13. **C.** The interest per month is $7,200 ÷ 9 = $800.
The interest per year is $800 × 12 = $9,600.
Then:
$80,000 (V) × ? (R) = $9,600 (I)
$9,600 ÷ $80,000 = 0.12 or 12%

14. **C.** $60,000 (V) × 0.1075 (R) = $6,450 (the
total *interest* for the year)
$6,450 ÷ 12 = $537.50 interest per month
$537.50 × 9 months = $4,837.50 total interest for 9 months
Balance: $60,000 + $4,837.50 = $64,837.50

15. **C.** $96,000 × 0.90 = $86,400 amount of loan
$86,400 × 0.12 = $10,368 interest for the year
$10,368 ÷ 12 = $864 interest per month
$864 × 2 months = $1,728

16. **D.** $15,000 (V) × 0.13 (R) = $1,950 interest per year
$1,950 ÷ 12 = $162.50 interest per month
$162.50 ÷ 30 = $5.42 interest per day
2 years: 2 × $1,950 = $3,900.
6 months: 6 × $162.50 = $975.00
10 days: 10 × $5.42 = $54.20
Total is $4,929.20

17. **B.** *First Payment:*
$30,000 (V) × 0.09 (R) = $2,700 (I)
$2,700 ÷ 12 = $225
$250 (payment) less $225 (interest) equals $25 (to balance)
$30,000 (old balance) less $25 (to balance) equals $29,975 (new balance)
Second Payment:
$29,975 (V) × 0.09 (R) = $2,697.75 (I)
$2,697.75 ÷ 12 = $224.81
$250 (payment) less $224.81(interest) equals $25.19 (to balance)
$29,975 (old balance) less $25.19 (to balance) equals $29,949.81 (new balance)
Third Payment:
$29,949.81 (V) × 0.09 (R) = $2,695.48 (I)
$2,695.48 ÷ $224.62
$250 (payment) less $224.62 (interest) equals $25.38 (to balance)
$29,949.81 (old balance) less $25.38 (to balance) equals $29,924.43 (new balance)

18. **C.** *Note:* A balloon payment is the final installment payment on a note that is greater than the preceding installment payments and pays the note in full.
$87,000 × 0.10 = $8,700
Second mortgage at interest only means that the entire amount (10% of the sales price) is due after 5 years—this is the balloon payment.

19. **C.** $87,000 × 0.80 = $69,600
$87,000 × 0.10 = $8,700
$69,600 + $8,700 = $78,300
$87,000 − $78,300 = $8,700 down payment

20. **B.** 94 × $10.90 = $1,024.60
$1,024.60 × 12 = $12,295.20
$12,295.20 × 25 = $307,380
$307,380 − $94,000 = $213,380 total interest paid (total payment less principal owed)

21. **D.** $68,000 × 0.085 = $5,780
$5,780 ÷ 12 = $481.67
$550 − $481.67 = $68.33
$68,000 − $68.33 = $67,932

Investment or Income

22. **B.** $120,000 (V) × 0.08 (R) = $9,600 (I)
$9,600 profit per annum
$9,600 ÷ 12 = $800 per month

23. **A.** $750 monthly earnings × 12 = $9,000 yearly earnings
$150,000 (V) × ? (R) = $9,000 (I)
$9,000 ÷ $150,000 = 0.06 or 6%

24. **D.** $1,050 profit per month × 12 = $12,600 profit per year
? (V) × 0.09 (R) = $12,600 (I)
$12,600 ÷ 0.09 = $140,000

25. **D.** $200 × 3 = $600
$150 × 3 = $450
$600 + $450 = $1,050 per month
$1,050 × 12 = $12,600 per year
? (V) × 0.09 (R) = $12,000 (I)
$12,600 ÷ 0.09 = $140,000

26. **A.** $50,000 × 0.08 = $4,000 yearly
$4,000 ÷ 12 = $333.33
$333.33 ÷ 5 = $66.67
Raise each rent $66.67
$600 (V) × ? (R) = $66.67 (I)
$66.67 ÷ $600 = 0.11 or 11% increase

27. **A.** $600 × 12 = $7,200 fixed rent
$250,000 − $150,000 = $100,000
$100,000 × 0.04 = $4,000
$7,200 + $4,000 = $11,200 yearly rent
$150,000 (V) × ? (R) = $11,200 (I)
$11,200 ÷ $150,000 = 0.074 or 7.5%

28. **C.** $180,000 (V) × 0.08 (old rate) = $14,400 (yearly investment)
$14,400 ÷ 12 = $1,200 monthly profit (old)
$180,000 × 0.10 (new rate) = $18,000 (yearly)
$18,000 ÷ 12 = $1,500 monthly profit (new)
$1,500 new monthly profit less $1,200 old monthly profit equals $300 gain
$1,200 (V) × ? (R) = $300 (I)
$300 ÷ $1,200 = 0.25 or 25%

29. **C.** $750 × 12 = $9,000 annual rent
$9,000 × 3 = $27,000 triplex
$27,000 – $1,600 = $25,400
price × 12% = $25,400
price = $25,400 ÷ 0.12 = $211,667

30. **C.** $61,000 ÷ $554,500 = 0.11; cap rate equals
net income divided by sales price
$68,000 ÷ $636,000 = 0.11; work this formula for each property (A, B, C)
$70,000 ÷ $618,000 = 0.11; all properties
have a cap rate of 11%

31. **A.** price × 12% = $21,000
price = $21,000 ÷ 0.12 = $175,000
price = $21,000 ÷ 0.11 = $190,909

32. **B.** $395 × 12 = $4,740 total monthly rent for
12 units
$4,740 × 12 = $56,880 total yearly rent for
12 units
price = $56,880 ÷ 0.095 = $598,737 price at
9.5% return (B is the closest answer)

Profit and Loss

33. **C.** $90,000 – $75,000 = $15,000 profit
$15,000 ÷ $75,000 = 0.20 or 20% profit and
loss
$75,000 (V) × ? (R) = $15,000 (I)
or
$75,000 × ? = $90,000
$90,000 ÷ $75,000 = 1.20 or 120% return

34. **C.** $50,000 × 1.05 = $52,500

35. **D.** $60,000 × 0.94 = $56,400 – $400 = $56,000
$50,000 × ? = $56,000
$56,000 ÷ $50,000 = 1.12 or 12% profit
(112% return)

36. **B.** ? × 1.15 = $92,000
$92,000 ÷ 1.15 = $80,000 purchase price
$92,000 – $80,000 = $12,000 gross profit
Loan:
$80,000 interest on loan × 0.90 = $72,000
$72,000 × 0.09 = $6,480
Commission:
$92,000 × 0.06 = $5,520
Total Expenses:

Interest	$6,480
Commission	$5,520
Tax	$350
Insurance	$150

Total is	$12,500

$12,000 gross profit less $12,500 expenses
= –$500 loss

37. **B.** $80,000 × 0.90 = $72,000 amount of loan
$72,000 × 0.03 points (3%) = $2,160
Commission:
$80,000 × 0.06 = $4,800 commission
$2,160 expenses + $4,800 = $6,960
Profit:
$30,000 – $6,960 = $23,040
$23,040 ÷ 5 = $4,608 profit per year
(B) $50,000 × ? = (A) $4,608
$4,608 ÷ $50,000 = 0.09 or 9%

38. **C.** $50,000 × .08 = $4,000 profit
$50,000 + $4,000 + (0.06 × SP) = SP
or $54,000 = 0.94 × SP
$54,000 ÷ 0.94 = $57,446.81 = selling price

39. **C.** $30,000 × 1.10 = $33,000 after 1 year
$33,000 × 1.20 = $39,600 after 2 years
$39,600 × 0.97 = $38,412 after 3 years

40. **B.** $80,000 – $70,800 = $9,200 profit from sale
$9,200 ÷ $70,800 = 0.13 or 13%; profit
divided by original price equals percent
profit

41. **C.** 1 – (sale price ÷ original price) = 14% original price ÷ original price = 1
1 – ($107,500 ÷ original price) = 14%
1 – 14 = $107,500 ÷ original price; switch
sides of formula
0.86 = $107,500 ÷ original price
original price = $107,500 ÷ 0.86 = $125,000

42. **B.** Sale price = (sale price × 7%) + $35,000 +
$1,140 + $55,000
Sale price = (sale price × 0.07) + $91,140
Sale price = (sale price × 0.07) = $91,140
1 – 0.07 (sale price) = $91,140
0.93 × sale price = $91,140
sale price = $91,140 ÷ 0.93 = $98,000

Depreciation and Appreciation

43. **C.** 3% × 7 years = 21%
100% – 21% = 79%
$90,000 × 0.79 = $71,100

44. **D.** 2½% × 4 years = 10%
100% – 10% – 90%

$? \times 0.90 = \$108,000$
$\$108,000 \div 0.90 = \$120,000$

45. **B.** $\$180,000 \times ? = \$153,000$
$\$153,000 \div \$180,000 = 0.85$ or 85%
$100\% - 85\% = 15\%$ for the 4 years
$15 \div 5 = 3$ or 3% depreciation per year

46. **A.** 100% in 10 years $= 10\%$ each year
$0.10 \times \$9,000 = \$900$ per year

47. **D.** *House:*
$\$40,000 \times 0.82 = \$32,800$
$3\% \times 6 = 18\%$
$100\% - 18\% = 82\%$
Lot:
$\$20,000 \times 1.30 = \$26,000$
$5\% \times 6 = 30\%$
$100\% + 30\% = 130\%$
Total:
$\$32,800 + \$26,000 = \$58,800$

48. **D.** $3\% \times 5 = 15\%$
$100\% - 15\% = 85\%$
$\$30,000 \times 0.85 = \$25,500$

49. **A.** With a financial calculator, enter $30,000 and then using the percent key touch minus 3% from the remaining number 4 more times.
$\$30,000 \times 0.97 = \$29,100$ after 1 year
$\$29,100 \times 0.97 = \$28,227$ after 2 years
$\$28,227 \times 0.97 = \$27,380.19$ after 3 years
$\$27,380.19 \times 0.97 = \$26,558.78$ after 4 years
$\$26,558.78 \times 0.97 = \$25,762.02$ after 5 years

50. **A.** $\$240,000 \times 0.04 = \$9,600$
$\$9,600 \times 6 = \$57,600$
$\$240,000 + \$57,600 = \$297,600$

51. **A.** $\$60,000 \times 2 = \$120,000$ appreciation of the house (doubled, went up 100%)
$\$40,000 \times 3 = \$120,000$ appreciation of lot (tripled)
$\$120,000 + \$120,000 = \$240,000$
$\$240,000 - \$100,000 = \$140,000$ total appreciation less original value
formula to determine % appreciation on house/lot appreciation $= \$140,000 \div \$100,000 = 1.4$ times or 140%

52. **A.** $\$180,000 \times 0.15 = \$27,000$
$\$180,000 - \$27,000 = \$153,000$
$\$153,000 + \$75,000 = \$228,000$

53. **C.** $\$9,000 \times .05 = \$450$ appreciation of lot per year
$\$450 \times 15 = \$6,750$ appreciation of lot over 15 years
$\$53,000 + \$6,750 = \$59,750$ original value of lot/house plus appreciation of lot
$\$98,250 - \$59,750 = \$38,500$ current value less original plus lot appreciation (house appreciation)
$\$38,500 \div 15 = \$2,567$ house appreciation per year (over 15-year time period)
appreciation $\times \$44,000 = \$2,567$; formula to determine what percentage the house appreciated
appreciation $= \$2,567 \div \$44,000 = 0.058$ or 5.8%

Taxes and Insurance

54. **A.** market value $\times \% =$ assessed value
$\$90,000 \times 0.40 = \$36,000$
assessed value (in thousands) $\times$ rate $=$ tax bill
$36 \times \$3.50 = \$126$ annual tax
quarterly tax: $\$126 \div 4 = \$31.50$

55. **D.** $\$243 \times 2 = \$486$ per year of tax
assessed value $\times$ rate $=$ tax
$? \times 6.75 = \$486$
$\$486 \div 6.75 = \$72$
assessed value is $\$72 \times \$1,000 = \$72,000$
market value $\times$ rate $=$ assessed value
$\$120,000 \times ? = \$72,000$
$\$72,000 \div \$120,000 = 0.60$ or 60%

56. **C.** $\$78.75 \times 2 = \$157.50$ tax per year
market value $\times \% =$ assessed value
$\$90,000 \times 0.50 = \$45,000$
assessed value $\times$ rate $=$ tax bill
$\$45$ (in thousands) $\times ? = \$157.50$
$\$157.50 \div 45 = \$3.50$

57. **A.** value $\times \% =$ insured value
$\$120,000 \times 0.80 = \$96,000$
insured value $\times$ rate $=$ premium
$\$96 \times 3.50 = \$336$ (for 3 years)
$\$336 \div 3 = 112$ yearly

58. **C.** $168.75 \times 2 = \$337.50$ for the 2 years
    insured value × rate = premium
    $? \times 3.00 = \$337.50$
    $\$337.50 \div 3 = \$112.50$ insured value (in thousands)
    market value × % = insured value
    $\$150,000 \times ? = \$112,500$
    $\$112,500 \div \$150,000 = 0.75$ or 75%

59. **B.** value × rate = tax
    $600 (in hundreds) × 0.07 = \$42$

60. **A.** value × rate = tax
    $1,100 (in hundreds) × ? = \$38.50$
    $\$38.50 \div \$1,100 = 0.035$ or 3.5¢

61. **B.** *Note:* 1 mill = 1/10 of 1 cent (or 0.001)
    90 mill × 0.001 = .09
    $\$63,000 \times 0.09 = \$5,670$
    $\$63,000 \times 0.10 = \$6,300$
    $\$63,000 + \$6,300 = \$69,300$; second year
    was 10% greater than first-year assessment
    90 mills × 0.10 = 9 mills; 10% of first-year
    mill rate
    90 mills − 9 = 81 mills; second year was
    10% less than first-year mill rate
    81 mills × 0.001 = 0.081 second-year mills
    $\$69,300 \times 0.081 = \$5,613.30$ tax rate for the
    second year
    $\$5,670 - \$5,613.30 = \$56.70$ amount taxes
    went down in the second year

62. **D.** market value × 0.65 = assessed value
    (assessed value ÷ 100) × 3.50 = tax
    (assessed value ÷ 100) × 3.50 = \$409.50
    (assessed value = $40,950 ÷ 3.50 = \$11,710
    market value = $11,710 ÷ 0.65 = \$18,015

63. **D.** $\$60,000 \times 0.55 = \$33,000$
    ($33,000 ÷ 10) × \$0.35 = \$1,155

64. **C.** 100 ft. × \$15 = \$1,500
    $\$1,500 + \$3,200 = \$4,700$
    ($4,700 ÷ 100) × \$4 = \$188

Prorations

65. **B.** (a) time period: 3 months (Oct., Nov., Dec.)
    (b) $390 per year ÷ 12 = \$32.50 per month
    (c) $32.50 × 3 = \$97.50

66. **D.** *Insurance:*
    $441 ÷ 36 months = \$12.25 per month
    $12.25 × 32 months remaining = \$392

Taxes:
$180 ÷ 6 = \$30 per month taxes
$30 × 2 months remaining = \$60
Total:
$392 + \$60 = \$452

67. **C.** $900 ÷ 12 months = \$75 per month
    $75 × 4.5 months = \$337.50

68. **C.** $195 ÷ 6 = \$32.50 per month
    Buyer pays for 3½ months
    $32.50 × 3.5 = \$113.75

69. **C.** $32,400 (V) × .0875 (R) = \$2,835 (I)
    $2,835 ÷ 12 = \$236.25 for the month
    $236.25 ÷ 30 = \$7.88 per day
    The seller owes for 20 days, $7.88 × 20 =
    $157.50

70. **D.** $426 ÷ 36 months = \$11.83 per month
    $11.83 × 20½ months remaining = \$242.52
    due the seller

71. **D.** *Taxes:*
    $600 ÷ 12 = \$50 per month
    8⅔ months remain $50 × \$8.67 = \$433.50
    Lease rent:
    $120 ÷ 6 = \$20 per month
    2⅔ months remain $20 × 2.67 = \$53.40
    Total:
    $433.50 + \$53.40 = \$486.90

72. **A.** January 1 to May 15 = 4 ½ months
    $760 ÷ 12 = \$63.33
    $80 ÷ 12 = \$6.67
    $63.33 + \$6.67 = \$70
    $70 × 4.5 = \$315
    $760 + \$80 = \$840
    $840 − \$315 = \$525

73. **D.** $130 ÷ 3 = \$43.33
    $43.33 ÷ 12 = \$3.64
    January 1 to August 15 = 7½ months
    $3.61 × 7.5 = \$27.10
    $625 ÷ 12 = \$52.08
    April 1 to August 15 = 4 1/2 months
    $52.08 × 4.5 = \$234.37
    $234.37 + \$27.10 = \$261.45 total amount of
    payments used by seller before sale
    $130 + \$625 = \$755 total prepaid by seller
    to cover insurance and taxes
    $755 − \$261.45 = \$493.55 amount not used,
    or owed to seller or buyer

74. **C.** $3,060 ÷ 12 = $255 monthly payments
January 1 to August 20 = 7⅔ months
$255 × 7.67 = $1,955 amount already used
by the seller
$3,060 – $1,955 = $1,105 yearly tax amount
paid – amount used (presale) = amount
owed seller

75. **B.** $441.60 ÷ 2 = $220.80; break annual tax
into two semiannual payments
$220.80 ÷ 6 = $36.80 amount due per
month, seller is responsible for one month
after July payment

76. **A.** $120,000 × 0.55 = $66,000
$66,000 ÷ 100 = 660
660 × $3.20 = $2,112
$2,112 × 12 = $176
$176 × 5.5 = $968 amount of tax accrued
until sale (5 ½ months)
$2,112 – $968 = $1,144 amount owed back
to seller (because whole amount was prepaid; also is the amount that buyer is
responsible for paying)

Ratio, Proportion, and Scale

77. **B.** 200/$900 = 350/?
900 × 350 = 200 × ?
900 × 350 = 315,000
315,000 ÷ 200 = $1,575

78. **D.** 9 × 12 = 108 sq. ft.
14 × 16 = 224 sq. ft.
Proportion:
108/$1,500 = 224/?
area/cost
$1,500 × 224 = 108 = ?
$1,500 × 224 = $336,000
$336,000 ÷ 108 = $3,111.11

79. **B.** 120/.25 = 150/?
150 × 0.25 = 37.50
37.50 ÷ 120 = .31 acre

80. **A.** *Note:* This is an inverse proportion (as number of people goes up, hours go down).
8 × 10 = 80 (This is number of "man-
hours.")
80 ÷ 15 = 5.33 hours

81. **C.** 3/5 = 0.60 and 0.60 × 120 = 72

82. **D.** 2/6 = ?/20
2 × 20 = 40
40 ÷ 6 = 6.67 inches

83. **C.** Scale ½ inch = 5 feet would be 1 inch = 10
feet
so
1/10 = 6½/?
10 × 6½ = 65 feet
1/10 = 3/?
3 × 10 = 30 feet
So the yard is 65 feet × 30 feet = 1,950
square feet.
Changing to square yards, there are 9 square
feet to a square yard.
9/1 = 1,950/?
1,950 ÷ 9 = 216.67 square yards
Each square yard costs $15, so 216.67
square yards cost 216.67 × 15 = $3,250.

Area

84. **A.** 70 ft. × 120 ft. = 8,400 sq. ft.
1 acre/43,560 sq. ft. × 8,400 sq. ft. = ? acres
8,400/43,560 = 0.193 (almost ⅕ acre)

85. **B.** area = rectangle – triangle
= 600 × 800 – ½ (300 × 200)
= 480,000 – 30,000
= 450,000

cost = no. of sq. ft. × cost per sq. ft.
= 450,000 × $2.50
= $1,125,000

86. **B.** area A = 40 × 20 = 800
area B = 50 × 30 = 1,500
area C = 10 × 20 = 200
total area = 2,500 sq. ft.
cost per sq. ft. = 150,000 ÷ 2,500 = $60

87. **D.** (a) Finding volume in cubic feet
V = 70' × 10' × 0.25'
(3 in. = 3/12 = 0.25 ft.)
V = 175 cu. ft.
(b) converting to cubic yards, 1 cu. yd. =
3' × 3' × 3' = 27 cu. ft.
?/175 = 1/27
? = 175 ÷ 27 = 6.48 cu. yd.
(c) at $30 per cu. yd. the cost will be: 6.48 ×
$30 = $194.40

88. **B.** (a) area of a rectangle = 240 x 150 = 36,000 sq. ft.
(b) value of rectangle per sq. ft. $12,000 divided by 36,000 = $0.33
(c) divide shaded area into two triangles:
1) ½ (90 × 150) = 6,750
2) ½ (30 × 150) = 2,250
6,750 + 2,250 = 9,000
9,000 × $0.33 = 3,000 + 10% = $3,300

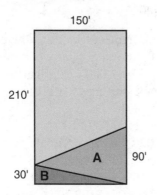

89. **A.** (a) no. of acres = total cost ÷ cost per acre
$120,000 ÷ $15,000/acre = 8 acres
(b) 1 acre = 43,560 sq. ft.
8 acres = 348,480 sq. ft.
(c) Area = base × height
348,480 = 500 × h
h = 696.96 ft.

90. **C.** 60 ft. × 104 ft. = 6,240 sq. ft.
6,240 sq. ft. × $0.17 = $1,060.80

91. **A.** In this problem you must assume that the 90 feet represents the frontage side (the lot being 120 feet deep).
90 ft. × $75 = $6,750
$12,750 – $6,750 = $6,000
(80 ft. × depth) × 0.75 = $6,000
(80 ft. × depth) = $8,000
depth = $8,000 ÷ 80 = 100 ft.

92. **D.** 42 ft. × 45 ft. = 1,890 sq. ft.
1,890 sq. ft. × 2 = 3,780 sq. ft.; the question tells you this is a two-story house
3,780 sq. ft. × $45.20 = $170,856

Miscellaneous

93. **B.** $1,000 shared by 8 apartments = $1,000 ÷ 8 = $125 each in 6 equal payments = $125 ÷ 6 = $20.83

94. **C.** 8 × 150,000 = $1,200,000
$1,200,000 – $1,000,000 = $200,000 increase
200,000/1,000,000 = 0.20 or 20%

95. **D.** $450 shared among 6 apartments = $75 per apartment; without utilities, the rent would be $500 – $75 = $425

96. **D.** $10,000 ÷ $100,000 equals the capitalization rate of 10%; $10,000 ÷ 9% is $111,111

97. **B.** 40% of 6% = 0.40 × 0.06 = 0.0240
? (sales) × 0.025 (rate) = $2,000 (income)
700 ÷ 0.024 = $83,333.33

98. **B.** $700 commission; 40% × 6% = 0.024
? (sales) × 0.024 (rate) = $700
$2,000 ÷ 0.025 = $83,333.33

99. **B.** P(1.1) × (1.1) × (1.1) × (1.1) × (1.1) = P(1.61) = 61%

100. **C.** $120,000 ÷ 3½ = $34,285.71 per year
$34,285.71 ÷ 52 = $659.34 per week

101. **A.** 1 acre = 43,560 sq. ft.
¼ acre = 10,890 sq. ft.
2,500 ÷ 10,890 = 0.229 = 23%

102. **B.** ¼ acre = ¼ × 43,560 sq. ft. = 10,890 sq. ft.
10,890 × $5 = $54,450
60' × 40' = 2,400 sq. ft.
2,400 × $30 = $72,000
$54,450 + $72,000 = $126,450

103. **D.** ? × 0.06 = $7,920
$7,920 ÷ 0.06 = $132,000

104. **B.** $110,000 × 0.11 = $12,100 ÷ 12 = $1,008.33
$1,047.56 – $1,008.33 = $39.23

105. **C.** *First year:*
100 + (0.10 × 100) = 110
Second year:
110 + (0.12 × 110) = 123.2
123.2 = 100 + (0.232 × 100)

106. **C.** Area $= 70 \times 50 - \frac{1}{2} (20 \times 30)$
$= 3,500 - 300 = 3,200$ sq. ft.
3,200 sq. ft. $\div$ 9 sq. ft./sq. yd. = 355.56 sq. yd.
$355.56 \times 100 = \$35,556$

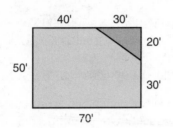

107. **D.** 1/3 acre = 14,520 sq. ft.
35 ft. $\times$ 40 ft. = 1,400 sq. ft.
1,400 $\div$ 14,520 = 0.096 = 10% house
Therefore: 90% not house

108. **C.** House $\$35,000 \times 2 = \$70,000$
Lot + 20,000 $\times$ 300% + 60,000
$\$130,000 - \$55,000$
$75,000 appreciation
$75,000 \div \$55,000 = 1.36$ or 136%

109. **B.** $600 - $260 (mortgage) = $340 - $60
(to broker) = $280 - $75 (repair) = $205
$205 \div \$68,000 = 0.0030147 \times 12 =$
0.03617 or 3.6%

110. **A.** $500 \times 12 = \$4,800$ per year
$4,800 \div 0.12 = \$40,000$

111. **B.** $336 \times 12 = \$4,032$ per year
$4,032 \div 0.125 = \$32,256$

112. **C.** 150 ft. $\times$ 220 ft. $-$ 33,000 ft.
70% of 33,000 = 23,100 sq. ft.

113. **A.** $30,000 \times 18\% = \$5,400$
$5,400 + \$4,200 = \$9,600$
$30,000 \times 14\% = \$4,200$
$60,000 - \$9,600 = \$50,400 \times 0.04 =$
$2,016

114. **D.** $37,500 \times 2.5 = \$93,750$ is the amount of
the loan they would qualify for; adding this
to their $35,000 equity would mean they
could purchase a $128,750 home.

115. **A.** $1,500 (deposit) + $260 (credit) = $1,760
$75,000 \times 80\% = \$60,000 \times 3\% = \$1,800$
points
$75,000 \times 20\% = \$15,000$ down payment $-$
$1,760 = \$13,240 + \$1,800 = \$15,040$

116. **A.** *Note:* Beware of unnecessary information.
The bank gave a loan of 75 percent of the
sale price of the home; the down payment
must be the difference between the loan
amount and the purchase price.
$120,000 \times 0.75 = \$90,000$
$120,000 - \$90,000 = \$30,000$
Alternate: 100% (sales price) $-$ 75% (loan
given from bank) = 25% (down payment)
$120,000 \times 0.25 = \$30,000$

117. **B.** *Note:* Payment factor of 7.69 refers to principal plus interest per month per $1,000.
$90,000 \div 1,000 = 90$; figure out loan
amount (see question 116) in terms of per
$1,000
$90 \times 7.69 = \$692.10$
$90,000 \times 0.085 = \$7,650$
$7,650 \div 12 = \$637.50$
$692.10 - \$637.50 = \$54.60$
$54.60 \times 2 = \$109.20$
$90,000 - \$109.20 = \$89,890.80$

118. **B.** *Note:* This problem assumes the monthly
payment includes insurance and taxes and
these are paid in equal installments.
($25,000 \div 1,000) \times \$8.50 = \$212.50$
$540 \div 3 = \$180$; break down 3-year loan to
yearly payment
$180 \div 12 = \$15$; break down yearly loan
payment to monthly
$405 \div 12 = \$33.75$ monthly tax payment
$212.50 + \$15 + \$33.75 = \$261.25$ total for
first month's payment

119. **A.** $95,000 \times 0.06 = \$5,700$
$95,000 - \$5,700 - \$33,000 - \$450 - \$90 -$
$15,000 = \$40,760$
$40,760 + \$750 = \$41,510$

120. **B.** $47,000 \times 0.9 = \$42,300$ mortgage loan
(90% of purchase price)
$47,000 - \$42,300 = \$4,700$
$4,700 - \$2,500 = \$2,200$
$2,200 - \$250 = \$1,950$
$1,950 + \$950 = \$2,900$
$42,300 \times 0.04 = \$1,692$
$2,900 + \$1,692 = \$4,592$

121. **A.** $90,000 \times 0.85 = \$76,500$
$76,500 \div 100 \times \$1.10 = \$841.50$

122. **A.** 40 years $\times$ 27.5% = 11 years

123. **C.** *Note:* Loan origination fee and discount points are on the insured portion of the $61,000 loan.

$35,000 × 0.03 = $1,050; amount first $35,000 is reduced (100% − 97% = 3% not covered)

$61,000 − $35,000 = $26,000 remainder of loan

$26,000 × 0.05 = $1,300; amount of remainder reduced (100% − 95% = 5% not covered)

$61,000 − $1,050 − $1,300 = $58,650; amount to apply to loan origination fee and discount points

$58,650 × 0.01 = $586.50 loan origination fee

$58,620 × 0.05 = $2,932.50 discount point fee (each discount point equals 1%)

$2,932.50 + $586.50 = $3,519 total buyer's loan costs

B

Salesperson's Practice Final Examination

This section contains a practice final examination for the salesperson candidate. The best way to prepare for the state exam is to work with exam material similar to what will appear on the actual test. This following test is not, however, a copy of the actual test. The actual test is copyrighted and may not be duplicated. The primary purpose of taking this practice test is to help you realize your weak areas so you can concentrate your studies on those areas.

GENERAL INFORMATION

1. The details about your state test may be found by contacting your state licensing agency at *www.arello.org*. In addition, each testing agency (as noted in the Introduction) prepares a special information bulletin concerning the exam.

2. Battery-operated, hand-held, non-programmable silent calculators may be used, and you will find that the use of a calculator cuts down the amount of time spent on the math questions.

SPECIFIC INFORMATION

The salesperson examination typically is divided into two separate tests, the national and the state portions. The national portion contains roughly 80 questions on a variety of subject areas. The approximate percentage distribution of each subject has been included.

The state portion tests your knowledge of the state legislation and real estate commission rules. Also included are questions dealing with transfer taxes, property taxes, civil rights, groundwater hazard statements, declarations of value, seller's property disclosure, and state-specific antitrust legislation.

EXAM CONTENT OUTLINE AND ALLOCATED PERCENTAGE

Your sales examination may contain five pretest questions that are *not* counted toward your score. These questions are used to gather statistics on performance and to help assess appropriateness for use on future examinations. Because pretest questions look exactly like questions that are scored, you should answer all the questions on the examination.

The following examination content outline and possible question count is appropriate for real estate salespersons.

    I.   **Real property characteristics, definitions, ownership, restrictions, and transfer (approximately 16 questions)**
- A. Definitions, descriptions, and ways to hold title
  1. Elements of real and personal property
  2. Property description and legal description
  3. Estates in real property
  4. Forms, rights, interests, and obligations of ownership
- B. Land use controls and restrictions
  1. Public (e.g., zoning, taxation, police power)
  2. Private (e.g., liens, encumbrances, recording and priorities, subdivision/association rules)
- C. Transfer/alienation of title to real property
  1. Voluntary and involuntary
  2. Deeds, warranties, and defects in title

  II.   **Assessing and explaining property valuation and the appraisal process (approximately 10 questions)**
- A. Principles, types, and estimates of property value
- B. Influences on property value
- C. Approaches to property valuation and investment analysis

 III.   **Financing the transaction and settlement procedures (8–12 questions)**
- A. Financing components
  1. Financing instruments (e.g., notes, mortgages, contract for deed, deed of trust)
  2. Sources (e.g., primary and secondary mortgage markets, seller financing)
  3. Types of loans
  4. Financing concepts and terminology
- B. Lender requirements and obligations
- C. Settlement procedures
- D. Settlement documents (e.g., title review, RESPA)
- E. Financing costs, property taxation, proration calculations, and other closing costs

  IV.   **Leases, rents, and property management (6 questions)**
- A. Types and elements of leasehold estates, leases, lease clauses, and rental agreements
- B. Lessor and lessee rights, responsibilities, and recourse
- C. Management contracts and obligations of parties

V. **Agency relationships with buyers and sellers, contracts, and federal requirements (28–32 questions)**
   A. Contract elements, types (e.g., valid, enforceable), and terminology
   B. Agency employment contracts, listing, and buyer
   C. Purchase/sales contracts and contingencies
   D. General agency relationships, fiduciary responsibilities, and ethical issues
   E. Property conditions and disclosures (e.g., property, environmental)
   F. Procedures and laws governing real estate activities (e.g., federal Fair Housing Act, Americans with Disabilities Act, antitrust, marketing controls)

VI. **Real Estate Calculations (5–10 questions)**

SAMPLE SALESPERSON REAL ESTATE LICENSING EXAMINATION

1. A buyer and a seller agree to the purchase of a house for $200,000 in which the buyer will make a $30,000 down payment and the seller will take back a ten-year purchase-money mortgage for the balance. There is nothing in the contract to indicate that time is of the essence. The sales contract will be valid even though the parties fail to provide for which of the following?
   A. Closing date
   B. Interest rate
   C. Signatures on the contract
   D. Term of loan

2. If an option to purchase is exercised, which of the following is *TRUE?*
   A. The option money is automatically applied to the purchase price.
   B. The optionor can be forced to sell the property.
   C. The notice to exercise must be in writing.
   D. Closing takes place the day the option is exercised.

3. A binder given by a buyer in a real estate transaction
   A. must be monetary.
   B. may be withdrawn by the buyer any time before the seller signs his or her acceptance.
   C. draws interest in favor of the broker.
   D. must exceed 5 percent of sales price.

4. Which of the following is *TRUE* under a contract of sale in which the date of occupancy is later than the settlement date?
   A. The buyer does not acquire legal title upon settlement.
   B. The contract should provide whether the seller is to pay any rent.
   C. The buyer cannot obtain hazard insurance.
   D. The seller is the legal owner until occupancy is ended.

5. If a lessee defaults on a lease and abandons the property in good condition, for which of the following could the lessee be held liable?
   A. Balance of the rent plus forfeiture of the security deposit
   B. Balance of the rent plus the cost to find a new tenant
   C. Decrease in the market value of the property
   D. Balance of the rent

6. Which of the following parties to a long-term ground lease is the holder of the leased fee?
   A. Lessor
   B. Lessee
   C. Grantee
   D. Grantor

7. A seller's broker was working with a buyer on an exclusive-authorization-to-sell listing, and presented an offer at less than the listed price. At the same time, the owner was dealing with another buyer who offered more money for the property and all in cash. The owner sold to the buyer at the higher price for all cash. The broker is entitled to
   A. a reasonable commission based upon the lower offer.
   B. stop the sale of the property.
   C. void the sale.
   D. a commission based upon the higher selling price.

8. Which one of the following is *TRUE* when the seller takes back a mortgage from the buyer as part payment for the sale?
   A. The seller is entitled to possession of the property until the debt is paid.
   B. The seller retains legal title.
   C. The buyer may place no second mortgage on the property.
   D. This is a purchase-money mortgage.

9. The standard of ethical behavior for REALTORS® is called
   A. agency law.
   B. contract law.
   C. the Code of Ethics.
   D. the Real Estate Code.

10. A mortgage that covers several parcels of land and contains a provision for partial release upon the sale of an individual parcel is a(n)
    A. direct-reduction mortgage.
    B. amortized mortgage.
    C. blanket mortgage.
    D. declining-balance mortgage.

11. Which of the following facts need *NOT* be disclosed?
    A. The seller has AIDS.
    B. Water leaks through a wall of the basement.
    C. There are high levels of radon.
    D. The existence of asbestos wrap around the heating pipes.

12. Brownfields refer to
    A. wetlands.
    B. tiled agricultural areas.
    C. deserted toxic industrial sites.
    D. new commercial developments.

13. In order to buy an investment property, a purchaser buys time to raise the money by entering into a(n)
    A. sale-leaseback.
    B. protection agreement.
    C. contract for deed.
    D. option to buy.

14. If the foreclosure sale proceeds are less than the outstanding debt and foreclosure expenses, which of the following remedies is available?
    A. There is no remedy.
    B. The mortgagee must absorb the loss, as the mortgagor is liable only for foreclosure expenses.
    C. Owner has the statutory right of redemption.
    D. Mortgagee may obtain a deficiency judgment against the mortgagor.

15. What type of report does a developer read to find population and median household income information?
    A. Neighborhood analysis
    B. Marketing analysis
    C. Traffic count
    D. Demographics

16. Fannie Mae can do all of the following *EXCEPT*
    A. purchase conventional loans.
    B. sell mortgages to institutions.
    C. buy FHA-VA loans.
    D. originate federal loans.

17. A land contract (installment contract or agreement of sale) and a purchase-money mortgage are similar in that
    A. the seller assumes no financial risk.
    B. the title is conveyed immediately to the buyer.
    C. the seller is the lender.
    D. a mortgage is required.

18. A VA loan may be granted for the purchase of a one-family to four-family dwelling if the
    A. veteran certifies the rent collected will equal the mortgage payments.
    B. loan will be amortized for not more than 20 years.
    C. veteran pays the points.
    D. veteran occupies one of the units.

19. The amount a lender will loan is generally based on the
    A. listed price.
    B. appraised value for loan purposes.
    C. appraised value for loan purposes or the sales price, whichever is lower.
    D. final sales price.

20. Under a Department of Veterans Affairs loan, a veteran can do which of the following?
    A. Transfer his or her VA loan to another home
    B. Sell his or her home and allow a nonveteran buyer to assume the loan without VA approval
    C. Require a veteran buyer to agree in the sale contract to assume the loan and substitute his or her VA eligibility
    D. Obtain the VA loan for a rental property

21. Regulation Z provides a right of rescission
    A. to first mortgages to finance the purchase of a residential condominium unit.
    B. that expires three business days after the date of consummation of the transaction, or the date on which the lender makes material disclosures, whichever is later.
    C. in all credit transactions.
    D. that does not apply to loans made by commercial banks.

22. A person borrowed $85,000 and agreed to repay in monthly installments of $823.76 at 11½ percent annual interest. Of her first month's payment, how much was applied to reduction of principal?
    A. $8.15
    B. $9.18
    C. $91.80
    D. $814.58

23. Serge and Ivana borrowed $85,000 at 11½ percent annual interest. Monthly payments on the loan are $823.76. In addition, they agreed to pay into the "customer trust fund" the pro-rated monthly share of the annual taxes of $625.32, the semiannual lease rent of $720, and a three-year homeowner's insurance policy totaling $586.22. Their monthly payment would be
    A. $1,012.15.
    B. $1,132.15.
    C. $1,164.71.
    D. $1,211.16.

24. On a long-term loan, the amount of semiannual interest is $5,400 at an annual interest rate of 12 percent. How much money is invested?
    A. $648
    B. $45,000
    C. $90,000
    D. $180,000

25. What federal legislation funds the clean-up of toxic waste site?
    A. HUD
    B. CERCLA
    C. Title VIII
    D. Title X

26. Edward and Donna agreed to buy an apartment on the following terms: first mortgage loan on a 90 percent loan-to-value ratio; seller to accept a second mortgage for one-half the remaining balance, the remainder to be paid in cash as down payment. If the down payment was $15,000, what was the amount of the first mortgage loan?
    A. $27,000
    B. $30,000
    C. $270,000
    D. $300,000

27. Which of the following statements regarding deeds is *TRUE?*
    A. The general warranty deed gives the least liability to the grantor.
    B. The quitclaim deed gives the least protection to the grantee.
    C. The special warranty deed gives the greatest protection to the grantor.
    D. The bargain and sale deed is unlawful.

28. Hank executes a deed of his farm to Sybil. Hank keeps the deed in his safe deposit box. Upon his death, the box is opened, and attached to the deed is a note to give the deed to Sybil. Who has title to the farm?
    A. Sybil
    B. Hank's heirs
    C. The state
    D. Sybil's heirs

29. Which of the following is covered by the covenant against encumbrances in a general warranty deed?
    A. Undisclosed subsurface waterpipe easement
    B. Restrictive zoning ordinance
    C. Rights of adverse possessor
    D. Mining and water claims

30. The clause that defines or limits the quantity of the estate being conveyed is the
    A. partition clause.
    B. revocation clause.
    C. habendum clause.
    D. reversion clause.

31. Which of the following parties is in the weakest position against a claim of title by a stranger?
    A. A nonoccupant holder of a warranty deed
    B. A nonoccupant holder of an unrecorded quitclaim deed
    C. One who holds an unrecorded deed
    D. One who holds a recorded quitclaim deed to the property

32. As far as its validity between grantor and grantee is concerned, a deed that is not dated, acknowledged, or recorded is
    A. invalid because of these omissions.
    B. void.
    C. revocable by the grantor.
    D. valid despite these omissions.

33. One who owns a life estate *CANNOT*
    A. sell one's interest.
    B. mortgage one's interest.
    C. devise one's interest.
    D. lease one's interest.

34. Restrictions in a deed that benefit only the grantor
    A. can be removed by the grantor's issuing a quitclaim deed.
    B. must be more lenient than the current zoning use.
    C. must be more strict than the current zoning use.
    D. are irrevocable.

35. To the holder of the dominant tenement, an easement is a(n)
    A. encumbrance.
    B. appurtenance.
    C. license.
    D. encroachment.

36. After Conrad purchases a property, he has a survey made and finds that his neighbor, through error, has recently built an ornamental fence two feet over on Conrad's land. This would be a basic example of
    A. a party wall.
    B. an encroachment.
    C. an appurtenance.
    D. adverse possession.

37. Riparian rights are those rights possessed by a(n)
    A. owner living in a townhouse subdivision.
    B. owner living on a waterway.
    C. corporation.
    D. business trust.

38. The word *fee* used in connection with real property means
    A. the money charged by a broker for services.
    B. an estate of inheritance.
    C. the charge made for searching title.
    D. the leased land.

39. When a person dies intestate and no heirs can be found for intestate succession, real property will revert to the government through a process known as
    A. reconveyance.
    B. reversion.
    C. escheat.
    D. succession.

40. What document is prepared to evidence that personal property is pledged to secure a loan?
    A. Bill of sale
    B. Chattel mortgage
    C. Bargain and sale deed
    D. Partial release

41. Which is *TRUE* about condominium or cooperative ownership?
    A. In a condominium, each owner is responsible for his or her own mortgage payments, as well as those of fellow owners.
    B. In a typical cooperative association, if one or more members fail to pay their share of the mortgage, the other owners must make payments for the defaulting members, or risk foreclosure on the entire property.
    C. In a condominium, usually there is a blanket mortgage on the common area.
    D. In a cooperative, each owner receives an apartment deed.

42. What can the taxing agency do when a condominium apartment owner defaults in paying state real property taxes?
    A. Seek to foreclose against the apartment
    B. Seek to recover from the condominium association
    C. Force the owner to forfeit a bond
    D. Place a lien on the common elements

43. Under the federal Fair Housing Act, it is permissible to
    A. approve a loan to a person who has stated the intention to rent the property only to members of a minority group.
    B. refuse to grant loans on the basis of the financial condition of an applicant who is a member of a minority group.
    C. require the applicant to sign a form that lists religion, sex, and marital status.
    D. deny housing to a pregnant woman.

44. Which of the following is permissible under the federal Fair Housing Act?
    A. Charging a higher interest rate on a loan by a savings association on the grounds the loan applicant intends to rent part of the subject property to members of a certain minority group
    B. Advertising property for sale only in publications primarily aimed at a particular ethnic group and using models of only that same ethnic group
    C. Refusing a loan on a house based on the religion of the applicant
    D. Denying housing based on a prior violent criminal conviction of the applicant

45. Sam decides to use the services of OK Realty to locate a suitable home for his minority family. OK Realty assigns Tom, its only minority salesperson, who avoids showing Sam any properties outside minority neighborhoods despite the fact Sam has indicated interest in houses in an all-white district. OK Realty's discriminating actions can be *BEST* described as
    A. redlining.
    B. blockbusting.
    C. steering.
    D. conciliation.

46. A salesperson gets 60 percent of the commission on property she lists and sells for the firm. Which of the following transactions will earn the *MOST* money for the salesperson?
    A. $60,500 at 7%
    B. $63,500 at 6.5%
    C. $63,750 at 6.5%
    D. $64,000 at 6%

47. Working for the A-1 Real Estate Agency, the listing salesperson gets 20 percent of the total commission on a sale. The selling salesperson gets 45 percent of the remainder. How much would Shay receive if he were both the listing and selling salesperson on a $115,500 sale at 6 percent commission?
    A. $2,494.80
    B. $3,880.80
    C. $4,504.50
    D. $6,930.00

48. An owner requests a broker to list a property for sale at $70,000. On inspection, the broker believes the property is worth $80,000. The broker should
    A. get a net listing for the property at $70,000.
    B. buy the property herself for $70,000.
    C. suggest that the owner list the property for $75,000 to have room for bargaining.
    D. inform the seller that the property is worth $80,000.

49. A fiduciary relationship could exist between a principal and all of the following *EXCEPT* a(n)
    A. trustee.
    B. administrator.
    C. appraiser.
    D. receiver.

50. A real estate salesperson might lawfully accept an extra commission in a difficult sale from
    A. an appreciative seller.
    B. a thankful buyer.
    C. an employing broker.
    D. the mortgage lender.

51. When money is deposited in a client trust account, part of which will be used to pay the broker's commission
    A. the broker can withdraw his or her share of the money before the real estate transaction is consummated or terminated.
    B. accurate records must be kept on the account.
    C. interest on the account is by law the property of the broker.
    D. the salespeople can withdraw money prior to closing.

52. One who has the right to sign the name of a principal to a contract of sale is a(n)
    A. attorney-in-fact.
    B. broker with a listing.
    C. special agent.
    D. attorney at law.

53. The relationship between a real estate agent and a principal is *MOST* similar to which of the following?
    A. Optionee and optionor
    B. Vendee and vendor
    C. Trustee and beneficiary
    D. Mortgagee and mortgagor

54. A property manager's duties typically include all of the following *EXCEPT*
    A. collecting rents.
    B. making minor repairs.
    C. marketing space.
    D. investing profits from client's properties.

55. All of the following are a valid operating expense for a building manager to put into a budget *EXCEPT*
    A. heating oil.
    B. cleaning supplies.
    C. foundation repairs.
    D. management fees.

56. A standard form policy of title insurance does *NOT* protect against loss resulting from
    A. encroachment on the property.
    B. liens and encumbrances of record.
    C. lack of capacity of the grantor.
    D. forgery in the chain of title.

57. Escrow or a settlement agent is often used for all of the following purposes *EXCEPT* to
    A. determine that outstanding and unpaid liens will be satisfied.
    B. see that the purchase price is paid and all checks have cleared the bank.
    C. handle the signing of documents and the closing.
    D. prepare the legal and tax documents.

58. A deed made and delivered but *NOT* recorded is
    A. valid between the parties and valid as to third parties with notice.
    B. valid between the parties and valid as to subsequent recorded interests.
    C. valid between the parties and invalid as to subsequent donees of the property.
    D. invalid between the parties.

59. Recordation of documents performs which of the following functions?
    A. Insures title against loss due to third-party claims
    B. Cures major defects in title
    C. Gives constructive notice of documents
    D. Handles the closing of real estate transactions

60. An insurance policy purchased January 10, 1989, was assumed by the purchaser effective October 30, 1990. Cost of the policy was $356.80 for a three-year period. The policy proration would be
    A. $142.05 credit to purchaser, debit to seller.
    B. $142.05 credit to seller, debit to purchaser.
    C. $214.75 credit to purchaser, debit to seller.
    D. $214.75 credit to seller, debit to purchaser.

61. Prorate the prepaid taxes as of settlement date (June 15) if a property is valued at $120,000 and assessed at 55 percent value with a tax rate of $3.20 per $100 of valuation on a calendar year basis.
    A. Debit both $968
    B. Credit both $968
    C. Credit buyer $1,144, debit seller $968
    D. Debit buyer $1,144, credit seller $1,144

62. Nicole sold her house August 31 for $112,000. Her mortgage balance is $63,200, and she has paid the taxes of $684 through December 31. She pays 6 percent commission to the agent. What is the amount due to the seller before other closing costs?
    A. $42,308
    B. $63,428
    C. $105,280
    D. $105,508

63. Buck, as manager of the Lua Overlook Apartments, collects $450 per month on each of six apartments. He makes monthly disbursements of $180 for utilities and $85 for insurance. If his management fee is 10 percent of gross rent per month, how much does he send the owner each month?
    A. $2,065
    B. $2,165
    C. $2,265
    D. $2,365

64. A house sold for $115,500, with the purchaser assuming a mortgage loan of $83,526.23. Tax rates were as follows: state recording tax, $0.05 per $100 or part thereof; local recording tax, $0.15 per $100 or part thereof; state transfer tax, $0.50 per $500 or part thereof, less assumed mortgage indebtedness. What were the total taxes applicable to this sale?
    A. $32
    B. $89.75
    C. $231
    D. $263

65. A 10-year-old, well-maintained house that is 36 ft. × 42 ft. is on a lot currently valued at $15,600. The current reproduction cost is $52 per sq. ft., excluding depreciation. The total depreciation for this structure is charged at $0.75 per sq. ft. What is the current value of the property to the nearest thousand?
    A. $79,000
    B. $93,000
    C. $94,000
    D. $95,000

66. Two years ago a property was assessed at $63,000. The tax rate was 90 mills. When the community was reappraised last year, the assessment was up 10 percent, but the tax rate was down 10 percent. The taxes paid were
    A. down by $56.70.
    B. the same.
    C. up by $47.80.
    D. up by $56.70.

67. Florinda is interested in an income property from which she would realize $1,500 per month net. If investment capital is attracted to a 15 percent return, what is the maximum she should pay for the property?
    A. $22,500
    B. $100,000
    C. $120,000
    D. $225,000

68. John is developing a subdivision with lots from ¼ to ¾ acre. There are four floor plans available for the houses—1,000 sq. ft., 1,450 sq. ft., 1,600 sq. ft., and 1,850 sq. ft. The lots sell for $65,000 an acre and the houses for $63.50 a square foot. What is the difference between the least and most expensive home?
    A. $79,750
    B. $86,475
    C. $93,432
    D. $166,225

69. Physical deterioration *MOST* closely means
    A. obsolescence.
    B. wear and tear.
    C. reversion.
    D. recapture.

70. If the reproduction cost shows a higher dollar amount than the appraised value, which of the following *MOST* probably has occurred?
    A. Accrued depreciation
    B. Excessive appraisal
    C. Economic obsolescence
    D. Capitalization

71. Which of the following is *TRUE* of real estate appraisers?
    A. They may not advertise.
    B. They usually base their fees on a percentage of appraised value.
    C. They must have a professional designation such as MAI, SREA.
    D. None of the above.

72. All of the following are examples of external obsolescence *EXCEPT*
    A. population density.
    B. direct effect of inclement weather.
    C. zoning.
    D. special assessments.

73. In using the market comparison approach to appraisal, the appraiser considers the
    A. sales price of comparable properties.
    B. acquisition cost to the present owner.
    C. property tax rates.
    D. tax benefits.

74. A variance could be which of the following?
    A. A large, new supermarket located in an area zoned for small retail shops
    B. An old grocery store located in an area recently rezoned residential
    C. A single-family home in a residential zone
    D. A home more expensive than adjacent homes

75. The difference between police power and eminent domain can be *BEST* determined by whether
    A. the action was by sovereign power or by statute.
    B. any compensation was paid to the owner.
    C. the owner's use was affected.
    D. the improvements are to be razed.

76. Which of the following statements is *TRUE?*
    A. All liens are encumbrances.
    B. All encumbrances are liens.
    C. Specific liens affect all property of the debtor located in the state.
    D. Judgments are specific liens.

77. Which of the following liens would have top priority in the event of foreclosure of the subject property?
    A. State income tax lien recorded first
    B. Federal estate tax lien recorded second
    C. Mechanic's lien for work commenced before any other lien was recorded
    D. State property tax lien recorded last

78. The lender wants to ensure the first priority of its lien. The lender should do all of the following *EXCEPT*
    A. make sure that all other liens are removed or subordinated from the property being used as collateral.
    B. make sure the borrower has an absolute estate with no liens.
    C. obtain an ALTA title insurance policy.
    D. verify the health of the borrower.

79. The gross income multiplier is calculated by dividing the sales price by the
    A. monthly net income.
    B. monthly gross income.
    C. annual net income.
    D. annual gross income.

80. All of the following appear in a promissory note *EXCEPT*
    A. interest.
    B. commencement date.
    C. term of loan.
    D. purchase price of property.

ANSWERS

Note: Where appropriate, assume V = Value, R = Rate, I = Income.

1. **A.** When a contract does not specify a date for performance, a court would probably consider the contract valid if the closing date was within a reasonable time. A court would not make the same assumption on an essential term, such as an interest rate or the parties' signatures.

2. **B.** Whether the option money is applied to the purchase price is a negotiable point. The optionee can obtain specific performance against the optionor.

3. **B.** A binder is like a deposit receipt. Although it usually is money, it could be some other form of valuable consideration (a boat or even a promise to do something).

4. **B.** In a late occupancy, the seller gets to stay in possession after closing. Some provision should be made as to rent, and the rental agreement should be in writing.

5. **D.** In no event could the lessee be responsible for more rent than if he or she had not

breached the lease and had remained for the full term. The key word here is *plus*.

6. **A.** The lessor holds the leased fee, which is valued as the discounted value of the rent plus the value of the reversionary interest. The lessee holds the leasehold estate.

7. **D.** Under the exclusive-authorization-to-sell listing, the broker earns commission based on the sales price, regardless of who is the procuring cause of the sale.

8. **D.** Possession and title pass to the buyer, but the seller retains a security interest pending full payment of the debt. Sellers usually do not restrict junior financing.

9. **C.** The Code of Ethics is the standard of ethical behavior for REALTORS®. Sometimes the Code of Ethics establishes obligations that are higher than those mandated by law and in those instances where the two may conflict, the obligations of the law take precedence.

10. **C.** Blanket mortgages are popular in subdivision developments. It is important to check if there are unambiguous partial release provisions.

11. **A.** People with AIDS are a protected class and would not be discussed. Known health and safety concerns must be disclosed.

12. **C.** Brownfields refer to deserted toxic industrial sites.

13. **D.** An option to buy allows the purchaser to line up financing or to continue looking during the option period.

14. **D.** In a few states, however, such as California, there can be no deficiency judgments on purchase-money mortgages. In effect, they are treated as nonrecourse loans.

15. **D.** Demographics are studies that identify population and median household income information.

16. **D.** Fannie Mae operates only in the secondary mortgage market.

17. **C.** Under a land contract, the seller retains legal title as security, whereas under the purchase-money mortgage, the seller retains no title interest in the property, only the lien interest of a mortgagee.

18. **D.** The only requirement is that the veteran certify he or she will occupy one of the units.

19. **C.** Typically, the appraised value is lower in a seller's market.

20. **C.** The VA loans are not transferable by the veteran to his or her new home. The veteran would need to have eligibility restored prior to getting a loan on another home. VA loans are assumable with prior approval.

21. **B.** First liens to acquire or construct a principal residence (including condominiums) would be exempt. The right of rescission is designed to protect the existing homeowner from losing his or her home (including condominiums and mobile homes) due to a credit transaction that uses a principal residence as security. Note that there is now a three-year statute of limitations if no disclosures are made.

22. **B.** $85,000 × 0.115 = $9,775/year
$9,775 ÷ 12 = $814.58
$823.76 − $814.58 = $9.18

23. **A.** Tax = $625.32 ÷ 12 = $52.11/month Lease = $720 ÷ 6 = $120/month
Insurance = $586.22 ÷ 36 = $16.28/month
Loan = $823.76/month
Payment = $1,012.15 total

24. **C.** ? × 0.12 = $10,800
$10,800 ÷ 0.12 = $90,000

25. **B.** CERCLA is the federal Comprehensive Environmental Response, Compensation, and Liability Act administered by the EPA. It funds the abatement of toxic sites (Superfund) and establishes a process for identifying responsible parties and forcing them to clean up or pay for the cleaning up of those toxic sites.

26. **C.** $15,000 down + $15,000 second mortgage = $30,000
? × 0.10 = $30,000
$30,000 ÷ 0.10 = $300,000 × 0.90 = $270,000

27. **B.** As far as the grantor's liability is concerned, the general warranty gives the most exposure, then comes the special warranty deed (only covers the time the grantor owned the property) and then the quitclaim deed (no liability).

28. **B.** There is no delivery because Hank did not give up control over the deed as he would have if he had handed it to Sybil or put it in an escrow. To accomplish his purpose, Hank should have prepared a will.

29. **A.** Because the easement was not disclosed, the grantee could recover for the loss in value caused by this easement, which is an encumbrance. Zoning laws are public restrictions and matters of public knowledge and thus not covered under this covenant.

30. **C.** Also called the "to have and to hold" clause, it is not an essential element for a valid deed but is customarily included. It would indicate if the grantor is conveying a fee simple or life estate, for example.

31. **B.** This grantee has given no constructive notice of his rights (recording or possession) and has no warranties to assert against the grantor in the event the stranger proves to have a superior title. Possession gives constructive notice (actual notice if a person is aware of the possession).

32. **D.** The date is useful to prove when it was delivered but it is not required, nor is recording or acknowledgment.

33. **C.** A *devise* is a transfer by will (do not confuse with *demise,* which is a transfer by lease). There is no estate left after the owner of the life estate (life tenant) dies. The buyer, lender, or lessee takes an interest subject to the life estate so each one's interest ceases when the life estate ceases. Lenders rarely lend on a life estate; and, if so, they may require a term life insurance policy as further security. Incidentally, the buyer would own a "life estate pur autre vie."

34. **A.** For example, assume a grantor of Lot 1 reserved an easement to benefit neighboring Lot 2. At any time, he could release the reservation interest in Lot 1 by way of a quitclaim deed. A more lenient deed restriction limiting a building to three stories would not control over a zoning law that permits only two stories, and vice versa.

35. **B.** To the servient tenement, the easement is an encumbrance. To the dominant tenement, it is something that attaches to the land and benefits it.

36. **B.** Conrad could bring a lawsuit to seek removal of the fence. Failure to do so for a long enough time might result in the neighbor obtaining title to the disputed land by adverse possession. This would be an encumbrance on Conrad's land, not an appurtenance. A party wall is located on the property line.

37. **B.** Such riparian owner would be the beneficiary of any increased land due to accretion.

38. **B.** Fee refers to a fee simple, which is a freehold estate of inheritance. The broker typically earns a commission.

39. **C.** Most state laws allow a long period between death and title passing to the government so that next of kin can file claims.

40. **B.** In those states that have adopted the Uniform Commercial Code, the chattel mortgage is called a *security agreement* and it is a financing statement that is recorded.

41. **B.** In a condominium, the owners are not responsible for the mortgage payments of other owners. But in a cooperative, there is usually one blanket mortgage, so all owners must make up the defaults of others to avoid foreclosure of the one mortgage. Of course, they would have a lien on the defaulting owner's interest to the extent of their cash advances. Co-op owners receive a proprietary lease, not an apartment deed.

42. **A.** Most state laws require that state real property taxes be assessed against individual units and not the property as a whole.

43. **B.** In choice (A), the borrower would be practicing discrimination in his or her rental program, so the lender cannot be a party to this. A lender can refuse a loan for valid credit reasons, but not to discriminate against minority groups.

44. **D.** The loan decision cannot be based on ethnic reasons, only economic reasons. The federal Fair Housing Act also prohibits discriminatory solicitation, which encompasses this type of selective advertising as indirect dis-

crimination—it is selected on ethnic grounds. A proposed tenant who poses a threat to others can be denied housing.

45. **C.** Steering is the unlawful practice of discouraging the sale or rental of a dwelling because of the presence or absence of minority neighbors. Referring minority prospects to minority salespersons may be unlawful, because it treats people differently because of minority status, even though there may be some valid business purpose.

46. **A.** $A = \$4,144 \times 0.60 = \$2,486$
$B = \$3,840 \times 0.60 = \$2,304$
$C = \$4,128 \times 0.60 = \$2,477$
$D = \$4,235 \times 0.60 = \$2,541$

47. **B.** $\$115,500 \times 0.06 = \$6,930$
$\$6,930 \times 0.20 = \$1,386$
$\$6,930 - \$1,386 = \$5,544$
$\$5,544 \times 0.45 = \$2,494.80$
$\$2,494.80 + \$1,386 = \$3,880.80$

48. **D.** The broker has a fiduciary duty to protect the best interests of the client, which, in this case, would be to inform the owner of the true worth of the property and then discuss an appropriate listing price.

49. **C.** The appraiser is hired to render an independent evaluation of the property and is generally not an agent entrusted with the client's properties.

50. **C.** A salesperson cannot receive compensation directly from anyone other than the broker.

51. **B.** The broker cannot withdraw money even though commission has been earned, unless the broker has the written consent of both seller and buyer.

52. **A.** Brokers have too limited an authority under most listings. They could sign if they were attorney-in-fact under a power of attorney.

53. **C.** The trustee in a deed of trust holds title to the secured property for the benefit of the beneficiary (lender).

54. **D.** Property managers handle rents, minor repairs, and marketing of leases. They are not responsible for making investment deci-

sions, such as handling real estate profits for their clients.

55. **C.** Foundation work would not be a regularly occurring expenditure.

56. **A.** Encroachments would be physical matters off the public records (such as overhanging eaves) that could be covered only in an extended title insurance policy.

57. **D.** Escrow will often use the buyer's money to pay off unpaid taxes and mortgages so the buyer will get the free and clear title promised by seller. Escrow does not act as the attorney or accountant.

58. **A.** If the deed is not recorded, a subsequent purchaser for value (from the original grantor) without notice of the first unrecorded deed could get superior title by recording this subsequent deed first. Donees are not protected under the recording law (nor are devisees).

59. **C.** The recording system neither insures nor corrects title defects; it merely gives constructive notice of the rights of people in certain property.

60. **B.** $21\frac{2}{3}$ months elapsed since January 10, 1989.
$\$356.80 \div 36 = \$9.91$ month
$21\frac{2}{3} \times \$9.91 = \$214.75$
$\$356.80 - \$214.75 = \$142.05$ seller has already paid for the unused period

61. **D.** $\$120,000 \times 0.55 = \$66,000$
$60 \times (320/100) = \$2,112/\text{year}$
$\$2,122 \div 12 = \$176/\text{month}$
$\$176 \times 6.5 \text{ months} = \$1,144$
Seller has prepaid for the whole year, and there is a 6.5-month unused portion that the buyer will benefit from unless some adjustment (proration) is made. In tax prorations, the debit and credit amounts are equal.

62. **A.** $\$112,000 \times 0.94 = \$105,280 - \$63,200 = \$42,080$
$\frac{1}{3}$ year: $\$684 \div 3 = \$228 + \$42,080 = \$42,308$

63. **B.** $\$450 \times 6 = \$2,700 - \$535 = \$2,165$
$\$2,700 \times 0.10 = \$270$
$\$270 + \$180 + \$85 = \$535$

64. **D.** $1,155 \times 0.05 = \$57.75$
$1,155 \times 0.15 = \$173.25$
$\$115,500.00 - \$83,526.23 = \$31,973.77$
$\$31,973.77 \div 500 = 63.9$ (approximately 64)
$64 \times 0.50 = 32$
$\$57.75 + \$173.25 + \$32.00 = \$263.00$

65. **B.** $36 \times 42 = \$1,512$
$\$1,512 \times 52 = \$78,624$
$\$78,624 + \$15,600 = \$94,224 - \$1,134 =$
$\$93,090$
$\$1,512 \times 0.75 = \$1,134$

66. **A.** First assessment—$\$63,000 \times 9\% = \$5,670$
Second assessment—$\$63,000 \times 1.10$
$= \$69,300 \times 8.1\% = \$5,613.30$
$\$5,670 - 5,613.30 = $ Down by $\$56.70$

67. **C.** $\$1,500/\text{month} \times 12 \text{ months} = \$18,000$
$? \times 0.15 = \$18,000$
$\$18,000 \div 0.15 = \$120,000$

68. **B.**   *Least:*

$0.25 \times \$65,000 = \$16,250$

$+ 1,000 \times \$63.50 = \underline{+63,500}$

$\$79,750$

Most:

$0.75 \times \$65,000 = \$ 48,750$

$+ 1,850 \times \$63.50 = \underline{+117,475}$

$\$166,225$

$\underline{- 79,750}$

Difference: $\$ 86,475$

69. **B.** Loss in value due to wear and tear is physical deterioration.

70. **A.** If it costs $100,000 to reproduce a five-year-old building valued at $92,000, there has been an adjustment made for $8,000 of depreciation over the five years.

71. **D.** Appraisers' fees are based upon the time and expenses; it would be unethical to have a contingent appraisal fee.

72. **B.** Population changes, changes in zoning, or an unusually high assessment might cause external obsolescence of the property. Direct effect of the elements (such as wind, snow) could result in physical deterioration.

73. **A.** Because the market comparison approach uses prices of recently sold comparables, the acquisition cost of the property is irrelevant.

74. **A.** Choice (B) is an example of a nonconforming use.

75. **B.** If the value of property is lessened by government regulation under the police power as opposed to taking under eminent domain, there is no just compensation paid.

76. **A.** Judgments are general liens. Easements are encumbrances but not liens.

77. **D.** Priority typically depends on date of recordation except in cases of state real property tax liens and special assessments.

78. **D.** Prior liens should be removed or placed junior through subordination. The lender usually would not want to lend on a conditional fee simple estate.

79. **D.** The gross income multiplier, used to compare investment property in the market comparison appraisal method, is the ratio between the gross income and the sales price.

80. **D.** The purchase price is found in the sales contract; the note states the amount of the loan.

C

Broker's Practice Final Examination

This section contains a practice final examination for the broker candidate. The best way to prepare for the exam is to work with test material similar to what will appear on the actual test. The purpose of this test is to help you realize your weak areas so you can better concentrate on those areas that need attention. For an additional exercise in test taking, broker candidates should consider taking the salesperson's practice final examination as well.

GENERAL INFORMATION

1. The details about your state test may be found by contacting your state licensing agency at *www.arello.org.* In addition, each testing agency (as noted in the Introduction) prepares a special information bulletin concerning the exam.

2. Battery-operated, hand-held, non-programmable silent calculators may be used, and you will find that the use of a calculator cuts down the amount of time spent on the math questions.

3. In most states, the required passing percentages are about 5 percent higher for brokers than salespersons.

4. The content for the broker's examination is pretty much the same as the salesperson's examination *except* there are more questions on the broker's test that deal with trust account laws, commercial and investment real estate, property management, and brokerage operations.

SPECIFIC INFORMATION

The broker's examination typically is divided into two separate tests, the national and the state portions. The national portion contains roughly 80 questions on a variety of subject areas. The approximate percentage distribution of each subject has been included.

The state portion tests your knowledge of the state legislation and real estate commission rules including trust account laws. Also included are questions dealing with transfer taxes, property taxes, civil rights, groundwater hazard statements, declarations of value, seller's property disclosure and state-specific antitrust legislation. Other areas to review include state statutes dealing with condominiums, subdivisions, local contracts, fair housing, and administrative hearing procedures.

EXAM CONTENT OUTLINE

The national portion of the real estate exam is made up of 80 scored questions, which are distributed as noted in the following content outline. Approximately 5 percent of the scored questions on the national examination will involve mathematical calculations.

The broker examination may contain five pretest questions that are *not* counted toward your score. These questions are used to gather statistics on performance and to help assess appropriateness for use on future examinations. Because pretest questions look exactly like questions that are scored, you should answer all the questions on the examination.

The following examination content outline is appropriate for real estate brokers.

  I.   **Real property characteristics, definitions, ownership, restrictions, and transfer (approximately 18 questions)**
     A. Definitions, descriptions, and ways to hold title
         1. Elements of real and personal property
         2. Property description and legal description
         3. Estates in real property
         4. Forms, rights, interests, and obligations of ownership
     B. Land use controls and restrictions
         1. Public (e.g., zoning, taxation, police power)
         2. Private (e.g., liens, encumbrances, recording and priorities, subdivision/association rules)
     C. Transfer/alienation of title to real property
         1. Voluntary and involuntary
         2. Deeds, warranties, and defects in title

  II. **Assessing and explaining property valuation and the appraisal process (approximately 8 questions)**
     A. Principles, types, and estimates of property value
     B. Influences on property value
     C. Approaches to property valuation and investment analysis

 III. **Agency relationships with buyers and sellers, contracts, and federal requirements (approximately 34 questions)**
     A. Contract elements, types (e.g., valid, enforceable) and terminology
     B. Agency employment contracts, listing, and buyer
     C. Purchase/sales contracts and contingencies
     D. General agency relationships and fiduciary responsibilities and ethical issues
     E. Property conditions and disclosures (e.g., property, environmental)

    F. Procedures and laws governing real estate activities (e.g., federal Fair Housing Act, Americans with Disabilities Act, antitrust, marketing controls)

IV. Financing the transaction and settlement procedures (approximately 7 questions)
    A. Financing components
        1. Financing instruments (e.g., notes, mortgages, contract for deed, deed of trust)
        2. Sources (e.g., primary and secondary mortgage markets, seller financing)
        3. Types of loans
        4. Financing concepts and terminology
    B. Lender requirements and obligations
    C. Settlement procedures
    D. Settlement documents (e.g., title review, RESPA)
    E. Financing costs, property taxation, proration calculations, and other closing costs

V. Leases, rents, and property management (approximately 5 questions)
    A. Types and elements of leasehold estates, leases, lease clauses, and rental agreements
    B. Lessor and lessee rights, responsibilities, and recourse
    C. Management contracts and obligations of parties

VI. Real Estate Calculations (approximately 8 questions)

SAMPLE BROKER REAL ESTATE LICENSING EXAMINATION—NATIONAL PORTION

1. After showing a property a number of times and not securing an acceptable offer, the broker, Lawrence, decides to buy the property himself. He must do which of the following?
   A. Wait until the listing expires and then make an offer to purchase
   B. Make his true position known to the seller
   C. Place his license on inactive status
   D. Use a strawman

2. A seller tells her broker that termites have destroyed the floor and the swimming pool is in violation of the city setback requirements. The broker's salesperson must disclose to a prospective buyer all of the following EXCEPT
   A. condition of the floor.
   B. pool violation.
   C. termite problem.
   D. the seller's lowest price.

3. It is an unethical practice for a broker representing a seller to do which of the following?
   A. Advise the seller of the highest price a prospective purchaser is willing to pay
   B. Advise a prospective purchaser of the lowest price the seller is willing to accept
   C. Advise a prospective purchaser of a cracked foundation
   D. Present written offers that are less than the listing price

4. When money is deposited in a client trust account, part of which will be used to pay the broker's commission
   A. the broker can withdraw his or her share of the money before the real estate transaction is consummated or terminated.
   B. accurate records must be kept on the account.
   C. the broker usually keeps interest earned on the account.
   D. the broker can keep earned commissions in the account.

5. In real estate transactions all of the following documents are usually recorded EXCEPT
   A. the deed.
   B. the offer to purchase.
   C. a second mortgage.
   D. a purchase-money mortgage.

6. The recordation of documents performs which of the following functions?
   A. Insures title against loss due to third-party claims
   B. Cures all defects in title
   C. Gives constructive notice of documents
   D. Guarantees good title

7. The Real Estate Settlement Procedures Act (RESPA) is designed to regulate which of the following?
   A. Disclosures of closing information
   B. Procedures for recording titles to real estate
   C. Disclosure of agency
   D. Proration of expenses

8. Except under specific conditions, an agent may serve only one principal at a time; however, a principal may have more than one agent. Which of the following would BEST describe such a situation?
   A. Multiple listing
   B. Open listing
   C. Exclusive agency
   D. Exclusive right to sell

9. A property owner who signed a listing with a broker for 60 days was killed in an accident before the broker procured a buyer. The listing is
   A. binding on the owner's heirs to carry out the owner's promises.
   B. no good as an authorization, but binding if a buyer is secured later.
   C. terminated immediately upon death.
   D. still in effect, as the owner's intent was clear.

10. The phrase "procuring cause" is *MOST* significant to a seller in relation to a(n)
    A. exclusive-agency listing.
    B. open listing.
    C. exclusive-right-to-sell listing.
    D. net listing.

11. A broker, Cynthia, is holding an earnest money deposit, equal to the amount of her commission. The seller, at the closing, not only refuses to pay the broker a commission but demands that the broker should pay him the entire deposit. The broker should
    A. refuse to permit the closing of the deal.
    B. retain the earnest money as commission.
    C. file a complaint with the real estate licensing agency.
    D. pay the earnest money to the seller and then sue for commission.

12. Which of the following would be a debit to the buyer on the settlement statement?
    A. Purchase price
    B. Earnest money deposit given by the buyer
    C. Assumed mortgage
    D. New mortgage

13. An owner's title insurance policy protects the owner against
    A. loss of property due to mortgage foreclosure.
    B. loss of title to a claimant with superior right of title.
    C. lawsuits based on property condition.
    D. loss due to a new tax law.

14. An abstract of title does which of the following?
    A. Insures the title
    B. Gives a history of the title, including the recorded encumbrances against the property
    C. Guarantees the title
    D. Covers encroachments

15. A property manager's duties typically include all of the following *EXCEPT*
    A. collecting rents.
    B. making minor repairs.
    C. marketing space.
    D. investing profits from clients' properties.

16. Arturo purchases a fee simple property for $70,000 by way of assuming a first mortgage of $50,000, paying $10,000 in cash and having the seller take back a purchase-money second mortgage for the balance. There is an existing $5,000 second mortgage on the property. At the close of escrow, what is the correct order in which to record the documents?
    A. The assumption mortgage, the deed, the purchase-money second mortgage
    B. The deed, release of existing second mortgage, assumption agreement, purchase-money mortgage
    C. The purchase-money second mortgage, the deed
    D. The release of existing second mortgage, the deed, the purchase-money second mortgage

17. Which of the following activities is a violation of the federal Fair Housing Act?
    A. A nonprofit church that denies access to its retirement home to a person because of race
    B. A private club that gives preference in renting units to its members at lower rates
    C. An owner-occupant of a duplex who refuses to rent to a woman
    D. Refusing to rent to a teacher

18. A religious group bought a house in a subdivision and organized it into a commune. A broker, eager to make some quick profits, began to canvass this neighborhood, soliciting listings, inquiring whether they knew who had just moved into the area and leaving his business card. Which term *BEST* describes the broker's marketing program?
    A. Redlining
    B. Lawful solicitation
    C. Panic peddling
    D. Steering

19. A broker is discussing a new listing with a prospective minority buyer. The buyer wants to inspect the property immediately, but the listing owner has instructed the broker not to show the house during the owner's three-week absence. The buyer insists on viewing the property. The broker should do which of the following?
    A. Show the property to avoid a violation of the federal Fair Housing Act
    B. Request the Real Estate Commission arbitrate the problem
    C. Explain to the buyer why the property cannot be shown
    D. Cancel the listing

20. A minority group is moving into an area immediately adjacent to an old subdivision. Xanadu Realty offers to list homes in the subdivision at a lower than usual rate if the owners list within 45 days. There is no mention of race, and the broker acts in good faith. Which of the following is *TRUE?*
    A. The broker's license can be revoked.
    B. This is blockbusting.
    C. Such practice is not illegal.
    D. Brokers cannot lower their standard rate of commission.

21. A properly drafted property management agreement should contain all of the following *EXCEPT*
    A. names of owner and manager.
    B. requirement that the manager provide periodic reports to the owner.
    C. fee payment schedule.
    D. list of approved appraisers.

22. A credit score contains how many digits?
    A. Two
    B. Three
    C. Four
    D. Five

23. Prorate the prepaid taxes as of settlement date (June 15) of a property valued at $120,000 and assessed at 55 percent value with a tax rate of $3.20 per $100 of valuation on a calendar year basis.
    A. Credit both $968
    B. Debit both $968
    C. Debit buyer $1,144, credit seller $968
    D. Credit seller $1,144, debit buyer $1,144

24. In order to close a $73,000 purchase of a home, the buyers paid a $5,000 earnest money deposit and secured a 75 percent conventional loan. The buyers' expenses included a 5 point loan discount charge and $425 survey, and they received a $275 credit on the tax proration. How much cash should the buyer bring to final settlement?
    A. $16,138
    B. $17,192
    C. $21,138
    D. $23,412

25. Lorrie sold her house August 31 for $112,000. Her mortgage balance is $63,200, and she has paid the taxes of $684 through the end of the calendar year. She pays 6 percent commission to the agent. What is the amount due Lorrie before other closing costs?
    A. $42,308
    B. $63,428
    C. $105,280
    D. $105,508

26. A lot sold for $1,200 an acre. What would be the minimum selling price for three acres after one year if expenses are $500 per acre and the subdivider wants to make a 10 percent profit?
    A. $4,510
    B. $4,960
    C. $5,100
    D. $5,610

27. Two lots with equal depth have front footages of 200 ft. and 350 ft. If the first lot has 20 acres, how many acres are in the second?
    A. 30
    B. 35
    C. 53
    D. 114

28. Which of the following transactions will net the seller the most money, assuming a broker's fee of 7 percent?
    A. $50,900 sales price and $15 in miscellaneous expenses
    B. $51,200 sales price and $110 in miscellaneous expenses
    C. $52,000 sales price and $294 in miscellaneous expenses
    D. $52,500 sales price and $492 in miscellaneous expenses

29. In which of the following tenancies could a husband or wife seek partition if they cannot agree on the sale of the property?
    A. Tenancy by entirety
    B. Joint tenancy
    C. Tenancy in severalty
    D. Tenancy for years

30. Tom and Sebastian take title to a farm as joint tenants. Assuming Sebastian dies, which of the following is true?
    A. Tom holds title with Sebastian's heirs.
    B. Tom holds title to the whole farm subject to the material interest of Sebastian's surviving wife.
    C. Tom holds title as a tenant in severalty.
    D. Sebastian's share passes according to his will.

31. A proper escrow, once deposited, should be
    A. managed by a licensed broker.
    B. void at the seller's option.
    C. voidable at option of either buyer or seller.
    D. not subject to the control of any one interested party.

32. A deed made and delivered, but not recorded, is
    A. valid between the parties and valid as to third parties with notice.
    B. valid between the parties and valid as to subsequent recorded interests.
    C. valid between the parties and invalid as to subsequent donees of the property.
    D. invalid between the parties.

33. A written and signed real estate contract can be voided for which of the following reasons?
    A. One of the parties failed to read the instrument before signing it.
    B. One of the parties was an unmarried minor at the time the contract was signed.
    C. The market value was less than the sales price.
    D. The market value declines.

34. If an option contract is duly executed by seller and buyer, which of the following is *TRUE?*
    A. The seller may sell or not at his or her option.
    B. The buyer must buy.
    C. The seller must sell, but the buyer need not buy.
    D. It is specifically enforceable by both parties.

35. A prospective purchaser has a legal right to demand which of the following?
    A. A copy of the broker's employment contract with the seller
    B. The return of the earnest money deposit prior to seller's acceptance of the offer to purchase
    C. A copy of the plans and specifications of the home
    D. A copy of the seller's financing statement

36. Which of the following is true regarding the assignment of a sales contract?
    A. An assignment of the sales contract by the buyer generally is valid.
    B. Only the original seller can assign rights.
    C. Assignments are illegal.
    D. Assignment requires the consent of the seller.

37. Homer executes a deed of his farm to Stanley. Homer keeps the deed in his safe deposit box. Upon his death, the box is opened, and attached to the deed is a note to give the deed to Stanley. Who has title to the farm?
    A. Stanley
    B. Homer's heirs
    C. The state
    D. Stanley's heirs

38. The covenant against encumbrances in a deed of conveyance warrants against the existence of all of the following undisclosed matters *EXCEPT*
    A. mortgages against the land.
    B. judgment liens against the land.
    C. easements that adversely affect the land.
    D. zoning ordinances that limit the use of the land.

39. The tenant in common attempts to convey the entire fee simple interest in the property to the grantee using a general warranty deed. Which covenant in the deed would be violated?
    A. Covenant of further assurance
    B. Covenant of seisin
    C. Covenant against encumbrances
    D. Covenant of loyalty

40. The term that *BEST* describes a tenant's interest in the property is a
    A. life estate.
    B. reversionary interest.
    C. remainder interest.
    D. leasehold estate.

41. Assume a mortgaged property is leased. Because of default in payment, the mortgagee forecloses on the mortgage. Which of the following statements is *TRUE* regarding rights under the lease?
    A. The lessee is automatically released from any further obligation on the lease.
    B. The lease continues in effect despite the foreclosure.
    C. The lease is void because the mortgagor has no right to give a lease on mortgaged property.
    D. The lease may be terminated by the mortgagee but not by the lessee.

42. The sale of a property that is under a long-term lease has which of the following effects?
    A. Terminates the lease upon 45 days' notice by new owner
    B. Has no effect on the term of the lease as far as the tenant is concerned
    C. Cannot be made unless the present tenant is notified of the intention to sell and given an opportunity to terminate the lease
    D. Terminates the lease and tenant must negotiate new lease with new owner

43. A tenant's rights under a lease are
    A. terminated when the property is sold.
    B. usually terminated when the lessor dies.
    C. terminated when the property is mortgaged.
    D. terminated upon a surrender.

44. Which of the following statements about types of leases is *TRUE?*
    A. A gross lease is one where the rent is based on an agreed percentage of the gross income.
    B. A net lease is one where the rent is based on a fixed percentage of the net income.
    C. A shopping center lease is often a percentage lease.
    D. An index lease requires constant payments over the term of the lease.

45. When leased premises reach a physical condition whereby the tenant is unable to occupy them for the purpose intended, the situation is legally recognized as a(n)
    A. dispossess eviction.
    B. actual eviction.
    C. constructive eviction.
    D. passive eviction.

46. You can be *MOST* assured that your ownership interest is protected in which of the following cases?
    A. If the owner will give a general warranty deed
    B. If the owner can furnish title insurance
    C. If you retain an attorney
    D. If you use an escrow company

47. All of the following are required for a valid bill of sale *EXCEPT*
    A. signature of the seller.
    B. description of the items.
    C. date of transaction.
    D. name of buyer.

48. When a person dies testate, his real property
    A. escheats and is sold at auction by the state.
    B. goes to the heirs.
    C. passes by devise.
    D. goes to the administrator.

49. If an area is rezoned industrial and a commercial establishment is given permission to continue its operation in that area, this is an example of which of the following?
    A. Variance
    B. Nonconforming use
    C. Conditional use permit
    D. Spot zoning

50. A condominium apartment owner can avoid payment of her share of the common expenses by doing which of the following?
    A. Not using certain common elements
    B. Abandoning her apartment
    C. Defaulting on mortgage payments
    D. Payment cannot be avoided

51. The economic life of a building has come to an end when the
    A. building ceases to represent the highest and best use of the land.
    B. value of the land and the building equals the value of the land only.
    C. rent produced is valued at less than a similar amount of money invested elsewhere could produce.
    D. reserve for depreciation equals the cost to replace the building.

52. A capitalization rate incorporates return on
    A. land and building and recapture of building.
    B. land and building and recapture of land.
    C. land and recapture of land and building.
    D. building and recapture of land and building.

53. If the replacement cost shows a higher value than the appraised value, which of the following MOST probably has occurred?
    A. Accrued depreciation
    B. Excessive appraisal
    C. Economic obsolescence
    D. Capitalization

54. Which of the following can be said of real estate appraisers in federally related loan transactions?
    A. They must have a real estate college degree.
    B. They usually base their fees on a percentage of the appraised value.
    C. They must belong to a professional organization.
    D. They need to be state licensed or certified.

55. All of the following are examples of external obsolescence EXCEPT
    A. population density.
    B. direct effect of the elements.
    C. zoning.
    D. special assessments.

56. The cost of new construction of the building having utility equivalent to the property under appraisal but built with modern materials according to current standards, design, and layout, is an appropriate definition of
    A. reproduction cost.
    B. replacement cost.
    C. duplication cost.
    D. redesign cost.

57. A residence located in an area where there are factories and plants and where there is much smoke and dust is suffering from
    A. physical depreciation.
    B. external obsolescence.
    C. wear and tear.
    D. functional obsolescence.

58. A house depreciated at 5 percent per year for the past seven years, and the lot has increased 10 percent per year for the same seven years. Originally, the house was worth $6,000 and the lot was worth $10,000. What is the current worth (simple interest)?
    A. $20,100
    B. $20,900
    C. $25,100
    D. $42,000

59. A house was assessed for tax purposes at 60 percent of market value and the tax rate was $3.72 per $100 of assessed value. Twelve years later the same ratios were used and the taxes went up by $400. How much did market value go up?
    A. $10,750
    B. $17,921
    C. $18,632
    D. $28,671

60. An existing commercial property has an average net monthly income of $600. With an additional $2,000 spent by the owner on repairs, the owner thinks that the net monthly income will rise to $800 after these repairs are made. What is the maximum an investor should pay for this property to earn the equivalent of 8½ percent return?
    A. $112,941
    B. $121,948
    C. $142,911
    D. $182,941

61. A building with a net income of $10,000 was appraised at $100,000. What would be the value if the capitalization rate has decreased by one percentage point?
    A. $90,909
    B. $100,000
    C. $105,263
    D. $111,111

62. A property sold for $75,000. This was 8 percent above the purchase price. The sales commission was 6 percent. What percentage over the original cost did the seller net?
    A. 1.5%
    B. 2%
    C. 2.5%
    D. 3.5%

63. Which of the following occurs when the mortgagor is declared bankrupt?
    A. Mortgagor retains equitable title to the property but forfeits legal title.
    B. Mortgagor no longer owes any money under the mortgage note.
    C. Mortgagee becomes a general creditor.
    D. Title passes to court trustee or receiver.

64. Which of the following parties to a real estate sales transaction would have the *MOST* exposure to liability?
    A. Grantor of quitclaim deed
    B. Grantor in a loan assumption
    C. Grantee taking subject to the loan
    D. Grantor selling subject to the loan

65. A mortgage banker can do all of the following *EXCEPT*
    A. service loans for its clients.
    B. use its own money to make loans.
    C. loan money and then sell the loan.
    D. prepare an appraisal for a fee.

66. A veteran seeking a VA loan to purchase a three-family structure must
    A. agree to a loan amortization not to exceed 15 years.
    B. sign a statement that there will be no negative cash flow.
    C. occupy one of the units.
    D. agree to sell with a loan assumption only to another veteran.

67. The VA
    A. regularly makes direct loans up to certain amounts.
    B. does not apply to women.
    C. charges interest on its loans.
    D. guarantees loans to eligible veterans.

68. Where a seller takes back a purchase-money second mortgage from the buyer, the seller is responsible for preparing and executing which of the following?
    A. Deed
    B. Second note
    C. Promissory mortgage
    D. Credit report

69. If a house burns to the ground prior to closing, the buyer may do all of the following *EXCEPT*
    A. delay closing until the seller builds a replacement.
    B. close the sale and obtain an assignment of the insurance proceeds.
    C. rescind the contract.
    D. renegotiate the price if seller agrees.

70. Which of the following is an element peculiar to the sale-leaseback transaction?
    A. The seller gets a return on the purchase in the form of rental.
    B. The property is sold on condition that the new owner leases it back to the seller at the time title passes.
    C. The buyer keeps capital in inventories, rather than in realty.
    D. The rental that the seller pays is not income-tax deductible.

71. A broker took a listing where the owner was shot and murdered inside the home. During the listing period, the broker received a call from a buyer's agent stating that they had a written offer to present. Prior to the presentation of the offer, what is the ethical dilemma?
    A. Disclosure of the situation on the listing contract
    B. Disclosure of the situation to the buyer's agent
    C. Disclosure of the situation to the MLS membership
    D. None, there is no dilemma.

72. Fannie Mae can do all of the following *EXCEPT*
    A. purchase conventional loans.
    B. sell mortgages to institutions.
    C. buy FHA/VA loans.
    D. originate federal loans.

73. The Truth-in-Lending Act is designed to do which of the following?
    A. Limit the amount of interest charged to the borrower
    B. Limit the amount of closing costs
    C. Disclose whom the lender represents
    D. Disclose the cost of borrowing

74. To qualify for the homeowner's capital gains exclusion, how long must you have occupied the property as your principal residence?
    A. Six months
    B. One year
    C. Two years
    D. Three years

75. Charles purchased a $92,500 home by making a $12,000 down payment, securing a conventional first mortgage and a $15,500 purchase-money second mortgage with the seller. What is the approximate loan-to-value ratio of the first mortgage?
    A. 66%
    B. 70%
    C. 75%
    D. 80%

76. A lending institution will make a 30-year 9½ percent loan for 70 percent of the first $50,000 and 40 percent of the next $45,000 of appraised value. If a house is appraised at $95,000, what will be the first month's interest charge?
    A. $300.83
    B. $419.58
    C. $526.46
    D. $752.08

77. A piece of income property has an annual income of $120,000 and monthly expenses of $875. What would be the maximum an investor would pay for the property to earn a minimum of 15 percent on the investment?
    A. $73,000
    B. $109,500
    C. $730,000
    D. $893,000

78. Real property taxes are $18 per $1,000 of assessed valuation, with the present assessed valuation at 45 percent. The state tax director has promised to increase the assessment ratio of buildings by an additional 15 percent. The property is presently fair market valued at $35,000 for the building and $10,000 for the lot. What is the promised increase in tax?
    A. $45.90
    B. $94.50
    C. $255.00
    D. $364.50

79. To purchase a house for $50,000, the lender requires a down payment of 4 percent of the first $25,000 and 8 percent of the next $25,000. In addition, the lender charges four discount points. What is the maximum amount of discount points paid?
    A. $1,880
    B. $1,920
    C. $1,960
    D. $2,000

80. In a 75-acre subdivision, 400 houses were built on 7,500-sq.-ft. lots. If the average size of the houses is 50×40 ft., what percentage of the subdivision is covered by the houses?
    A. 12.25%
    B. 20%
    C. 24.5%
    D. 49%

ANSWERS

Note: Where appropriate, assume *V* = Value, *R* = Rate, *I* = Income.

1. **B.** It is not necessary that the listing first expire, but the broker must be extremely careful to disclose his interest in writing and avoid any possibility of self-dealing or secret profiting.

2. **D.** Failure to disclose material defects in a property for sale could be grounds for misrepresentation by the agent (concealment of material fact), especially in view of the present consumer trend of the courts away from the former caveat emptor doctrine ("let the buyer beware").

3. **B.** The broker would be breaching his or her duty of loyalty and confidentiality to reveal a price to a buyer other than that agreed on by the owner in the listing or modification thereof. Rather than say, "The property is listed at $100,000, but I know the owner will take $90,000," the broker *should* say, "The property is listed at $100,000, and if you are going to submit an offer of less than that, I'll take the offer to the seller and see what he or she says."

4. **B.** Unless he or she has the written consent of both seller and buyer, the broker cannot withdraw money even though he or she has earned his or her commission.

5. **B.** Most sales contracts involve a short-lived executory transaction and are not recorded. When performed, the deed is recorded.

6. **C.** The recording system neither insures against nor corrects title defects; it merely gives constructive notice of the rights of people in certain property.

7. **A.** RESPA is a federal law requiring certain disclosures of closing data to consumers.

8. **B.** Only the agent under an open listing who is the procuring cause will be entitled to the commission. Under a multiple listing, there is only one listing and only one agent; the cooperating brokers would be subagents working with the listing broker.

9. **C.** Under general agency principles, death terminates an executory listing agreement.

10. **B.** The only broker entitled to the commission under an open listing is the one who is the procuring cause of the sale. This is not a requirement under exclusive listings (which might also be net listings).

11. **D.** The broker has a fiduciary duty of obedience and a duty to account for all monies of her client. She cannot use client monies to set off or satisfy her own claims. A lawsuit may be the only answer.

12. **A.** The deposit money is credited against the total amount of money by which the buyer is indebted to purchase the property.

13. **B.** Mortgage foreclosures would occur when the owner defaults on the mortgage. Title insurance is concerned with title losses.

14. **B.** The abstract would reveal such recorded encumbrances as judgment liens or mortgages.

15. **D.** Property managers handle rents, minor repairs, and marketing of leases. They are not responsible for making investment decisions, such as handling real estate profits for their clients.

16. **D.** The existing second mortgage will be paid off, so a release or satisfaction piece must be recorded. Nothing need be recorded concerning the assumption because the obligation to assume will be stated in the deed, which is recorded the instant before the purchase-money second mortgage is recorded.

17. **A.** The church could be selective on the basis of religion but not race. There is a specific private club exemption under the federal Fair Housing Act.

18. **C.** *Panic peddling* is defined as soliciting of sales or rental listings, making written or oral statements creating fear or alarm, transmitting written or oral warnings or threats,

soliciting prospective minority renters or buyers, or acting in any other manner so as to induce or attempt to induce the sale or lease of residential property, either (a) through representations regarding the present or prospective entry of one or more minority residents into an area or (b) through representations that would convey to a reasonable person under the circumstances, regardless of whether overt reference to minority status is made, that one or more minority residents are or may be entering the area.

Note: The term *minority* means any group that can be distinguished because of race, sex, handicap, familial status, religion, color, or national origin. Vigorous solicitation of sellers in the context of a rapidly changing neighborhood frequently is panic peddling.

19. **C.** An agent must obey the instructions of her or his principal except where there is an illegal intent or act involved. Here, the owner is acting reasonably with no indication of any unlawful bias.

20. **C.** For blockbusting to exist, there must be some actual or implied representation about the effect of the entry of minority groups into the area.

21. **D.** The property management agreement is a contract, so the parties must be named. It is in the best interest of the owner to receive periodic reports.

22. **B.** A credit score contains three digits.

23. **D.** $120,000 \times 0.55 = \$66,000$
$\$660 \times 3.20$ per $100 = \$2,112$ per year
$\$2,112 \div 12 = \$176 \,/$ month
$\$176 \times 6.5$ (months) $= \$1,144$
Seller has prepaid for the whole year, and there is a 6.5-month unused portion the buyer will benefit from unless some adjustment (proration) is made. In tax prorations, the debit and credit amounts are equal.

24. **A.** $\$73,000 \times 75\% = \$54,750$ loan
$\$54,750 \times 5\% = \$2,737.50 + \$425.00 - \$275 = \$2,887.50$
$\$73,000 - \$54,750.00 = \$18,250 + \$2,887.50 = \$21,137.50$
$\$21,137.50 - \$5,000.00 = \$16,137.50$

25. **A.** $\$112,000$ Proration tax $\frac{1}{3}$ year (V) $\times 0.94$ (R) $= \$105,280$ (I) $- \$63,200 = \$42,080 + \$228 = \$42,308$
$\$684 \div 3 = \$228 + \$42,080 = \$42,308$

26. **D.** $\$1,200 \times 3 = \$3,600 + \$1,500 = \$5,100$
$\$500 \times 3 = \$1,500$
$\$5,100 \times 1.10 = \$5,610$

27. **B.** $200/20 = 350/? = (350 \times 20) \div 200 = 35$

28. **D.** $\$48,333$

29. **B.** Choice (A) is not correct because the marital unit owns the property as tenancy by the entirety and one spouse cannot seek partition.

30. **C.** Joint tenants hold the property free from claims of dower or curtesy of spouses, as well as free from claims of creditors or heirs of a deceased joint tenant.

31. **D.** Escrow does not take "change orders" from either party (i.e., both parties must consent to any change in the original contract or escrow instructions).

32. **A.** If the deed is not recorded, a subsequent purchaser for value (from the original grantor) without notice of the first unrecorded deed could get superior title by recording her subsequent deed first. Donees are not protected under the recording law (nor are devisees).

33. **B.** A person who signs a contract without reading it or the fine print does so at his own risk. Most contracts of minors are voidable at the election of the minor. In some states, a minor who marries is treated as an adult. Contracts for necessities are not voidable in some states.

34. **C.** Because an option is a unilateral contract, the optionee is not obliged to perform but, if the optionee does not elect to purchase, then the seller is bound to sell.

35. **B.** The listing is a confidential employment agreement between the seller and the broker and should not be shown to the buyer. There could be inaccurate information on the listing that has not yet been verified.

36. **A.** Assignments by the buyer are valid unless in violation of a clear antiassignment clause in the contract.

37. **B.** There is no delivery. Homer did not give up control over the deed as he would have if he had handed it to Stanley or put it in an escrow. To accomplish his purpose, Homer should have prepared a will.

38. **D.** Zoning ordinances are matters of public knowledge.

39. **B.** Because the grantor does not have the complete estate (i.e., the other tenants in common would have to join in the deed), then she would be liable under the covenant of seisin.

40. **D.** It might be noted, however, that a lessor has a reversionary interest in the leased fee.

41. **D.** The mortgagee has the choice of whether to terminate the lease because the lessee acquired the leasehold estate subject to the existing mortgage.

42. **B.** The purchaser takes the property subject to the rights of the lessee under the existing lease (which explains why it is important to inspect the property to discover the rights of parties in possession).

43. **D.** Neither death, mortgage, nor sale of the property will terminate the lease. Surrender involves a release of rights under a lease.

44. **C.** A percentage lease is based on a percentage of gross income.

45. **C.** The tenant is thereafter relieved of rent payments once he moves out.

46. **B.** While no title is certain, title insurance does provide the best assurance of good title.

47. **C.** While the date is frequently given, it is not as essential as these other items.

48. **C.** *Testate* means to die with a will in which real property is passed by way of a devise.

49. **B.** A *variance* would be the introduction of a new use that varies from the current zoning; a *nonconforming use* is the continuation of a use that was permissible prior to the recent zoning change.

50. **D.** If owners were allowed to reduce their monthly maintenance expenses (association dues) by electing not to use the swimming pool, for example, there would be much chaos in managing the condominium. Likewise, until title to the abandoned apartment was transferred, the owner would still be liable for common expenses.

51. **B.** Economic life is the period over which a building can be profitably utilized.

52. **A.** An investor would get a return *on* his or her investment in the land and building (similar to receiving interest) and a return *of* his or her investment in the building through recapture (similar to depreciation rate).

53. **A.** If it costs $100,000 to reproduce a five-year-old building valued at $92,000, there has been an adjustment made for $8,000 of depreciation over the five years.

54. **D.** Appraisers' fees are based upon time and expenses; it would be unethical to have a contingent appraisal fee.

55. **B.** Population changes, changes in zoning, or an unusually high assessment might cause external obsolescence of the property. Direct effect of the elements (such as wind, snow) could result in physical deterioration.

56. **B.** Reproduction cost is the present cost of reproducing the improvement with an exact replica, not just one with similar utility as in replacement cost.

57. **B.** External obsolescence is loss in value due to conditions of the surrounding neighborhood. The question does not present any facts indicating this house suffered physical damage caused by the dust and smoke.

58. **B.** *House:*

$6,000 × 0.05 = $300

$300 × 7 = $2,100

$6,000 − $2,100 = $3,900

Lot:

$10,000 × 0.10 = $1,000

$1,000 × 7 = $7,000

$10,000 + $7,000 = $17,000

$3,900 + $17,000 = $20,900

59. **B.** ? × $3.72/100 = $400

? × .60 = $10,753

$400 ÷ $3.72 = $107.53 × 100 = $10,753

$10,753 ÷ 0.60 = $17,921

60. **A.** $800/month × 12 = $9,600/year

? × 0.085 = $9,600

$9,600 ÷ 0.085 = $112,941

61. **D.** $100,000 × 0.10 = $10,000

? × 0.09 = $10,000

$10,000 ÷ 0.09 = $111,111

Income divided by capitalization rate equals value.

62. **A.** ? (V) × 1.08 (R) = $75,000 (I)

commission $75,000 × 0.06 = $4,500 to seller

$70,500 − $69,444 = $1,056

$69,444 × ? = $1,056

$75,000 ÷ 1.08 = $69,444

$1,056 ÷ $69,444 = 0.0152 = 1.5%

63. **D.** The title passes to the receiver. The mortgagor still owes the debt, but the lenders most likely rely on the sale of the secured property to obtain reimbursement for the loan. As a secured creditor, the mortgagee would receive a preference in the bankruptcy distribution.

64. **D.** The grantor selling subject to a loan would remain primarily liable for the debt, whereas he or she would be secondarily liable as a surety in a loan assumption. The grantor of a quitclaim deed would have the least exposure.

65. **D.** Mortgage bankers often originate loans and then package them (warehousing) to larger investors and continue to service the loans regularly.

66. **C.** Most VA loans are amortized for longer than 15 years. Frequently, the expenses will exceed the income on the rented units, but there is no prohibition on negative cash flow. The veteran must occupy one of the units.

67. **D.** Direct loans are made in exceptional circumstances with the current limit around $35,000. VA loans apply to female veterans and certain unremarried widows of veterans.

68. **A.** The buyer benefits by having a mortgage loan to purchase the property, so the buyer would pay for the cost of preparing the mortgage. Also, the seller does not sign the mortgage. The seller is obligated by contract to convey title to the buyer, so the seller pays for cost of the deed.

69. **A.** The seller has the risk of loss until closing so the buyer can rescind or accept the deed and insurance proceeds.

70. **B.** Rent is tax deductible as a business expense. The buyer is relatively confident the seller will become a triple-A tenant.

71. **B.** The dilemma is whether or not to tell the buyer's agent before the buyer's offer is presented. If told, the buyer could remove the offer from the table and the seller's property would still be for sale. However, if the buyer isn't told about the murder, then hard feelings could be created between the buyer's agent and the uninformed buyer. Legally, it isn't the buyer's agent's duty to discover if a property has been stigmatized. However, if the buyer's agent knew about the murder, then the buyer's agent would be required to disclose the material fact. The dilemma then rests with the listing broker to tell or not to tell the buyer's agent about the murder. The golden rule suggests that the listing broker tell the buyer's agent in advance of the offer presentation to protect everyone in this scenario.

72. **D.** Fannie Mae only operates in the secondary mortgage market.

73. **D.** The law does not limit costs or charges; it merely requires their full disclosure. RESPA also regulates disclosure of closing costs.

74. **C.** The homeowner's tax exclusion applies if the taxpayer occupies the property as his or her principal residence for two out of the last five years.

75. **B.** $92,500 – $12,000 = $80,500 – $15,000 = $65,000
$92,500 × ?% = $65,000 ÷ $92,500 = 0.702 = 70.2%

76. **B.** $50,000 × 0.70 = $35,000
$45,000 × 0.40 = $18,000
$35,000 + $18,000 = $53,000 total loan
$53,000 × 0.095 = $5,035 ÷ 12 = $419.58

77. **C.** $875 × 12 = $10,500 expenses
$120,000 – $10,500 = $109,500
? × 0.15 = $109,500
$109,500 ÷ 0.15 = $730,000

78. **B.** *Present tax:*
$45,000 × 45% = $20,250
$20.25 × 18 = $364.50
$459.00 – $364.50 = $94.50
Proposed tax:
$35,000 × 60% = $21,000 + $4,500 = $25,500
$10,000 × 45% = $4,500
$25.50 × 18 = $459

79. **A.** $50,000 – $3,000 down payment = $47,000 loan × 4 discount points = $1,880

80. **C.** 50' × 40' = 2,000 sq. ft./house
400 × 2,000 = 800,000
75 × 43,560 = 3,267,000
3,267,000 × ? = 800,000
800,000 ÷ 3,267,000 = 0.245 = 24.5%

Review Exams

Appendix D contains three review exams to help you finalize your preparations for the state licensing examination. The first two exams each contain 80 miscellaneous questions so you can practice your timing for taking the national portion of the exam. The last exam is a bonus quiz consisting of 60 questions.

REVIEW EXAM 1 QUESTIONS

1. Which is *TRUE* regarding the recording of a deed?
   A. If the actual deed is lost, the recorded copy will be proof of the grantee's title.
   B. The deed becomes valid on recording.
   C. Recording requires actual notice.
   D. Deeds from the U.S. government must be recorded in federal court.

2. One may acquire title or ownership in real property by all of the following *EXCEPT*
   A. deed.
   B. inheritance.
   C. adverse possession.
   D. lease.

3. At what time is a properly drawn and executed deed first considered to have transferred legal title to the grantee?
   A. When the grantee's name is filled in
   B. When it is signed by the grantor
   C. When it is delivered to the grantee
   D. When it is found in the possession of the grantee

4. A man whose wife recently died is thinking about moving to his son's home. He is hesitant about renewing his lease at the expiration date, but if he stays on after the expiration date, he will be a
   A. tenant at will.
   B. life tenant.
   C. tenant in common.
   D. joint tenant.

5. Which of the following is *NOT* a private restriction on the use of real property?
   A. Zoning laws
   B. Condominium bylaws
   C. Restrictive covenants
   D. Subdivision restrictions

6. Changing a building use from apartments to condominiums would be accomplished by which of the following?
   A. Condemnation
   B. Sale-leaseback
   C. Conversion
   D. Rent with option to buy

7. A buyer is interested in purchasing an interest in a resort condominium that will guarantee her a specific two-bedroom unit during March of every year. Which of the following forms of ownership might a broker recommend?
   A. Time-sharing
   B. Corporate
   C. Cooperative
   D. Syndication

8. All of the following violate the federal Fair Housing Act *EXCEPT*
   A. steering.
   B. blockbusting or panic selling.
   C. redlining.
   D. denying a lease to military personnel.

9. Two brokers know of a house that was recently sold to members of a socialist commune. The brokers sense a quick gain and call the other owners in the neighborhood to get them to sell, telling them, "It's becoming a communal neighborhood, and everyone knows members of this commune can't take care of property." This behavior is
   A. unethical behavior.
   B. unlawful panic peddling.
   C. unlawful discrimination.
   D. unlawful intimidation.

10. A minority person offered to buy a vacant lot in a residential subdivision for $25,000 in cash. The offer was refused, but two days later the developer accepted an offer from a non-minority buyer for $10,000 in cash. Which is *TRUE* under the federal Fair Housing Act?
    A. This discrimination does not violate the federal act because it involves vacant land.
    B. The developer is exempt from the law.
    C. The law applies only to transactions over $50,000.
    D. The minority person may have a valid claim under the act.

11. A bank's refusal to consider making a real estate loan to which of the following groups *MOST* likely would be a violation of the federal Fair Housing Act?
    A. Multiple couples seeking to live in one residence
    B. Three rock stars taking title as joint tenants
    C. Military officers
    D. Several priests buying a condominium apartment

12. Which of the following is racial steering?
    A. Salesperson introduces minority buyer to minority lender who will give buyer a loan.
    B. Salesperson shows minority buyer homes only in minority section of town even though buyer wants to see homes in other areas.
    C. Salesperson directs minority buyer to minority attorney.
    D. Salesperson directs minority buyer to minority appraiser.

13. In an old area of Baltimore there have been a large number of defaults in multifamily housing loans held by Armbreaker Savings and Loan. Armbreaker decides to hold off making any more loans on multifamily housing projects until it can discover the reason why there are so many delinquent loans. Such a decision would violate the
    A. federal Fair Housing Act.
    B. Equal Credit Opportunity Act.
    C. Truth-in-Lending Act.
    D. Not a violation

14. Which practice violates the federal Fair Housing Act?
    A. A minority mother owns a fourplex, lives in one unit, and gives preference to having minority mothers rent the other three units.
    B. A broker takes a listing from a minority mother in which she can sell the single-family home only to another minority mother.
    C. A nonprofit retirement home rents to members of one religious denomination only.
    D. A minority owner refuses to sell to a lawyer.

15. All of the following are important elements to establish a real estate agent as an independent contractor *EXCEPT*
    A. a written contract between agent and broker.
    B. agent compensation based on performance and not on number of hours worked.
    C. the agent is properly licensed to sell real estate.
    D. agent's successfully closing a minimum of two transactions per year.

16. A minority group is moving into an area immediately adjacent to the Devil Estates development. Xanadu Realty offers to list homes in Devil Estates at a lower than usual rate if the owners list within 45 days. There is no mention of race and the broker acts in good faith. Which of the following is *TRUE?*
    A. The broker's license can be revoked.
    B. This is blockbusting.
    C. Such practice is legal.
    D. Brokers cannot lower their standard rate of commission.

17. Craig obtains an exclusive listing in which the owner instructs him not to sell to anyone who is a certain religion. Craig shows the property to people of this religion but does not present any of their offers to the owner. Which is *TRUE* under the federal Fair Housing Act?
    A. Craig is not obliged to show any offer that he feels the owner will reject.
    B. Craig must present all offers.
    C. Craig must get instructions from the owner about presenting offers to members of the religion.
    D. Craig could be punished by HUD if a complaint is filed against him.

18. Which of the following activities is permissible under the federal Fair Housing Act?
    A. Taking into consideration the borrower's race in fixing the terms of a loan
    B. Inquiring into the financial capacity of a prospective purchaser of a dwelling who belongs to a minority group
    C. Using a form that contains a fill-in section for applicant's religion and national origin
    D. Refusing to rent to a pregnant woman

19. Which of the following facts is *LEAST* important for an appraiser of a commercial shopping center to discover?
   A. Person(s) entitled to possession and ownership
   B. Rents and operating expenses
   C. Zoning
   D. Original cost of the center

20. Which is *TRUE* concerning an agency coupled with an interest?
   A. It can be revoked by the principal.
   B. It is terminated by the death of the principal.
   C. It is illegal.
   D. It generally is irrevocable.

21. If an agent purchases his client's real property by having his wife secretly act as the buyer, using her maiden name, the agent would *MOST* likely breach which one of these duties?
   A. Obedience
   B. Care
   C. Loyalty
   D. Skill

22. Which of the following acts of a broker is *NOT* an example of an agency relationship?
   A. Signing listings
   B. Leasing property
   C. Selling the broker's own property
   D. Representing the purchaser

23. What type of agency relationship *MOST* likely exists between a property manager and the owner?
   A. Special
   B. Limited
   C. Indirect
   D. General

24. A property manager is *LEAST* likely to be concerned with a prospective tenant's
   A. physical appearance.
   B. credit rating.
   C. profession.
   D. understanding of the house rules.

25. If there is a break or gap in the chain of title, it is usually necessary to
   A. rely on a warranty deed as proof of title.
   B. establish ownership by a suit to quiet title.
   C. prepare and record a new abstract of title.
   D. secure an affidavit from the grantor.

26. Which one of the following expenses is *MOST* likely to be paid outside of closing (POC)?
   A. Title insurance
   B. Lender's credit report fee
   C. Attorney's fees for preparing the closing document
   D. The conveyance tax

27. All of the following would appear on the RESPA settlement statement required by HUD *EXCEPT*
   A. tax prorations.
   B. the escrow fee.
   C. income tax deductions.
   D. closing costs.

28. Inspection of the seller's settlement or closing statement (*not* the HUD-1 RESPA form) will indicate which of the following to the seller?
   A. Amount the seller will receive from the sale
   B. Amount the buyer will pay at closing
   C. Interest rate on the buyer's loan
   D. Buyer's attorney's fee

29. RESPA forms must be used in all of the following loans *EXCEPT*
   A. FHA.
   B. Farmer's Home Administration (FmHA).
   C. VA.
   D. seller financing.

30. Written documents affecting title to real estate are recorded where
   A. the titleholder resides.
   B. the titleholder has legal residence.
   C. the real estate is located.
   D. due legal process is to be served.

31. Which of the following is a typical purpose of the closing statement?
   A. Determine how title is to be held by buyer
   B. Show how expenses are to be paid
   C. Show the chain of title
   D. Show the location of the property

32. A broker obtained a 120-day exclusive-right-to-sell listing but did absolutely nothing to market the property for 60 days. Any of the following is true *EXCEPT* the
    A. seller can cancel the listing prior to the 120th day.
    B. seller can withdraw the property from the market.
    C. broker has earned a commission.
    D. broker has breached the contract.

33. In which one of the following cases can commission rates be legally set?
    A. At a real estate commission hearing
    B. At an informal meeting of real estate brokers
    C. At a formal meeting of real estate brokers of their firm
    D. At a meeting between the seller and listing broker

34. Which of the following statements about an open listing is *TRUE?*
    A. An open listing may be terminated by the owner at any time prior to performance.
    B. An owner may not enter into an open listing contract with more than two brokers at a time.
    C. An open listing must contain a definite termination date.
    D. An open listing is illegal.

35. Automobile expenses of a salesperson accrued in the act of listing a property are typically paid by the
    A. principal broker whether or not a sale results.
    B. seller if a sale results.
    C. buyer.
    D. salesperson whether or not a sale results.

36. An open listing on residential real estate is generally considered to be which type of contract?
    A. Voidable
    B. Executed
    C. Bilateral
    D. Unilateral

37. A seller wants to list a property with a broker but wants to reserve the right to sell it himself without being obligated to pay a commission. What type of listing would allow what the seller wants?
    A. Exclusive agency
    B. Exclusive right to sell
    C. Multiple listing
    D. Net listing

38. A broker advertises a "Guaranteed Sale" as a means of obtaining listings. This means that if an owner lists the property for sale with the broker for 120 days
    A. if the property does not sell in 120 days, the listing period is extended for an additional period of time, until the property is sold.
    B. if the property is not sold within the 120-day period, the broker will buy it.
    C. title is guaranteed.
    D. the property is guaranteed against any defects.

39. Which of the following is the *BEST* example of rescission of a contract?
    A. A lease is canceled by mutual agreement of the lessor and lessee.
    B. An offer to purchase is revised by a counterproposal.
    C. An option to purchase is transferred to a new buyer.
    D. A listing results in a commission to a broker.

40. Concerning an option on a parcel of real property, which of the following is *TRUE?*
    A. It is voidable by the optionor.
    B. It can be made binding on the optionee.
    C. It usually is given by the owner.
    D. It can be enforced by a suit filed by the optionor.

41. Juanita has an option to purchase a property at $120,000 for 180 days. Which is *TRUE?*
    A. Juanita may assign the option to a third party only with the optionor's consent.
    B. Juanita may offer a lower price prior to the expiration of the option without losing her right to exercise the option.
    C. Only Juanita must sign the option agreement.
    D. Juanita can exercise the option within a reasonable time after the 180th day.

42. A buyer makes an offer of $155,000 on a $170,000 listed property. The seller gives the broker a counteroffer of $169,999.99. What should the embarrassed broker do?
   A. Refuse to present the counteroffer
   B. Alter the counteroffer
   C. Follow the seller's instructions
   D. Persuade the buyer to recounter at a middle price

43. In selling a condominium including all fixtures and furnishings, the seller should give the buyer which of the following?
   A. Inventory of the furnishings
   B. Affidavit as to the condition of the furnishings
   C. Truth-in-Lending disclosure
   D. Promissory note

44. A buyer who has put up $10,000 earnest money on a sales contract for a $200,000 property decides to default. The seller may keep the $10,000 as
   A. punitive damages.
   B. liquidated damages.
   C. consequential damages.
   D. special damages.

45. Which one of the following is *TRUE* about real estate options?
   A. The optionee must sign the option and have it acknowledged.
   B. The option money is applied to the purchase price if the option is exercised.
   C. The optionee must pay the full purchase price before the option expires.
   D. If the option is not exercised, the option money is forfeited.

46. If the parties to a contract are of legal age and of sound mind, they are said to have
   A. consideration.
   B. legality of object.
   C. reality of consent.
   D. legal capacity.

47. Cynthia rents space to use for a restaurant and installs counters, booths, stoves, and other fixtures necessary for business use. These fixtures will become the property of the lessor
   A. once they are connected to the real estate.
   B. if they are not removed by Cynthia upon the expiration of the lease.
   C. if the lessee is late with one rent check.
   D. if the lessor pays for their upkeep.

48. To say that a landlord is bound by an implied covenant of quiet enjoyment to a lessee is to say that the landlord
   A. will not allow the lessee to be disturbed by strangers coming upon the property.
   B. is obligated to make all necessary repairs to the leased premises.
   C. promises that the lessee will not be evicted by a person who has title superior to that of the landlord.
   D. undertakes to protect the lessee from loud noises caused by other tenants.

49. A client wants to purchase land under a ground lease from the lessor-owner. The client is purchasing a
   A. leasehold estate.
   B. contingent fee.
   C. leased fee.
   D. reverter.

50. The largest source of funds for secondary mortgage money is which of the following?
   A. Private parties
   B. FHA
   C. Mortgage insurance companies
   D. Freddie Mac

51. A means by which a business can free money invested in its plant for use as working capital is called a(n)
   A. sale-leaseback.
   B. land contract of sale.
   C. real estate investment trust.
   D. assignment of rents.

52. A conventional guaranteed mortgage is a mortgage that is
   A. insured by a private mortgage insurance company.
   B. insured by the FHA.
   C. guaranteed by the seller.
   D. guaranteed by the VA.

53. As far as the owner of a parcel of real property is concerned, which of the following would *MOST* likely result in a reduction of equity?
    A. Liquidation
    B. Refinancing
    C. Exchanging
    D. Leasing

54. An FHA conditional commitment is an agreement by the FHA to
    A. indemnify the lender on a defaulted loan.
    B. qualify the buyer for a new loan.
    C. insure a loan made to a qualified buyer.
    D. guarantee the value of the property.

55. Financing real estate through a group of persons who pool their funds to purchase or make a down payment on investment properties is *BEST* described as
    A. a syndicate.
    B. growing equity.
    C. a participating group.
    D. an investment trust.

56. The primary function of the Federal Housing Administration is to
    A. insure real estate loans.
    B. build public housing.
    C. act as a secondary mortgage market.
    D. establish discount points.

57. Assume Barb refinanced her home and received $30,000 in cash. Which one is *TRUE?*
    A. Barb's monthly payments are lower than before.
    B. Barb's tax depreciation allowance is increased.
    C. A capital gains tax is due.
    D. Barb's debt service is higher than before.

58. A veteran would have to make a down payment to buy a residence using a VA loan in which of the following cases?
    A. The veteran owns investment property.
    B. The sales price exceeds the Certificate of Reasonable Value.
    C. The veteran is in the National Guard.
    D. The veteran is unmarried.

59. A veteran who agrees to buy, subject to obtaining an FHA loan, can get his or her money refunded under all of the following circumstances *EXCEPT* if the
    A. veteran cannot qualify for the loan.
    B. sales price exceeds the FHA appraisal.
    C. property cannot be repaired to meet minimum property requirements.
    D. veteran decides the house is too small.

60. The sellers were a married couple when they executed a three-year land contract to sell their house. On satisfaction by the buyer, the sellers are divorced and the wife refuses to sign the deed. Which is *TRUE?*
    A. The buyer must accept the deed signed only by the husband.
    B. The buyer can sue the wife for breach of contract.
    C. The husband must reduce the balance due.
    D. The husband can rescind the contract.

61. All of the following are true about federal Farmer's Home Administration (FmHA) loans *EXCEPT*
    A. they are specifically designed for farmers, rural residents, and communities seeking money to finance housing, farms, and business opportunities.
    B. FmHA loans can be made for housing located in open country and in rural communities with small populations, such as under 10,000.
    C. FmHA loans are typically set at more favorable terms than conventional loans.
    D. FmHA loans are for veterans only.

62. To be relieved of the primary responsibility of a loan, a seller must find a buyer who will
    A. be willing to subordinate.
    B. purchase subject to the loan.
    C. buy on land contract.
    D. assume the loan.

63. All of the following in a real estate advertisement require full disclosure under the Truth-in-Lending Act, *EXCEPT*
    A. monthly payments of $275.
    B. 360 monthly payments.
    C. no charge for credit.
    D. financing by Second Federal Savings.

64. An ad states that the monthly mortgage payments on an assumed loan are $634. Regulation Z requires further disclosure of all of the following *EXCEPT*
   A. terms of repayment.
   B. amount of down payment.
   C. simple interest rate.
   D. annual percentage rate.

65. A real estate broker, who is also a mortgage broker, regularly negotiates the loans for her buyer-clients. Under the Truth-in-Lending Act, the broker would be considered a(n)
   A. customer.
   B. arranger.
   C. lender.
   D. borrower.

66. Regulation Z requires that the lender disclose which of the following to a borrower when a first mortgage is made to finance the purchase of a residence?
   A. Appraised value of the residence
   B. Total charges required for settlement of a real estate transaction
   C. Total finance charges
   D. Cost of a survey

67. After a judicial foreclosure sale, the court would most likely arrange for the purchaser to receive which one of the following?
   A. Sheriff's deed
   B. Commissioner's deed
   C. Quitclaim deed
   D. Guardian's deed

68. When a borrower makes $100 amortized loan payments, it means that
   A. each payment has the same amount applying to principal.
   B. there will be a balloon payment.
   C. the amount applying to principal increases with each payment.
   D. there is a lump sum payment.

69. Which is *TRUE* concerning a real estate mortgage?
   A. It must be signed by all owners for it to be an effective lien against the entire property.
   B. Upon the death of one out of two tenants-in-common mortgagors, one-half of the property would pass to the mortgagee.
   C. It must be signed by each mortgagee.
   D. Only the promissory note is recorded.

70. A principal difference between a mortgage and a deed of trust concerns which of the following?
   A. Amortization
   B. Redemption
   C. Acceleration
   D. Capitalization

71. An amortized mortgage loan is one that is paid in monthly payments
   A. with interest in addition.
   B. of interest only.
   C. of principal only.
   D. that include both principal and interest.

72. A lender might require a 100-percent performance bond from a contractor building an addition to your home
   A. as added assurance the building will be built.
   B. to reduce the risk of subordination.
   C. to eliminate forfeiture.
   D. as a hedge against inflation.

73. Assume that a property is encumbered by a second deed of trust with a subordination clause. If the owner refinances the first deed of trust with a new lender, which one of the following is *TRUE*?
   A. The second deed of trust is now the first lien, since it was recorded first.
   B. The original first deed of trust is still a lien.
   C. The second deed of trust is no longer a lien.
   D. The new deed of trust takes priority over the second deed of trust.

74. The priority of mortgages may be reversed with the execution of a(n)
   A. partial release agreement.
   B. assignment agreement.
   C. subordination agreement.
   D. release agreement.

75. The legal process of defeating a debtor's interest in property as a result of default on the loan is called
   A. defeasance.
   B. defect of title.
   C. redemption.
   D. foreclosure.

76. Which of the following can be said of a mortgage?
    A. A mortgage creates a lien even if it does not convey title to the holder.
    B. A mortgage is secured by a promissory note.
    C. A mortgage is not needed if the loan is under $10,000.
    D. Only banks use a mortgage.

77. Which of the following is *LEAST* likely to be present in a wraparound mortgage?
    A. All-inclusive monthly payments
    B. An existing underlying mortgage
    C. Profit from interest override
    D. Priority of lien by wraparound mortgage

78. The distinguishing feature of an adjustable-rate mortgage is that the interest rate
    A. changes depending on the borrower's income.
    B. never varies.
    C. varies one time each year.
    D. varies according to an agreed-on market indicator.

79. A mortgage with a variable interest rate that is determined by economic indicators would be a(n)
    A. FHA loan.
    B. fixed-rate loan.
    C. adjustable rate indexed loan.
    D. flexible-payment loan.

80. A seller owns a property and has an $80,000 first mortgage and a $30,000 second mortgage. The seller is willing to sell to a buyer, who has $30,000 ready cash as a down payment to buy the property. The sales price is $130,000, and the seller agrees to take back a wraparound mortgage for $100,000. What is the proper advice for the buyer?
    A. Use the $30,000 as an earnest money deposit
    B. Have the seller apply at least $10,000 of the down payment to reduce the mortgage balance
    C. Have the buyer refuse to sign the note
    D. Put all mortgage payments into a trust account until maturity of the loan

REVIEW EXAM 1 ANSWERS

Note: Where appropriate, assume V = Value, R = Rate, I = Income.

1. **A.** Because the deed itself is not the title (it is evidence of title), there is no loss of title merely because the deed is lost. However, it is to the grantees's advantage to have a copy on record. Even U.S. patent deeds must be recorded in the local record office where the property is located.

2. **D.** Under a lease, one acquires a right of exclusive possession—not title or ownership, which remain with the lessor.

3. **C.** Delivery is the key because the deed could have been signed by the grantor, then stolen by the grantee who filled in his own name.

4. **A.** Depending on the facts, the tenant also could have been a tenant at sufferance or a holdover tenant. Choices (B), (C), and (D) are concerned with methods of ownership.

5. **A.** Zoning laws are public restrictions. Condominium bylaws often restrict the type of uses in the project.

6. **C.** Condominium conversion involves the transformation of a rental apartment building under single ownership to a building in which the individual apartment units are separately owned as condominium apartments. The building remains basically the same.

7. **A.** Under time-sharing, the owners have specific rights of possession in a particular project. In some cases, they have rights to a particular unit for a particular time period; in other cases, both the unit and the time period may vary according to a prearranged schedule.

8. **D.** While it is not a specified discriminatory act under the federal Fair Housing Act to refuse to rent to military, it is not a recommended practice and may involve violation of other federal laws.

9. **A.** Though nothing in the facts indicates unlawful discrimination based on sex, color, religion, handicap, familial status, race, or national origin, it would be considered an unethical practice.

10. **D.** The federal law applies to developers and to sales of vacant land that may be used for residential purposes.

11. **D.** It is no violation to discriminate against groups of people so long as it is not based on race, sex, color, religion, national origin, familial status, or handicap (physical or mental).

12. **B.** Steering is the practice of directing a prospect into or away from certain areas based on ethnic considerations.

13. **D.** Armbreaker's decision is based on sound business judgment rather than discriminatory reasons, so there is no violation. Note that the Equal Credit Opportunity Act, unlike the federal Fair Housing Act, also prohibits discrimination based on age.

14. **B.** There is a "Mrs. Murphy" exemption, whereby an owner who occupies at least one unit in up to a fourplex can discriminate (except on race), provided he or she does not use the services of a broker.

15. **D.** Federal regulations now require only choices (A), (B), and (C).

16. **C.** Because there is no apparent connection between the lower commission rates and race, there is no illegal act. If the broker, however, were to emphasize the need to sell due to increased crime caused by the presence of this minority group, then this would be blockbusting.

17. **D.** The mere acceptance of a listing with a discriminatory restriction is an illegal act. Not presenting all offers involves licensing law.

18. **B.** Race is not a proper factor, but financial capacity is proper regardless of whether the borrower is from a minority group.

19. **D.** The appraiser must know, for example, whether he or she is appraising the leasehold estate (lessee) or the leased fee (lessor). Rents and operating expenses are vital in the capitalization or income approach to valuation.

20. **D.** An agency coupled with an interest is different from a normal listing in that the agent has some direct interest in the property. Assume a broker owns a parcel that the broker sells to a developer on the condition that the developer give the broker an exclusive listing to sell the completed condominium development. This unique type of agency cannot be revoked nor is it terminated by death.

21. **C.** While all the choices are fiduciary duties, this question describes the duty of loyalty. The activity described would violate most licensing laws as well.

22. **C.** In selling his or her own property, the broker is acting as a principal, not an agent. Brokers can represent buyers, but they should clearly disclose this representation in the sales contract.

23. **D.** The property manager typically has continuing duties to manage and maintain the property, unlike a broker who has limited or special duties to find a ready, willing, and able buyer.

24. **A.** Too much attention to physical appearance may imply some preference based on discriminatory grounds, and this is a violation of the federal Fair Housing Act.

25. **B.** The best way to clear up the title gap is to get a court opinion rather than just an opinion from the grantor. A new abstract won't be able to show why there was a break in the chain of title.

26. **B.** Some lenders collect their own fees and give escrow only the *net* loan amount.

27. **C.** The RESPA statement would include choices (A), (B), and (D), but not all tax deductions such as depreciation.

28. **A.** The seller's statement reflects only the seller's obligations, not the buyer's.

29. **D.** RESPA is mandatory in all federally related loan transactions.

30. **C.** If, for example, Adam and Bernard sign a contract of sale in Florida for property located in Alaska, the deed should be recorded in Alaska.

31. **B.** The closing statement is the financial blueprint of the transaction. Choices (A) and (C) concern a title report, and (D) is a tax map.

32. **C.** The broker has a duty to use good-faith efforts to sell the property. Failure to do so is a breach justifying cancellation or withdrawal.

33. **D.** Only broker and seller can negotiate the commission rate. If two or more conspire to fix rates in their community, this attempt to fix commission will violate state and federal antitrust laws.

34. **A.** Open listings are generally unilateral contracts that can be canceled prior to substantial performance. A seller can give many open listings but owes a commission only to the broker who is the procuring cause of the sale.

35. **D.** The salesperson, especially if an independent contractor, pays for most out-of-pocket expenses in connection with a listing, except that the broker often pays for advertising.

36. **D.** The broker generally is under no obligation to find a buyer. If, however, the broker is the procuring cause of the sale, then the seller owes a commission.

37. **A.** The seller can reserve the right to sell the property under an exclusive agency (where the seller agrees not to list with other brokers) and under an open listing (in which it can be given to any number of brokers).

38. **B.** The broker must fully disclose any limitations on his or her obligation to purchase in the event the property is not sold.

39. **A.** A rescission is a return to the status quo. Choice (A) is also called a *surrender;* choice (B) is a counteroffer; choice (C) is an assignment.

40. **C.** The optionor is typically the owner, who receives option money in return for the promise to sell at a specified price to the optionee in the event the optionee decides to buy.

41. **B.** Juanita's lower offer is an independent act and not relevant. Options are contracts and thus are generally assignable unless restricted.

42. **C.** It is the broker's duty to follow his principal's instructions after explaining all the ramifications of this type of counteroffer.

43. **A.** It is common practice to itemize the personal property but not to make a sworn statement as to its condition.

44. **B.** Earnest money is usually a good-faith deposit that can be used by the seller to liquidate the debt in the event the buyer breaches the contract and fails to perform.

45. **D.** Option money is forfeited if the option is not exercised. If the option money were to be refunded, then the option would not have been enforceable because there really was no consideration—it was illusory. Because the optionee is usually given a short period of time to close after the option is exercised, the full price is often not paid until after the option's expiration date. Choice (B) is a matter of agreement and should be covered in the option.

46. **D.** Legal capacity refers to competency. Reality of consent refers to genuine consent in an offer and acceptance (no fraud, misrepresentation, or duress).

47. **B.** These fixtures belong to the tenant under the trade fixtures exception, although the tenant must remove them by the time the lease expires.

48. **C.** This covenant is breached if the lessee is evicted by the true owner other than the landlord. Under choice (A), if the stranger has no valid claim to the property, then the lessee will have to take her or his own protective measures.

49. **C.** The leased fee is the lessor's interest, which represents the fee simple title subject to the lease. The lessee's interest is called the *leasehold estate.*

50. **A.** Private parties include individuals and corporations, and they buy the mortgages, including FHA mortgages that are sold in

the secondary mortgage market by organizations like Freddie Mac. While insurance companies are a good source, mortgage insurance companies insure loans.

51. **A.** By selling its plant and then renting it back, the seller gains funds yet does not have to relocate; otherwise, the owner would have to refinance its plant to raise the money.

52. **A.** A popular private insurance program is that of the Mortgage Guaranty Insurance Corporation, or MGIC, which enables a lender to make a 90 percent loan despite the lender's policy of usually making only 70 percent loans, because the insurance (paid for by the borrower) would insure the lender for that additional 20 percent. FHA has an insurance program for its nonconventional loans.

53. **B.** In a typical refinancing, the borrower receives cash for part of the equity in the property. For example, assume a property owner has a property worth $100,000 with a $40,000 mortgage. The owner might refinance for a $60,000 loan, thus raising $20,000 in cash (after paying off the $40,000 mortgage) but reducing the equity from $60,000 to $40,000.

54. **C.** Under a conditional commitment, the FHA agrees to insure a loan (usually for a certain period such as six months), provided the buyer meets FHA qualification standards.

55. **A.** Syndications are usually set up in the form of a limited partnership where the limited partners pool their money and have the real estate venture managed by a general partner.

56. **A.** Under the Mutual Mortgage Protection Plan, the FHA insures loans made by approved lenders to qualified borrowers.

57. **D.** Barb's monthly principal and interest payments will increase because she's increased her loan amount by the $30,000 equity she received in cash.

58. **B.** While a 100 percent loan is possible under VA, the loan cannot exceed the appraisal as indicated by the Certificate of Reasonable Value.

59. **D.** FHA sales contracts usually contain a contingency provision allowing the buyer to cancel either if the buyer cannot qualify for the loan or if the sales price exceeds the FHA appraisal.

60. **B.** To get clear title, the buyer needs a deed from both husband and wife and can sue the wife for specific performance. The divorce had no legal effect on the transaction.

61. **D.** FmHA is a federal agency under the U.S. Department of Agriculture and makes guaranteed loans and insured loans.

62. **D.** In a true assumption, the buyer replaces the seller for primary responsibility on the loan, but the seller remains secondarily liable (unless there is a novation).

63. **D.** (D) is such a general statement that it does not trigger the required disclosures that a specific statement such as choice (A), (B), or (C) would trigger.

64. **C.** It should also state whether any increase in the annual percentage rate is possible.

65. **B.** If deemed an "arranger," the broker is required to make the necessary disclosures concerning credit terms.

66. **C.** Regulation Z is concerned with credit disclosure only, not appraisal amount or closing costs (covered by RESPA).

67. **B.** The court appoints a commissioner to conduct the public auction and sale, including executing the commissioner's deed transferring legal title to the purchaser.

68. **C.** With amortized payments, the monthly amount remains the same, but a portion of that amount is applied each month to reduce principal. In the early years, most of the payment is applied to interest; in the later years most is applied to principal, with no balloon payment due at the end of the loan term.

69. **A.** Because all owners must sign, most lenders require a title policy to see who the owners are. Death of a mortgagor does not trigger any survivorship rights in the mortgagee.

70. **C.** The equitable redemption period is typically shorter with a deed of trust. Choices (A) and (B) refer to the provisions of note.

71. **D.** With an amortized loan, there is a zero balance of interest and principal at the end of the loan term.

72. **A.** Sometimes contractors get into financial difficulty. The performance bond is designed to provide funds to get the job completed.

73. **D.** If it were not for the subordination clause, choice (A) would be correct.

74. **C.** With a subordination clause, the lender under a first mortgage may agree to become junior to a subsequent mortgage. This agreement is often used when the holder of raw land sells it by way of a deed and purchase-money mortgage to a buyer who will later go out and obtain a construction loan from a lender who requires that it be in a first lien position.

75. **D.** The foreclosure process is structured to close off any rights of the mortgagor/debtor to redeem his or her property.

76. **A.** In title theory states, the mortgage actually conveys legal title; most states are lien-theory states in which the mortgage creates a lien even though no legal title is transferred. The mortgage secures the note.

77. **D.** The wraparound mortgage is typically junior to the underlying mortgage that it wraps around.

78. **D.** The rate may, for example, be subject to change according to changes in the U.S. Treasury Bill rate. Such changes may occur several times a year, although there are specified ceilings on the amount of change.

79. **C.** The specific index used, however, differs from lender to lender.

80. **B.** The down payment is $30,000; it is too much for the buyer to put up as a good-faith deposit. The first and second mortgage total $100,000, so the buyer should have $10,000 applied to reduce the mortgage balance. The danger in allowing the underlying mortgage balance to exceed the balance owed to the seller is that the buyer could pay off the seller who then leaves town. The buyer is left with the outstanding balance on the property even though he or she has met all his or her obligations to the seller.

REVIEW EXAM 2 QUESTIONS

1. A mortgage clause that gives the mortgagee the right to declare the whole sum due in the event that the borrower sells to another who assumes the loan without the mortgagee's consent is called a(n)
   A. release clause.
   B. alienation clause.
   C. subordination clause.
   D. prepayment clause.

2. An acceleration clause is *BEST* defined by which of the following?
   A. Mortgagor's right to prepay
   B. Mortgagee's demand for full payment
   C. Foreclosure
   D. Promissory note

3. A buyer pays $25,000 as a down payment and agrees to pay the balance of $150,000 at 12 percent interest over ten years to a seller who has a $100,000 first mortgage at 10 percent interest. If the seller gives the buyer a deed, what type of financing device is *MOST* likely involved?
   A. Agreement of sale
   B. Assumption of mortgage
   C. Wraparound mortgage
   D. Conventional mortgage

4. An acceleration clause inserted in a note to benefit a lender covers which of the following?
   A. A procedure for declaring a debt due and payable upon default
   B. A penalty for early payment of the note
   C. A gradually increasing interest rate
   D. A method of foreclosure

5. All of the following are methods used in estimating replacement costs for a commercial building *EXCEPT*
   A. unit-cost-in-place.
   B. quantity survey.
   C. comparative unit.
   D. engineering breakdown.

6. The term *reproduction cost new,* as used in the cost approach to estimating value, means the present cost of reproducing the subject improvement
   A. minus depreciation.
   B. plus land value.
   C. with one having the same utility.
   D. with the same or very similar materials.

7. Given the annual income of a property, what is the *BEST* method to determine its value?
   A. Capitalization method
   B. Comparison method
   C. Replacement cost method
   D. Summation method

8. All of the following would be considered in the cost approach to appraisal *EXCEPT*
   A. operating expenses.
   B. depreciation.
   C. land value.
   D. replacement cost.

9. All of the following should be considered when appraising real property *EXCEPT*
   A. owner's rights and interests.
   B. easements and adequacy of public improvements and utilities.
   C. zoning.
   D. foreclosure rights.

10. A building ten years old is being appraised today. It has a useful remaining life of 25 years. The applicable recapture rate is
    A. 2.5%.
    B. 4%.
    C. 20%.
    D. 25%.

11. All of the following are examples of physical deterioration as defined by the cost approach to value *EXCEPT*
    A. poor condition of floors, ceilings, beams, and other structural elements.
    B. basement damage due to flooding.
    C. peeled paint on the exterior and siding.
    D. rundown neighborhood.

12. Sigmund decides to exchange his rental property with Heinrich. As an appraiser you would be guided in your evaluation of the appropriate exchange value by which of the following?
    A. Market data comparables
    B. Sigmund's demands
    C. Heinrich's demands
    D. Lender's opinion

13. In seeking a listing, the owner tells the broker that the larger house next door recently sold for $135,000. The suggested listing price for the owner's house would be
    A. $135,000.
    B. $135,000 plus commission.
    C. based on the square-foot cost of the house next door.
    D. based on more comparables.

14. An appraiser is interested in all of the following *EXCEPT*
    A. zoning of the property.
    B. a stated definition of value and the purpose of the appraisal.
    C. a description of the property and type of title.
    D. the types of financing that are available for the property.

15. The operating practices of a manufacturing business and of the management of rental properties differ in that
    A. the real estate manager is not concerned with the economic utilization of capital.
    B. the manufacturer can curtail supply in a falling market.
    C. the manufacturer must be licensed.
    D. there is no difference.

16. Functional obsolescence can be corrected with
    A. capitalization.
    B. modernization.
    C. depreciation.
    D. specialization.

17. When determining the net operating income of a property in using the income approach to value, it is proper to
    A. omit a management fee if the property is managed by the owner.
    B. include the owner's income taxes.
    C. deduct the owner's income taxes.
    D. deduct typical vacancy and bad debt collection losses.

18. The highest and best use of a site for light industry would have all of the following criteria *EXCEPT*
    A. financially feasible use.
    B. compatibility with surrounding land uses.
    C. legally permissible use.
    D. production of highest gross income.

19. Which factor is *LEAST* important in evaluating a property for a manufacturing site?
    A. Pedestrian traffic
    B. Ceiling height
    C. Capacity of water and electrical services
    D. Capacity of floor load factors

20. Which of the following is the effect of neglect on a building?
    A. The rate of depreciation is speeded up.
    B. The rate of obsolescence is speeded up.
    C. The rate of depreciation is slowed down.
    D. The rate of obsolescence is slowed down.

21. Which subject would *LEAST* likely be found in a prospectus marketing a time-share condominium?
    A. Interval ownership
    B. Floating-use periods
    C. Prepaid vacations
    D. Escalating rents

22. In an appraisal using the market comparison approach, appraisers must take into account special features and make the necessary addition or subtraction adjustments to which property?
    A. Subject property
    B. Comparable property
    C. Both properties
    D. Neither property

23. The gross income multiplier is calculated by dividing the sales price by the
    A. monthly net income.
    B. monthly gross income.
    C. annual net income.
    D. annual gross income.

24. The principle of "high leverage" is involved when a buyer can control an expensive property with
    A. a small mortgage.
    B. a 60 percent loan.
    C. a large mortgage.
    D. no mortgage.

25. Which one is *MOST* likely treated as an independent contractor?
    A. Principal broker
    B. Salesperson
    C. Broker in charge
    D. Secretary

26. The collection of data and the analysis of different approaches to value is known as
    A. depreciation.
    B. amortization.
    C. reconciliation.
    D. accrual.

27. Assume there is a five-year lease at $5,000 per year. The lessor in year three usually *CANNOT*
    A. mortgage.
    B. sell.
    C. raise rent.
    D. devise.

28. In a Section 1031 exchange, the basis for the old property becomes the basis for the new property and the capital gains tax is
    A. exchanged.
    B. deferred.
    C. forgiven.
    D. compounded.

29. In appraising investment property, what does the owner deduct to arrive at the net operating income?
    A. Federal income taxes
    B. Capital improvements
    C. Vacancy and debt losses
    D. All ordinary expenses to the property

30. Which one of the following types of mortgages enables elderly homeowners to borrow against the equity in their homes?
    A. Sweat equity
    B. Reverse annuity
    C. Balloon
    D. Graduated payment

31. In times of inflation, who suffers *MOST* from rent control?
    A. Tenant
    B. Hotel industry
    C. Lessor
    D. Optionee

32. Which of the following types of ownership is *LEAST* likely to be subject to regulation by the securities law?
    A. Limited partnership
    B. Syndication
    C. S corporation
    D. Joint tenancy

33. A sales associate is employed by a listing broker to sell a home. The sales associate is a subagent of
    A. the seller.
    B. the buyer.
    C. the broker.
    D. escrow.

34. In a city's master development plan, all of the following are analyzed and included *EXCEPT*
    A. population growth.
    B. transportation and traffic patterns.
    C. study of blighted areas.
    D. state's usury laws.

35. What advantage would the developer/lessee gain if the owner/lessor subordinated her fee simple interest?
    A. Land values would increase.
    B. Interim construction loan would be on better terms.
    C. The owner would avoid foreclosure.
    D. The purchaser could rescind sale.

36. If a person selling real estate securities in the form of a Real Estate Investment Trust (REIT) is guilty of fraud, all of the following could occur *EXCEPT*
    A. criminal penalty.
    B. civil penalty.
    C. rescission of contract.
    D. actual damages multiplied by five.

37. Which one of the following types of loans would a borrower want to cover the period between the end of one loan and the beginning of another?
    A. Filler loan
    B. Bridge loan
    C. Subordinate loan
    D. Conversion loan

38. All of the following is true about surveys *EXCEPT* they
    A. are useful in revealing encroachments.
    B. are likely to be used when lenders are making a loan on real property.
    C. may reveal zoning and setback violations.
    D. are required in every real estate transaction.

39. Which of the following is *FALSE* about FHA loans?
    A. The interest rate and points are negotiable.
    B. Points are based on the amount of the mortgage.
    C. The insurance premium is payable upfront or added to the loan balance at 3.8% on a maximum loan of $135,000.
    D. They are restricted to veterans.

40. Al sees Sid's ad that says "For Sale by Owner." Al asks Sid if he can show his buyer the property. Sid leaves Al the key. Which is true?
    A. Al is the subagent of Sid.
    B. Sid is Al's principal.
    C. No agency exists.
    D. An implied agency exists.

41. A real property tax appraiser would consider all of the following *EXCEPT*
    A. years left on the building lease.
    B. zoning.
    C. condition of structure.
    D. location.

42. When determining the highest and best use of a property, an appraiser would consider all of the following *EXCEPT*
    A. original purchase price.
    B. zoning.
    C. setback requirements.
    D. restrictions on record.

43. After the buyer visits the property at an open house, the owner decides to leave extra paint cans and firewood. The broker should do which of the following?
    A. Make a mental note to see if these items are still there at closing.
    B. Do nothing because they were not on the listing.
    C. Write them into the offer because they are personal property.
    D. Do nothing because they are fixtures.

44. Which of the following sales is *MOST* likely used in the market comparison approach to value?
    A. Probate sale
    B. Comparable sale
    C. Foreclosure sale
    D. Tax sale

45. A broker examining the seller's conveyance document would likely discover all of the following information *EXCEPT*
    A. legal description.
    B. nonconforming use.
    C. restrictive covenants.
    D. estate of ownership.

46. A buyer made a $32,000 down payment on an $80,000 purchase. Payments on a 25-year mortgage were $587 a month. What was the total amount of interest paid over the life of the loan?
    A. $81,000
    B. $112,000
    C. $128,100
    D. $144,100

47. When the broker reviews the closing statement, she or he notices that the seller pays the attorney's fee to draw up the purchase-money mortgage. The sales contract did not state who is to pay this fee. What should the broker do?
    A. Keep silent
    B. Tell the seller to pay
    C. Tell the buyer to pay
    D. Point out to the closing agent that there may be a problem

48. All of the following are true about nonconventional loans *EXCEPT*
    A. FHA loans for nonowner occupants are assumable in the first 24 months without lender approval.
    B. the maximum VA guaranty is set by law.
    C. VA loans can be assumed and the veteran released from liability if the buyer is proven to be creditworthy.
    D. under a FHA formal assumption, the original borrower can be released from liability.

49. A ceiling beam in a condo unit is classified as a common element. Who is normally responsible for termite damage?
    A. Unit owner
    B. Management company
    C. Association of owners
    D. Real estate broker

50. An FHA conditional commitment is an agreement by the FHA to
    A. insure a loan made to a qualified buyer.
    B. guarantee the value of the property.
    C. make a loan subject to a mortgage.
    D. indemnify the lender on a defaulted loan.

51. All of the following own a future interest in real property *EXCEPT* a
    A. remainderman.
    B. holder of a reversion.
    C. grantor of a life estate.
    D. life tenant.

52. Which of the following is considered a sound office management procedure for the principal broker to adopt?
    A. Bimonthly payroll
    B. Graduated commission scale
    C. Preparation of monthly statements that account for expenses on each listing
    D. Newspaper ads at the discretion of the listing salesperson

53. Mud tunnels at the foundation of a home indicate
    A. soil settlement.
    B. ground termites.
    C. cracked foundation.
    D. inadequate footing.

54. What is *MOST* likely to occur when salesperson Salvador moves to a new broker?
    A. Salvador takes his listings with him.
    B. His listings are terminated.
    C. His errors and omissions policy is automatically transferred.
    D. His broker can pay him commissions that he earned.

55. Which statement is *TRUE* concerning the Accelerated Cost Recovery System (ACRS)?
    A. Appraisers favor this method of valuing commercial properties.
    B. Taxpayers can switch from straight line to accelerated depreciation after four years.
    C. Contractors use this system to recoup expenses.
    D. Under the Tax Act, the typical method of recovery of depreciation is straight line.

56. Homeowner Arlin refinances his home and takes out $5,000 due to the appreciation in value. Which is *TRUE* about the $5,000?
    A. It is subject to capital gains tax.
    B. It is tax free to the homeowner.
    C. It reduces the tax basis in the home.
    D. It increases the equity in the home.

57. The seller is usually responsible for which of the following at closing?
    A. Cost to draft note and mortgage
    B. Unpaid charges that accrue on the day of closing
    C. Real estate licensing fees
    D. Cost of appraisal

58. A metal tool shed is set on wooden blocks in the backyard. Nothing is said in the sales contract about the tool shed. Which is *TRUE?*
    A. A bill of sale is needed to transfer title to it.
    B. It is a fixture that belongs to the buyer.
    C. It is personal property that belongs to the seller.
    D. It is an encumbrance that runs with the land.

59. The real estate salesperson has primary fiduciary duty to which one of the following?
    A. Supervising broker
    B. Buyer
    C. Seller
    D. Sales manager

60. To determine net operating income, all of the following is deducted from gross income *EXCEPT*
    A. real property taxes.
    B. insurance costs.
    C. debt service.
    D. utility costs.

61. A salesperson who has listed a seller's house owes a fiduciary duty directly to which one of the following?
    A. Seller
    B. Broker
    C. Buyer
    D. Escrow

62. The loan reserve account (customer trust fund) balance is $1,000. Real property taxes are due in December and closing is July 15. The closing statement entry would be which of the following?
    A. Credit seller $1,000
    B. Credit buyer $1,000
    C. Debit seller $1,000 and credit buyer $1,000
    D. Credit seller $1,000 and debit buyer $1,000

63. The buyer assumes a ten-year sewer assessment in its third year. At closing the correct practice is to prorate
    A. annual interest due.
    B. interest and principal.
    C. principal only.
    D. seller to pay balance due.

64. While observing market conditions, a property manager would be aware that an increased demand for rental property would *MOST* likely be caused by which of the following?
    A. An increase in the mortgage rate
    B. An increase in disposable income
    C. A decrease in mortgage rates
    D. An increase in urban clearance

65. Under a property management agreement, the property manager representing the owners most likely would do all of the following, *EXCEPT*
    A. negotiate maintenance service fees.
    B. rehabilitate and convert property.
    C. initiate action for recovery of rent.
    D. file required federal and state reports.

66. If a commercial building is leased on an "absolute" net lease (triple net), for which of the following expenses is the lessor responsible?
    A. Lease rent
    B. Insurance
    C. Maintenance
    D. Property management fee

67. A house was purchased for $100,000. Improvements of $25,000 were added. The house sold for $250,000 ten months later. How much was the seller's capital gain?
    A. $25,000
    B. $50,000
    C. $75,000
    D. $125,000

68. What is a good example of leverage?
    A. Control of a large asset with a small mortgage
    B. Ability to change loan terms
    C. Control of a large asset with little money down
    D. Purchase of a security

69. Real estate commissions are
    A. fixed by law.
    B. determined by agreement of brokers in the community.
    C. sometimes set by company policy but could be further negotiated by the seller and broker.
    D. agreed upon at closing.

70. The government survey system uses which of the following to describe real property?
    A. Lot and block number
    B. Ranges, townships, and sections
    C. Plat and parcel
    D. Metes and bounds

71. In an FHA mortgage, the mortgagee does which of the following?
    A. Requires the same amount of mutual mortgage insurance for both the first and second mortgages
    B. Allows unlimited assumptions of the loan
    C. Collects discount charges from either buyer or seller
    D. Charges a prepayment penalty

72. Last year a taxpayer, Samantha, paid $800 in real property taxes on her home and $5,800 in mortgage payments ($5,100 interest and $700 principal). She added a $3,000 room. How much deduction can she take on her tax return?
    A. $700
    B. $800
    C. $5,900
    D. $6,400

73. Two married couples buying an investment property want to retain their inheritance rights in ownership. What type of tenancy might suit their need?
    A. Joint tenancy
    B. Tenancy in common
    C. Tenancy by entirety
    D. Tenancy in severalty

74. A mortgage tied to an economic indicator is called a(n)
    A. index mortgage.
    B. open-end mortgage.
    C. balloon mortgage.
    D. escalation mortgage.

75. All of the following are essential for a valid real estate sales contract *EXCEPT*
    A. names and signatures of parties to be bound.
    B. provision for broker's commission.
    C. consideration.
    D. description of property.

76. On March 5, Jake agrees to sell his home to Carl with a closing date of April 10. Carl will assume Jake's 11 percent, 30-year mortgage that has 21 years to go and a balance, after the March 25 amortization date, of $48,500, with principal and interest payments of $525 per month. The loan balance at closing is
    A. $46,558.
    B. $47,652.
    C. $47,975.
    D. $48,500.

77. A seller makes a counteroffer. During the time the buyer is deciding what to do, the broker can do all of the following *EXCEPT*
    A. continue to show the property.
    B. present additional offers.
    C. answer questions about the property.
    D. recommend the seller accept another offer.

78. A sale of property in which the lender agrees to release its mortgage lien even though the lender will not be paid in full is called a
    A. deficiency judgment.
    B. lis pendens.
    C. short sale.
    D. court sale.

79. Which one of the following is *TRUE* concerning RESPA?
    A. The seller can require that the buyer use a specific title company.
    B. It applies to VA and FHA loans.
    C. It applies to seller wraparound loans.
    D. It is the responsibility of the seller.

80. A mortgage with interest-only payments for five years and a payoff in the fifth year is called a(n)
    A. payoff mortgage.
    B. budget mortgage.
    C. straight mortgage.
    D. amortized mortgage.

REVIEW EXAM 2 ANSWERS

Note: Where appropriate, assume V = Value, R = Rate, I = Income.

1. **B.** The alienation clause is also called the *acceleration clause* or *due-on-sale clause*. It has been upheld by the U.S. Supreme Court as an enforceable device for the lender to call in the loan if the property is transferred without the lender's consent.

2. **B.** The acceleration clause may be triggered by default or by transfer of the property. Choice (A) refers to the privilege of prepayment.

3. **C.** The sales price is $175,000 with the seller carrying back a second mortgage from which the seller will make the payments on the $100,000 first loan at 10 percent. (The $150,000 mortgage wraps around the seller's $100,000 first mortgage, although the buyer does not assume the first mortgage.)

4. **A.** Choice (B) is a prepayment penalty clause; choice (C) may be a variable rate mortgage. Choice (D) could be a power of sale clause in a mortgage.

5. **D.** Engineering breakdown refers to a method of estimating accrued depreciation. Choice (C) would cover component costs such as cost per square feet of foundation. Choice (B) involves a more detailed analysis of the cost of each material used in construction, and choice (A) involves estimating the unit cost of each component section in place, including labor and materials.

6. **D.** Reproduction cost involves the cost to make an exact replica. Replacement cost involves producing a replacement structure with similar utility. After this cost is determined, the appraiser subtracts a figure for accrued depreciation in arriving at an estimate of value under the cost or summation approach.

7. **A.** The capitalization approach converts income into value.

8. **A.** Operating income is only relevant when using the income or capitalization approach to value.

9. **D.** Foreclosure rights aren't relevant, but choices (A), (B), and (C) all have an impact on value.

10. **B.** Recapture rate is designed to give a return of the investment in a building that will be theoretically worth zero at the end of its useful life. Thus each year the building will depreciate 4 percent.

11. **D.** This is an example of external obsolescence.

12. **A.** Market value is determined by an analysis of market conditions, not the personal desires of the parties.

13. **D.** Listing prices should be based on several comparable sales and not just one, especially where the properties are different sizes.

14. **D.** Financing is not relevant to an appraisal, but zoning is because it affects the highest and best use. The appraiser also needs to know whether to look for insurance value, market value, loan value, and so on.

15. **B.** In a falling market, the manager of real estate cannot decrease the supply of unrented units.

16. **B.** Certain outdated design problems can be corrected by modernization such as expanding a room or replacing an obsolete plumbing system.

17. **D.** Vacancy and bad debt losses must be taken into consideration, whereas personal income tax aspects are not relevant. Under choice (A), even though the present owner does his own management, the next owner might want to hire a manager to perform this function.

18. **D.** The highest and best use is concerned with that use which will produce the highest *net* income or yield.

19. **A.** Pedestrian traffic patterns are more appropriate for a retail establishment like a shopping center.

20. **A.** Neglect will speed up the rate of physical deterioration.

21. **D.** There are many forms of time-share ownership—time interval (like tenants in common), license to use, vacation lease, and club members. Often the time periods fluctuate over the years, and they can be exchanged. The concept is attractive to people who vacation frequently in the same resort (and get tired of increased hotel rates).

22. **B.** The value of the comparable is adjusted upward or downward, depending on whether it has a feature different from the subject property.

23. **D.** The gross income multiplier, used to compare investment property in the market comparison appraisal method, is the ratio between gross income and sales price.

24. **C.** The larger the loan amount, the less cash the buyer has invested in the property—the less cash, the greater leverage (or use of other people's money, OPM).

25. **B.** The salesperson must not be compensated on a hourly basis. Choices (A) and (C) act in a supervisory capacity. The secretary is also an employee.

26. **C.** Reconciliation, formerly called *correlation,* is more than just averaging the three approaches to value; it weighs many factors.

27. **C.** The rent is fixed for five years. If the lessor mortgages, sells, or wills the property, it will be taken subject to the lease.

28. **B.** Taxes are deferred until the new property is sold.

29. **D.** Expenses are deducted to arrive at net operating income. Vacancy and bad debt losses are deducted to reflect the gross effective income.

30. **B.** The reverse annuity mortgage allows the homeowner to receive monthly payments to help meet living costs. Thus, the inflow and outflow of funds is the reverse of the standard loan.

31. **C.** With inflation, expenses increase while income is frozen by rent control, in which the government puts a lid on rent increases.

32. **D.** A security often involves stock or an investment contract, as when one invests in a venture with the expectation of making profits through the efforts of the promoter. The sale of an investment condominium with a mandatory rental pool arrangement involves the sale of a security and thus requires registration with federal and state securities agencies.

33. **A.** The sales associate is the agent of the broker, who is the agent of the seller. Thus, the sales associate is subagent of the seller.

34. **D.** City planning is not concerned with laws regulating the amount of interest charged on loans.

35. **B.** By subordinating the fee, the collateral or security for the loan now includes both the leasehold and the fee simple estates. The owner would do this only after consulting legal counsel. The prime motivation would be to help the project get completed and thus result in a greater sales price to the owner for the property.

36. **D.** The antifraud provisions of the *federal* securities laws provide for stiff penalties, but not multiplied by five. The law applies to the seller and the broker.

37. **B.** A bridge, or swing, loan is often used to carry the property from the time of acquisition until it can be improved or developed, so it can qualify for a permanent loan.

38. **D.** Many transactions close without a survey being ordered. Most lenders require an extended title insurance policy. The policy covers rights of parties in possession, so a survey is usually ordered.

39. **D.** VA loans are restricted to veterans. FHA loans have an MIP—mortgage insurance premium—paid by the borrower to cover the cost of insurance (payable in one lump sum upfront or financed).

40. **C.** Agency is a consensual relationship. Giving Al the key is inadequate to evidence an intent to have Al act on behalf of Sid.

41. **A.** The tax assessor is concerned with the value of the fee simple interest.

42. **A.** The original purchase price has no effect on present value.

43. **C.** The personal property will not pass to the buyer unless included in the sales contract.

44. **B.** Involuntary sales are *not* included in the market comparison approach, which stresses sales to ready, willing, and able buyers by sellers not compelled to sell.

45. **B.** The nonconforming use status is revealed by a comparison of the existing use with the permitted use under the zoning.

46. **C.** $80,000 - $32,000 = $48,000
$25 \times 12 \times $587 = $176,100$
$176,100 - $48,000 = $128,100

47. **D.** The problem is that the buyer customarily pays for the cost of drafting the mortgage because the buyer benefits by being able to obtain the loan.

48. **A.** FHA loans are no longer automatically assumable. There can be no simple assumption in the first 24 months (one year for owner-occupants), and only formal assumptions are allowed. This change is in response to the high number of foreclosures within the first two years of an FHA loan.

49. **C.** The association of owners is responsible for repairs to common elements.

50. **A.** Provided the borrower is qualified, the FHA commits to insure the loan.

51. **D.** A future interest is one that occurs in the future on the happening of some event such as the default of a life tenant. A life tenant owns a present interest.

52. **C.** Brokers need to be careful that expenses don't get out of control or too much money is spent on ads.

53. **B.** Subterranean land or ground termites move through mud tunnels.

54. **D.** The listings belong to the broker, not the salesperson.

55. **D.** The 1986 Tax Reform Act basically limited depreciation to straight line, thus eliminating the ACRS methods developed under the 1981 Tax Act.

56. **B.** The $5,000 is not taxable, but it reduces the owner's equity in the home.

57. **B.** A question sometimes arises whether the seller or the buyer is responsible for the expenses (like real property taxes, interest, maintenance fees) on the day of closing. Typically, the seller's obligations run up to and *include* the day of closing.

58. **C.** The tool shed is easily removable and not permanently attached to the property.

59. **A.** The salesperson is the agent of the listing broker, who is the agent of the seller.

60. **C.** Under the income (capitalization) approach, effective gross income is determined by deducting from potential gross income an allowance for bad debts and vacancy. To determine net operating income, deduct fixed and operating expenses but not financing costs (debt service).

61. **B.** The salesperson is the agent of the listing broker and the subagent of the seller.

62. **D.** This is a double entry with the seller being returned the funds the seller had advanced at the start of the loan—funds that the buyer will receive later at loan payoff.

63. **A.** Only interest, not principal, is prorated.

64. **A.** Higher interest rates usually mean marginal buyers can't buy and have to rent instead.

65. **B.** Clients make the major decisions, such as converting a rental building into a condominium.

66. **D.** Under the terms of a typical triple net lease, the tenant pays all the carrying charges. The lessor pays for its own property managers.

67. **D.** Because the seller's basis was $100,000 plus $25,000, the taxable capital gain is $125,000. The prior tax law permitted a deferment of capital gain if a replacement property was acquired within 24 months.

68. **C.** Leverage involves the use of other people's money to control an asset (e.g., buy real estate with little money down).

69. **C.** Price fixing is illegal under antitrust laws. Some firms prefer a certain fee but recognize that the commission is negotiable between buyer and seller.

70. **B.** The survey system creates a checkerboard of identical squares covering a given area—also called *rectangular survey system.*

71. **C.** Whether buyer or seller pays, the discount charged is subject to negotiation. FHA restricts assumption in the first 24 months of a loan on an investment property.

72. **C.** Samantha can deduct interest and real property taxes.

73. **B.** They could choose any tenancy among themselves; but as to the share of each couple, that should be a tenancy in common. If they were all to be joint tenants, then one could survive the other, thus leaving nothing for the heirs to inherit.

74. **A.** An example is an index mortgage whose interest rate is tied to the rate of U.S. Treasury bills.

75. **B.** The broker's fee is often set in the listing agreement. It may also appear in the sales contract but is not necessary.

76. **D.** Principal is not prorated on a daily basis, only interest.

77. **D.** Unless instructed otherwise by the seller, the broker should continue to market the property. The seller needs to be careful about accepting additional offers without first revoking the counteroffer.

78. **C.** Normally the lender will require full payment before releasing its lien. In a short sale, the lender may feel market conditions are such that it will net more money faster from the defaulting mortgagor by taking the proceeds from a short sale rather than seeking foreclosure through the courts.

79. **B.** RESPA applies to any federally related loan. The *lender* is the party responsible that RESPA disclosures are made.

80. **C.** A straight mortgage is an interest-only mortgage, also called a *term mortgage.*

REVIEW EXAM 3 QUESTIONS

1. A home was purchased for $100,000, and $10,000 of improvements were added. The home sold for $130,000 with a 6.5 percent commission. What is the tax basis of the property?
   A. $100,000
   B. $110,000
   C. $120,000
   D. $121,500

2. Property taxes for the current year are due on December 31. One property has an assessed value of $42,000 with a tax mill rate of 0.075. If the house was sold on July 15, what is the proration?
   A. Credit the seller $1,444
   B. Credit the buyer $1,706
   C. Debit the buyer $1,181
   D. Debit the seller $1,968

3. Selwyn bought a house for $130,000. He paid $30,000 down and took out a $100,000 mortgage at 9½ percent for 30 years. His monthly principal and interest payments were figured at $8.20 per thousand dollars. How much interest had he paid at the end of the 30 years?
   A. $127,500
   B. $195,200
   C. $285,000
   D. $310,220

4. A business leases store space for which it pays base rent of $7,200 and 5 percent on sales over $200,000. If last year the business paid total rent of $37,465, what was the amount of sales last year?
   A. $590,300
   B. $605,300
   C. $749,300
   D. $805,300

5. It is estimated that the reproduction cost of a building 32' by 50' will be $32 per square foot, and that the subject property has depreciated $15,000. What will be the value of the property?
   A. $35,200
   B. $36,200
   C. $41,200
   D. $51,200

6. Which of the following prorated items is typically paid in arrears?
   A. Interest
   B. Lease rent
   C. FHA points
   D. Private mortgage insurance

7. A seller agrees to finance a buyer for $35,000 of the purchase price on an unsecured promissory note. This agreement is entered on the closing statement as which of the following?
   A. Debit to buyer; debit to seller
   B. Credit to buyer; credit to seller
   C. Debit to buyer; credit to seller
   D. Credit to buyer; debit to seller

8. Items marked POC (paid outside of closing) may be paid to all *EXCEPT*
   A. seller.
   B. lenders.
   C. escrow office.
   D. appraiser.

9. A buyer offered $140,000 to purchase a house. The buyer offered to pay the seller $15,000 down and $10,000 a year at 12 percent until paid off. What is the appropriate entry on the settlement statement?
   A. Credit $125,000 to buyer; debit $125,000 to seller
   B. Debit $125,000 to seller; credit $125,000 to seller
   C. Credit $140,000 to seller; debit $15,000 to seller
   D. Debit $140,000 to buyer; credit $10,000 to seller

10. When a buyer is to assume the seller's mortgage balance, escrow is to account for the customer trust account by which entry in the settlement statement?
    A. Debit buyer
    B. Credit seller
    C. Debit buyer; credit seller
    D. Credit buyer; debit seller

11. The closing statement shows an entry of
    $64,000 credit to buyer for a loan and a $640
    debit for a loan fee. The $64,000 loan is the
    A. net loan amount.
    B. gross loan amount.
    C. prorated amount.
    D. adjusted loan amount.

12. All the following expenses are prorated
    between buyer and seller *EXCEPT*
    A. rental income.
    B. real property tax.
    C. recording fees.
    D. assigned insurance policy.

13. In preparing a settlement statement on the
    sale of a rental property, what is the appropri-
    ate entry for any security deposits?
    A. Debit seller and credit buyer
    B. Credit seller and debit buyer
    C. Debit seller only
    D. Credit buyer only

14. If a house burns to the ground prior to closing,
    the buyer may do all of the following
    EXCEPT
    A. delay closing until seller builds a replace-
       ment.
    B. close the sale and obtain an assignment of
       the insurance proceeds.
    C. rescind the contract.
    D. renegotiate the price if seller agrees.

15. The seller's conveyance document would
    likely reveal all of the following *EXCEPT*
    A. boundaries.
    B. estate.
    C. restrictive covenants.
    D. nonconforming use.

16. If the property already has the maximum
    improvements permitted under the zoning but
    the owner wants to add a new structure, the
    owner would need to first apply for a
    A. building permit.
    B. variance.
    C. nonconforming use.
    D. special use permit.

17. All of the following can file a mechanic's lien
    EXCEPT
    A. prime contractor.
    B. subcontractor.
    C. architect.
    D. real estate broker.

18. After a partition of property between several
    joint tenants or tenants in common, the ten-
    ancy is
    A. entirety.
    B. joint.
    C. severalty.
    D. common.

19. The principle of "leverage" is involved when
    a buyer can control an expensive property
    with
    A. a small mortgage.
    B. a 60 percent loan.
    C. a large mortgage.
    D. no mortgage.

20. Any of the following is protected under the
    "familial status" provision of the federal Fair
    Housing Act *EXCEPT* a person
    A. who is pregnant.
    B. in process of securing legal custody of a
       child.
    C. with a child 19 years old.
    D. who has written permission of a child's
       parents to keep temporary custody of the
       child.

21. Which of the following is an acceptable busi-
    ness practice for a real estate agent working
    with a buyer?
    A. Filling out a loan application form for the
       buyer
    B. Selecting the lender for the borrower
    C. Advising the buyer about possible loans
       available in the market
    D. Cosigning a promissory note in order for
       the buyer to qualify for a loan

22. Once a licensee has prequalified a client,
    which of the following can the licensee do?
    A. Promise the client the availability of a
       specified loan amount
    B. Show the client houses within the proba-
       ble price range indicated by the prequali-
       fication
    C. Require the client to use a specific lender
       before the sales contract is drafted and
       presented to the seller
    D. Require the use of the lender who
       prequalified the client

23. Alejandro owns a duplex building. He occupies one of the units. On what basis may he *NOT* discriminate in renting the other unit?
    A. Race
    B. Religion
    C. National origin
    D. Sex

24. Any of the following is required of new multifamily dwellings under the 1988 "handicap" amendments to the federal Fair Housing Act *EXCEPT*
    A. reasonable modifications at expense of tenant.
    B. reasonable accommodations in the rules and policies.
    C. premises that are newly designed must meet certain accessibility requirements.
    D. lower rent payments charged to handicapped tenants.

25. All of the following supporting documents are normally required by the lender to verify income and employment *EXCEPT*
    A. college transcripts.
    B. pay stubs.
    C. last two years' personal income tax returns.
    D. current business financial statements.

26. Which of the following practices is discriminatory under the federal Fair Housing Act?
    A. Refusing to make any modifications in a unit that will add to the comfort and safety of a handicapped tenant
    B. Refusing permission to a handicapped tenant to make modifications unless the tenant pays the cost
    C. Refusing permission to a handicapped tenant to make modifications unless the tenant agrees to restore the premises to approximately the same condition at the end of lease
    D. Refusing permission to a tenant who pays the cost and agrees to restore the property to its original condition

27. Which of the following steps can a borrower take to expedite the processing of a loan application?
    A. Provide all of the information to the licensee so that the licensee can fill out the application for the borrower
    B. Submit all account numbers and branch locations and addresses of banks and lenders with application
    C. Provide the lender with a photograph of the borrower
    D. Disclose all physical handicaps of borrower

28. A borrower is not obligated to disclose which of the following to a lender when applying for a loan?
    A. Receipt of alimony
    B. Payment of child support
    C. Car loan payments
    D. Second mortgage obligations

29. Which type of loan has its interest rate based on some type of index?
    A. Adjustable-rate mortgage
    B. Graduated-payment mortgage
    C. Rollover mortgage
    D. Reverse-annuity mortgage

30. Which of the following mortgages has negative amortization?
    A. Growing equity mortgage
    B. Biweekly fixed rate
    C. Level payment, fixed rate
    D. Reverse annuity mortgage

31. Under RESPA, when escrow is used, how many business days in advance of settlement does the borrower have the right to inspect the HUD-1 Settlement Statement?
    A. One day
    B. Three days
    C. Five days
    D. No advance inspection required

32. Under what conditions will a real estate salesperson who drafts a complex original contract for a client be guilty of negligence?
    A. If the salesperson does not meet the professional standards of a licensed attorney
    B. If the client fails to make a profit on the deal
    C. If the salesperson does not have the contract reviewed by his or her employing broker
    D. If the salesperson fails to get written permission, in advance of drafting the contract, from the Board of REALTORS®

33. A buyer and seller want the agent to draft a purchase-money mortgage to include a subordination agreement and a partial release clause. The real estate salesperson should
    A. suggest that the parties consult an attorney.
    B. disclose that this would make the salesperson a mortgage broker.
    C. fill out a standard purchase-money mortgage form.
    D. obtain the proper language from a bank.

34. If a licensee who is a buyer's agent shows an in-house listing, which of the following is TRUE?
    A. The licensee is a dual agent.
    B. The buyer is now a "customer."
    C. The seller is now a "customer."
    D. The buyer is unrepresented.

35. Which of the following are material facts that must be disclosed by the listing broker?
    A. The seller is dying of AIDS.
    B. The building does not conform with tax records.
    C. The price the seller paid for the property.
    D. The seller is about to obtain a divorce.

36. All of the following are practical rules in dealing with contingencies EXCEPT
    A. making sure the contingency is properly and clearly stated.
    B. making sure the client diligently adheres to all time provisions.
    C. obtaining all receipts, satisfactions, waivers, approval and failure notices, and other matters in writing.
    D. requiring an additional earnest money deposit for each contingency.

37. An "as is" clause is designated to cover
    A. disclosed and obvious defects.
    B. any hidden defects.
    C. affirmative misrepresentation.
    D. all property defects.

38. A licensee who is selling an in-house listing and has accepted a power of attorney from the buyer is all of the following EXCEPT
    A. a dual agent.
    B. an attorney-in-fact.
    C. required to make disclosure of the dual agency to the seller.
    D. a single agent.

39. Which of the following is the MOST true with respect to the area of fair housing laws?
    A. Federal law always prevails.
    B. State law always prevails.
    C. The law that gives the most protection to the consumer prevails.
    D. The law that gives the most protection to the homeowner prevails.

40. Any of the following can be considered discriminatory advertising EXCEPT
    A. ads using words like "private," "integrated," or "traditional."
    B. a series of ads using models but failing to include some representation of other major racial groups.
    C. advertising limiting housing to people of a particular religion.
    D. ads for low-income housing.

41. Using several methods of appraisal to arrive at an estimate of value is BEST called
    A. reconciliation.
    B. weighted analysis.
    C. adjustment.
    D. assemblage.

42. Changing the zoning from commercial use to single-family residential use is BEST called
    A. consolidation.
    B. downzoning.
    C. spot zoning.
    D. restrictive zoning.

43. The capitalization method is designed to do which of the following?
    A. Determine net income
    B. Evaluate commercial joint ventures
    C. Select the proper capitalization rate
    D. Convert a property's net income into market value

44. The sublessor is *MOST* likely which one of the following?
    A. Tenant
    B. Lessee
    C. Lessor
    D. Owner

45. The lessee would *MOST* likely pay for real property taxes under which type of lease?
    A. Percentage
    B. Gross
    C. Triple net
    D. Index

46. The gross rent multiplier is a less reliable measurement of value than the capitalization or cost approach because it does *NOT* consider
    A. location.
    B. comparable sales.
    C. amenities.
    D. extraordinary expenses.

47. What would happen to the value of a fixed-rent property if expenses increased by $8,000, using a capitalization rate of 10 percent?
    A. Increases $80,000
    B. Decreases $8,000
    C. Decreases $80,000
    D. No change

48. The Real Estate Settlement Procedures Act requires that the lender do all of the following *EXCEPT*
    A. provide borrower with a copy of HUD booklet within three business days.
    B. allow borrower to inspect HUD settlement statement one business day before settlement.
    C. charge a reasonable fee for preparation of RESPA form.
    D. provide borrower with further estimate of likely settlement charges.

49. Which party benefits most from an assignment of rents provision in a mortgage?
    A. Trustee
    B. Mortgagee
    C. Mortgagor
    D. Lessee

50. Any of the following is involved with the government's handling of nonconforming uses *EXCEPT* a(n)
    A. ban on expanding use.
    B. eventual time for the use to stop.
    C. ban on rebuilding once the structure deteriorates.
    D. requirement to switch to a permitted use immediately.

51. Tearing down a corner gas station and convenience store to allow the construction of a shopping center and office building is an example of which appraisal principle?
    A. Progression
    B. Substitution
    C. Highest and best use
    D. Regression

52. Compound interest is used in connection with which one of the following types of loans?
    A. Partial amortization loan
    B. Fully amortized loan
    C. Reverse annuity loan
    D. Adjustable rate loan

53. The phrase "blind ads" refers to ads that omit the
    A. price of the property.
    B. fact an agent placed the ad.
    C. location of the property.
    D. fact the owner is leaving the state.

54. If nothing is stated in a short-term apartment lease regarding rent renegotiation, which of the following is *TRUE* at the end of the lease?
    A. Lessor can increase the rent to any amount
    B. Mandatory arbitration is required to set the new rent
    C. Court appoints a commissioner to set rent
    D. Litigation is needed if agreement is not reached within 180 days

55. An elderly retired person is planning her estate with the expectation that she will live comfortably and then leave all to her children. In evaluating the purchase of several properties, this person would be interested most likely in which one of the following appraisal approaches?
    A. Capitalization
    B. Direct sales comparison
    C. Cost
    D. Summation

56. A broker purchased one of his listings that was on the market for one year. The seller, who was behind in paying taxes and mortgage, carried back a second mortgage at a low rate of interest. The broker painted the house and re-sold it three months later for a $35,000 profit. How could the broker have reduced the likelihood of a suit by the seller to obtain the $35,000?
    A. Retained an attorney
    B. Used a salesperson to represent him
    C. Terminated the listing and advised the seller to retain other counsel
    D. Avoided giving the seller a second mortgage

57. What is the gross rent multiplier if the sale price is $70,000, the gross monthly rent is $525, and the monthly expenses are $125?
    A. 0.0006
    B. 0.0008
    C. 133.33
    D. 175

58. In a subdivision with homes in the $140,000 range, a person constructs a home in the $160,000 range. In appraising the new home what appraisal principle would the appraiser need to consider?
    A. Progression
    B. Reconciliation
    C. Regression
    D. Substitution

59. A loan in which the lender agrees not to seek a deficiency judgment against the borrower is *BEST* called
    A. fixed.
    B. nonrecourse.
    C. adjusted.
    D. nonmonetary.

60. Which type of foreclosure requires a power of sale clause in the mortgage?
    A. Nonrecourse
    B. Judicial
    C. Deed in lieu of foreclosure
    D. Nonjudicial

REVIEW EXAM 3 ANSWERS

Note: Where appropriate, assume V = Value, R = Rate, I = Income.

1. **B.** $100,000 cost plus $10,000 in improvements

2. **B.** $42,000 × 0.075 = $3,150
   $3,150 ÷ 12 = $262.50/month × 6.5 = $1,706.25

3. **B.** 8.20 × 100 = $820/month × 12 = $9,840
   $9,840 × 30 = $295,200 – $100,000 = $195,200

4. **D.** $37,456 – $7,200 = $30,265
   $30,265 ÷ 5% = $605,300 + $200,000 = $805,300

5. **B.** 32' × 50' = 1,600 sq. ft. × $32 = $51,200 – $15,000 = $36,200

6. **A.** The September mortgage payment, for example, includes the interest for August. FHA points are now paid upfront.

7. **D.** It is debited to the seller because it is money not yet received.

8. **C.** The HUD settlement statement is designed to reflect all closing charges, even those that are not paid through the escrow agent.

9. **A.** The $125,000 represents the financing carried back by the seller and is used to offset the $140,000 purchase price credited to the seller.

10. **C.** The customer trust account (impound or reserve account) is money advanced by the seller to make sure there is enough to pay taxes, condo maintenance fees, insurance, and so on. Because the money won't be returned to the seller by the lender until the end of the loan, an adjustment is made at closing and the assuming buyer will be entitled to the refund when the loan is paid off.

11. **B.** If the lender deducted the loan fee before depositing the funds into escrow, then the statement would show a credit to the buyer of only $63,360.

12. **C.** Recording fees are a single-entry expense of either the seller or the buyer, depending upon custom or agreement.

13. **A.** The seller has possession of the tenant's money, which the buyer will have to return to the tenant if the tenant leaves the property in good condition.

14. **A.** The seller has the risk of loss until closing, so the buyer can rescind or accept the deed and insurance proceeds.

15. **D.** While the fact that a property is nonconforming should be disclosed in the sales contract, it does not appear on the deed.

16. **B.** The owner is looking for an exception to the zoning.

17. **D.** Brokers cannot file a lien for unpaid commission for sales or for rental management.

18. **C.** Each parcel is now held in sole ownership.

19. **C.** The larger the loan amount, the less cash the buyer has invested in the property—the less cash, the greater leverage (or use of other people's money, OPM).

20. **C.** The age of majority under the law is 18.

21. **C.** The agent's role is to give advice, not to make decisions for the buyer.

22. **B.** Because many things can cause a loan to fall through, the agent should caution the buyer not to count on the loan until a final commitment is obtained. Prequalification helps to set the range of properties to preview.

23. **A.** Alejandro is exempt under the federal Fair Housing Act but is still covered by the Civil Rights Act of 1866 (racial discrimination).

24. **D.** The law does not regulate amount of rent.

25. **A.** Lenders are concerned with financial data, not educational background.

26. **D.** The landlord does not have to make modifications to accommodate a handicapped person but does have to agree to modifications paid for by the tenant.

27. **B.** This information is required to obtain a credit history of the borrower.

28. **A.** Payments need to be disclosed, not all sources of income.

29. **A.** The ARM is based on some predetermined index such as the U.S. Treasury Bill rate.

30. **D.** As payments are made, the principal increases. In a GEM the loan is paid off early because principal payments are increased during the term of the loan.

31. **A.** Escrow sends the HUD-1 Settlement Statement, a disclosure document, but no right of rescission exists.

32. **A.** If the salesperson is practicing law without a license, the salesperson is held to the standards of an attorney.

33. **A.** These provisions are too complex for the untrained salesperson and require the use of a legal expert.

34. **A.** As a dual agent, the licensee needs to obtain the written informed consent of both the buyer and seller clients.

35. **B.** This indicates there may be a building code violation. In most states, AIDS is not deemed to be a material fact—disclosure may invade the seller's privacy.

36. **D.** If the buyer fails to meet the contingency despite good-faith efforts, the buyer is entitled to the return of all the deposit money.

37. **A.** The "as is" clause relates to obvious and disclosed defects. If a seller knows of hidden defects, the "as is" clause won't free the seller of liability for affirmative concealment of such facts.

38. **D.** A single agent represents either a buyer or a seller, never both as in this case.

39. **C.** In some cases state law is more strict than federal law (e.g., federal law doesn't involve "marital status" as a basis for discrimination but state law may).

40. **D.** The fact that housing is directed at low-income prospects is not discriminatory. Choice (A) implies that the housing is not open to all.

41. **A.** Different weights are assigned to each method, depending on the particular cir-

cumstances. Assemblage is the increased value created by consolidating several lots.

42. **B.** Downzoning is a change from a higher use classification to a lower one, often causing a devaluation in property value.

43. **D.** This method considers the property's net operating income and the expected return (cap rate) to arrive at an estimate of value.

44. **B.** The sublessor is the lessee under the original lease; the tenant occupying the property is the sublessee.

45. **C.** Under a net lease the lessee typically pays the carrying charges on the property, such as taxes and insurance.

46. **D.** If a building incurs large expenses, the gross revenues will bear little relationship to the net.

47. **C.** Because rents are fixed, there is an $8,000 loss in income. $8,000 ÷ 0.10 = $80,000.

48. **C.** No fee may be charged by a lender for preparing required RESPA forms.

49. **B.** The assignment of rents provision allows the mortgagee (lender) to collect rent during the default of the loan.

50. **D.** Laws generally permit the nonconforming use to continue until such time as the structure needs to be rebuilt.

51. **C.** Highest and best use is that use which at a given time produces the best net return for the property.

52. **C.** Under a reverse annuity loan, the lender pays the borrower a certain amount each month. The borrower eventually will pay back principal plus interest on the interest portion of the payments.

53. **B.** Licensing laws require that brokers placing ads must identify themselves as licensees; otherwise, a buyer might think this was a "for sale by owner."

54. **A.** At the end of the lease the landlord is not required to renegotiate, unless the lease contains specific provisions.

55. **A.** The capitalization or income approach analyzes the net operating income and the expected rate of return on the investment.

56. **C.** The risk of buying an in-house listing is that the seller will later claim breach of the fiduciary duties of loyalty and full disclosure. While not foolproof, the best technique is to terminate the agency relationship and advise the seller to retain an attorney or another broker.

57. **C.** $70,000 ÷ 525 = 133.33

58. **C.** Regression states that as between dissimilar properties, the worth of the better property is adversely affected by the presence of the lesser-quality property. Progression is the opposite.

59. **B.** The lender agrees to limit its recovery to the money generated at the foreclosure sale. Some states have antideficiency legislation to curb selling at speculative prices.

60. **D.** A nonjudicial foreclosure requires a special clause in the mortgage that would permit a sale to take place without the need for a more time-consuming and expensive court action. No deficiency judgment can be obtained, however.